RESEARCH METHODS:
EXPLORING THE SOCIAL WORLD

FIRST EDITION

DIANE SYMBALUK

McGraw-Hill Ryerson

Research Methods
Exploring the Social World
First Edition

The Internet addresses listed in the text were accurate at the time of publication. The inclusion of a Web site does not indicate an endorsement by the authors or McGraw-Hill Ryerson, and McGraw-Hill Ryerson does not guarantee the accuracy of the information presented at these sites.

ISBN-13: 978-0-07-096878-3
ISBN-10: 0-07-096878-0

1 2 3 4 5 6 7 8 9 10 QGF 1 9 8 7 6 5 4

Printed and bound in the United States of America

Care has been taken to trace ownership of copyright material contained in this text; however, the publisher will welcome any information that enables them to rectify any reference or credit for subsequent editions.

Director of Product Management: *Rhondda McNabb*
Senior Product Manager: *Marcia Siekowski*
Marketing Manager: *Stacey Metz*
Senior Product Developer: *Jennifer Cressman*
Senior Product Team Associate: *Marina Seguin*
Supervising Editor: *Graeme Powell*
Copy Editor: *Janice Dyer*
Proofreader: *Rodney Rawlings*
Production Coordinator: *Sheryl MacAdam*
Permissions Editor: *Derek Capitaine*
Cover Designer: *Dianne Reynolds*
Cover Image: *Celine Ramoni/Getty Images (RF)*
Page Layout and Interior Design: *Laserwords Private Limited*
Printer: Quad/Graphics Fairfield (U.S.)

Library and Archives Canada Cataloguing in Publication

Symbaluk, Diane, 1967-, author
  Research methods : exploring the social world / Diane
Symbaluk.—First edition.

Includes bibliographical references and index.
ISBN 978-0-07-096878-3 (pbk.)

  1. Sociology—Research—Methodology. I. Title.

HM571.S94 2014   301.072   C2013-906332-3

Dedication

This book is dedicated to curious students, many of whom will come to realize that research methods are more than a practical means for finding answers to questions of interest. Research methods are also an integral part of an interesting and challenging process of discovery that involves learning skills through practice, sometimes even career-determining skills you wish you had developed sooner.

About the Author

I am an associate professor in the Department of Sociology at MacEwan University in Alberta where I teach a range of courses, including introductory sociology, second year lecture-based classes (e.g., social psychology and criminology), third- and fourth-year research methods classes (social research methods and advanced qualitative methods), a senior seminar, and an advanced social psychology seminar.

I earned all three of my degrees at the University of Alberta, where I was fortunate enough to be mentored by professors with expertise in a range of methods, including behaviourists who conducted experiments (Drs. W. David Pierce and the late W. Frank Epling), demographers who specialized in survey research (Drs. Frank Trovato and Parameswara Krishnan), criminologists who worked with data on risk assessment and offenders or studied victims and vulnerable populations (Drs. Robert Silverman, Leslie W. Kennedy, Helen Boritch, and James Creechan), sociologists recognized for their contributions in evaluation research (Dr. John Gartrell) and human factors research (Dr. W. Andrew Harrell), and an educational psychologist who helped me understand the merits of using a statistical methodology called meta-analysis (Dr. Judy Cameron).

I began teaching social research methods in the winter of 1997 and added advanced qualitative methods to the course offerings in 2010. While I have conducted experiments, designed surveys, carried out observational studies, facilitated focus groups, and given in-depth interviews as part of my own scholarly activity and service, my primary passion is teaching. As a result, most of my published research centres on the scholarship of teaching and learning, culminating in tools designed to aid instructors and students, including manuals, student engagement activities, study guides, test banks, chapter resources, and online supplements. For more information on my research interests and recent work, visit my home page at academic.macewan.ca/symbalukd.

Brief Contents

Contents

Preface

GOALS AND APPROACH OF THE BOOK

The purpose of this book is to introduce post-secondary students in Canada to a variety of social research methods as framed by research questions and objectives, as opposed to a particular qualitative, quantitative, mixed, or multiple method approach. Students are more apt to want to learn about research methods and practise them if they are personally relevant and interesting. By framing research topics within a Canadian context and drawing upon research conducted by Canadian scholars at universities and research institutes in Canada, students will be able to identify with the learning material. While primarily directed at students in second-, third-, or fourth-year sociology classes who have yet to conduct research, this book will be of equal benefit to students in anthropology, criminology, social work, psychology, or political science who are interested in learning more about social science research through examples drawn from their disciplines. Also, given its emphasis on current ethical standards, this book is instrumental for students who plan to carry out research and write research proposals or reports as part of an honour's program, independent study, or graduate school requirement.

Through my teaching experience, I have discovered there is substantial variation in the way students learn. Accordingly, I have incorporated multiple learning strategies into this textbook. I hope my passion for teaching is evident and the pedagogy in this book helps students to succeed in research methods by bringing the material alive. I firmly believe that one of the best ways to learn about research methods is to practise them. Reading about recommendations for how to structure survey questions may help you prepare a draft survey, but a pilot test will confirm whether you are asking the right questions and whether people understand the questions. Similarly, while you can create an interview guide with key questions to indicate what you plan to do for an in-depth interview, it is only through experience that you will learn how to actively listen and create impromptu follow-up questions as an interview unfolds. Although this book provides you with steps for applying different methods, please appreciate that research is a process and as such, it seldom conforms to ideal types in the real world. Again, it is only through experience that you will begin to understand the subtleties that underlie research processes.

I am the first to admit I have learned more about research from being engaged in it than reading about it, and I have similarly learned more about research processes through my errors and omissions than my initial successes. The Learning Through Practice exercises and step-by-step instructions for planning and designing studies provided throughout this book provide a starting point for inexperienced researchers. Beyond this book, you can continue to develop your research skills through educational pursuits such as a thesis-based master's program or through work-related experiences such as a research assistantship.

ORGANIZATION

PART 1: PREPARING FOR RESEARCH

The first part of this book prepares you for research by outlining considerations and processes that take place in the planning stage prior to the collection of data.

- Chapter 1 is on research foundations and it begins with a consideration of the various strategies we have for finding things out. Chapter 1 also discusses the limitations to alternatives to social research methods and the common errors associated with reasoning processes. Finally, Chapter 1 introduces you to social science research, helps you to understand the goals of social science research, and distinguishes between qualitative and quantitative approaches to research.

- Chapter 2 details the importance of theory, beginning with the main assumptions of positivist, interpretive, critical, and pragmatic paradigms. This chapter differentiates between theoretical frameworks and theories and deductive and inductive forms of reasoning. Chapter 2 helps you to formulate research questions and explains the importance of existing literature for framing research assumptions. Finally, this chapter teaches you how to locate appropriate literature and evaluate sources of information found on the Internet.
- Chapter 3 introduces you to research ethics through historical examples of unethical treatment of humans in military and medical cases, along with the regulatory outcomes. This chapter also discusses classic research examples to help you understand how ethical considerations arise in studies that include humans as participants. Ethical issues that relate to social science research are discussed in detail in this chapter, along with the core principles of the current Tri-Council Policy Statement (TCPS-2) on ethically responsible research.
- Chapter 4 covers the main components of a research design and explains conceptualization and operationalization processes. In addition, this chapter differentiates between levels of measurement, explores techniques used to assess reliability and validity, and identifies sources of measurement error. Finally, this chapter explores means for achieving rigour in qualitative research.
- Chapter 5 teaches you about sampling techniques, including when and under what circumstances a researcher might choose a probability-based or a non-probability-based sampling method. This chapter distinguishes between probability-based methods including simple random sampling, systematic random sampling, stratified random sampling, and cluster sampling, and it also explores non-probability methods including convenience sampling, snowball sampling, purposive sampling, and quota sampling.

PART 2: APPROACHES TO RESEARCH

With the who, what, where, when, and why components of research covered, Part 2 focuses on how to collect data using a variety of research methods, beginning with quantitative approaches.

- Chapter 6 explores the rationale underlying an experimental method and teaches you about the criteria needed to establish causality and how to test hypotheses using various experimental designs. This chapter also examines potential threats to internal and external validity.
- Chapter 7 focuses on asking questions through survey methods. This chapter examines the key methodological considerations that precede survey research, describes the two main survey methods used by quantitative researchers, and provides survey construction guidelines.
- Chapter 8 introduces four indirect methods used to gather information about people: physical trace analysis, archival analysis, content analysis, and secondary analysis of existing data. All of these methods are considered to be unobtrusive because the source of data is something created by or for people, as opposed to information obtained directly from people.
- Chapter 9 moves into qualitative approaches for learning about people through a direct method called qualitative interviewing. This chapter describes the structure of qualitative interviews and explains how to conduct an in-depth interview. In addition, this chapter outlines focus groups, comparing and contrasting them to qualitative interviews.
- Chapter 10, on ethnography, outlines the main features of ethnographic studies and explains the main roles of ethnographers engaged in fieldwork. In addition, this chapter looks at the techniques used by ethnographers to blend into a group under investigation and the ethical issues raised in fieldwork.

- Chapter 11 examines the merit of including both qualitative and quantitative approaches within a single study and introduces you to mixed-methods research designs. In addition, this chapter shows how researchers can combine multiple methods to collect information on people and organizations using case study research, evaluation research, and action research.

PART 3: WRITING UP RESEARCH

Finally, the book concludes with Chapter 12 on how to write research proposals and reports and an Appendix containing a sample research report.

- Assuming you have a firm understanding of the preliminary chapters and have settled on the most appropriate method or methods needed to answer a research question of interest, Chapter 12 helps you translate your research ideas into a technical plan that can be submitted to a research ethics board or your supervisor for approval or grading. If you have already carried out research as part of a class project or thesis requirement, this chapter also provides you with guidance and suggestions for how to structure and write a formal report, similar to a published journal article.
- The Appendix includes a research report written by a student in a third-year social research methods course. The sample report demonstrates that students can and do carry out research projects. Readers benefit from being able to follow the same topic through the various stages of an actual research process. Finally, students can see how the report writing guidelines provided in Chapter 12 are adhered to in an actual research report.

PEDAGOGY

Opening Quotes

Each chapter begins with a selected quote by a scholar or research organization to provide you with focus and insight into what I consider to be the underlying meaning or importance of the topic material covered in the chapter.

Canadian Content

Students and instructors at Canadian colleges and universities will be pleased to learn this book is written from the ground up with intentional emphasis on Canadian content. The vast majority of research examples are based on empirical research carried out in Canada by Canadian researchers.

Learning Objectives

Each chapter begins with a brief set of four to six learning objectives, consisting of statements that spell out the core skills or knowledge students should be able to demonstrate after carefully reviewing the chapter.

Test Yourself

Test Yourself questions are built-in open-ended review questions designed to help students gauge their understanding of the learning objective covered in a main section before proceeding to the next one.

Research on the Net

Research on the Net boxes contain information on and links to recommended websites that are particularly useful for understanding key concepts, providing additional resources, or demonstrating key ideas from the chapter.

Research in Action

Research in Action boxes include descriptions of research, documentaries/feature films, news stories, YouTube videos, and other examples that illustrate the relevance of particular methods and research concepts in everyday life.

Key Terms

Throughout each chapter, key terms are indicated in boldface font and defined in the margins as well as at the end of the textbook in a Glossary.

Chapter Summary

Chapter summaries consist of brief statements that are illustrative of the kinds of responses students should be able to provide as evidence that they have achieved the learning objectives.

Research Reflection

Research Reflection questions provided at the end of each chapter are designed to help students think critically about the material covered in the chapter. Reflection question can be used in any number of ways, including as a basis for class discussion, for use by instructors as short assignment questions, and/or by students to help them prepare for short answer and essay questions on exams.

Learning Through Practice

Each chapter contains a practice exercise designed to help students understand the chapter material through direct engagement. Some instructors may assign this exercise as a short laboratory assignment, a research assignment, a class demonstration, or as part of group work. An expanded version of this exercise forms the basis of the online laboratory exercises that accompany this book on Connect.

Research Resources

References to articles, book chapters, and websites that provide a more in-depth understanding of the key concepts and issues are included as recommended readings at the end of each chapter.

ANCILLARIES

McGraw-Hill Connect™ is a web-based assignment and assessment platform that gives students the means to better connect with their coursework, with their instructors, and with the important concepts that they will need to know for success now and in the future. With Connect, instructors can deliver assignments, quizzes and tests easily online. Students can practice important skills at their own pace and on their own schedule. With Connect, students also get 24/7 online access to an eBook—an online edition of the text—to aid them in successfully completing their work, wherever and whenever they choose.

INSTRUCTOR RESOURCES

Instructor's Manual

The Instructor's Manual includes learning objectives, a chapter outline and brief chapter summary, lecture ideas, in-class activities, and discussion topics.

Computerized Test Bank

The Test Bank contains 600 multiple-choice, true/false, and short essay questions, each categorized according to learning objective and level of Bloom's taxonomy. The Test Bank is available within Connect and through EZ Test Online—a flexible and easy-to-use electronic testing system—that allows instructors to create tests from book-specific items. Test items are also available in Word (Rich text format).

PowerPoint Presentations

Prepared by the text author, the PowerPoint presentations cover the key concepts in each chapter and include visual elements as well as figures from the text.

Superior Learning Solutions and Support

The McGraw-Hill Ryerson team is ready to help you assess and integrate any of our products, technology, and services into your course for optimal teaching and learning performance. Whether it's helping your students improve their grades, or putting your entire course online, the McGraw-Hill Ryerson team is here to help you do it. Contact your Learning Solutions Consultant today to learn how to maximize all of McGraw-Hill Ryerson's resources!

For more information on the latest technology and Learning Solutions offered by McGraw-Hill Ryerson and its partners, please visit us online: **www.mcgrawhill.ca/he/solutions**.

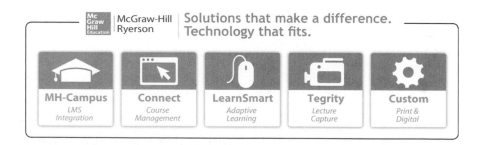

Acknowledgements

This text is the end result of a collective effort put forth by many individuals. First, I respectfully thank the reviewers who examined early draft chapters and offered numerous helpful suggestions:

Colin Campbell, *Douglas College*

Isabelle Carrier, *Dawson College*

Dawne Clark, *Mount Royal University*

Dale Dearden, *Kwantlen Polytechnic University*

David Desjardins, *John Abbott College*

Kimberley Ducey, *University of Winnipeg*

Sheri Fabian, *Simon Fraser University*

Elizabeth Finnis, *University of Guelph*

Elizabeth Flynn-Dastoor, *Wilfrid Laurier University*

Sylvia Hale, *St. Thomas University*

John Irwin, *University of Guelph-Humber*

Renan Levine, *University of Toronto Scarborough*

William Marshall, *University of Western Ontario*

Tara-Leigh McHugh, *University of Alberta*

Alissa Overend, *MacEwan University*

Detelina Radoeva, *York University – Glendon College*

Vincent Sacco, *Queen's University*

Michael Seredycz, *MacEwan University*

Joanne van Dijk, *McMaster University*

Philip Wilson, *Brock University*

In addition, special thanks go to Marcia Siekowski (Senior Product Manager) and Jennifer Cressman (Senior Product Developer) at McGraw-Hill Ryerson who worked closely with me to help steer the course of this book from its inception to the final draft version.

Finally, I wish to acknowledge my students, from whom I continue to learn valuable teaching and research lessons.

—Diane Symbaluk

Research Foundations

Learning Objectives

After reading this chapter, students should be able to do the following:

LO1 Explain why it is important to learn about social research methods.

LO2 Identify various "ways of knowing" and note their limitations.

LO3 Recognize common errors in reasoning.

LO4 Define social science research, distinguish between primary and secondary research, and differentiate between basic and applied research.

LO5 Explain the goals of research.

LO6 Differentiate between qualitative and quantitative research methods.

"The most beautiful thing we can experience is the mysterious. It is the source of all true art and science." (Albert Einstein)[1]

Introduction

LO1

Many students enroll in an introduction to social research course only because the course is required for their program of study. Some dread the thought of having to read about and carry out academic research, and others worry about how they will perform in what they perceive is going to be a highly laborious and boring course. I know this because students routinely admit these reservations, and they also ask why they need to take such a course and what value it will have for them in their everyday lives. My response is this: Though you may be skeptical now, what you will learn in this research methods book and in a research methods course has practical and relevant implications for you—for understanding people and events around you, for earning a living, and especially for making informed choices. After taking a research methods course, one of my students wrote in the course evaluation: "This class should be the last one that anyone completing an undergraduate degree takes. . .the skills learned and the knowledge acquired directly translate into the real world."

Research informs practice. Regardless of the career path you take, research has already played and continues to play an integral role in the proficiency of the skill set practised within that occupation. For example, health care professionals such as family physicians, nurse care practitioners, and dentists rely upon best practices as identified by researchers in the discipline. Similarly, teachers base

Research on the Net

Statistics Canada

One of the leading sources for information on Canada and Canadians is Statistics Canada. Statistics Canada, originally called the Dominion Bureau of Statistics, was established in 1918 as a federal government department that is mandated under the Statistics Act to "collect, compile, analyze, abstract and publish statistical information relating to the commercial, industrial, financial, social, economic and general activities and conditions of the people of Canada" (Statistics Canada, 2012). Here, various economists, mathematical statisticians, programmers, demographers, sociologists, senior methodologists, and others are employed in a realm of social research describing Canada and its people. For example, among other facts, you can learn about the population and characteristics of Aboriginal peoples; the health and well-being of children and youth; the economic viability of Canada's economy; the average annual income of families; trends in labour, energy supply, and demand; and commuting patterns.

One of the most important functions of Statistics Canada is to generate research to help inform policy that is developed at the provincial and federal levels of government. The information collected about Canadian citizens, businesses, departments,

Statistics Canada is the main federal government source for economic, social, and census data.

and programs helps to provide direction for decision making involving the prioritization of issues, the allocation of funding, and the development of rules and strategies. This occurs through the analysis of economic performance, the shaping of trade negotiations, the monitoring of the effectiveness of the justice system, the assessment of program funding, the maintenance of education and health care policies, and other regulatory systems involving the government. For more information on Statistics Canada and its research-based career opportunities, visit the Statistics Canada website at www.statcan.gc.ca.

lesson plans on an established curriculum that is continuously monitored and evaluated, peace officers interview eyewitnesses based on methods designed to maximize recall and minimize errors, social workers employ proven crisis intervention strategies to assist families and individuals in need, and lawyers argue points based on their prior research into similar cases with specific outcomes. Moreover, successful businesses frequently invest in research to learn about existing customers, satisfaction with current products and services, and the potential for market growth (e.g., this is how Apple® comes up with ideas for its newest iPhones).

In addition to describing people and processes, applied research also helps us evaluate whether the course of action we take is the most appropriate in a given circumstance, and it provides direction for how we might make improvements in the future. Summing up, research methodology can be best viewed as a practical means for acquiring relevant knowledge that is used to make informed decisions. As implied by Einstein's opening quote, anybody who is curious about people or events around them can be considered a potential social researcher. This book is specifically designed to help these individuals to use the most appropriate methods in their quest to find answers.

Ways of Knowing and Their Limitations as Sources of Knowledge

LO2

Each of us has accumulated knowledge based on ideas and events we have heard about, read about, witnessed, and/or experienced that we use at different times to make choices. As you will discover, many of these ways of knowing have limitations that detract from our ability to make sound and informed choices.

Tradition, Common Sense, and Authority

Tradition A familiar compilation of beliefs and practices passed down from one generation to the next.

One of the earliest ways of knowing lies in **tradition**—the compilation of beliefs and practices passed down from one generation to the next that everyone knows about and often adheres to, though rarely questions. Without delving into anyone's personal preferences or religious views about what marriage should or might entail, consider what our gendered tradition tells us about the main performers in traditional wedding ceremonies in Western culture. We know, for example, that there is usually a bride and a groom who are part of a larger wedding party consisting of a maid of honour, a best man, bridesmaids, and groomsmen. Similarly, there are various well-established customs associated with weddings, including the groom asking the bride's father for permission to marry his daughter and the bride wearing a white dress, a bridal veil, a garter belt, and other articles that represent something old, something new, something borrowed, and something blue. Other common features include the exchange of wedding vows and the placing of wedding bands, the first kiss as a newlywed couple, the bouquet toss, the cutting of a wedding cake, the first dance as a couple, and the departure for a honeymoon. While tradition as a form of knowledge might be important for teaching religious doctrine or helping maintain certain cultural practices, it is often passed on and adhered to without consideration of what the practices mean historically, or even in the present-day context. For instance, it is unlikely that a modern groom seen tossing the bride's garter belt into a crowd on their wedding day would be trying to stave off a group intent on tearing at his bride's clothing. Instead, the couple is likely mindlessly observing the norms of tradition.

Common sense Practical knowledge based on adaptive forms of prior learning.

Another source of information is **common sense**, which is a form of practical knowledge based on adaptive prior learning that can generalize to novel situations. Common sense is often relied upon to make sound judgments that will benefit us or that will help to keep us out of harm's way, often through recognition of our physical, emotional, and/or cognitive limits. For example, my common sense tells me to opt for intermediate (or blue) downhill ski runs over expert (black diamond) trails given my current abilities at this stage in my life. And, if I felt out of control while skiing down an intermediate run, as might be the case if I picked up too much speed or slid on an icy patch and was thrown off course, I would again rely upon my common sense to help guide me back to safety by perhaps seeking out deeper-looking snow that might provide some traction or by looking for ways to traverse across the mountain. Common sense also plays a role in the establishment and maintenance of intimate relationships, where a person might end a relationship when there are too many "red flags" or obstacles to overcome. Of course, our common sense might also be misguided, such as when we believe that "opposites attract for a reason" and stay in an unfulfilling relationship. A limitation of common sense is that it doesn't articulate when and under what specific circumstances our generalized beliefs will actually hold true. In some cases opposing traits may foster attraction in a partner; however, research shows that people who are similar to one another (e.g., in looks and with respect to values) fare much better when it comes to establishing relationships (Berscheid & Reis, 1998). Common sense may even provide false hope as we cling to the belief that "absence makes the heart grow fonder," while research indicates that distance relationships seldom work. Instead, close proximity is the key antecedent for establishing relationships (Aronson, Wilson, Akert, & Fehr, 2013).

Authority A source of information that is perceived to possess specialized knowledge.

We also learn new things through the teachings of **authority** figures or experts who share their knowledge and experience with us. Beginning with early socialization in our families of origin, we receive imparted wisdom from our parents and relatives who teach us about the importance of eating well-balanced meals, of looking both ways before we cross the road, of respecting our teachers and peers, and of obeying the rule of law. Of course, the same authorities may pass on erroneous information and/or model less appropriate forms of conduct, such as poor eating habits and disregard for the law. Beyond the family, we also obtain information from various credentialled professionals, academics, institutions, and organizations (e.g., a dentist who indicates root canal therapy is necessary, a political science professor who predicts provincial budget cuts, and Health Canada's food guidelines for healthy eating). Although many of the teachings offered by authority figures are helpful and even necessary to our well-being, we often fail to follow expert advice. For example, the World Health Organization informs us how an inadequate intake of fruits and vegetables is linked to heart disease (the second leading cause of death in Canada after cancer), while a Canadian Community Healthy Survey indicates that half of adult Canadians do not eat enough fruits and vegetables (Symbaluk & Bereska, 2013). In addition, some authority figures offer opinions on issues outside of their realm of expertise, as in the case of professional athletes who are paid to endorse particular views and products.

Half of Canadian adults do not eat enough fruits and vegetables.

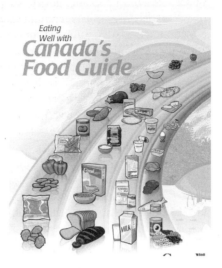

Finally, we tend to over-rely on the mass media as a source of authority without questioning the legitimacy of the messages provided. The mass media is an authority for informing us about local and international events in the form of communications we receive in newspapers, on television, and especially over the Internet. However, the media is also a profit-based business with highly concentrated ownership. For example, Bell Media owns the CTV Network and its affiliates, including 27 TV channels, six A-Channel affiliates, and 30 specialty channels (e.g., Discovery Channel and TSN). In addition to television, the company controls part of *The Globe and Mail,* along with 33 radio stations and even some web properties (e.g., Sympatico). Quebecor Media is also a big contender, owning eight major daily newspapers as well as 200 local papers, along with Quebec's largest cable company and French-language TV network, book publishing, video stores, and web interests (CBC News, 2010). Media giants set the agenda, thereby determining what we are exposed to when we watch television or read the newspapers. Thus, it is important to critically assess the messages we are exposed to, as well as their originating sources.

Experience

Experience First-hand observations or recollections of events that serve as sources of knowledge.

Lastly, much of what we believe we gain through first-hand **experience**. You probably understand more about the complexities of single parenthood or divorce if this is something you personally have experienced. Similarly, if you are considering whether divorce is becoming increasingly common in Western culture, you may rely upon your own personal knowledge of couples who have divorced to get a sense of whether this assumption is plausible. While you may be able to recall several recent instances of divorce among friends, family members, and work associates, does this really provide evidence for a claim that divorce is becoming more common? It could be that you are better able to remember recent cases of divorce than ones that occurred much earlier on. It could also be that your particular friends are not representative of the general population (e.g., they may possess shared characteristics by association that put them at greater risk for divorce, such as being of an age where they are more likely to have young children, having fewer financial resources, or holding an occupation that is less conducive to a stable marriage or family life).

© Aaron Warner. www.Cartoonstock.com

Test Yourself

- What are the four ways of knowing that do not involve scientific research?
- Why might it be problematic to rely upon common sense as a source of knowledge?
- Why is it especially important to critically assess information gleaned from the mass media?

Common Errors in Reasoning

First-hand experience, common sense, authority, and tradition are all important sources of knowledge that help inform what we know about the social world. However, each has particular limitations that can lead to a narrow or even inaccurate understanding. As humans we are subject to a number of errors in reasoning, since we pay more careful attention to certain people and events than others. Some of the more common errors in reasoning that result from reliance on unscientific or everyday ways of knowing include: imprecise observation, illogical reasoning, overgeneralization, selective observation, and premature closure.

Imprecise Observation

Imprecise observations
Everyday errors made as a function of our limited ability to perceive, store, and later accurately recall information.

Although we do pay attention to the people and events going on around us, there is so much information that it is impossible to take in everything at once, let alone process that information accurately, store all of the details, and recall it at a later point in time. **Imprecise observations** are the inevitable result. As you will learn in later chapters, our ability to observe can be greatly improved when we use a careful, systematic process in which we look for particular things that are precisely defined ahead of time. In addition to our tendency to make errors while observing, humans are also prone to making errors in their consideration of what they have observed. For example, people over-rely on what they can bring to mind (i.e., what is available in memory) as an indication of the frequency for that event (Tversky & Kahneman, 1973).

Illogical Reasoning

Illogical reasoning
Faulty decision making based on a failure to take into account the most appropriate sources of information.

Another of the more common errors has to do with **illogical reasoning**, where people make decisions based on faulty logic. This underlies what is referred to as a "gambler's fallacy," where a gambler will place a bet believing that a particular outcome is "due," such as a "red number" on a roulette table following a run of several "black numbers." In reality, the odds of a red number coming up are based on the overall quantity of numbers (i.e., there are 18 red numbers, 18 black numbers, and two green numbers [i.e., a zero and a double zero] in most North American versions). The odds of a red (or black) number occurring are 1 in 2.11 every time, regardless of previous events. Illogical reasoning results from a failure to take into account the true odds or probability of an event occurring.

Gamblers often fail to take into account the true probability of an event occurring.

Overgeneralization

Overgeneralization
The tendency to assume the existence of a general pattern based on a limited number of observed cases.

Overgeneralization refers to the tendency to assume the existence of a general pattern or trait based on a limited number of observations (Babbie & Benaquisto, 2014). For example, recall the global Occupy movement against economic and social inequality initiated by a Canadian activist organization called the Adbusters Media Foundation in September, 2011 (refer to www.adbusters.org). Reporters highly sensationalized the fact that a few of the students in attendance at New York's financial district protests were from highly privileged backgrounds as evidenced by their clothes and belongings, including expensive laptop computers and cell phones. This led to overgeneralizations about who the protestors actually were, reflected in headlines such as "The Rich Kids Occupy Wall Street" and stories depicting protestors as sharing "more in common with that top one percent than with the bottom one percent" (Flynn, 2011). This type of faulty logic is the basis for stereotypes, which involve overgeneralizations made about entire groups of people on the basis of shared group characteristics such social class, race, or ethnicity.

Selective Observation

Selective observation The tendency to assume a general pattern exists based on factors other than objective frequency.

A related error is made when the search for a pattern is undertaken by specifically seeking out instances that confirm an existing belief. **Selective observation** refers to the tendency to assume a general pattern exists based on factors other than objective frequency. For example, suppose you recently purchased a new car. After deliberating for days, you decide to order your new vehicle in the colour red. During the first couple of weeks, it may appear to you that the majority of vehicles on the road are red! This is because your attention is drawn to that colour (i.e., it is now salient for you) and you are inadvertently seeking out red vehicles while ignoring the higher prevalence of other vehicles which are not red. In reality, due to its high visibility, white is the most common colour for vehicles that display business signs. Moreover, white is also the most popular colour for new cars, followed by black and then silver (De Paula, 2012). Similarly, when seeking to support a particular viewpoint, observers may be biased (even unknowingly) toward certain observations in their quest to find confirming evidence.

Research in Action

Selective Observation

If you don't believe you are prone to selective observation, try completing Christopher Chabris and Daniel Simon's two minute Original Selective Attention Test found under videos and demos on the website for their recent book, *The Invisible Gorilla,* at www.theinvisiblegorilla.com.

- Try it: Click on the YouTube clip of the Original Selective Attention Test located at the authors' site. (The instructions are provided at the start of the clip. You are asked to count the number of basketball passes made by players wearing white.).
- Hint: Concentrate only on the players wearing white shirts and ignore those who are wearing black shirts to see whether you can obtain the correct answer, which is one of the following: 13, 14, 15, 16, or 17 passes.

- Were you correct? Where you surprised by what you learned from completing this test? Are you, in fact, prone to selective attention?

To learn more about the processes underlying perception and attention, I highly recommend Christopher Chabris's (2010) Authors@Google talk. The YouTube video for this fascinating lecture is posted at the web address above under the title "Chris's 2010 presentation at Google."

Premature Closure

Premature closure
The tendency to stop searching for necessary observations due to an erroneous belief that the answer has already been determined.

Premature closure refers to a tendency to stop searching for necessary observations due to an erroneous belief that an answer has already been determined. This is similar to overgeneralization and selective observation because in all three cases, a social perceiver fails to locate the most appropriate answer by short-cutting the process and limiting a search to a small number of observations. In an analysis of 100 medical cases of injuries and death involving diagnostic errors, the most common error made by internists was premature closure, or the failure to search for alternatives after making an initial (albeit incorrect) diagnosis (Graber, Franklin, & Gordon, 2005). Premature closure can also foster what Chambliss and Schutt (2013) call "resistance to change," when people are reluctant to modify their assumptions in the face of new information.

Test Yourself

- What are the five common errors that result from reliance on unscientific forms of reasoning?
- What does overgeneralization refer to?
- In what way is selective observation similar to premature closure?

Scientific Reasoning

Empirical methods
Data collection techniques carried out using logical and systematic procedures that are widely recognized by other researchers.

What sets scientific reasoning apart from the other ways of knowing with their corresponding limitations is the reliance on empirical methods. **Empirical methods** refer to data collection techniques carried out using logical and systematic procedures that are widely recognized by other researchers (Symbaluk & Bereska, 2013). Researchers in the social sciences use empirical methods to study individuals, groups, societies, and social processes in a manner that helps to overcome the limitations of other ways of knowing. Specifically:

- Social researchers seek to find answers through a careful examination of the social world. They do not assume that their initial beliefs or ideas are necessarily correct, and this reduces the likelihood of unquestioning faith in the teachings of tradition or authority. Similarly, while common sense and prior experience can aid scientific inquiry, these forms of knowledge do not substitute for observations that take place in the social world. The importance of theory and prior research for informing the development of new research is the topic of Chapter 2.
- Social researchers also rely upon systematic procedures and processes that contribute to quality observations focused on particular areas of interest. This lessens the likelihood of imprecise observation, selective observation, and illogical reasoning since researchers are very clear about what they are studying and how they will go about collecting, analyzing, and making sense of their observations. The main components of a research design and the features of sound measurement are covered in detail in Chapter 4.

- Social researchers limit the tendency to make overgeneralizations by ensuring they collect information from individuals or sources that appropriately represent the group or targeted area of interest (see Chapter 5 on sampling). In addition, their findings are also open to scrutiny and verification by other researchers in their field of study.

LO4

Social science research A process in which people combine a set of principles, outlooks, and ideas with a collection of specific practices, techniques, and strategies to produce knowledge.

Primary research First-hand data collection and data analysis that is undertaken to answer an original research question.

Secondary research The summation or analysis of research already collected by others.

Applied research Scientific research that is conducted to address a problem or issue.

Social Science Research

Both the social and natural sciences use empirical methods in their endeavour to understand and explain the world around us. The _natural sciences_ focus on laws that govern nature (e.g., plants and animals) from within various branches such as the biological sciences, physical sciences, and earth and planetary sciences. In contrast, the _social sciences_ study human nature and society from within various disciplines such as economics, education, criminology, sociology, psychology, political science, anthropology, and archeology. **Social science research** is "a process in which people combine a set of principles, outlooks, and ideas (i.e., methodology) with a collection of specific practices, techniques, and strategies (i.e., a method of inquiry) to produce knowledge" (Neuman & Robson, 2012, p. 2). The generation of new knowledge is often the end result of **primary research**, or first-hand data collection and data analysis that is undertaken to answer an original research question. Primary research is the focus of much of this book and most courses on research methods. Primary research can be contrasted with **secondary research**, which is the summarizing or analysis of research already collected by others. An essay you write on a topic summarizing what is already known about a particular issue or a published review of research findings in a particular area would be examples of secondary forms of research. Regardless of whether it is collected first or examined second-hand, all research in the social sciences is conducted in a way that attempts to reveal knowledge and increase our understanding, while minimizing the likelihood of errors. Generally, social science research takes one of two broad forms as described in the next section.

Applied and Basic Research

Applied research refers to scientific research that is conducted to specifically address a problem or issue. Applied research has a practical and often more immediate intention, such as when it is initiated on behalf of an employer or business to learn how to improve services at a particular location or how to better advertise a specific product. Applied research may be carried out within post-secondary institutions to evaluate internal programs, policies, or services (e.g., How could we improve a registration process or service for students?). In addition, a government or social agency may sponsor applied research to evaluate a program, a policy, or a community service (e.g., Is this treatment program working or not working?). Finally, applied research is also carried out to find a solution to a particular issue of concern. For example, Genome British Columbia, a not-for-profit organization that invests in and manages applied research projects dealing with large-scale issues of concern, recently committed $60 million dollars to 16 applied research projects on various topics, including saving endangered bee populations, improving the Canadian cattle herd, and reclaiming polluted land sites (Genome British Columbia, 2011; Genome Canada, 2010).

Basic research
Scientific research that is conducted to advance knowledge.

Basic research, in contrast, is research that is conducted to advance knowledge for its own sake. Most of the research conducted in universities and published in academic journals is considered to be a form of basic research. Basic research usually stems from a researcher's own curiosity, interest, and area of expertise, as opposed to the commercial interests of a business or the more narrow agenda of an organization-sponsored applied project. Basic research can span an infinite number of topics and issues. For example, researchers interested in home births assisted by midwives studied the views and birthing experience of 559 Canadian women who underwent this practice (Janssen, Henderson, & Vedam, 2009); those interested in identity and appearance interviewed Canadian men about their experiences with cosmetic surgery (Ricciardelli & White, 2011); and researchers wanting to learn more about structural and social barriers to housing conducted interviews with Canadian "street-involved" youth (Krüsi, Fast, Small, Wood, & Kerr, 2010).

Research on the Net

Social Sciences and Humanities Research Council

The Social Sciences and Humanities Research Council (SSHRC) is a federal government agency that promotes research in the humanities and social sciences on a diverse range of social, cultural, economic, environmental, technological, and wellness issues (Social Sciences and Humanities Research Council, 2013). SSHRC funds basic research projects at post-secondary institutions through graduate scholarships, postdoctoral fellowship programs, and research grants. When you are entering a masters or doctoral program, you can apply to SSHRC for a scholarship to assist you financially while you design basic research in support of your degree. Since the awarding of scholarships is a highly competitive process, it might be helpful to note that SSHRC prioritizes research projects in particular areas (e.g., Aboriginal Research, Digital Economy, and Canadian Environmental Issues). SSHRC also funds applied research through partnership development grants where industry partners with universities. For more information on the Social Sciences and Humanities Research Council and its funding, visit their website at www.sshrc-crsh.gc.ca.

Test Yourself

- What sets scientific research apart from other ways of knowing?
- How can social science methods reduce the risk of selective observation?
- What is social science research?
- What is the main difference between basic and applied research?

Goals of Social Science Research

Social science research is usually conducted to accomplish one of the four following goals: to explore, to describe, to explain, or to critically evaluate a phenomenon of interest.

Exploration

Exploratory research Research undertaken to find out more about a particular area of interest.

Exploratory research is undertaken to learn about a particular area of interest that is relatively new or not well-understood, or to find out more about an existing area using a novel approach. An underlying question of interest in an exploratory study centres on the notion of *what is X?* (where *X* can be anything of interest, such as what is it like to serve out a life sentence for murder while on parole?). Even areas of interest that are already fairly well-established can benefit from the fresh perspective afforded by exploratory research, which Stebbins (2001) claims is designed to examine an issue using "broad" and "unspecialized terms." For example, Bansal and Eiselt (2004) conducted exploratory research to learn more about tourist motivation and planning in New Brunswick. Although previous research had already established various highly specialized reasons for travel often linked to complex concepts such as "socioeconomic status," the authors opted for an exploratory approach to reassess vacation motives using five broad categories: climate, relaxation, adventure, personal, and education. The researchers selected these categories specifically because they were readily amenable to field research and they would be easily understood by an average tourist (Bansal & Eiselt, 2004). As it turned out, many of the tourists vacationing to New Brunswick claimed they were primarily seeking adventure—an area in which vacation/tour companies might benefit from further exploratory research. Listed below are additional examples of research questions that underlie exploratory forms of research:

- What are the factors affecting individual food choice and availability in Inuit communities in Nunavut? (Mead, Gittelsohn, Kratzmann, Roaches, & Sharma, 2010)
- What are the main barriers to organic farming practices in Saskatchewan, Canada? (Khaledi, Weseen, Sawyer, Ferguson, & Gray, 2010)
- What are some of the barriers to employment experienced by disabled Canadians? (Shier, Graham, & Jones, 2009)
- How can digital gaming serve as a learning environment for promoting sustainability? (Fabricatore & López, 2012)

Description

Descriptive research Research undertaken to identify the main traits or characteristics of a particular population or phenomenon.

While most research has a descriptive component, **descriptive research** is specifically undertaken to establish the main traits or characteristics of a particular population or phenomenon. A question of interest within descriptive research is: *What are the main features of X?* For example, Mcdonald, Reeder, Chen, and Després (1997) undertook descriptive research to learn more about obesity in Canada. By examining the body mass index of Canadians between the ages of 18 and 74, the researchers were able to describe the prevalence of obesity in the adult population. Results showed that obesity increased with age, and that men had higher rates of obesity (35 percent) than women (27 percent). Additional examples of research questions examined in descriptive research include:

- What features describe the sexual offending committed by Canadian teachers? (Moulden, Firestone, Kingston, & Wexler, 2010)
- What are the social, health, and drug use characteristics of crack cocaine users in British Columbia? (Fischer, Rudzinski, Ivsins, Gallupe, Patra, & Krajden, 2010)
- How do police officers administer the right to silence and legal counsel cautions? (Snook, Eastwood, & McDonald, 2010)
- Have breastfeeding policies and practices in Canadian hospitals changed from 1993 to 2007? (Levitt, Hanvey, Kaczorowski, Chalmers, Heaman, & Bartholomew, 2011)

Body mass index is one measure used to describe obesity among Canadians.

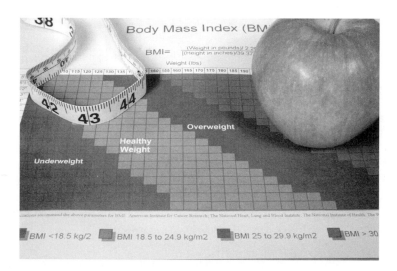

Explanation

Explanatory research Research undertaken to clarify the variation found between groups on some dimension of interest.

Explanatory research is conducted to clarify the variation found between groups on some dimension of interest. The central question underlying explanatory research is *"why?"* and the goal is to explain an outcome. For example, in trying to explain why some people are more likely than others to become compulsive gamblers, Callan, Ellard, Shead, and Hodgins (2008) found support for a hypothesis that gambling served a justice-seeking function in certain people. That is, compulsive gamblers try to obtain rewards through gambling that they feel they deserve since they have not obtained success through more conventional means, such as earning a decent income and investing wisely over time.

In addition, explanatory research may be directed at better understanding the factors that influence some process, condition, or state of being. For example, during my graduate program, I (along with a team of researchers) sought to explain how social modelling (i.e., watching others who serve as role models) might influence people's ability to tolerate the pain of a new exercise. Initially we thought it might work though self-efficacy (people's beliefs in their ability), but we found out it worked through pain perception instead. We discovered that prior exposure to pain intolerant social models (i.e., people who display signs of pain early and make the exercise appear difficult to do) led participants to also feel pain immediately, and this produced poor endurance. Conversely, exposure to pain tolerant models (i.e., people who manage the pain of exercise and last a long time at it) enabled participants to stave off feelings of pain and last longer at the same exercise (see Symbaluk, Heth, Cameron, & Pierce, 1997). Other examples of research questions from explanatory research are:

- Why are bystanders less likely to intervene in an emergency situation while in the presence of others? (Darley & Latané, 1968)
- Why don't boys like to read and why do girls outperform boys on Canadian reading assessment tests? (Canadian Council on Learning, 2009)
- Why are U.S. health care expenditures so different from Canada's? (Spithoven, 2011)
- Why have real wages lagged behind labour productivity growth in Canada? (Sharpe, Arsenault, & Harrison, 2008)

Evaluation

Evaluation research
Research undertaken to assess whether a program or policy is effective in reaching its desired goals and objectives.

Evaluation research seeks to assess whether a program or policy is effective in reaching its desired goals and objectives. Central questions for evaluation research include: *Is this policy working* and/or *What is the impact of this program?* McDonald and colleagues (2009) evaluated a community-based group intervention strategy called Families and Schools Together (FAST) that was designed to help teenage mothers and their infants in 11 Canadian communities. Data collected from mothers and grandmothers before and after the intervention indicated positive improvement as a result of the program on a number of original aims, including improved parent–child bonds, reduced stress and family conflict, and increased parental self-efficacy (McDonald et al., 2009). Evaluation research is sometimes more generally referred to as "critical research" when it is designed to assess an aspect of the social world as opposed to a particular program or policy. Examples of additional questions framed within evaluation research include:

- Is methadone maintenance a cost-effective form of drug rehabilitation in Ontario? (Zaric, Brennan, Varenbut, & Daiter, 2013)
- Does videoconferencing provide timely, cost-effective, and convenient professional development opportunities for English as an Additional Language literacy tutors? (Hare & Eaton, 2010)
- Did the Canada–U.S. Wheat Trade Agreement of 1994 benefit Canada? (Carter & MacLaren, 1997)
- Is the Continuing Medical Education program an effective approach for delivering road safety information to health professionals? (Dow & Jacques, 2012)

Test Yourself

- What is a central question of interest in exploratory research?
- Why is descriptive research undertaken?
- What central question underlies explanatory research?
- When would it be appropriate to use evaluation research?

Qualitative and Quantitative Research Methods

LO6

Research methods
Techniques for carrying out research to answer questions of interest.

Data Information gathered through research techniques.

Quantitative research method A technique that seeks to describe, explain, or evaluate a phenomenon of interest and produces numerical data.

Qualitative research method A technique that seeks to explore, interpret, explain, or evaluate a phenomenon of interest and produces non-numerical data.

Research methods are the specific tools or techniques used to carry out the research that obtains the information needed to answer questions of interest and achieve the goals discussed in the previous section. The information gathered through these techniques is collectively referred to as **data**. Chapters 6 through 10 each focus exclusively on specific data gathering techniques used in the social sciences (e.g., experiments, surveys, unobtrusive methods, qualitative interviews, ethnography). At a broader level, consider for now that a **quantitative research method** is one that seeks to describe, explain, or evaluate some phenomenon using numerical data that is amenable to statistical analyses. In contrast, a **qualitative research method** is one that seeks to explore, interpret, explain, or evaluate a phenomenon of interest using non-numerical data, often in the form of words, patterns, and/or themes that are generally not amenable to statistical analyses. Let's look at both types in more detail, beginning with quantitative methods.

Quantitative Methods

Quantitative methods are often used to obtain information or data that can be counted or "quantified" in some way. The findings from a quantitative study usually tell us the percentage of people who feel a particular way about a topic, the number of times a certain event occurred, or the amount of time it took the average person to complete some kind of task under certain conditions. The most commonly used quantitative methods are experiments and surveys, followed by a few unobtrusive methods. Experiments are studies carried out in carefully designed environments that allow researchers to test cause–effect relationships where one variable of interest is believed to be the cause and the other is believed to be the effect or outcome (see Chapter 6). Surveys are studies used to gather people's views or opinions on a range of issues (see Chapter 7). Unobtrusive methods are techniques that do not directly involve people as research participants in the data collection process (see Chapter 8). For example, we can systematically observe people from a distance without asking them directly for information, we can conduct secondary data analysis on existing forms of primary data, and we can examine various social mediums such as television programs or song lyrics for the presence or absence of some phenomenon of interest (e.g., alcohol, violence, or gender stereotypes). Note that each of these methods will be discussed in detail in later chapters. For now, I just want you to start associating these techniques with the quantitative realm of the research world.

Qualitative Methods

In contrast, qualitative methods are particularly useful for learning more about the nature or "quality" of some phenomenon of interest. Qualitative techniques underlie a desire to better understand how people are experiencing events and why people feel the way they do or why they do the things they do. The form of the data collected tends to be words as opposed to amounts or counts. Commonly used techniques include qualitative interviewing and ethnography, as well as unobtrusive methods. Qualitative interviewing is used to gather in-depth information from the perspective of the participant to reveal meaning (e.g., what is it like to be a single parent of a child with special needs?) (see Chapter 9). Ethnography is a multi-method approach that combines techniques such as participant observation and qualitative interviewing to learn about a group in its natural setting (e.g., what can be learned about interactions among group members by joining a religious cult?) (see Chapter 10). Finally, qualitative methods also include unobtrusive methods such as content analyses where the purpose is often exploratory and involves looking for patterns and themes; archival analyses, which involves looking at existing information including written documents (e.g., letters, records); historical analyses, which involves an examination of historical documents; and/or secondary analysis of other phenomenon that can be considered a data source, including traces left behind by people (e.g., garbage and graffiti). Refer to Table 1.1 for a comparison and overview of the two main methods.

Qualitative methods include observations in natural settings.

TABLE 1.1   Overview of Qualitative and Quantitative Methods

	Method	
	Qualitative	**Quantitative**
Objective	• to learn about the nature of some phenomenon • to "qualify" or explain • to explore • to interpret	• to describe some phenomenon • to quantify • to count • to explain
Aim	• understanding • meaning	• description • cause–effect relationships
Focus	• human-centred	• objective reality
Research techniques	• qualitative interviews • ethnography/field research • unobtrusive methods (e.g., content analyses, naturalistic observation)	• experiments • surveys • unobtrusive methods (e.g., secondary analysis of existing data)
Data	• words • pictures • patterns • themes	• numerical • counts • ratings • amenable to statistical analyses

Qualitative Versus Quantitative: An Unnecessary Divide

I do not wish to leave you with the impression that all research is qualitative or quantitative and that researchers necessarily should be of one type or the other. Particular research interests may be amenable to both quantitative and qualitative techniques, and some researchers may use both approaches within the same study. For example, in 2001, Dr. Andrew Howell and I surveyed faculty and students at a Canadian university to determine views toward published student ratings of instruction. Using a primarily quantitative approach, we asked faculty and students to rate their level of agreement on a number of items on a questionnaire to describe views (e.g., whether instructor ratings should be published and whether different forms of published ratings jeopardize instructor privacy). To provide answers, respondents mainly checked off boxes that corresponded to their level of agreement with each statement (e.g., strongly disagree, disagree, neutral, agree, or strongly agree). Most of the data collected was coded into numbers and analyzed using descriptive and inferential statistics. Results indicated widespread support for disclosure of all forms of evaluation by students and widespread opposition from instructors (Howell & Symbaluk, 2001).

However, the survey also included open-ended items where respondents were asked to list the advantages and disadvantages of published ratings. Faculty and student comments in their own words constituted qualitative data. Patterns and themes in the data highlighted the nature of potential benefits for students who, for example, were interested in learning more about an instructor's particular teaching style. Qualitative data also identified the main concerns of instructors, who, for example, worried that an instructor's reputation could be tarnished by a posted negative evaluation that might persist over time even if an instructor changed (Howell & Symbaluk, 2001).

Qualitative methods are not better or worse than quantitative ones. There is an ongoing and even sometimes highly contentious debate concerning the relative merit of quantitative versus qualitative methods, where some quantitative researchers dismiss qualitative approaches as being less scientific and qualitative researchers accuse quantitative approaches as being unable to tell us about the true nature of things. I, along with several other authors of textbooks on research methods, find this dichotomy to be unwarranted and unnecessary (e.g., see also Bouma, Ling, & Wilkinson, 2009; Palys & Atchison, 2014). While it is common practice to determine in advance whether you are using a more qualitative or quantitative approach, it is the nature of the research issue itself (e.g., an interest in understanding the experiences of a group versus a desire to quantify the prevalent views of a group on an issue), as well as many other aspects of any given study (e.g., the availability of resources, time restraints, and the willingness of the participants), that determine the exact method(s) used. Refer to Chapter 11 for a comprehensive overview of the use of mixed methods and multiple methods within a single study.

Research in Action

The Blonde Mystique

The Blonde Mystique (Telefilm Canada, 2006) is a documentary that provides a light-hearted look at research by showing how just about any topic can underlie a research question, including whether there is such a thing as a "blonde mystique." Over the course of their study, three women set out to test whether a blonde mystique exists by using a number of research techniques, from interviews with men on the street, to field research conducted in bars, to staged roadside experiments. They even change their own hair colour in an attempt to determine if people treat them differently if they go from blonde to brunette, or brunette to blonde! Discover whether men really have a preference for fair (blonde) hair over darker shades in women.

Test Yourself

- Which type of research method typically produces numerical data?
- Which type of research method is best suited to revealing the meaning of events as experienced by particular individuals?
- Which type of research method uses experiments to test causal relationships?
- Which type of research approach is more appropriate for studying groups in natural settings?

Chapter Summary

LO1   **Explain why it is important to learn about social research methods.**

Social research methods are a practical means for acquiring knowledge and developing an informed opinion that is useful in a range of contexts, from everyday curiosity to skills that underlie most forms of employment.

LO2   **Identify various "ways of knowing" and note their limitations.**

Four common ways of knowing include the use of tradition, common sense, authority, and personal experience. While highly informative and convenient, these sources of knowledge are fraught with errors as we learn accurate and inaccurate information as part of tradition; common sense fails to hold true under many circumstances; authority figures often speak well beyond their level of experience; and personal experience is restricted to our recollections of observations.

LO3   **Recognize common errors in reasoning.**

Imprecise observation refers to the everyday errors we make as a function of our ability to accurately take in, store, and later recall an overwhelming amount of information. Illogical reasoning refers to decision making based on a failure to take into account the most important sources of information. Overgeneralization is the tendency to assume a general pattern or trait exists based on a limited number of observations, while selective observation is the tendency to assume a general pattern exists based on factors other than objective frequency. Premature closure refers to a tendency to stop searching for necessary observations due to an erroneous belief that an answer has already been determined.

LO4   **Define social science research, distinguish between primary and secondary research, and differentiate between basic and applied research.**

Social science research is a process where a set of principles, outlooks, and ideas are combined with a collection of specific practices, techniques, and strategies to produce knowledge. Primary research refers to first-hand data collection and data analysis that is undertaken to answer an original research question. Secondary research refers to the summarizing or analysis of research already collected by others. Applied research refers to scientific research that is conducted to specifically address a problem, while basic research is conducted to advance knowledge for its own sake.

LO5   **Explain the goals of research.**

Social science research is usually conducted to explore, to describe, to explain, or to critically evaluate a program or phenomenon of interest (i.e., evaluation or critical research). Exploratory research is carried out to learn more about an area of interest. Descriptive research is undertaken to establish the main traits of a population. Explanatory research is conducted to clarify the variation found between groups on some dimension of interest. Evaluation research assesses whether a program or policy is effective.

LO6   **Differentiate between qualitative and quantitative research methods.**
Quantitative research methods are techniques that seek to describe, explain, or evaluate a phenomenon of interest, while qualitative research methods are tools that seek to explore, interpret, explain, or evaluate a phenomenon of interest. Quantitative methods produce numerical data amenable to statistical analyses, while qualitative methods produce non-numerical data often in the form of words, patterns, or themes.

Research Reflection

1. Identify one traditional belief or idea that was passed on to you from a family member or close friend as a form of advice. Are there any obvious limitations to that information as a means of knowing about the world? Do any of the common errors in reasoning apply to this example? If you were going to examine this assumption using a scientific approach, what is one technique you could use to test it in the real world? Describe how you would carry out such a study.

2. Suppose you were interested in studying homelessness in a large city such as Toronto, Montreal, Calgary, Vancouver, or Ottawa. Develop one research question you could attempt to answer in a study. Which of the four goals of social science research is most closely aligned with the question you created? Defend your answer.

3. Starting with the general topic area of health, develop a specific research question to highlight each of the four distinct goals of social science research. Which of the questions holds the most interest to you? Which research technique is best suited to gather data to answer your preferred question of interest?

Learning Through Practice

Objective: To familiarize students with social science research.
Directions:

1. Locate and print off a scholarly article of interest based on primary research in an academic journal from a social science database (e.g., Social Sciences Citation Index, JSTOR, Web of Science, ScienceDirect, PsychINFO, SocIN-DEX with full text, Criminology: A SAGE Full-Text Collection, Family and Society Studies Worldwide, or Anthropology Plus).

2. Describe the social issue that underlies the research interest of the article. How is the main research question framed?

3. Are the researchers conducting mainly qualitative, mainly quantitative, or both types of research? How do you know?

4. Which main goal of social science research does the objective of this study best align with? Explain your answer.

5. Describe one of the techniques used by the researchers to obtain information on their question of interest.

Research Resources

1. For an overview of qualitative research techniques, I recommend: Berg, B. L., & Lune, H. (2012). *Qualitative research methods for the social sciences* (8th ed.). Upper Saddle River, NJ: Pearson Education.

2. For an overview of quantitative research techniques, I recommend: Cozby, P. C. (2012). *Methods in behavioral research* (11th ed.). New York, NY: McGraw-Hill.

3. To find scholarly research articles, refer to Thomson Reuter's *Social Sciences Citation Index,* the largest full-text database for social science journals. You can usually access this database for free through the library at your post-secondary institution.

4. For the most comprehensive source of data on virtually all aspects of Canadian lives, refer to Statistics Canada at www.statcan.gc.ca. Note that restricted forms of data may be accessible through library licenses and agreements at your post-secondary institution.

 For more information on the resources available from McGraw-Hill Ryerson, go to www.mcgrawhill.ca/he/solutions.

References

Aronson, E., Wilson, T., Akert, R., & Fehr, B. (2013). *Social pychology* (5th ed.). Toronto, ON: Pearson Education Canada.

Babbie, E., & Benaquisto, L. (2014). *Fundamentals of social research* (3rd Can. ed.). Toronto, ON: Nelson Education, Ltd.

Bansal, H., & Eiselt, H. A. (2004). Exploratory research of tourist motivations and planning. *Tourism Management, 25*(3), 387–396.

Berscheid, E., & Reiss, H. T. (1998). Attraction and close relationships. In D. Gilbert, S. Fiske, & G. Lindzey (Eds.), *The handbook of social psychology* (4th ed., pp. 193–281). New York, NY: McGraw-Hill.

Berg, B. L., & Lune, H. (2012). *Qualitative research methods for the social siences* (8th ed.). Upper Saddle River, NJ: Pearson Education.

Bouma, G. D., Ling, R., & Wilkinson, L. (2009). *The research process: Canadian edition.* Don Mills, ON: Oxford University Press.

Callan, M. J., Ellard, J. H., Shead, N. W., & Hodgins, D. C. (2008). Gambling as a search for justice: Examining the role of personal relative deprivation in gambling urges and gambling behavior. *Personality and Social Psychology Bulletin, 34*(11), 1514–1529.

Canadian Council on Learning (2009, February 18). Why don't boys like to read: Gender differences in reading achievement. *Lessons in Learning.* ERIC. Retrieved from http://www.eric.ed.gov/PDFS/ED519285.pdf

Carter, C. A., & MacLaren, D. (1997). An evaluation of the Canada-U.S. Wheat agreement of 1994. *American Journal of Agricultural Economics, 79*(August), 703–714.

CBC News (2010, April 30). Media convergence, acquisitions and sales in Canada. CBC News online. Retrieved from http://www.cbc.ca/news/business/story/2010/04/29/f-media-ownership-canada.html

Chambliss, D. F., & Schutt, R. K. (2013). *Making sense of the social world* (4th ed.). Thousand Oaks, CA: Pine Forge Press.

Cozby, P. C. (2012). *Methods in behavioral research* (11th ed.). New York, NY: McGraw-Hill.

Darley, J. M., & Latané, B. (1968). Bystander intervention in emergencies: Diffusion of responsibility. *Journal of Personality and Social Psychology, 8*(4), 377–383.

De Paula, M. (2012, December 21). Top ten most popular car colors. In Vehicles. *Forbes.* New York, NY: Forbes.com. Retrieved from http://www.forbes.com/sites/matthewdepaula/2012/12/21/top-10-most-popular-car-colors/

Dow, J., & Jacques, A. (2012). Education doctors on evaluation of fitness to drive: Impact of a case-based workshop. *Journal of Continuing Education in the Health Professions, 32*(1), 68–73.

Fabricatore C., & López X. (2012). Sustainability learning through gaming: An exploratory study. *Electronic Journal of e-Learning, 10*(2), 209–222.

Fischer, B., Rudzinski, K., Ivsins, A., Gallupe, O., Patra, J., & Krajden, M. (2010, August). Social, health, and drug use characteristics of primary crack users in three mid-sized communities in British Columbia, Canada. *Drugs: Education, Prevention, and Policy, 17*(4), 333–353.

Flynn, D. (2011, November 4). The rich kids of Occupy Wall Street. In Daily Mailer. *FrontPage Magazine.* Retrieved from http://frontpagemag.com/2011/11/04/the-rich-kids-of-occupy-wall-street/

Genome British Columbia (2011, March 25). *News releases.* Genome Canada announces $60 million for 16 new applied research projects. Vancouver, BC: Genome British Columbia. Retrieved from http://www.genomebc.ca/media/news-releases/2011/genome-canada-announces-60m-for-16-new-applied-research-projects/

Genome Canada (2010). *Research Portfolio.* 2010 Large-scale applied research project competition summaries of successful projects. Ottawa, ON: Genome Canada. Retrieved from http://www.genomecanada.ca/data/Nouvelles/Fichiers%5Cen%5C378_1_Project%20summaries%20LSP%202010.pdf

Graber, M. L., Franklin, N., & Gordon, R. (2005). Diagnostic error in internal medicine. *Archives of Internal Medicine (165),* 1493–1499.

Hare, C., & Eaton, S. (2010). Evaluation of a videoconferencing pilot project: Training for volunteer literacy tutors for speakers of English as an Additional Language (EAL). An iCCAN pilot project in collaboration with the Rural

Routes Initiative. Final Report. Retrieved from http://www.eric.ed.gov/PDFS/ED508253.pdf

Howell, A. J., & Symbaluk, D. G. (2001). Published student ratings: Reconciling the views of students and faculty. *Journal of Educational Psychology, 93,* 790–796.

Janssen, P. A., Henderson, A. D., & Vedam, S. (2009). The experience of planned home birth: Views of the first 500 women. *Birth, 36*(4), 297–304.

Khaledi, M., Weseen, S., Sawyer, E., Ferguson, S., & Gray, R. (2010). Factors influencing partial and complete adoption of organic farming practices in Saskatchewan, Canada. *Canadian Journal of Agricultural Economics, 58,* 37–56.

Krüsi, A., Fast, D., Small, W., Wood, E., & Kerr, T. (2010). Social and structural barriers to housing among street-involved youth who use illicit drugs. *Health and Social Care in the Community, 18*(3), 282–288.

Levitt, C., Harvey, L., Kaczorowski, Chalmers, B., Heaman, M., & Bartholomew, S. (2011). Breastfeeding policies and practices in Canadian hospitals: Comparing 1993 with 2007. *Birth, 38*(3), 228–237.

McDonald, L., Conrad, T., Fairtlough, A., Fletcher, J., Green, L., Moore, L., & Lepps, B. (2009). An evaluation of a groupwork intervention for teenage mothers and their families. *Child and Family Social Work, 14,* 45–57.

McDonald, S. M., Reeder, B. A., Chen, Y., & Deprés, J. P. (1997, July 1). Obesity in Canada: A descriptive analysis. *Canadian Medical Association Journal, 157*(1 Suppl.), S1–S9.

Mead, E., Gittelsohn, J., Kratzmann, M., Roaches, C. & Sharma, S. (2010). Impact of the changing food environment on dietary practices of an Inuit population in Arctic Canada. *Journal of Human Nutrition and Dietetics, 23*(Suppl. 1), 18–26.

Moulden, H. M., Firestone, P., Kingston, D. A., & Wexler, A. F. (2010). A description of sexual offending committed by Canadian teachers. *Journal of Child Sexual Abuse, 19,* 403–418.

Neuman, W. L., & Robson, K. (2012). *Basics of social research: Qualitative and quantitative approaches* (2nd Can. ed.). Toronto, ON: Pearson Canada Inc.

Palys, T., & Atchison, C. (2014). *Research decisions: Quantitative and qualitative perspectives* (5th ed.). Toronto, ON: Nelson Education.

Ricciardelli, R., & White, P. (2011). Modifying the body: Canadian men's perspectives on appearance and cosmetic surgery. *The Qualitative Report, 16*(4), 949–970.

Sharpe, A., Arsenault, J., & Harrison, P. (2008). Why have real wages lagged labour productivity growth in Canada? *International Productivity Monitor, 17*(Fall), 16–27.

Shier, M., Graham, J. R., & Jones, M. E. (2009). Barriers to employment as experienced by disabled people: A qualitative analysis in Calgary and Regina, Canada. *Disability and Society, 24*(1), 63–75.

Snook, B., Eastwood, J., & McDonald, S. (2010). *Canadian Journal of Criminology and Criminal Justice,* October, 545–560.

Social Sciences and Humanities Research Council (2013). About us. Ottawa, ON: Author. Retrieved from: http://www.sshrc-crsh.gc.ca/about-au_sujet/index-eng.aspx

Spithoven, A. (2011). It's the institutions, stupid! Why U. S. health care expenditure is so different from Canada's. *Journal of Economic Issues, Vol. XLV*(1), March, 75–95.

Statistics Canada. (2012). About us. Ottawa, ON: Author. Retrieved from: http://www.statcan.gc.ca/about-apercu/mandate-mandat-eng.htm

Stebbins, R. A. (2001). *Exploratory research in the social sciences: Qualitative research methods series 48.* Thousand Oaks, CA: Sage Publications.

Symbaluk, D. S., & Bereska, T. M. (2013). *Sociology in action: A Canadian perspective.* Toronto: Nelson Education.

Symbaluk, D. S., Heth, C. D., Cameron, J., & Pierce, W. D. (1997). Social modeling, monetary incentives, and pain endurance: The role of self-efficacy and pain perception. *Personality and Social Psychology Bulletin, 23*(3), 258–269.

Telefilm Canada (2006). *The blonde mystique.* A. Mehler and L. Nault (Producers). Vancouver, BC: Paperny Films.

Tversky, A., & Kahneman, D. (1973). Availability: A heuristic for judging frequency and probability. *Cognitive Psychology, 5,* 207–232.

Zaric, G. S., Brennan, A. W., Varenbut, M., & Daiter, J. M. (2013). The cost of providing methadone maintenance treatment in Ontario, Canada. *The American Journal of Drug and Alcohol Abuse, 38*(6), 559–566.

Endnote

[1] Opening quote retrieved December 29, 2011 from www.quotationspage.com.

The Importance
of Theory

Learning Objectives

After reading this chapter, students should be able to do the following:

LO1 Outline the main assumptions of positivist, interpretive, critical, and pragmatic paradigms.

LO2 Define and differentiate between theoretical frameworks and theories.

LO3 Distinguish between deductive and inductive reasoning and explain how the role of theory differs in qualitative and quantitative research.

LO4 Formulate social research questions.

LO5 Explain the importance of a literature review.

LO6 Locate appropriate literature and evaluate sources of information found on the Internet.

"There is nothing more practical than a good theory."(Kurt Lewin, 1951, p. 169)[1]

Introduction

In Chapter 1 you were introduced to scientific reasoning as a desirable alternative to learning about the social world through tradition, common sense, authority, and personal experience. In addition, you learned to distinguish between basic and applied research, and that research methods are used to collect data for a variety of purposes (e.g., to explore, describe, explain, or evaluate some phenomenon). In this chapter, you will learn about paradigms that shape our views of social science research, you will learn about theoretical frameworks, and you will find out about the importance of theory and prior research for informing the development of new research. Finally, this chapter helps you locate and evaluate sources of information you find in the library and on the Internet.

Paradigm A model or framework for observation and understanding, which shapes both what we see and how we understand it.

Inquiry Paradigms in the Social Sciences

LO1

At the most general level, a **paradigm** is a set of "basic beliefs" or a "worldview" that helps us understand "the nature of the world," including our own place in it (Guba & Lincoln, 1994). Earl Babbie and Lucia Benaquisto (2014) define a paradigm as a "model or framework for observation and understanding, which shapes both what we see and how we understand it" (p. 32). As a broad framework, a paradigm includes assumptions about the nature of knowledge (a branch of philosophy called epistemology), assumptions about the nature of reality or the way things are (a branch of philosophy called ontology), and assumptions about how we go about solving problems and gathering information (a system of principles or practices collectively known as methodology). As Egon G. Guba and Yvonna S. Lincoln (1994) explain, paradigms are "basic belief systems based on ontological, epistemological, and methodological assumptions" (p. 107). The assumptions are interrelated in the sense that how one views the nature of reality (an ontological stance) influences beliefs about one's relationship to that reality (an epistemological stance) and how one would go about examining that reality (a methodological stance). This will become clearer as we compare the assumptions of four distinct and competing inquiry paradigms.

Research findings may alter widely shared worldviews, bringing about what late American philosopher Thomas Kuhn (1962) termed a "paradigm shift."

Positivist Paradigm

French philosopher Auguste Comte (1798–1857) first used the term "social physics" (later called "sociology") to describe a science of society used to study people in a single objective reality he called positivism (Wernick, 2005). The **positivist paradigm** is a philosophical approach–based inquiry aimed at discovering universal laws. Positivists hold a worldview similar to that of the natural sciences, which stresses objectivity and truth as discovered through direct empirical methods. The goal is to search for antecedent causes that produce outcomes. From this perspective, "only phenomenon and regularities confirmed by the senses (sight, hearing, etc.) can be accepted as knowledge" (Bryman, Bell, & Teevan, 2012, p. 8). Hence, this paradigm emphasizes observable phenomenon, while rejecting feelings and subjective interpretations of events, as credible forms of reality. Within a positivist paradigm, the search for empirical truth begins with what is already known about an area. From that starting point, probable causes are "deduced" using logical reasoning, and then theories are tested for accuracy.

Positivist paradigm A worldview that upholds the importance of discovering truth through direct experience using empirical methods.

Systematic observation and experimental methods are commonly employed modes of inquiry and the data obtained is quantifiable.

Interpretive Paradigm

Interpretive paradigm A worldview that rests on the assumption that reality is socially constructed and must be understood from the perspective of those experiencing it.

The **interpretive paradigm** (also called constructivism) arose in part as a critique of positivism for its failure to recognize the importance of subjectivity in human-centred approaches. The interpretive paradigm worldview rests on the assumption that reality is a social construction. As such, there are "multiple individual reconstructions" not a "single" reality (Guba & Lincoln, 1994). The focus of the interpretive paradigm is on understanding individuals' perceptions of reality as opposed to identifying objective phenomenon or social facts that exist outside of individuals. This understanding "involves being able to explain unique behaviour in context, after investigating the ways in which reality is constructed and negotiated" (Palys & Atchison, 2014, p. 23). This generally necessitates a qualitative research strategy, such as ethnography, which brings the researcher in close contact with those being studied for a prolonged period of time. As Palys and Atchison (2014) put it: "good theory is not imposed; rather, it emerges from direct observation and contact with people in context" (p. 23).

Critical Paradigm

Critical paradigm A worldview that is critical of paradigms which fail to acknowledge the role of power in the creation of knowledge and is aimed at bringing about empowering change.

Another worldview that emphasizes interpretation and understanding is the **critical paradigm.** The critical paradigm rests on an assumption that "human nature operates in a world that is based on a struggle for power" (Lincoln, Lynham, & Guba, 2011, p. 102). The critical paradigm focuses specifically on determining the role power plays in the creation of knowledge, often through the use of qualitative strategies. The critical approach is more of a critique concerning how and why particular views become the dominant ones and how privilege and oppression interact, often "based on race or ethnicity, socioeconomic class, gender, mental or physical abilities, or sexual preference" (Lincoln, Lynham & Guba, 2011, p. 102). In addition, this paradigm has an explicit aim involving "emancipation," or the "empowering of subordinated groups in society" (Symbaluk & Bereska, 2013, p. 10). In other words, to the extent that research can identify ways in which particular groups are disadvantaged and identify the causes of subordination, it can also be used to help resolve the inequities. Various paradigms stem from a critical-interpretative stance, including feminist, Marxist cultural studies, and queer theory.[2]

Pragmatic Paradigm

Pragmatic paradigm A worldview that rests on the assumption that reality is best understood in terms of the practical consequences of actions undertaken to solve problems.

Finally, in contrast to the dichotomy between the objectivity of positivism and the subjectivity of interpretive approaches, a more impartial outlook is offered by a more recent paradigm called the **pragmatic paradigm.** The pragmatic view "arises out of actions, situations, and consequences rather than antecedent conditions" and is more concerned with what is the most practical route to fully understanding a problem and finding a solution that will work for that problem at that time (Creswell, 2014, pp. 10–11). This problem-centred worldview is not based in any particular philosophy, nor does it necessitate the use of a particular form of reasoning or research technique. It does, however, emphasize the importance of methodology for solving problems and advocates for the use of combined qualitative and quantitative approaches for a more complete understanding. Historically, combining qualitative and quantitative approaches has proven problematic given the opposing assumptions upon which each approach is based. The pragmatic paradigm offers a solution to the dichotomy. As Creswell (2014) notes, "pragmatists do not see the world as an absolute unity. In a similar way, mixed methods researchers look to many approaches for collecting and analyzing data rather than subscribing to any one way (e.g., quantitative or qualitative)" (p. 11). Thus, the starting point is the issue or research problem, which itself suggests the most applicable means for further research exploration. Mixed method approaches to research that are grounded in a pragmatic paradigm are discussed in more detail in Chapter 11.

FIGURE 2.1   Comparison of Positivist, Interpretive, Critical, and Pragmatic Paradigms

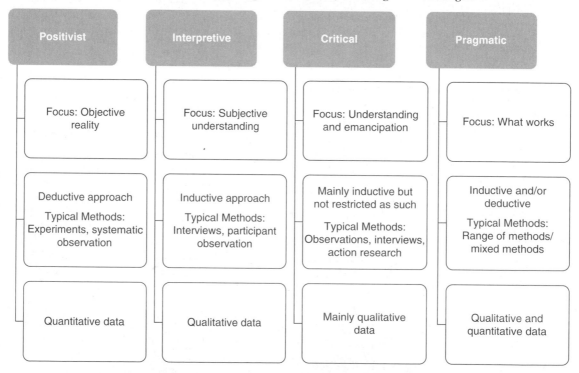

the social world, whether sociology should be considered a science, and why theories are important for framing social facts. The positivist and interpretive paradigms are compared and contrasted based on how issues are framed in the real world. Finally, a third paradigm called the "realist" approach is offered as a bridging view focused on the interplay between individuals and social structures. Using suicide as a case study, this program demonstrates how researchers ask very different questions and make very different assumptions depending on the paradigm that is their starting frame of reference. This program is available from Films on Demand at http://digital.films.com.

Test Yourself

- Which paradigm seeks to discover universal laws?
- Which paradigm is most concerned with objective reality?
- Which paradigm is problem-centred?
- Which paradigm rests on the assumption that reality is socially constructed?

Theoretical Frameworks and Theories

LO2

Theoretical framework A perspective based on core assumptions.

Macro level The level of broader social forces.

Micro level The level of individual experiences and choices.

Positivist, interpretive, critical, and pragmatic paradigms all offer a broad world-view from which theoretical frameworks emerge. **Theoretical frameworks** are perspectives based on core assumptions that provide a foundation for examining the social world at a particular level. Theoretical frameworks that operate at the **macro level** tend to focus on "broad social forces," while those dealing with the **micro level** are aimed at understanding "individual experiences and choices" (Symbaluk & Bereska, 2013, p. 5).

© Mike Flanagan. www.Cartoonstock.com

Within the discipline of sociology, the functionalist, conflict, interactionist, feminist, and postmodern frameworks provide different lenses from which we can view society. The functionalist framework is a macro level perspective that views society as being made up of certain structures such as the family, education, and religion, which are essential for maintaining social order and stability. The functionalist framework is rooted in positivism in its focus on observables in the form of social facts and universal truths. The conflict framework is also a macro level perspective, but it is rooted in the critical paradigm in its examination of power and its emphasis on the prevalence of inequality in society as groups compete for scarce resources.

The symbolic interactionist framework is a micro level perspective attributed to the early work of sociologists George Herbert Mead (1863–1931) and Herbert Blumer (1900–1987). The symbolic interactionist framework "depicts society as consisting of individuals engaged in various forms of communication that come to have particular meanings" (Symbaluk & Bereska, 2013, p. 17). The emphasis here is on how individuals create meaning through the use of symbols and language. Note how this framework emerges from interpretivism, with its emphasis on the importance of subjective meaning for individuals that is constructed and interpreted within interactions. The symbolic interactionist perspective often guides qualitative researchers as they design strategies for uncovering meaning in particular groups and contexts.

With roots in the critical paradigm, the feminist framework rests on the premise that men and women should be treated equal in all facets of social life (e.g., employment, law, and policy). The feminist framework operates at both the micro and macro level in an effort to demonstrate ways in which society is structured on the basis of gender. Finally, emerging post–World War II, the postmodern framework supports the worldview of the interpretive paradigm. The postmodern framework speaks out against singular, monolithic structures and forces. It traces the intersectional features of inequality, including race, class, and gender, and focuses specifically on the effects of the digital age. This framework complicates dualistic boundaries between the micro and macro (arguing that they are one and the same) and calls into question the singular truths of Marxism and functionalism.

Drilling down another layer, within broader theoretical perspectives, we can locate particular theories. Within the functionalist framework, for example, we find Robert Merton's (1938) strain theory of deviance, which explains how people adapt when there is a discrepancy between societal goals (what we are supposed to aspire to) and the legitimate means for obtaining them. Or, within the symbolic interactionist perspective, we locate Edwin Lemert's (1951) labelling theory of deviance, which explains a process whereby people may come to view themselves as lifelong deviants. Theories are discussed in more detail in the next section.

Test Yourself

- Which level of theorizing focuses on broad social forces?
- How does a theoretical framework help us to examine the social world?

The Role of Theory in Research

Theory A set of propositions intended to explain a fact or phenomenon.

A **theory** "is a set of propositions intended to explain a fact or a phenomenon" (Symbaluk & Bereska, 2013, p. 10). The propositions are usually expressed as statements that reflect the main assumptions of the theory. For example, Edwin Sutherland's (1947) differential association theory is a theory about crime. Differential association theory explains how crime is learned through interactions with others in much the same way as noncriminal behaviour is learned. That is, members of small groups with whom we spend time, and who we feel are important, teach us the techniques and motives needed to develop criminal tendencies as summarized in the following nine propositions provided by Sutherland (1947):

1. Criminal behaviour is learned.
2. Criminal behaviour is learned in interactions with other persons in a process of communication.
3. The principal part of the learning of criminal behaviour occurs within intimate personal groups.
4. When criminal behaviour is learned, the learning includes (a) techniques of committing the crime, which are sometimes very complicated, sometimes very simple and (b) the specific direction of motives, drives, rationalizations, and attitudes.
5. The specific direction of motives and drives is learned from definitions of the legal codes as favourable or unfavourable.
6. A person becomes delinquent because of an excess of definitions favourable to violation of law over definitions unfavourable to violation of law.
7. Differential associations may vary in frequency, duration, priority, and intensity.

Deductive reasoning A theory-driven approach that typically concludes with empirical generalizations based on research findings.

8. The process of learning criminal behaviour by association with criminal and anti-criminal patterns includes all of the mechanisms that are involved in any other learning.
9. Although criminal behaviour is an expression of general needs and values, it is not explained by those general needs, because noncriminal behaviour is an expression of the same needs and values. (Pp. 6–7)

Deductive Forms of Reasoning

Hypothesis A testable statement that contains at least two variables.

Variable A categorical concept for properties of people or events that can differ and change.

Theory doesn't happen in isolation from research; it can inform the research process, and it may develop from it. Theory that informs the research process is known as deductive reasoning. **Deductive reasoning** is a "theory-driven approach that typically concludes with [empirical] generalizations based on research findings" (Symbaluk & Bereska, 2013, p. 24). A deductive approach to social research is often a "top-down" linear one that begins with a research idea that is grounded in theory. A **hypothesis** or "testable statement that contains at least two variables" is derived from the theory, and this sets the stage for data collection (Symbaluk & Bereska, 2013, p. 27). A **variable** is a "categorical concept for properties of people or things that can differ and change" (Symbaluk & Bereska, 2013, p. 24) (as discussed in more detail in Chapter 4). In a study on crime, criminal behaviour (e.g., the presence or absence of it) or a certain type of crime is likely to be a main variable of interest, along with another variable regularly associated with crime such as age, sex, or race. For example, based on a theory of aggression, a hypothesis could be that men are more likely than women to commit physical assaults.

Testing Hypotheses Derived from Theories

Based on the tenants of Sutherland's (1947) differential association theory, Reiss and Rhodes (1964) "deduced" that delinquent boys are likely to engage in the same acts of deviance as their closest friends, since this is from whom they learn the techniques, motives, and definitions favourable to committing crimes as outlined in the main propositions. Specifically, they tested a hypothesis that the probability of an individual committing a delinquent act (e.g., auto theft, assault, and vandalism) would be dependent upon his two closest friends also committing that act. The researchers looked at six different delinquent acts among 299 triads (i.e., groups of three) wherein each boy reported on his delinquency and indicated whether he committed the act alone or in the presence of others. In support of the theory, Reiss and Rhodes (1964) found that boys who committed delinquent acts were more likely to have close friends that committed the same acts. Figure 2.2 summarizes the logic of a typical research process based on deductive reasoning.

Inductive Forms of Reasoning

An **inductive** approach is more "bottom-up," beginning with observations and ending with the discovery of patterns and themes that are usually informed by theory or help establish and thereby "induce" new theory (see Figure 2.3).

Inductive reasoning A bottom-up approach beginning with observations and ending with the discovery of patterns and themes informed by theory.

FIGURE 2.2
A Research Process Based on Deductive Reasoning

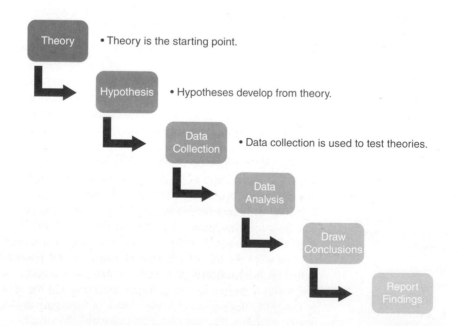

- Theory is the starting point.
- Hypotheses develop from theory.
- Data collection is used to test theories.

FIGURE 2.3
**A Research Process
Based on Inductive
Reasoning**

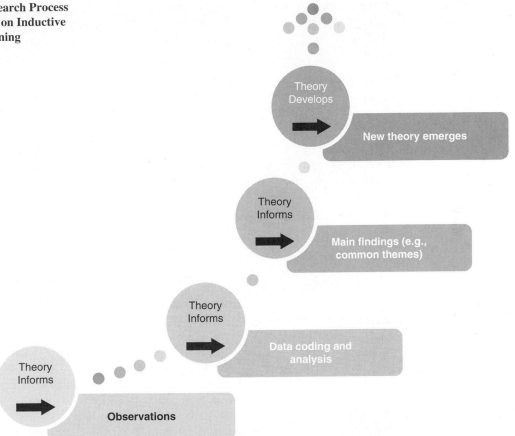

For example, Lowe and McClement (2011) examined the experience of spousal bereavement through interviews with young Canadian widows. Over the course of data collection, the researchers identified various common themes, including "elements of losses" such as the loss of companionship and the loss of hopes and dreams for the future. They also identified a notion of "who am I?" as the widows relayed their attempts to redefine themselves as single, in relation to other men, with their friends, and as single parents. Although the lived experience of young Canadian widows as a specific group of interest had not been previously explored, the researchers interpreted their findings within the context of previous studies and theoretical frameworks, such as Bowman's (1997) earlier research on facing the loss of dreams and Shaffer's (1993) dissertation research on rebuilding identity following the loss of a spouse. Lowe and McClement (2011) also identified the importance of making connections through memories as a means of adapting, suggesting a direction for additional research and the potential for an eventual theory on the development of relationships following the loss of a spouse.

The Role of Theory in Quantitative and Qualitative Research

Note that the role and use of theory differs depending on whether the study is quantitative (i.e., based on deductive reasoning) or qualitative (i.e., based on inductive reasoning). Recall from Chapter 1 that qualitative research often seeks to provide an in-depth understanding of a research issue from the perspective of those who are affected first-hand. The research process begins with an interest in a particular research area and a research question (e.g., What are the long-term implications of prior attendance in Canadian residential schools for Aboriginal people?). Data collection is often undertaken through a technique such as qualitative interviews, where a researcher asks open-ended questions, and depending on the answers given, formulates new ones in an attempt to learn as much as possible from an interviewee. Theory is usually brought into an analysis to help make sense of the narrative responses collected. For example, how does what this respondent is saying about former abuses and neglect suffered in residential schools and current reoccurring nightmares parallel what other researchers in this area have already reported on? Can the patterns and trends in this data be understood through concepts developed in other areas of existing research (e.g., post-traumatic stress)? In some cases, new theory develops out of the research findings. The "discovery of theory from data systematically obtained from social research" is better known as **grounded theory** (Glaser & Strauss, 2007, p. 2) since it is intricately linked to the data and context within which it developed. For example, in the case of residential schools, as a result of the severe abuse and neglect suffered, some former students developed what has come to be known as "residential school syndrome," a condition similar to post-traumatic stress disorder, involving reoccurring nightmares, memories, and the avoidance of anything that is a reminder of residential schooling (Brasfield, 2001). In most instances of qualitative research, theory plays a central role at various stages (e.g., in the formulation of the research question, in the initial stages of data coding, and especially toward the end of the data analysis process).

Grounded theory
Theory discovered from the systematic observation and analysis of data.

In contrast, theory is the starting point for most quantitative studies. On one hand, a theory provides a set of interrelated ideas that organize the existing knowledge in a meaningful way and help to explain it (Cozby, 2012). For example, demographic transition theory helps to identify universal stages of population change as countries progress from pre-industrial societies through to post-industrial economies (Notestein, 1945; Landry, 1934). In countries characterized by the more advanced industrial stage of development, birth rates are fairly low, corresponding to people having fewer children due to various considerations (e.g., birth control, female participation in the workforce, reliance on exported manufactured goods, greater emphasis on higher educational attainment, etc.). Despite the specificity of economic and social issues that vary from one country to the next, we can still identify broader commonalities such a declining birth rate coupled with an already low death rate in all countries that have reached the industrial stage of development, including Canada. Hence, this early theory is still useful today for explaining differences between countries in early industrial, industrial, and post-industrial stages of development.

In addition, a theory provides a focal point that draws our attention to particular issues and events in a manner that helps to generate new interest and knowledge (Cozby, 2012). For example, conflict theorists showed us how capitalism and its focus on economic productivity is linked to major environmental issues, including the high extraction of natural resources and the high accumulation of waste (Schnaiberg, 1980). Schnaiberg's early framing of capitalism as a "treadmill of production" spawned additional interest in the study of modern industry, highlighting ways in which current environmental issues are constructed as "proeconomic" measures in part because of alliances formed between capitalists, workers, and the state (Gould, Pellow, & Schnaiberg, 2008). Conflict theorists now direct our attention to the capitalist "treadmill of accumulation," which in its reliance on ever-increasing amounts of expansion and exploitation, may render any attempts at sustainable capitalism unattainable from an environmental standpoint (Foster, Clark, & York, 2010).

On the other hand, using theory as a starting point necessitates the development of specific propositions and the prior classifications of key concepts and assumptions before data collection begins. As David and Sutton (2011) explain, "there are advantages and disadvantages here. Those who seek to classify their qualities prior to data collection can be accused of imposing their own priorities, while those who seek to allow classifications to emerge during the research process are thereby unable to use the data collection period to test their subsequent theories. They too can then be accused of imposing their own priorities because it is hard to confirm or disprove their interpretations as no 'testing' has been done" (p. 92). You will learn more about the criteria used to evaluate research in Chapter 4. For now, consider that the two approaches, while different, have equal merit and drawbacks. Walter Wallace (1971) suggested that inductive and deductive approaches are probably best viewed as different components of the same research cycle, with some researchers beginning with theories and others starting with observations as shown in Figure 2.4.

FIGURE 2.4
Deductive and Inductive Reasoning Based on Wallace's Wheel of Science

Source: Schutt (2012). *Investigating the Social World: The Process and Practice of Research*, p. 41.

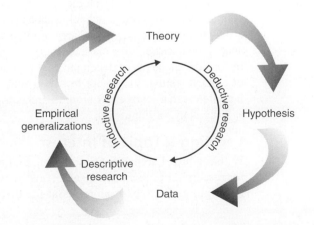

Research on the Net

SocioSite

SocioSite is an online social science information system based out of the University of Amsterdam and edited by Albert Benschop. Here, you can explore sociological theories and perspectives, as well as find links to research centres, data archives, associations, and a multitude of resources on a range of social issues (e.g., gender studies, population studies, research methodology and statistics, power, poverty, and racism). For an online tour of various Internet resources on social theories and perspectives, visit SocioSite at www.sociosite.net.

Test Yourself

- What is a theory?
- What does a hypothesis contain?
- In what ways is a research process based on deductive reasoning different from one based on inductive reasoning?
- How does the role and use of theory differ in a qualitative versus quantitative study?
- What is grounded theory?

Formulating Research Questions

LO4

Although most of this chapter has focused on the role of theory for guiding the development of research and helping to inform research outcomes, research actually begins before this with a general area of interest. Every research study begins with a topic of interest. Similar to the starting point of a very general worldview working down to a specific theory, a general area of interest must be shaped into a specific social research question. Think about the last time you were asked to write an essay on a topic of interest, or if you are considering continuing your studies into graduate school, what a general area of interest might entail. For a student in sociology, a broad area of interest could be the family, gender, deviance, globalization, or social inequality. A student in psychology is more likely to consider the areas of developmental psychology, cognition, neuropsychology, or clinical testing, to name a few. Someone in anthropology may have a starting interest that lends itself more to archeology, physical anthropology, cultural anthropology, or linguistics.

Locating a Topic of Interest

Within a broad area of interest, there are topics or issues that are focus points for research. For example, a sociologist working in the area of social inequality might wish to learn more about the distribution of poverty in Canada, or the barriers to housing experienced by those who are homeless. A developmental psychologist may be studying the intellectual, emotional, or perceptual development of children. Someone in anthropological linguistics might be interested in the evolution of particular language dialects or the loss of a mother tongue over time. Regardless of the topic you choose, your research interest is likely to centre on social groups (e.g., homeless people, children with developmental delays, Aboriginal Canadians who speak an endangered language) or social structures, policies, and processes that affect particular groups (e.g., barriers to housing, definitions of poverty, residential schooling practices, health benefit coverage).

Framing an Interest into a Social Research Question

Social research question A question about the social world that is answered through the collection and analysis of first-hand, verifiable, empirical data.

Recall from Chapter 1 that a social research question is designed to explore, describe, explain, or critically evaluate a topic of interest. This means that as you consider your topic of interest, you also have to think about how the wording of the question suggests the most appropriate course of action for answering it. A **social research question** is "a question about the social world that is answered through the collection and analysis of firsthand, verifiable, empirical data" (Schutt, 2012, p. 27). A question beginning with "What is it like to…" often implies an exploratory purpose, inductive reasoning, and a qualitative research method. A question beginning with "Why" may presuppose a search for causes, and this is generally undertaken for an explanatory purpose based on deductive reasoning and quantitative methods, such as an experiment. Alternatively, "Why" might also imply inductive reasoning that is designed to get the essence of a first-hand experience using a qualitative approach. Research questions designed to evaluate a program or service are likely to be formulated along the lines of "Is this working?" Program evaluations are often based on qualitative methods, but the approaches and methods vary considerably and may include mixed methods, depending on the nature of the particular program or policy. Descriptive studies, often beginning with a research question such as "What are its main features?," tend to be heavily represented in the quantitative realm (especially when the data is gathered through surveys). However, like evaluation research, descriptive studies are amenable to qualitative methods, especially in the case of field observation, which can produce highly descriptive forms of data.

Framing an interest is not a process that occurs instantly; rather, it is one that you develop over a period of time, eventually shaping your interest into a manageable research question that will direct a study that contributes worthwhile information to the existing body of knowledge. You will need to start with a general area, select a topic, issue, or focus within that area, and then look at the literature before refining your topic into a central social research question. Figure 2.5 provides two examples of the progression from a general area to a more specific question.

FIGURE 2.5   **Developing an Area of Interest into a Research Question**

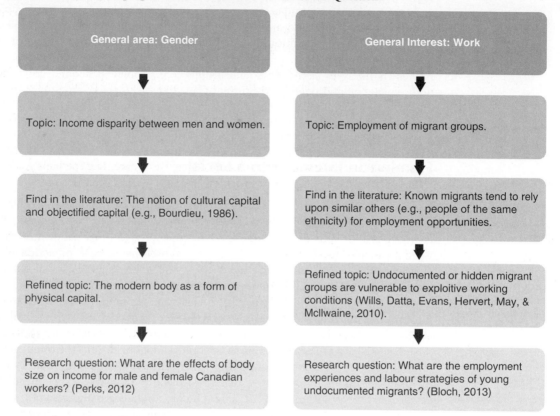

Test Yourself

- What does a research study begin with?
- What is a social research question?

The Importance of a Literature Review

LO5

Just as every study originates with a topic of interest, every research-based study that is published in an academic journal is based on at least one central research question. The odds are very high that you will be able to find existing research on any topic you wish to learn more about. In fact, if you plan to conduct research, you will need to be familiar with what is already known about your research interest *before* you finalize your research question. It is important that you at least examine the literature before you commit to a specific social research question (and hopefully before you mention your specific research question to your instructor). You are very likely to modify your research question once you learn more about the topic from a literature review.

A literature review is essential for a number of reasons:

1. First, a literature review tells you how much has already been done in this area. For example, if you are interested in carrying out a study on the portrayal of gender stereotypes in the media, it is important for you to know that this topic has been heavily researched for decades. There are literally millions of studies on gender stereotypes in movies, on television, in magazines, and on the Internet. In this case, your research question would not be exploratory in nature. One of your next steps with this topic would be to identify a more narrow area (e.g., perhaps you are more interested in male stereotypes portrayed in magazine advertisements).

2. Second, a literature review helps familiarize you with what is already known in the area. Continuing with an interest in stereotyped depictions of males, the literature can help you learn more about the construction of masculinity and how the male body is depicted in advertising. For example, Mishkind, Rodin, Silberstein, and Striegel-Moore (1986) note that advertising has increasingly come to celebrate a young, lean, and highly muscular body. This helps you choose an area that most interests you and that you can build upon with your own research (or that you can identify for an area of future research).

3. Third, a literature review helps you understand the debates and main points of interest within an area of study. Existing literature can inform you about how the portrayal of gender stereotypes in the media can lead people to become dissatisfied with their body image or engage in extreme practices and measures designed to obtain an ideal body image (e.g., dieting, fitness, cosmetic surgery). The literature can also help you understand similarities and differences in the ways in which men and women are portrayed, or how depictions of men have changed over time. These considerations may further shape the direction you elect to take with a current or future research project.

4. Fourth, a literature review highlights what still needs to be done in an area of interest. By examining previous research, you can find out researchers' suggestions for additional studies, where replications would be helpful, or areas that still need to be addressed. In particular, the discussion section at the end of most academic articles includes a few sentences that explicitly address how the current study could have been improved upon and/or point out a direction for future research. This is where you will obtain a sense of how you could design a study that builds on the existing literature but also contributes something new.

5. Lastly, a literature review can help you define important concepts and establish guidelines for how you will need to carry out your own study. For example, if you wish to clarify how male bodies are depicted in magazine advertisements, it would be practical to locate examples by other researchers that have already established standard ways to describe and code the body of a central character in a magazine advertisement.

Test Yourself

- Why is a literature review essential?

Locating Relevant Literature

Resist the temptation to simply Google the Internet to find any available resources on your topic of interest. Search engines prioritize links from paid sponsors, so the resources that appear first are likely not the most relevant or even appropriate references for your area of interest. In addition to commercial interests, the Internet also suffers from a lack of quality control; the information from web pages and articles you find on the Internet can be obsolete, and worse, fraught with errors.

Searching for Books

The best sources of information for a literature review include periodicals, e-books, books, and government documents located in or accessed through a library in a post-secondary institution. You can probably browse an online catalogue system for your post-secondary institution's library from any computer, as long as you can access the Internet and you are officially registered as a student. The library home page will direct you to library resources and provide you with more specific instructions on how to search for holdings by subject, title, and/or author. Subject areas tend to correspond with main concepts or key words in an area of interest. If you find you are obtaining too many resources using a fairly general search term, try combining two terms joined by "and." For example, if you try searching for a book using the combined subject search terms "male and stereotypes," you will probably locate a list of starting resources. If there are more than 50 books on this topic, you might try "male and stereotypes and media" to narrow your search a bit further. Conversely, if you are finding too few resources with even just one search term, try using two concepts joined by "or" to broaden the search.

Searching for Periodicals

Periodicals
Publications that contain a number of articles written by different authors and are released at regular intervals.

Periodicals (including magazines, newspapers, and scholarly journals) are publications that contain a number of articles written by different authors. Periodicals are released at regular intervals such as daily, weekly, monthly, semi-annually, or annually. Popular press periodicals (e.g., *Maclean's, Reader's Digest,* newspapers, and news websites) contain articles that are less scientific and more general interest–focused than scholarly articles published in peer-reviewed periodicals. Scholarly journals published by academic and professional organizations (e.g., universities) are the form of periodical most often cited by your instructors as credible sources for you to use in writing essays and research reports. Scholarly journals contain articles on basic research authored by academics and researchers with particular expertise in a subject matter. Articles found in scholarly journals have undergone considerable scrutiny in a competitive selection process that rests on peer review and evaluation prior to publication. This helps to ensure that only up-to-date, high-quality research, based on sound practices, makes it to the publication stage. Examples of Canadian sociological periodicals include the *Canadian Journal of Sociology* and the *Canadian Review of Sociology and Anthropology.* Note that hundreds of periodicals span a range of related disciplines (e.g., *Canadian Journal of Criminology, Canadian Journal of Economics, Canadian Journal of Political Science,* and *Canadian Psychology*) and more specialized topics (e.g., *Sex Roles, Child Abuse and Neglect, Contemporary Drug Problems,* and *Educational Gerontology*).

In many cases you can access journals online through a database. If it is available in "full text," you can usually download the entire article onto a storage device or email it yourself so you can later retrieve it for further reading. Comprehensive databases for locating articles on research in the social sciences include: Academic Search Premier, Social Sciences Full Text, PsychINFO, JSTOR, and the Social Sciences Citation Index. For example, Academic Search Premier is dubbed the most comprehensive multidiscipline full-text database. It contains abstracts for more than 8500 journals, with full-text available for more than 4600 of them (EBSCO Industries, 2012).

Research in Action

Evaluating Sources Found on the Internet

It is not enough to simply locate sources of information on a particular topic and assume that you have appropriate materials for learning about the area of interest. While academic journals undergo a peer-review process that helps to provide a check on the quality, accuracy, and currency of the published materials, the Internet has little or no quality control. If you use the Internet to find sources of information, such as web pages with links to various articles and other resources, it is important to evaluate that information before using it to inform your research. MacEwan University's Library (2013) suggests that you assess the quality of information you find on the Internet by asking the following questions about the site's authority, accuracy, objectivity, currency, coverage, and ease of use. A site that obtains many "yes" responses would be considered good enough for you to include in your literature review.

Authority

- Is it clear who is sponsoring the page or what institution/organization the author is affiliated with?
- Is there a link describing the purpose of the sponsoring organization?
- Is this organization recognized in the field of study?
- Is it clear who wrote the material and what the author's qualifications are?
- Is there an address to contact for more information?
- If the material is protected by copyright, is the name of the copyright holder given?

Accuracy

- Are sources of any factual information listed in a clear and complete manner so that they can be verified if necessary?

- Is the information free of grammatical, spelling, and other typographical errors?
- If statistical data is presented in graph or chart form, is it clearly labelled and easy to read?

Objectivity

- Is the information provided as a public service?
- Is the information free of advertising, or if there is any advertising on the page, is it clearly differentiated from the informational content?
- Are the organization's biases (if any) clearly stated?

Currency

- Are there dates on the page to indicate
  - when the page was written?
  - when the page was first placed on the web?
  - when the page was last revised?
- Are there any other indications that the material is kept current?

Coverage

- Is there an indication that the page has been completed, and is not under construction?

- If external links are provided, are they evaluated and do they relate to the purpose of the website?
- Are any references to other sources cited correctly?
- If there is a print equivalent to the web page, is there a clear indication of whether the entire work is available on the web or only parts of it?

Ease of Use

- Is it usually easy to connect to the site? Is it relatively free of technical difficulties?
- Is it attractive with clearly marked internal links and appropriate graphics?
- Are there tools, such as a help screen, a site map, or an internal search engine to guide you around the site?

For more information on assessing information found on the Internet and suggestions for research help, visit: http://library.macewan.ca/any_good.

Source: © MacEwan University, 2012. "Is it any good? Evaluating information on the World Wide Web." Retrieved Sep 9, 2012 from http://library.macewan.ca/any_good

Test Yourself

- What are the best sources of information for a literature review?

Chapter Summary

LO1   **Outline the main assumptions of positivist, interpretive, critical, and pragmatic paradigms.**

The positivist paradigm emphasizes objectivity and the importance of discovering truth through the use of empirical methods. The interpretive paradigm stresses the importance of subjective understanding and discovering meaning as it exists for the people experiencing it. The critical paradigm focuses on the role of power in the creation of knowledge. The pragmatic paradigm begins with a research problem and determines a course of action for studying it based on what seems most appropriate given that particular research problem.

LO2 **Define and differentiate between theoretical frameworks** **theories.**

Theoretical frameworks are perspectives based on core assumptions that provide a foundation for examining the social world at a particular level. For example, theoretical frameworks at the macro level tend to focus on broader social forces, while those at the micro level emphasize individual experiences. Theories develop from theoretical perspectives and they include propositions that are intended to explain a fact or phenomenon of interest.

LO3 **Distinguish between deductive and inductive reasoning and explain how the role of theory differs in qualitative and quantitative research.**

Deductive reasoning is a top-down theory-driven approach that concludes with generalizations based on research findings. Inductive reasoning is a bottom-up approach that begins with observations and typically ends with theory construction. Inductive approaches to reasoning guide qualitative research processes, while deductive approaches guide the stages of quantitative research. Theory tends to be the starting point for quantitative research, while it is interspersed throughout and emphasized more in the later stages of qualitative research.

LO4 **Formulate social research questions.**

Based on a broad area of interest and a careful literature review, a researcher eventually shapes a research interest into a social research question, which is a question about the social world that is answered through the collection and analysis of data. For example, a researcher might begin with an interest in gender that develops into an examination of the effects of body size on income for male and female workers, as demonstrated earlier in the chapter.

LO5 **Explain the importance of a literature review.**

A literature review is the starting point for formulating worthwhile social research questions. A literature review helps to identify what is already known about and still needs to be done in an area of interest. A literature review also points out debates and issues in an area of interest, along with the most relevant concepts and the means for going about studying the issue in more depth.

LO6 **Locate appropriate literature and evaluate sources of information found on the Internet.**

Appropriate literature sources include periodicals, books, and government documents, most of which can be accessing online through the library at post-secondary institutions. You should evaluate the quality of information gleaned from Internet websites prior to using that information as a primary source in a literature review. Evaluating information on the Internet generally takes the form of asking questions that centre on the authority, accuracy, objectivity, currency, coverage, and overall ease of use of the site and information located at that site. For example, in assessing objectivity, you can ask: "Is the information provided as a public service?"

Research Reflection

1. Which of the four main paradigms introduced at the beginning of the chapter do you think best represents your own personal views? Explain why this is the case.

2. Suppose you were interested learning more about the ways in which people experience major food allergies. For example, in what ways do food allergies impact people's lives? Which of the four main paradigms discussed in this chapter has basic beliefs that would be compatible with such a study?

3. Develop two social research questions—one that implies an exploratory purpose and one that implies an explanatory purpose.

4. In what ways is an article found in a scholarly journal likely to be more appropriate as a reference source for a research topic than one located using a search engine such Yahoo! or Google?

Learning Through Practice

Objective: To assess information on the Internet.
Directions:

1. Use a search engine to locate a website that contains factual information on a topic of interest.

2. Assess the web source using the following ten questions:
   1. Can you determine who is responsible for maintaining the site?
   2. Is there a way to contact the authors of the site?
   3. Is it possible to verify the accuracy of any of the claims made on this site?
   4. Is there an evident educational purpose for this site?
   5. Is the site objective (or free from bias)?
   6. Is the site free of advertisements?
   7. Can you tell when the site was created?
   8. Was the site recently updated?
   9. Are there properly cited references on the site?
   10. Is the site relatively easy to navigate?

3. What rating would you give this site out of 100, if 100 is perfect and 0 stands for without any merit? Explain why you think the site deserves this rating.

Research Resources

1. For an in-depth look at the qualitative approach to the development of grounded theory, refer to: Glaser, B. G. & Strauss, A. L. (2007). *The discovery of grounded theory: Strategies for qualitative research.* Piscataway, NJ: Aldine Transaction.

2. To learn more about the philosophical views that underlie the selection of a research design, the importance of a literature review, and the use of theory in research, I recommend: Creswell, J. W. (2014). *Research design: Qualitative, quantitative, and mixed method approaches* (4th ed.). Thousand Oaks, CA: Sage Publications.

3. To learn more about social theorists and the underpinnings of social theory, refer to: Ritzer, G. (Ed.). (2005). *Encyclopedia of social theory* (Vols. 1 & 2). Thousand Oaks, CA: Sage Publications.

connect For more information on the resources available from McGraw-Hill Ryerson, go to www.mcgrawhill.ca/he/solutions.

References

Babbie, E., & Benaquisto, L. (2014). *Fundamentals of social research* (3rd Can. ed.). Toronto, ON: Nelson Education.

Bloch, A. (2013). The labour market experiences and strategies of young undocumented migrants. *Work, Employment and Society, 27*(2), 272–287.

Bourdieu, P. (1986). The forms of capital. In J. G. Richardson (Ed.), *Handbook of theory and research for the sociology of education* (pp. 241–258). New York, NY: Greenwood Press.

Bowman, T. (1997). Facing loss of dreams: A special kind of grief. *International Journal of Palliative Nursing, 3*(2), 76–80.

Brasfield, C. (2001). Residential school syndrome. *British Columbia Medical Journal, 43*(2), 78–81.

Bryman, A., Bell, E., & Teevan, J. J. (2012). *Social research methods* (3rd Can. ed.). Don Mills, ON: Oxford University Press.

Cozby, P. C. (2012). *Methods in behavioral research* (11th ed.). New York, NY: McGraw-Hill.

Creswell, J. W. (2014). *Research design: Qualitative, quantitative, and mixed method approaches* (4th ed.). Thousand Oaks, CA: Sage Publications.

David, M., & Sutton, C. (2011). *Social research: An introduction* (2nd ed.). Thousand Oaks, CA: Sage Publications.

EBSCO Industries (2012). *Academic Search Premier.* Ipswich, MA: EBSCO Publishing. Retrieved from http://www.ebscohost.com/academic/academic-search-premier

Films Media Group (1996). *Sociological theory and methods.* Films on Demand. Retrieved from http://digital.films.com/PortalPlaylists.aspx?aid=8751&xtid=40133

Foster, J. B., Clark, B., & York, R. (2010). *The ecological rift: Capitalism's war on the earth.* New York: Monthly Review Press.

Glaser, B. G., & Strauss, A. L. (2007). *The discovery of grounded theory: Strategies for qualitative research.* Piscataway, NJ: Aldine Transaction.

Gould, K., Pellow, D. N., & Schnaiberg, A. (2008). *The treadmill of production: Injustice and unsustainability in the global economy.* Boulder, CO: Paradigm Publishers.

Grant MacEwan University (2013). Is it any good? Evaluating information on the World Wide Web. In *Research Help: Evaluate Web Information.* Edmonton, AB: Grant MacEwan University. Retrieved from: http://library.macewan.ca/any_good

Guba, E. G., & Lincoln, Y. S. (1994). Competing paradigms in qualitative research. In N. K. Denzin & Y. S. Lincoln (Eds.), *Handbook of qualitative research* (pp. 105–117). Thousand Oaks, CA: Sage.

Guba, E. G., (1990). The alternative paradigm dialog. In E. G., Guba (Ed.). *The paradigm dialog* (pp. 17–30). Newbury Park, CA: Sage.

Hennink, M., Hutter, I., & Bailey, A. (2011). *Qualitative research methods.* London, UK: Sage Publications.

Kuhn, T. S. (1962). *The structure of scientific revolutions.* Chicago, IL: University of Chicago Press.

Landry, A. (1934). *La révolution démographique.* Paris: Sirey.

Lemert, E. M. (1951). *Social pathology: A systematic approach to the study of sociopathic behavior.* New York: McGraw-Hill.

Lincoln, Y. S., Lynham, S. A., & Guba, E. G. (2011). Paradigmatic controversies, contradictions, and emerging confluences, revisited. In N. K. Denzin & Yvonna S. Lincoln (Eds.), *The Sage handbook of qualitative research* (4th ed., pp. 97–128). Thousand Oaks, CA: Sage Publications.

Lowe, M. E., & McClement, S. E. (2010–2011). Spousal bereavement: The lived experience of young Canadian widows. *OMEGA, 62*(2), 127–148.

Merton, R. K. (1938). Social structure and anomie. *American Sociological Review, 3,* 672–682.

Mishkind, M. E., Rodin, J., Silberstein, L. R., & Striegel-Moore, R. H. (1986). The embodiment of masculinity: Cultural, psychological, and behavioral dimensions. *American Behavioral Scientist, 29(5),* 545–562.

Notestein, F. (1945). Population: The long view. In Theodore W. Schultz (Ed.), *Food for the world* (pp. 36–57). Chicago, IL: University of Chicago Press.

Palys, T., & Atchison, C. (2014). *Research decisions: Quantitative, qualitative, and mixed methods approaches* (5th ed.). Toronto, ON: Nelson Education.

Perks, T. (2012). Physical capital and the embodied nature of income inequality: Gender differences in the effect of body size on workers' incomes in Canada. *Canadian Review of Sociology, 49*(1), 1–25.

Reiss, A. J., & Rhodes, A. L., (1964). An empirical test of differential association theory. *Journal of Research in Crime and Delinquency, 1,* 5–18.

Schnaiberg, A. (1980). *The environment: From surplus to scarcity.* New York: Oxford University Press.

Schutt, R. K. (2012). *Investigating the social world: The process and practice of research* (7th ed.). Thousand Oaks, CA: Sage Publications.

Shaffer, S. L. (1993). *Young widows: Rebuilding identity and personal growth following spousal loss.* Unpublished doctoral dissertation. California: University of San Francisco.

Sutherland, E. H. (1947). *Principles of criminology.* Philadelphia, PA: J. B. Lippincott.

Symbaluk, D. S., & Bereska, T. M. (2013). *Sociology in action: A Canadian perspective.* Toronto: Nelson Education.

Wallace, W. (1971). *The logic of science in sociology.* Hawthorne, NY: Transaction Publishers.

Wernick, A. (2005). Comte, August. In George Ritzer (Ed.), *Encyclopedia of social theory* (Vol. 1., pp. 128–134), Thousand Oaks, CA: Sage Publications, Inc.

Wills J., Datta, K., Evans, Y., Herbert, J., May, J., & McIlwaine, C. (2010). *Global cities at work: New migrant divisions of labour.* London, UK: Pluto.

Endnotes

[1] Lewin, K. (1951). In D. Cartwright (Ed.), *Field theory in social science: Selected theoretical papers.* New York: Harper & Row.

[2] For more information on paradigms based on feminism, Marxism, cultural studies, and queer theory, refer to *The Sage Handbook of Qualitative Research* (2011) edited by Norman K. Denzin and Yvonna S. Lincoln.

Research Ethics

3

"Many research textbooks explain research methods and their ethical aspects as logical processes that follow a given number of steps. Research, however, does not take place in a vacuum. It is imagined, designed, planned, funded (or not), executed and reported in a complex world by and with people with a whole range of viewpoints, values, needs, beliefs and agendas." (Martin Johnson, 2007, p. 29)[1]

Introduction

Ethics Conduct that is considered "morally right" or "morally wrong" as specified by codified and culturally ingrained principles, constraints, rules, and guidelines.

From medical breakthroughs to technological innovations to discoveries in the social sciences, few would argue against the importance of including humans in research. Along with the need to involve humans in research is a corresponding ethical obligation on the part of physicians and researchers to treat participants in a safe, dignified, and well-informed manner. **Ethics** refer to "conduct that is considered 'morally right' or 'morally wrong' as specified by codified and culturally ingrained principles, constraints, rules, and guidelines" (Rosnow & Rosenthal,

Research ethics An
array of considerations
that arise in relation to
the morally responsible
treatment of humans in
research.

2013, p. 41). **Research ethics** refer to an array of considerations that arise
tion to the morally responsible treatment of humans in research, including
for protecting the welfare and dignity of participants and procedures for asses
the overall risks and benefits. For example, where possible, researchers carefully
explain the procedures, risks, and benefits of a study to potential participants prior
to their participation in the study. Researchers also obtain consent or permission
from participants prior to their enlistment in a study, they make participants aware
that their participation is voluntary, and they make sure participants understand
that they are free to withdraw from the study at any time without penalty. Ethical
conduct also includes designing research procedures in a manner that minimizes
the potential for causing harm and maintains the privacy of individual participants.
However, as implied by the opening quote, while ethical principles and procedures
may appear straightforward from a moral perspective, researchers are people with
divergent interests, agendas, and even flaws. They may intentionally or inadvertently place participants in situations that they are ill-informed about ahead of
time, or that inflict harm, invade privacy, or otherwise compromise human dignity.

This chapter examines historical and social science cases involving the
unethical treatment of humans in research, along with the development of principles and procedures used to help guide ethical human-based research. In later
chapters, you will see how particular research techniques may pose special ethical
dilemmas for researchers, such as when researchers try to balance the trust established with participants against their research objectives in field studies where a
researcher joins a group to study it (see Chapter 10).

Unethical Treatment of Humans and Regulatory Outcomes

LO2

Numerous military and medical cases involve the unethical treatment
of unsuspecting citizens, soldiers, prisoners of war, and various vulnerable populations. These studies provide a historical context for understanding the ethical principles that regulate and govern research involving humans today.

Military Research: Nazi Experiments 1939–1945

Medical experimentation on human prisoners was routinely conducted during
World War II. German physicians, military officials, and researchers subjected
men, women, and children from concentration and death camps to all sorts of
torturous treatments to learn how to carry out medical practices, to find out more
about the course of disease pathology, to test the limits of human suffering, and
even to establish means for eliminating the Jewish race.

Famous examples include Professor Carl Clauberg, who developed a technique for the mass non-surgical sterilization of Jewish women using chemical
irritants; SS-Sturmbannfëhrer Horst Schumann, who induced sterilization by
subjecting women's ovaries and men's testicles to repeated radiation via x-rays;
chief SS physician Dr. Eduard Wirths, who studied contagious diseases by first
inflicting them upon prisoners (Auschwitz-Birkenau State Museum, 2012);
and Dr. Josef Mengele (i.e., the "Angel of Death"), whose interest in genetic
abnormalities led him to carry out often fatal surgical procedures on sets of twin

children, including the removal and exchange of internal organs and tissues (Lagnado & Dekel, 1991). Experiments were also routinely conducted to inform the German army about health issues, to help the government advance anti-Semitism plans involving racism and hatred toward people of Jewish descent, and to aid academics and physicians in furthering their own personal or professional agendas (Auschwitz-Birkenau State Museum, 2012).

This photo depicts the unloading ramp and the main entrance (or "Gate of Death") to Auschwitz-Birkenau, the largest network of German concentration and extermination camps during World War II.

The Nuremberg Code

Many of the physicians, political leaders, and researchers implicated in the inhumane examples provided above were prosecuted for their actions in a series of military tribunals. The Nuremburg trials, which began in 1945 at the Palace of Justice in Nuremberg, Bavaria in Germany, defined the Nazi medical experiments as "war crimes" and "crimes against humanity," and resulted in lengthy prison and/or death sentences for guilty defendants. Another important outcome was the establishment of a set of ten directives for human experimentation called the **Nuremberg Code.** The Nuremberg Code (1949) is among the first published set of ethical guidelines. It is summarized in the excerpts below:

Nuremberg Code
A set of ethical directives for human experimentation.

1. The voluntary consent of the human subject is absolutely essential.
2. The experiment should be such as to yield fruitful results for the good of society.
3. The experiment should be so designed and based on the results of animal experimentation.
4. The experiment should be so conducted as to avoid all unnecessary physical and mental suffering and injury.
5. No experiment should be conducted where there is an a priori reason to believe that death or disabling injury will occur.
6. The degree of risk to be taken should never exceed that determined by the humanitarian importance of the problem to be solved by the experiment.

7. Proper preparations should be made and adequate facilities provided to protect the experimental subject against even remote possibilities of injury, disability, or death.

8. The experiment should be conducted only by scientifically qualified persons.

9. During the course of the experiment the human subject should be at liberty to bring the experiment to an end.

10. During the course of the experiment the scientist in charge must be prepared to terminate the experiment at any stage. (Pp. 181–182)

Research on the Net

Canadian World War II Veterans Exposed to Mustard Gas

Military experimentation extended beyond Germany and prisoners of war to include Canadian soldiers who volunteered for studies designed to help military warfare. Many participants maintained oaths of secrecy despite long-standing suffering, and even eventual death in some cases from related health implications. In May 2004, the Canadian government released a $24,000 compensation payment to retired Master Corporal Roy Wheeler and retired Flight Sergeant Bill Tanner (CBC News, 2004). The two soldiers were the first of about 2500 remaining World War II veterans to receive an official apology and reparation on behalf of an estimated 3500 men exposed to mustard gas and other deadly chemicals. Experiments on the effects of chemical warfare agents were conducted by the Canadian military at Canadian Forces Base Suffield near Medicine Hat in Alberta for a thirty-year period from 1940 to 1970 (CBC News, 2004). While the compensation acknowledges unethical treatment, it cannot repair lasting health implications suffered by the soldiers, including infertility, heart disease, and lung complications. Learn more by going to CBC News Online at cbc.ca and searching for the news article title "Vets exposed to mustard gas receive compensation."

Biomedical Research: The Tuskegee Syphilis Study

The unethical treatment of patients is not limited to prisoners of war and military personnel. In 1932, 600 low-income, African-American men from Macon County, Alabama were recruited by the United States Public Health Service for a study on the natural (i.e., untreated) progression of the sexually transmitted disease syphilis (Tuskegee Syphilis Legacy Committee, 1996). Although 399 of the men had syphilis at the onset of the study, they were never informed about their condition and they never received treatment for it. Instead, the men were told they were being treated for "bad blood." They were monitored over a period of almost 40 years during which they were not given the standard therapy for syphilis of the time nor the penicillin that was developed as a cure for syphilis in 1947. Researchers even persuaded local doctors to withhold standard antibiotics (Stryker, 1997). In exchange for their willingness to participate, the men were provided with free meals, free medical examinations, and free burials (Tuskegee Syphilis Legacy Committee, 1996). Note that the study continued long after the establishment of the Nuremberg Code. In fact, the research went on for four decades until lawyer Peter Buxton took the case to the media. The Tuskegee study came to an end in 1972 when Jean Heller of the Associated Press released the story, making the true purpose of the research apparent along with the fact that the cure for syphilis had been withheld from the participants (Stryker, 1997).

An obvious implication of the withholding of knowledge of the disease in conjunction with the prevention of treatment was that all of the men suffered prolonged physical symptoms and many eventually died, passed the disease onto their wives, and even in some cases, onto their children as congenital syphilis. Survivors and their families eventually received financial compensation resulting from a class-action suit. On May 16, 1997, then-President Bill Clinton formally apologized on behalf of the government to the remaining survivors, their families, and the community for wrongdoings carried out at Tuskegee (Tuskegee University, 2013).

Participants in the Tuskegee Syphilis Study thought they were being treated for "bad blood."

The Belmont Report

In response to the Tuskegee study, the United States Congress passed the *National Research Act* in 1974 that created the National Commission for the Protection of Human Subjects of Biomedical and Behavioral Research. Since medical practices and research often occur together, the Commission outlined boundaries between medical practices and research to help determine conditions under which the actions of physicians and researchers would require review (National Commission for the Protection of Human Subjects of Biomedical and Behavioral Research, 1979). A summary of the recommendations by the Commission, called the Belmont Report, outlines three basic ethical principles meant to guide all future research involving humans:

- Principle 1: Respect for Persons
- Principle 2: Beneficence
- Principle 3: Justice

Respect for persons A moral principle stressing that researchers respect the human participants in their investigations as persons of worth whose participation is a matter of their autonomous choice.

Respect for persons is a moral principle stressing the importance of people being treated as "autonomous agents." This means that all participants should be valued as individuals who are free to make choices for themselves, including whether or not they wish to participate in a study. **Beneficence** is a term that describes the general personal safety and well-being of research participants.

Beneficence A moral principle outlining that in the planning and conduct of research with human participants, the researcher maximizes the possible benefits and minimizes the potential harms from the research.

Justice A moral principle of rightness claiming that in the course of research, researchers behave and make decisions in a manner that demonstrates social responsibility in relation to the distribution of harm versus benefits.

Beneficence as a moral principle refers to the dual notions of 1) "do no harm" and 2) "maximize possible benefits and minimize potential harms" (National Commission for the Protection of Human Subjects of Biomedical and Behavioral Research, 1979). **Justice** is a moral principle based on "fairness" attributed to common sense adages such as "to each person an equal share" and "to each person according to individual need." In this case it is expected that researchers will make decisions and behave in socially responsible ways. For example, "an injustice occurs when some benefit to which a person is entitled is denied without good reason or when some burden is imposed unduly" (National Commission for the Protection of Human Subjects of Biomedical and Behavioral Research, 1979, p. 5).

Research on the Net

Recruiting the Poor for Clinical Drug Trials

Unfortunately the principle of justice is not always upheld, as evidenced by the ongoing exploitation of disadvantaged groups for the advancement of science. On March 4, 2012, Dateline NBC correspondent Chris Hansen reported on the exploitation of poor people living in Ahmedabad, India by U.S. pharmaceutical companies who pay participants to undergo drug testing in clinical trials. Some of the test subjects are recruited by Rajesh Nadia, who is paid for every person he finds on behalf of the drug companies. In his interview with Chris Hansen,

Nadia admits the recruits often disregard the potential health risks and sometimes even enlist in overlapping studies for financial incentives (Sandler, 2012). How can pharmaceutical companies get away with this? In reference to the clinical drug trials taking place in India, Satinath Sarangi, director of the Bhopal Group for Information and Action, noted that, "you can do it cheaply, do it with no regulation, and even if there are violations, get away with it" (Sandler, 2012). For more information, visit the home page for Open Channel at msnbc.com and search for the news title "People keep falling sick."

Test Yourself

- What do research ethics refer to?
- What is the name for the ethical guidelines that developed out of the Nazi war trials?
- What features of the Tuskegee study illustrate unethical biomedical research?
- What three ethical principles are highlighted in the Belmont Report?

Unethical Treatment of Participants in Social Science Research

The unethical treatment of humans also extends into the realm of social research, as demonstrated in the following three studies.

Stanley Milgram's Experiments on Obedience to Authority

In what proved to be among the most controversial set of studies ever conducted in the social sciences, Yale University Professor Stanley Milgram (1961) devised a procedure while still in graduate studies for examining obedience. In this study, a naïve participant followed orders to administer increasingly painful electric shocks to a fellow participant serving as the "learner." In one of the earliest versions of what turned out to be a series of experiments, Milgram (1963) recruited participants through a newspaper advertisement for a paid study on memory conducted at Yale University. When a participant arrived at the university, he was greeted by an experimenter and an accomplice posing as the other participant in a two-person study of the effects of punishment on learning. After a brief overview, participants were asked to draw slips of paper from a hat to determine who would assume the role of the "teacher" and who would become the learner. The draw was fixed so that both slips of paper said "Teacher," ensuring that that the participant would always end up in the role of the teacher while the accomplice would assume the role of the learner.

The participant and accomplice were then taken to adjacent rooms where the learner was "strapped into an electric chair apparatus" designed to "prevent excessive movement" while also indicating to the teacher that the victim would be unable to depart the experiment of his own accord (Milgram, 1963, p. 373). The naïve participant was shown the shock generator apparatus consisting of a series of lever switches marked in increments of 15 and labelled with descriptors to indicate increasing voltage from 15 (slight), to 75 (moderate), to 135 (strong), to 195 (very strong), to 255 (intense), to 315 (extreme intensity), to 375 (Danger: Severe Shock), up to 420, where the descriptor was Xs. To add credibility, the teacher was then given a sample shock of 45 volts.

Throughout the word task, the teacher was instructed to give a shock by pressing down a lever on the shock generator each time the learner provided an incorrect answer. Importantly, the teacher was instructed to increase the shock level after each error and call out the value, such that the voltage increases by 15 each time and the increased voltage was salient to the teacher. At pre-planned intervals according to a script, the victim (learner) protested the shock treatment using various forms of feedback, such as pounding on the wall and screaming out in pain, until the shock value of 300 volts was reached. After that, the learner no longer responded. If at any point during the experiment the teacher stopped giving shocks and/or sought guidance on how to proceed, the experimenter followed a sequence of scripted prods including, "Please continue," or "Please go on," "The experiment requires that you continue," "It is absolutely essential that you continue," and "You have no other choice, you *must* go on" (Milgram, 1963, p. 374).

Results indicated that participants believed they were administering real shocks and they showed signs of extreme tension (e.g., sweating, stuttering, and trembling). Of the 40 participants included in the original version, five refused to obey commands to shock to the end beginning at 300 volts, two more stopped at 330 volts, and one more quit at each level of 345, 360, and 375 volts, for a total of 14 who defied the experimenter and 26 who obeyed orders to the very end.

This procedure was replicated by Milgram in more than 20 variations, including conducting the experiment in different countries (e.g., Norway and France), introducing group dynamics (e.g., the teacher was part of a small group obeying or breaking off from the experimenter's orders), introducing varied elements of the assumed responsibility (e.g., the learner made it evident he did not wish to

A participant in Milgram's study administers a shock to the learner while carrying out a word task.

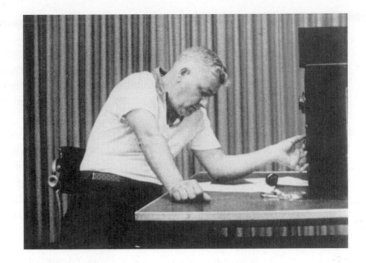

continue but was unable to get out of the study without help, the experimenter claimed full responsibility for the situation), and changing the salience or immediacy of victim (e.g., the victim was placed within view of the teacher) (Russell, 2010). In most cases, large numbers of participants obeyed the experimenter, providing what would be severely painful shocks to an innocent victim (i.e., the learner), and completing the study to the end. The fact that about two-thirds of the participants obeyed orders to the end goes against what we might consider common sense, which tells us that only in rare cases involving a highly sadistic or evil sort of person should this happen. Zimbardo (2004) explains that even 40 psychiatrists who were given a description of Milgram's procedures ahead of time failed to account for situational determinants and predicted that fewer than 1 percent of participants would shock to the maximum of 450 volts.

Milgram's experiments were widely criticized for their use of deception that evoked prolonged periods of distress where participants believed they were harming another individual. Milgram (1963) reported that "in a large number of cases the degree of tension reached extremes that are rarely seen in sociopsychological laboratory studies. Subjects were observed to sweat, tremble, stutter, bite their lips, groan, and dig their fingernails into their flesh. These were characteristic rather than exceptional responses to the experiment" (p. 375). Milgram (1963) went on to say that "one sign of tension was the regular occurrence of nervous laughing fits. Fourteen of the 40 subjects showed definite signs of nervous laughter and smiling. The laughter seemed entirely out of place, even bizarre. Full-blown, uncontrollable seizures were observed for three subjects. On one occasion we observed a seizure so violently convulsive that it was necessary to call a halt to the experiment" (p. 375). Many readers are left wondering if the "friendly reconciliation" between the learner and teacher that Milgram arranged at the end of the study was enough to disengage the tension produced throughout the study. As Diana Baumrind (1964) noted in an article questioning the ethics of Milgram's research, "It would be interesting to know what sort of procedures could dissipate the type of emotional disturbance just described. In view of the effects on subjects, traumatic to a degree which Milgram himself considers nearly unprecedented in sociopsychological experiments, his casual assurance that these tensions were dissipated before the subject left the laboratory is unconvincing" (p. 422). Baumrind (1964) added that Milgram had no way of determining how this study might negatively impact on the self-image of participants or their future views of authority figures.

In addition to the potential for lasting distress suffered by participants, the very topic of Milgram's studies (i.e., obedience) warranted a type of procedure that necessarily impinged on the voluntary nature of participation. That is, teachers were ordered to continue and told they must go on even when they said they wished to stop. This practice clearly goes against voluntary participation since the teachers were not free to withdraw from the study at any time without penalty.

Philip Zimbardo's Stanford Prison Study

In an attempt to study the interpersonal nature of prison life, Philip Zimbardo, Craig Haney, and Curtis Banks set out in 1971 to design a simulated prison in which participants would be randomly assigned the role of "prisoner" or "guard" (Haney, Banks, & Zimbardo, 1973). The procedures for this study were relatively straightforward. Participants were recruited through a newspaper advertisement seeking paid volunteers for a "psychological study of prison life." Of the 75 respondents, 21 were selected based on extensive background screening to determine those with the most "stable" and "mature" and least "anti-social" tendencies. Participants were informed that they would be assigned either a guard or prisoner role, and that they would be paid $15 per day for a period up to two weeks. They signed a contract "guaranteeing a minimally adequate diet, clothing, housing, and medical care as well as the financial remuneration in return for their stated 'intention' of serving in the assigned role for the duration of the study" (p. 74). No instructions were given for how to carry out a prisoner role, although participants were forewarned that they would have little privacy and they could expect to have their "basic civil rights suspended during their imprisonment, excluding physical abuse" (p. 74). Those serving as guards were given vague instructions to "maintain the reasonable degree of order within a prison necessary for its effective functioning" (p. 74).

With assistance from the Pala Alto City Police Department, participants assigned to the prisoner role were unexpectedly arrested at their homes and taken to the mock prison to begin the study, which took place in the basement of the psychology building at Stanford University. When the prisoners arrived, they were "stripped, sprayed with a delousing preparation (a deodorant spray) and made to stand alone naked for a while in the cell yard" (p. 76). Following this they were issued a uniform, had their ID picture taken, were taken to a cell, and were "ordered to remain silent." As part of the administrative routine, the warden, played by an undergraduate assistant, then explained rules for prisoners that the guards and the warden had created. These rules included being referred to as only a number, the granting of minimal supervised toilet breaks and limited scheduled visits, and compliance with regular "count" lineups, among other things.

This photo depicts a distinction between prison and guard roles that developed during the Stanford Prison Study.

Results showed that over time, guards became increasingly negative, aggressive, and dehumanizing, while prisoners became increasingly passive and in some cases, distressed. Haney, Banks, and Zimbardo (1973) noted that "extremely pathological reactions which emerged in both groups of subjects testify to the power of the social forces operating" (p. 81), and "the most dramatic evidence of the impact of the situation is seen in the gross reactions of five prisoners who had to be released because of extreme emotional depression, crying, rage and acute anxiety" (p. 81). Anyone who has seen video footage from the study is likely to question why the study was not stopped sooner or why particular prisoners who showed signs of extreme distress and begged to be let out of the study were not immediately allowed to do so. Even Zimbardo admits that it should have been his "job to hold in check the growing violence and arbitrary displays of power of the guards rather than to be the Milgramesque authority who, in being transformed from just to unjust as the learner's suffering intensified, demanded ever more extreme reactions from the participants" (Zimbardo, Maslach, & Haney, 2000, p. 194). It was not until after his soon-to-be-wife's tearful admonishment, "What you are doing to those boys is a terrible thing!" (p. 216), followed by a heated argument, that Zimbardo detached from his role as the prison superintendent and more fully appreciated how the power of the situation had taken over those in it, including himself (Zimbardo, Maslach, & Haney, 2000). For more information on the prison study, to view slides from the study, or to examine the documentary *Quiet Rage* produced by Musen & Zimbardo (1991), refer to the official website for the Stanford Prison Study at prisonexp.org.

Laud Humphreys's Tearoom Trade

One other well-known social science example deserves mention for unethical practices. In 1965, R. A. Laud Humphreys embarked upon a field study for his doctoral research of illegal and impersonal homosexual exchanges among males in park public washrooms. Because Humphreys was interested in learning about the practices and rules surrounding the homosexual behaviour of men who otherwise had no "homosexual identity," he needed to find a way to be included in the secret exchanges designed to maintain privacy (Humphreys, 1970). To accomplish this, Humphreys posed as a "voyeur-lookout"—someone interested in homosexual exchanges but not a direct participant—who could help alert the participants to potential detection by police or unsuspecting passersby. Thus, Humphreys carried out observational analyses in the field as a covert deviant. In his role as a participant observer, Humphreys discovered that silence was the main feature of the environment used to uphold privacy. That is, the men who had impersonal sex in "tearooms" (the name for public washrooms in which these exchanges took place), did so in silence specifically to ensure that the interaction was limited to that secret exchange and would not in any way impede on their regular lives that included wives, children, and so on. Over time, Humphreys realized that this silence constituted a significant impediment to his learning more about the participants. To resolve this, Humphreys decided to make contact with some of the regulars that he referred to as the "intensive dozen."

Upon making contact, Humphreys (1970) disclosed the true nature of his study and "with the help of some meals together and a number of drinks" persuaded the men to "cooperate in subsequent interviewing sessions" (p. 36). Although Humphreys now had detailed data from his interviews, he felt these men were not "representative of the tearoom population," and he then came up with a plan for contacting 100 other participants. First, he followed unsuspecting men to their vehicles where he recorded their license plate numbers. Next, he persuaded local police officers to give him access to their license registers under the auspices of "market research" where he obtained the names and home addresses of the men (Humphreys, 1970, p. 38). After verifying their addresses in the phone book, Humphreys then altered his appearance and showed up at their homes to interview the men to learn more about their regular lives under the pretext of a larger health survey. While several ethical issues are clearly evident in this study, a few of the most notable pertain to the way in which Humphreys misrepresented himself—first as a voyeur and then as a social worker—to gain access to the tearooms and later the participants' homes. Deception can be highly problematic for undermining the voluntary nature of participation in research, and it is generally used only in rare cases where disclosing the true nature of the study would negate or change the behaviour being studied. While this is likely the case with Humphrey's research, we are still left considering whether the invasions of privacy were warranted and whether the study contributed more overall benefit relative to its potential harm for participants.

Test Yourself

- What features of Milgram's study posed ethical concerns?
- What features of Zimbardo's study posed ethical concerns?
- What features of Humphreys's study posed ethical concerns?

Ethical Issues Common to Social Science Research

The historical medical, military, and social science examples discussed thus far all help to illustrate key ethical issues that arise in research. This section discusses five recurring concerns in more detail, including the potential for harm, risk-benefit analysis, informed consent, privacy and confidentiality, and debriefing. These issues are still prevalent today, and they need to be specifically addressed by researchers who plan to apply for ethical approval for any kind of research involving humans as participants in the social sciences.

1. The Potential for Harm

Perhaps the most essential consideration in any study is its potential to produce harmful outcomes for participants. Any procedure that requires participants to engage in physical activity has the potential, even if slight, for someone to incur an injury. Similarly, a clinical drug trial might require participants to ingest a medicine that could produce physical side effects, such as sweating, blurred vision, or an increased heart rate. In most cases where there is the potential for physical harm, researchers attempt to design their study in a manner that minimizes the risk. For example, in research on factors influencing participants' willingness to endure the pain of an isometric sitting exercise, we included only physically active, healthy individuals aged 18 to 25 years who were continuously monitored and whose heart rates were assessed every 20 seconds to ensure their ability to continue safely to a maximum of six minutes (Symbaluk, Heth, Cameron, & Pierce, 1997). Harmful studies such as those conducted by the Nazi doctors or the researchers in the Tuskegee Syphilis Study would never receive ethical approval today.

It is possible for participants to experience psychological forms of harm, as in case of the severe stress experienced by some of the subjects in Milgram's experiments who believed they were giving painful electric shocks to an innocent victim, or the "prisoners" in Zimbardo's experiment who were verbally abused and degraded by the "guards." Participants may also experience stress as a function of being asked personal questions during an interview or disclosing particular responses on a questionnaire. In addition, being provided with certain kinds of feedback during a study, such as a participant determining he or she is performing extremely poorly relative to the other participants on some kind of task, can lead to feelings of stress. In cases where procedures have the potential to evoke high levels of stress (e.g., the roles of prisoners and guards), safeguards need to be built into the study, such as careful monitoring, the ability to readily terminate a study, and ways to assess the stress. Where stressful reactions become apparent especially if they were unanticipated ahead of time (e.g., as a function of a question being asked during an interview), the onus is on the researcher to respond in a timely and appropriate manner.

2. Risk-Benefit Analysis

Studies should be designed to minimize harm and maximize benefits. Through risk-benefit analysis, studies that necessitate the use of known harm but contribute little to our understanding are usually considered unethical, while studies that minimize the potential for harm or result in negligible harm but greatly improve programs, help to reduce suffering, or have a widely applicable benefits are more apt to be deemed ethical.

While Milgram's experiments clearly caused harm, they must be evaluated in historical context. These studies were the only ones to examine obedience at a time when science had yet to explain how millions of innocent people had lost their lives at the hands of otherwise "ordinary" Nazi soldiers and officials, many who claimed they were simply following orders. Similarly, while participants in Zimbardo's study were also negatively affected by their experience, the researchers could not anticipate the severity of the situation or how they themselves would be carried away by situational forces. In both cases, the importance of the findings for teaching us about obedience and situational forces, as well as how to build in participant safeguards in subsequent research, cannot be understated. Finally, although it is tempting to paint Humphreys as an unethical researcher, it is important to note that homosexuality was considered a crime at that time and such deviant exchanges had not been previously studied. Humphreys can just as readily be viewed as a pioneer in furthering knowledge by refuting popular misconceptions of the time by revealing that many of the men who engaged in homosexual exchanges were "normal" and even "exemplary" educated people with wives, full-time jobs, and strong religious ties. While much of the information presented above is in hindsight, the point is that all research has benefits and drawbacks, which need to be carefully weighed out to determine the merit of any given study at a particular place and point in time.

3. Informed Consent

Informed consent
A process where potential participants are provided with all of the relevant details of the study needed to make a knowledgeable judgment about whether or not to participate in it.

Under no circumstances should people be coerced, misled, or otherwise forced to take part in research. The indictment of the physicians implicated in Nazi medical experiments during the Nuremberg trials was less based on the harm incurred than the fact that victims were forced into the experiments against their will. **Informed consent** refers to a process where potential participants are provided with all of the relevant details of a study needed to make a knowledgeable judgment about whether or not to participate in it.

Informed consent is usually obtained with a written consent form that discloses all of the relevant details of the study and clearly establishes the voluntary nature of participation. The form includes a statement indicating that the study constitutes research; a description of the nature and purpose of the research; an outline of the procedures, including the anticipated timelines; a disclosure of any potential risks and benefits; alternatives to participation; measures taken to ensure privacy, anonymity, and confidentiality; details of any reimbursement or compensation for participating; assurances that participation is voluntary; and contact information for the researchers.

Note that a number of factors can challenge the process for obtaining informed consent. For example, participants with limited or impaired cognitive ability may lack the capacity to understand the risks and benefits of a study or what is required in the role of a participant. Similarly, consent cannot be obtained from children without both their approval and the approval of adults who are responsible for them. Finally, individuals in vulnerable positions, such as persons who are serving time in prison or employees being asked to take part in a study by their employers, may be informed that participation is voluntary, but still may believe that a failure to participate could have negative repercussions.

According to Cozby (2012), informed consent should be obtained in a manner that is readily understood by the general public and aimed at an education level of about grade six to eight. In addition, the form should be written as an informal letter to the participant as opposed to a legal document. The letter should be free of any kind of technical terms specific to a research area or discipline. Finally, it should be apparent to the potential participant that he or she is free to withdraw consent at any time, without penalty. Importantly, signing a consent form is not the same thing as signing a waiver form where a person absolves all others of blame. A researcher remains responsible and may incur later legal liability for actions taken or not taken during a study that result in harm to the participant (see Figure 3.1).

4. Privacy and Confidentiality

Another key ethical issue in research concerns the loss of privacy and confidentiality. Although researchers try to uphold the privacy of participants, in many instances social research itself necessitates an invasion of privacy. From the completion of a relatively harmless online survey that intrudes into a respondent's personal time, to highly personal questions about one's private experiences asked by a qualitative researcher in a face-to-face interview, research spans a continuum when it comes to loss of privacy. Sometimes a researcher may be more interested in the responses than in the respondents in a given study. In such cases, researchers may be able to maintain the **anonymity** of participants by keeping their name off any of the materials that could be used to identify a response to a given person. Anonymity exists if a researcher cannot link any individual response to the person who provided it. This is similar to student evaluations of courses and instructors where student responses are anonymous because they do not include their names or any other identifying information on the evaluation instruments.

Confidentiality is an ethical principle referring to the process enacted to uphold privacy (Sieber, 1992). For example, a researcher may be able to identify a person from his or her responses if an interviewer can clearly see who is

Anonymity A state of being unknown. In the case of research, this means a researcher cannot link any individual response to its originator.

Confidentiality The process of maintaining privacy. In research, this means even when a participant's identity is known to the researcher, steps are taken to make sure it is not made public.

FIGURE 3.1
Sample Informed
Consent Form

Sample Informed Consent Form

You are invited to participate in research by Dr. xxx in the Department of Psychology at xxx University. This research is examining people's views toward others, and people's responses to different descriptions of others. Participants will be asked to complete a number of ratings, such as judging how much you like various newspaper headlines that describe people in different ways. Participants will also be asked to report their age, sex, their program of study, whether they were born inside or outside of Canada, and year of study.

Participation will be anonymous. Only aggregate (group) data will be examined and reported. The recording of your ID number for the purpose of receiving course credit for your participation will be kept entirely separate from your questionnaire responses.

You will be credited with 2 percent toward your final course grade by participating in this research. Participation is voluntary, and you are free to withdraw at any time, for any reason, without a loss of credit. Additionally, if you choose to participate and find a question you would prefer not to answer, you are free to skip that question and continue on with the rest of the items.

Participation will take about 30 minutes. If you choose to participate, not only will you make a valuable contribution to scientific advancement, but you will experience what it is like to be a participant in psychological research and come to more fully appreciate and understand the research processes fundamental to the field of psychology. There are no anticipated risks of participating in this research.

If you choose not to participate in this study, you can obtain the same course credit by participating in another study, or by completing the alternative, non-research activity.

If you have any further questions feel free to contact Dr. xxx by email at xx@xxx.ca or by phone at (xxx) xxx–xxx. You can also contact the chair of the research ethics board with any questions or concerns (Dr. xxx; email: xxx@xxx.ca).

Consent to Participate

I hereby give my consent to participate in the research described above. I realize that by signing I have not waived my right to legal action should I be harmed in any way by participating in this study.

Signature of Participant: _____   Date: _____

---

providing the responses; however, the researcher promises not to later disclose information that would identify that person publicly. Confidentiality can often be upheld by reporting collected data in an aggregate (i.e., grouped), rather than individual format. In other cases, information may need to be omitted to preserve privacy. For example, a published report that indicates that a participant held a position as mayor or was a director of human resources at a university would inadvertently reveal the identity of participants. Researchers routinely use pseudonyms in place of actual names, and they may even change a few details, such as the sex or age of a participant, to respect privacy.

Research in Action

The Russel Ogden Case

Confidentiality was put to the most extreme test in early 1994 in the only Canadian case in which a researcher was ever subpoenaed to appear in court to provide evidence that would identify research participants (Palys & Atchison, 2014). The researcher was Russel Ogden, a then–MA student in the School of Criminology at Simon Fraser University, who was carrying out controversial research on assisted suicide among individuals suffering from HIV/AIDS. Ogden guaranteed his research participants "absolute confidentiality" and therefore refused to provide any identifying information on ethical grounds. Although he was threatened with a charge of contempt of court, he eventually won his case. The riveting case, the legal and ethical implications, and the controversy involving Simon Fraser University for its initial lack of support is described by Palys and Atchison (2014) and is outlined in detail in a web page posted by Ted Palys that you can access at sfu.ca/~palys/OgdenPge.htm.

5. Debriefing

Debriefing The full disclosure and exchange of information that occurs upon completion of a study.

Debriefing refers to the full disclosure and exchange of information that takes place upon completion of a study. Debriefing is required in all situations where participants are not told all of the details of the study or are misled about details of the study prior to participating in the study. In psychological research in particular, deception is sometimes required to maintain the integrity of the main variable under consideration. For example, suppose you wish to conduct an experiment on helping and want to see how many students are willing to help classmates who request to borrow their notes under the pretense of missing class due to an illness. If you informed participants ahead of time that someone was going to approach them at the end of class and ask to borrow their notes so you could measure whether they actually helped or not, this knowledge would likely affect their willingness to help in a manner and would negate the purpose of the study.

Test Yourself

- Is harm always of a physical nature? Explain your answer.
- How is beneficence a risk-benefit calculation?
- What is informed consent and what details are included in a consent form?
- How is anonymity different from confidentiality?
- What is debriefing and when is it a requirement?

Tri-Council Policy Statement

LO5

Research ethics regulations in Canada arose in the late 1970s largely in response to U.S. policies stemming from the Tuskegee study, controversies surrounding deception in social psychological experiments including Milgram's, and calls for greater accountability by government funding agencies (Adair, 2001). Canada's three federal research funding agencies include the Canadian Institutes of Health Research (CIHR), the Natural Sciences and Engineering Council of Canada (NSERC), and the Social Sciences and Humanities Research Council of Canada (SSHRC). In 1998, these agencies collectively adopted the Tri-Council Policy Statement: Ethical Conduct for Research Involving Humans (TCPS or the Policy). The policy is meant to guide researchers in the design of their studies, to promote ethical conduct in the carrying out of research projects, and to establish a process for the ethical review of research involving humans. Research on animals is not considered in this policy, although separate, extensive ethical guidelines exist with respect to animal rights, animal care, and the use of animals in research. The TCPS was expanded into a revised, second edition in 2010 and it is now referred to as the Tri-Council Policy Statement: Ethical Conduct for Research Involving Humans (TCPS 2). The TCPS 2 serves as the guide to official policies at universities in Canada where research takes place.

Respect for human dignity A value necessitating that research involving humans be conducted in a manner that is sensitive to the inherent worth of all human beings and the respect and consideration that they are due.

The overarching value of the TCPS 2 is **respect for human dignity**. Respect for human dignity necessitates that "research involving humans be conducted in a manner that is sensitive to the inherent worth of all human beings and the respect and consideration that they are due." Respect for human dignity is expressed in the three principles you were introduced to earlier in this chapter: respect for persons, a concern for welfare, and justice.

Respect for Persons

As noted in the Belmont Report, respect for persons recognizes the value of human worth as well as the dual need to respect autonomy and protect those with diminished autonomy. The TCPS 2 additionally includes as persons, "human biological materials" such as "materials related to human reproduction." Respect for persons is demonstrated through the establishment of consent to participate in a study.

Establishment of Consent

Three important principles underlie the establishment of consent. First, consent is given voluntarily. This means a subject freely chooses to participate in the research. Consent is not voluntary in cases where, for example, soldiers are coerced into a study by their superior officers or prisoners participate in a study out of fear of negative implications that might result if consent is not provided.

Second, consent is informed by the disclosure of all relevant information needed to understand what participation entails, including all foreseeable risks and benefits. For research intended to involve individuals who lack the capacity to provide informed consent, the individuals must be involved—to the extent possible—in the consent decision-making process, consent must be obtained from "authorized third parties" who are not affiliated with the research team, and the research must have direct benefit for the intended participants (CIHR, NSERC, and SSHRC, 2010, p. 41).

Third, consent is an ongoing process. This does not imply that once a person signs a consent form, he or she has consented to finish the study. Rather, "the researcher has an ongoing ethical and legal obligation to bring to participants' attention any changes to the research project that may affect them" throughout the course of the study (CIHR, NSERC, and SSHRC, 2010, p. 34). A participant may or may not choose to start a study and may elect to discontinue his or her involvement at any time after starting, without penalty. In cases where a participant discontinues involvement, data collected up to the point may also be withdrawn at the discretion of the participant.

Concern for Welfare

Concern for welfare
Steps taken to protect the welfare of research participants both in terms of harm and in terms of other foreseeable risks associated with participation in a given study.

Harm has already been discussed in detail so I won't reiterate this issue here. In addition to minimizing harm, a **concern for welfare** entails efforts to mitigate other foreseeable risks associated with participation, such as to housing, employment, security, family life, and community membership. The protection of privacy also falls under a concern for welfare: "Privacy risks arise in all stages of the research life cycle, including initial collection of information, use and analysis to address research questions, dissemination of findings, storage and retention of information, and disposal of records or devices on which information is stored" (CIHR, NSERC, and SSHRC, 2010, p. 56). In this case, the promise of keeping data confidential is expanded to include an obligation on the part of the researcher to put safeguards in place for all "entrusted information" so that it is protected from "unauthorized access, use, disclosure, modification, loss, or theft" (CIHR, NSERC, and SSHRC, 2010, p. 56). Typical security measures include the storage of data on password-protected computers and in locked file cabinets away from the public, such as in the private office of a researcher.

Another concern related to welfare is the special consideration of particular individuals or groups "whose circumstances may make them vulnerable in the context of research," as in the case of impoverished groups where even a slight participation incentive could negate the voluntary manner in which consent is supposed to be given (CIHR, NSERC, and SSHRC, 2010, p. 52). An example of this is the use of paid participants from poor areas in India, as described in the Research on the Net box "Recruiting the Poor for Clinical Drug Trials."

A final application of welfare extends to research with Aboriginal peoples, or First Nations, Inuit, and Métis peoples. Traditionally, much of the research carried out on Aboriginal peoples has been undertaken by non-Aboriginal researchers. This is problematic as researchers may overlook how core ethical principles correspond to and in some cases fail to adequately take into account community customs, concerns, relationships, and values. The TCPS 2 dedicates an entire chapter (Chapter 9) to research involving First Nations, Inuit, and Métis peoples of Canada in an effort to interpret the ethics framework within Aboriginal contexts.

Justice

Recall that justice refers to "the obligation to treat people fairly and equitably" (CIHR, NSERC, and SSHRC, 2010, p. 10). Fairness means equal concern and respect is shown to all research participants, while equity relates more to considerations of the overall distribution of benefits versus "burdens" incurred by participants in research. Stemming from this is a concern that certain groups are not given the opportunity to participate in research on the basis of attributes unrelated to the research. For example, women, children, and the elderly are sometimes inappropriately excluded from research on the basis of sex, age, or disability (see Chapter 4 in the TCPS 2).

Finally, researchers seeking to carry out projects that target Aboriginal participants, affect Aboriginal communities, or are conducted on First Nations, Inuit, or Métis lands, must first be informed about rules and customs that apply to Aboriginal peoples and their land, and must engage directly with the implicated community in the design and implementation of the project. For example, the TCPS 2 notes that a comparative study of access to public housing in Prince Albert, Saskatchewan would meet the criteria since Aboriginal people or an Aboriginal community would necessarily make up a significant portion of the study on which conclusions would be reached (CIHR, NSERC, and SSHRC, 2010).

Test Yourself

- What is the all-encompassing value of the TCPS 2?
- What three principles underlie the consent process?
- In what ways might a concern for welfare extend beyond physical and psychological harm?
- What are privacy risks and when do they arise?
- Why are certain individuals and groups especially vulnerable in the context of research?

Research Ethics Boards and the Ethical Review Process

LO6

Research ethics board A committee whose mandate is to review the ethical acceptability of research on behalf of the institution, including approving, rejecting, proposing modifications to, or terminating any proposed or ongoing research involving humans.

The TCPS 2 mandates that all research involving humans be subject to an ethical review by an institutional **research ethics board.** A research ethics board (REB) is a committee whose role is to "review the ethical acceptability of research on behalf of the institution, including approving, rejecting, proposing modifications to, or terminating any proposed or ongoing research involving humans" (CIHR, NSERC, and SSHRC, 2010, p. 69).

Membership Requirements

Members on a REB must be qualified to judge the ethical provisions of the research as guided by the TCPS 2. At least some of the members of the committee are required to have expertise in research methodologies of the relevant disciplines of the researchers likely to submit applications. In addition, the group must contain ethical and legal expertise, as well as someone who can represent the interests of the general public, such as a community member not affiliated with the institution.

Ethical Review Process

All research that is conducted by individuals affiliated with an institution, such as faculty members or professors, is conducted at a university using that institution's assets (e.g., a classroom, equipment, etc.), or includes students or staff members from a university as participants needs to be approved in advance by an REB. The formal process begins with the researcher completing an application for review.

Ethical Review Application Form

As directed by the TCPS 2, an ethical review application at a university in Canada includes the following information:

- background information on the main or principal researcher, including name, email address, department or program, mailing address, telephone number, and affiliated institution;
- a list of other investigators on the project;
- details about the proposed project, including the project title, the proposed start and end date, the institution at which the project will be conducted, and other relevant specifics such as ethical approval received or sought from other institutions and any applicable sources of funding;
- a summary of the proposed project objectives;
- a relevant literature review on the topic;
- the hypotheses or research questions examined;
- detailed information about the research participants, such as the number sought and characteristics relevant to recruitment (e.g., age range or type of participant);
- the manner in which the participant will be solicited, including disclosure of any inducements or promises offered for participation;
- details of all known risks, including physical and psychological, as well as any other foreseeable concerns stemming from participation;
- justifications for any harm incurred and explanations of how safeguards or resolutions will be built into the study;
- a detailed description of the procedures to be used in the study, including how informed and voluntary consent will be secured, how privacy will be respected, and how consent will be obtained if there are exceptions to anonymity and confidentiality;
- explicit justification in cases where information is withheld from participants, along with indications of how and when the concealed information will be shared;
- details regarding when and how participants are debriefed;
- an indication of how participants can contact the researchers at a later date to ask questions or learn more about their role in the study; and
- details on plans for the retention and disposal of data.

The application is submitted to the chair of the REB, along with any other supporting documents as deemed relevant in relation to the particular study, such as an advertisement for participant recruitment, an indication of ethical approval from another institution, an interview script or interview question guidelines, a participant informed consent form, and/or a questionnaire or survey items.

Research Ethics Board Decision

An REB usually meets on a published schedule (e.g., once a month) to review research applications and render a decision about the ethical acceptability of the proposed research, taking into account all of the guidelines outlined in the TCPS 2. The decision is provided in writing to the researcher on behalf of the institution. It generally takes the form of an approval with no conditions, an approval subject to the conditions outlined in the decision provided by the committee, or the research project is deemed unethical and is not granted ethical approval for the reasons listed.

Research in Action

Acres of Skin: Medical Abuse Behind Bars

Acres of Skin: Medical Abuse Behind Bars (Films for the Humanities and Science, 2004) is a documentary that describes decades of medical experiments conducted by dermatologist Dr. Albert Kligman on inmates from Philadelphia's Holmesburg Prison. The film is an excellent resource on research ethics because it demonstrates how the absence of strict regulations can make vulnerable populations especially susceptible to unethical treatment. Through first-hand examples of unethical behaviour by researchers, this film highlights the significance of ethical considerations discussed in this chapter with special emphasis on the use of vulnerable populations, the need for full disclosure of medical procedures and risks, and a consideration of the mental capacity required for informed consent.

Test Yourself

- What is an REB?
- What kinds of study details are included in an ethical review application form?

Chapter Summary

LO1 **Define research ethics and provide examples of research-related ethical conduct.**

Research ethics refer to an array of considerations that arise in relation to the morally responsible treatment of humans in research. For example, ethical conduct includes minimizing the risk of harm to participants; treating participants fairly, equitably, and with respect; ensuring participants have provided informed and voluntary consent; and safeguarding privacy.

LO2 **Recognize links between early military research and regulatory outcomes.**

Much of the early research conducted by Nazi doctors and military personnel involved severe injury or death for victims who were forced to participate in experiments against their will. The Nuremberg Code consists of ten ethical guidelines outlining safeguards for experiments, including the importance of obtaining informed and voluntary consent, providing justification for a study based on its overall merits versus potential for causing harm, minimizing the potential for harm, and giving subjects the liberty to withdraw their participation at any time. The Belmont Report comprises three main principles: respect for persons (a principle recognizing the autonomy and worth of individuals), beneficence (a principle stressing the importance of maximizing benefits and minimizing harm), and justice (a principle underlying socially responsible behaviour).

LO3   **Discuss ethical considerations raised by Milgram's, Zimbardo's, and Hymphreys's early research.**

In Stanley Milgram's experiments on obedience to authority, participants were harmed by the belief that they were administering painful electric shocks to another participant. In Philip Zimbardo's simulated prison study, prisoners were harmed by the aggressive and abusive tendencies that developed in the guards. In Laud Humphreys's study, deception was repeatedly used to secure access to participants and to obtain data from them.

LO4   **Discuss the potential for harm, risk-benefit analysis, informed consent, privacy and confidentiality, and debriefing as major ethical considerations in social science research.**

Researchers attempt to design studies in a manner that minimizes the risk of any form of harm, such as physical or psychological. Informed consent refers to an autonomous process where participants are provided with all of the relevant details needed to make a judgment about whether or not to participate in a study. Anonymity exists if a researcher cannot link individual responses to the person who provided them. Confidentiality is a process for maintaining privacy where the researcher ensures that a participant's identity will not be publicly disclosed. Debriefing refers to a full disclosure and exchange of information regarding all aspects of the study.

LO5   **Identify the core principles of the current Tri-Council Policy Statement (TCPS 2).**

The overarching value of the TCPS 2 is respect for human dignity expressed as respect for persons (i.e., human worth), concern for welfare (i.e., quality of life), and justice (i.e., fair and equitable treatment).

LO6   **Describe the role of a research ethics board and outline the process for undergoing an ethical review of research.**

The role of a research ethics board (REB) is to review the ethical acceptability of research on behalf of an institution, including approving, rejecting, proposing modifications to, or terminating any proposed or ongoing research involving humans. Researchers submit an application that summarizes a proposed study, along with all of the relevant ethical considerations to the chair of the REB, the REB reviews the application, and the researcher is provided with a written decision.

Research Reflection

1. Imagine you are a member of a research ethics board. The chair of the REB has asked you to come up with criteria for assessing the level of risk in social science research. Develop criteria and/or provide examples to illustrate "low or minimal risk," "moderate risk," and "probable harm or high risk."

2. Using Zimbardo's Stanford Prison experiment as a case study, provide an assessment of beneficence in terms of benefits and risks. If you were going to replicate Zimbardo's study, how would you change the procedures to minimize the potential for harm?

3. Become an expert on the TCPS. The Government of Canada's Interagency Advisory Panel on Research Ethics offers a TCPS 2 online tutorial free of charge. The tutorial is a condensed Course on Research Ethics (CORE) designed to help researchers, members of research ethics boards, educators, students, and others become familiar with the TCPS 2. Try completing this course on your own time and receive an official certification of completion. You can access the TCPS tutorial at pre.ethics.gc.ca.

4. To learn about responsible conduct for researchers in relation to conflicts of interest and competing interests, authorship and publication, intellectual property, research misconduct, and liability read Chapter 8 in Unger, D. (2011). *The Canadian bioethics companion: An online textbook for Canadian ethicists and health care workers*. See canadianbioethicscompanion.ca.

Learning Through Practice

Objective: To evaluate ethical issues in social science research.
Directions:

1. Locate and read Burger, J. M. (2009) Replicating Milgram: Would people still obey today? *American Psychologist, 64*(1), 1–11.

2. Describe the central research question and summarize the main procedures used to carry out the study on obedience.

3. Explain how the replication attempts to resolve for specific ethical implications raised in Milgram's original experiment. Do you think the changes accomplish this? Why or why not?

4. If you were a member of an institutional REB, would you grant approval to this study with no conditions, provide approval but require changes to the study, or fail to grant approval? Justify your answer making reference to the main ethical issues discussed in this chapter.

Research Resources

1. For more information on the mustard gas compensation package and the subsequent class-action suit, search "mustard gas and war veterans" on CBC News: cbc.ca.

2. For more information on the Tuskegee Syphilis Study, refer to: Jones, J. H. (1993). *Bad blood: The Tuskegee's syphilis experiment*. New York, NY: The Free Press or Gray, F. D. (1998). *The Tuskegee Syphilis Study*. Montgomery, AL: NewSouth Books.

3. To learn more about Stanley Milgram and his research on obedience, I recommend social psychologist Thomas Blass's website on the legacy of Stanley Milgram: stanleymilgram.com.

4. If you are interested in learning more about the data collection techniques and findings in Laud Humphreys's study, refer to: Humphrey, R. A. L. (1970) *Tearoom trade: Impersonal sex in public places.* Chicago, IL: Aldine Publishing Company.

5. To learn about ethical issues in research on vulnerable and marginalized groups of people, I recommend: Liamputtong, P. (2007). *Researching the vulnerable: A guide to sensitive research methods.* Thousand Oaks, CA: Sage Publications.

6. To learn more about the role of institutional research ethics review boards and how they carry out and assess applications, I recommend: Mazur, D. J. (2007). *Evaluating the science and ethics of research on humans: A guide for IRB members.* Baltimore, MD: The John Hopkins University Press.

For more information on the resources available from McGraw-Hill Ryerson, go to www.mcgrawhill.ca/he/solutions.

References

Adair, J. G. (2001). Ethics of psychological research: New policies, continuing issues; new concerns. *Canadian Psychology, 42*(1), 25–37.

Auschwitz-Birkenau State Museum (2012). Medical experiments in Auschwitz. In *History.* Oświęcim, PO: Państwowe Muzeum Auschwitz-Birkenau w Oświęcimiu. Retrieved from en.auschwitz.org/h/index.php?option=com_content&task=view&id=12&Itemid=10&limit=1&limitstart=0

Baumrind, D. (1964). Some thoughts on ethics of research: After reading Milgram's "Behavioral Study of Obedience." *American Psychologist, 19*(6), 421–423.

Burger, J. M. (2009). Replicating Milgram: Would people still obey today? *American Psychologist, 64*(1), 1–11.

Canadian Institutes of Health Research, Natural Sciences and Engineering Research Council of Canada, and Social Sciences and Humanities Research Council of Canada. (2010, December). *Tri-Council Policy Statement: Ethical conduct for research involving humans.* Her Majesty the Queen in Right of Canada. Catalogue no. MR21-18/2010E-PDF

CBC News. (2004, May 12). Vets exposed to mustard gas receive compensation. In Canada: Calgary. CBC News online. Retrieved from www.cbc.ca/news/canada/calgary/story/2004/05/12/ca_suffield20040512.html

Cozby, P.C. (2012). *Methods in behavioral research* (11th ed.). New York, NY: McGraw-Hill.

Films for the Humanities and Sciences. (2004). *Acres of skin: Medical abuse behind bars.* Hamilton, NJ: Films Media Group.

Gray, F. D. (1998). *The Tuskegee syphilis study.* Montgomery, AL: NewSouth Books.

Haney, C., Banks, C., & Zimbardo, P. (1973). Interpersonal dynamics in a simulated prison. *International Journal of Criminology and Penology, 1,* 69–97.

Humphreys, R. A. L. (1970). *Tearoom trade: Impersonal sex in public places.* Chicago, IL: Aldine Publishing Company.

Jones, J. H. (1993). *Bad blood: The Tuskegee syphilis experiment.* New York, NY: The Free Press.

Lagnado, L. M., & Dekel, S. C. (1991). *Children of the flames: Dr. Joseph Mengele and the untold story of the twins of Auschwitz.* New York: William Morrow and Company.

Liamputtong, P. (2007). *Researching the vulnerable: A guide to sensitive research methods.* Thousand Oaks, CA: Sage Publications.

Mazur, D. J. (2007). *Evaluating the science and ethics of research on humans: A guide for IRB members.* Baltimore, MD: The John Hopkins University Press.

Milgram, S. (1963). Behavioral study of obedience. *Journal of Abnormal and Social Psychology, 67*(4), 371–378.

Milgram. S. (1961). Nationality and conformity. *Scientific American, 205*(6), 45–51.

Musen, K., & Zimbardo, P. G. (1991). *Quiet rage: The Stanford prison study.* Video recording. Stanford, CA: Psychology Dept., Stanford University.

National Commission for the Protection of Human Subjects of Biomedical and Behavioral Research. (1979, April 18). *The Belmont Report: Ethical principles and guidelines for the protection of human subjects of research.* Department of Health, Education, and Welfare. Washington, DC: U.S. Government Printing Office.

Nuremberg Code. (1949). Nuremberg Code. *Trials of war criminals before the Nuremberg Military Tribunals Under Control Council Law. No. 10,* Vol. 2. Washington, DC: US Government Printing Office, pp. 181–182.

Palys, T., & Atchison, C. (2014). *Research decisions: Quantitative, qualitative, and mixed methods approaches.* Toronto, ON: Nelson Education.

Rosnow, R. L., & Rosenthal, R. (2013). *Beginning behavioral research: A conceptual primer* (7th ed.). Toronto, ON: Pearson Education.

Russell, N. J. C. (2010). Milgram's obedience to authority experiments: Origins and early evolution. *British Journal of Social Psychology, 50,* 140–162.

Sandler, T. (2012, March 2). "People keep falling sick": How poor Indians are recruited for clinical drug trials. NBC News: msnbc.com. Retrieved from openchannel.msnbc.msn.com/_news/2012/03/02/10561824-people-keep-falling-sick-how-poor-indians-are-recruited-for-clinical-drug-trials?chromedomain=insidedateline

Sieber, J. E. (1992). *Planning ethically responsible research.* Newbury Park, CA: Sage Publications.

Stryker, J. (1997, April 13). Tuskegee's long arm still touches a nerve. In Health: Week in Review. *The New York Times:* NYTimes.com. Retrieved from www.nytimes.com/1997/04/13/weekinreview/tuskegee-s-long-arm-still-touches-a-nerve.html

Symbaluk, D., Heth, C. D., Cameron, J., & Pierce, W. D. (1997). Social modeling, monetary incentives, and pain endurance: The role of self-efficacy and pain perception. *Personality and Social Psychology Bulletin, 23*(3), 258–269.

Tuskegee Syphilis Study Legacy Committee (1996, May 20). Final Report of the Tuskegee Syphilis Study Legacy Committee. In *Historical Collections.* Charlottesville, VA: Claude Moore Health Sciences Library. Retrieved from www.hsl.virginia.edu/historical/medical_history/bad_blood/report.cfm

Tuskegee University (2013). *Coverage of the apology.* Tuskegee, AL: Tuskegee University. Retrieved from www.tuskegee.edu/about_us/centers_of_excellence/bioethics_center/coverage_of_the_apology.aspx

Unger, D. (2011). *The Canadian bioethics companion: An online textbook for Canadian ethicists and health care workers.* Retrieved from http://canadianbioethicscompanion.ca

Zimbardo, P. G. (2004). A situationist perspective on the psychology of evil: Understanding how good people are transformed into perpetrators. In A. G. Miller's (Ed.), *The social psychology of good and evil* (pp. 21–50). New York, NY: Guilford Press.

Zimbardo, P. G., Maslach, C., & Haney, C. (2000). Reflections on the Stanford Prison Experiment: Genesis, transformations, consequences. In T. Blass (Ed.), *Obedience to authority: Current perspectives on the Milgram paradigm* (pp. 193–237). Mahwah, NJ: Erlbaum.

Endnote

[1] Johnson, M. (2007). The theoretical and social context of research ethics. In T. Long & M. Johnson, *Research ethics in the real world: Issues and solutions for health and social care* (pp. 29–46). Philadelphia, PA: Churchill Livingstone.

Research Design and Measurement

Learning Objectives

After reading this chapter, students should be able to do the following:

LO1 Describe the main components of a research design.

LO2 Explain what conceptualization and operationalization processes entail.

LO3 Explain how the purpose of a variable is directly related to how it is measured in research.

LO4 Outline the main techniques used to assess reliability and validity.

LO5 Distinguish between random and systematic errors.

LO6 Explain how rigour is achieved in qualitative research.

"In any discussion about improving measurement, it is important to begin with basic questions. What exactly are we trying to measure, and why?" (Christine Bachrach, 2007, p. 435)[1]

Introduction

After carefully considering research foundations, the importance of theory, and the ethics involving research with human participants, you are almost ready to delve into the techniques used for obtaining answers to social research questions. But before you can start collecting data, you need to develop a research plan that outlines who or what it is you are studying, and how you will go about measuring and evaluating the attitudes, behaviours, or processes that you want to learn more about.

Main Components of a Research Design

LO1

Research design
The plan or blueprint for a study outlining the who, what, where, when, why, and how of an investigation.

Unit of analysis The object of investigation.

Linked to a specific research question, a **research design** is "the plan or blueprint for a study and includes the who, what, where, when, why, and how of an investigation" (Hagan, 2010, p. 65). Beginning with the "who"—researchers in the social sciences most often study people, so individuals are usually the main focus of investigation, called the **unit of analysis**. Individuals are often studied as part of a collective or group. For example, the unit of analysis could be students, employees, single-parent-headed families, low-income earners, or some other group of interest. Researchers also compare groups of individuals along particular variables of interest, such as a sample of individuals with less than a high school education relative those who have a Grade 12 diploma, single versus dual-income families, or patients who completed a treatment program versus ones who dropped out. Social institutions and organizations that guide individuals and groups can also make up the units of analysis for research in the social sciences, such as the university or college you are attending, a not-for-profit agency such as the Canadian Red Cross, or a health care organization such as the Canadian Medical Association. Finally, social researchers are sometimes interested in artifacts created by people rather than people themselves. For example, researchers might examine newspapers, television shows, motion pictures, personal diaries, profiles on an online dating site, YouTube videos, Facebook postings, or Twitter trends.

The "what" component of research design refers to whatever is specifically examined and measured in a study, such as attitudes, beliefs, views, behaviours, outcomes, and/or processes. The measured component is usually referred to as the "unit of observation" since this is what the data is collected on. For example, a researcher might be interested in factors affecting instructors' views on published ratings of instruction at a particular university. The instructional faculty members who take part in the study constitute the unit of analysis from whom the views on published ratings are obtained (i.e., the more specific focus of the research that comprises the data). Similarly, a researcher might be interested in dating preferences of individuals who use online match-making sites such as lavalife® or PlentyofFish (POF)™. The individuals seeking to find dates online are the units of analysis, while their posted profiles containing the characteristics of interest in the study are the units of observation.

The "where" pertains to the location for a study. The possibilities are endless, from research conducted first-hand in the field to studies conducted in the home of participants or even in the office of the principal researcher. The location for a study is closely linked to the unit of analysis since the researcher often needs to go to the individuals, groups, or organizations to collect information from them or about them. For example, a researcher interested in interviewing couples who met online might set up appointments to visit dating couples in restaurants or coffee shops near to where the couples reside, at the discretion of the participants. Alternatively, a researcher interested in online dating relationships might choose to gather information in a virtual environment by posting a survey on the Internet.

The "when" relates to an important time consideration in the research design. Some studies are conducted once at a single point in time, and others are carried out at multiple points over time. Most often, when social researchers carry out a study, it takes place at a single point in time or within a single time frame, such as when a researcher develops a questionnaire about Internet dating and administers it to a group of people attending a singles' social function. This is called **cross-sectional research** because the study is made up of a cross-section of the dating population taken at a point in time, similar to taking a photo that captures a person or group at a single point in time. Alternatively, social researchers sometimes study individuals or groups at multiple points in time using what is called **longitudinal research**. For example, a sample of dating couples might be surveyed shortly after they meet and again after dating for one year to capture their initial viewpoints and to see how their perceptions might change once they get to know each other better. Four longitudinal designs are discussed below.

Cross-sectional research Research conducted at a single point in time.

Longitudinal research Research conducted at multiple points in time.

Panel study Research on the same unit of analysis carried out at multiple points in time.

A **panel study** is a longitudinal study in which a researcher observes the same people, group, or organization at multiple points in time. A new phase of a large-scale panel study called The Tomorrow Project was launched in 2013 in Alberta to learn more about the causes of cancer. The study aims to include 50,000 cancer-free Albertans aged 35 to 69 years for up to 50 years to see who does and does not develop cancer over time (The Tomorrow Project, 2013). Researchers from The Tomorrow Project collect information on participants' health and lifestyle through surveys, blood samples, and the collection of other specimens at regular intervals. Going back to the dating example, by collecting information on the same dating couples at various intervals, a researcher could use a panel study to examine how relations evolve or change over time.

Cohort study Research on the same category of people carried out at multiple points in time.

A **cohort study** is similar to a panel study, except rather than focusing on the same people, it focuses on comparable people over time. "Comparable" refers to a general category of people who are deemed to share a similar life experience in a specified period. The most common example of this is a birth cohort. Think about the classmates you went through school with. Although there were obviously various individual differences between you and your classmates, you also shared some common life events, such as the music that topped the charts at that time, the clothing fads and hairstyles, and the political events that occurred during that era. Following the earlier example, a researcher might include people who met and married an online dating partner in 2010 as a unit of analysis. Several couples might be studied in 2010 shortly after they were married, several other couples who also married in 2010 might be studied in 2011, another group in 2012, another group in 2013, and so on over a period of five years.

Time-series study Research on different units of analysis carried out at multiple points in time.

A **time-series study** is a longitudinal study in which a researcher examines different people at multiple points in time. Every year, Statistics Canada gathers information from thousands of people in Canada using what is called the General Social Survey. Although the participants are different each time, similar forms of information are gathered over time to detect patterns and trends. For example, we can readily discern that Canadians today are delaying marriage (i.e., getting married for the first time at a later age) and they are having fewer children relative to twenty years ago. Going back to the online dating example used throughout this section, a researcher might use a time-series study to gather information from new dating couples at an online site each year for five years. Looking at the data over time, a researcher would be able to determine if there are changes in the overall profiles of online daters at that site. For example, the use of the site might be increasing for particular groups, such as highly educated women or single individuals over the age of 60 years.

Case study Research on a small number of individuals or an organization carried out over an extended period of time.

Lastly, a **case study** is a research method in which a researcher focuses on a small number of individuals or even a single case over an extended period of time. You'll learn more about this method later in the text. For now, you can think of a case study as a highly detailed study of a single person or organization over time. For example, a researcher might study an alcoholic to better understand the progression of the disease over time, or join a subculture such as a magic card club that meets every Friday night to gain an insider's perspective of the group. Similarly, a researcher could examine the experiences of a frequent online dater over time to get a sense of how online dating works at various sites. See Figure 4.1 for an overview of time considerations in relation to units of analysis.

Research in Action

Longitudinal Panel Study of Self-Rated Health

The National Population Health Survey (NPHS) is a longitudinal study on the health of Canadians administered to the same sample of Canadians by Statistics Canada every two years from 1994/1995 to present. The intent is to gather health-related information on the same sample for a period of up to 20 years. Shooshtari, Menec, and Tate (2007) compared predictors of positive and negative self-rated health between younger (25–54 years) and older (55+ years) Canadians using data from the first of three cycles of the NPHS (i.e., 1994/1995; 1996/1997; and 1998/1999). Health was measured by a self-rating of poor, fair,

good, very good, or excellent. The researchers found that the strongest predictors of positive (very good or excellent) and negative (poor or fair) health were chronic conditions and individual health and functioning measures, including perceived level of physical health, psychological distress, and pain. They also identified differences between the groups, such as an association between a history of premature death of a parent and perceived negative health, and an association between factors related to the social environment, such as perceived emotional support and positive health for younger Canadians only (Shooshtari, Menec, & Tate, 2007).

FIGURE 4.1
Time Considerations by Units of Analysis

Cross-Sectional Research

Same people at a single point in time.

Longitudinal Research

Panel Study
Same people over time.
Example: Same dating couples at Time 1 and Time 2.

Cohort Study
Similar people over time.
Example: Couples who met online in 2010 at Time 1 and other couples who met online in 2010 at Time 2.

Time-Series Study
Different people over time.
Example: Couples who met online at Time 1 and other couples who met online at Time 2.

Case Study
One person over time.
Example: A regular user of online dating sites over the course of a year.

In addition to the time dimension, a research design also takes into account the "why" and the "how" plan for a study. "Why" relates to the purpose of a study as discussed in Chapter 1. A study on Internet dating could focus on exploring ways in which people represent themselves in posted profiles; describing who uses Internet dating sites; explaining the importance of including certain types of information such as appearance or personality factors for attracting dates; or evaluating the effectiveness of a given site in matching suitable partners. The nature of the study really depends on the interests of the researcher and the nature of the issue itself.

"How" refers to the specific method or methods used to gather the data examined in a particular study. With an interest in the merit of including certain items in a dating profile, a researcher might opt for an experimental design to explain, for example, whether certain characteristics in posted dating profiles are better than others for eliciting potential dates (see Chapter 6 for a discussion of different types of experiments). An experiment is a special type of quantitative research design in which a researcher changes or alters something to see what effect it has. In the dating example, an experimenter might compare the number of responses to two profiles posted at an Internet dating site. If the profiles are virtually identical with the exception of one trait—for example, one profile might contain an additional statement saying the person has a great sense of humour—it would be possible to determine the importance of that one trait for attracting potential partners.

Recall from Chapter 1 that the specific methods or techniques differ depending on whether a researcher adopts a qualitative or quantitative orientation, and the approach itself links back to the research interest. A researcher interested in learning more about why people make dates online or how people define themselves online is more apt to use a qualitative approach. Qualitative researchers tend to engage in research that seeks to better understand or explain some phenomenon through the use of field research and in-depth interviews, as well as strategies involving discourse analyses and content analyses that can be used to help to uncover meaning. Regardless of the approach taken and specific methods used, all researchers must work through various design considerations and measurement issues in their quest to carry out scientific research. Similarly, both qualitative and quantitative researchers undertake a process of conceptualization and measurement—it just occurs differently and at different stages within the overall research process, as discussed in the next section.

Test Yourself

- What does a research design tell us?
- What is the main difference between cross-sectional and longitudinal research?
- What is the name for research on the same unit of analysis carried out at multiple points in time?
- In what ways will a quantitative research design differ from a qualitative one?

Conceptualization and Operationalization

LO2

Concepts Abstract mental representations of important elements in our social world.

Conceptualization The process where a researcher explains what a concept means in terms of a particular research project.

Researchers in the social sciences frequently study social issues, social conditions, and social problems that affect individuals, such as environmental disasters, legal policy, crime, health care, poverty, divorce, marriage, or growing social inequality between the rich and poor, within a particular conceptual framework. Their quest is to explore, describe, explain, and evaluate the experiences of particular individuals or groups. A conceptual framework is the more concentrated area of interest used to study the social issue or problem, which includes the main objects, events, or ideas, along with the relevant theories that spell out relationships. Terms like "family," "social inequality," and "power" are broad **concepts** that refer to abstract mental representations used to signify important elements of our social world. Concepts are very important because they form the basis of social theory and research in the social sciences. However, as often with abstract representations, concepts like power can be vague since they mean different things to different people. Consider what the concept of family means to you. Does your notion of a family include aunts and uncles or second cousins? What about close friends? How about pets? People have very divergent views about what a family is or is not. The concept of family also has very different meanings depending on the context in which it is applied. For example, there are rules about who is or is not considered eligible to be sponsored under family status for potential immigration to Canada, or who may or may not be deemed family in regards to visitation rights involving prisoners under the supervision of Corrections Canada. Because concepts are broad notions that can take on various meanings, researchers need to carefully define the concepts that underlie their research interests as part of the conceptualization and operationalization process.

Conceptualization, in research, is the process where a researcher explains what a concept means in terms of a particular research project. For example, a researcher studying the impact of education cutbacks on the family, with a particular interest in the negative implications for children, might adopt the broad conceptualization of family provided by Statistics Canada (2013a):

> A census family is defined as a married couple and the children, if any, of either or both spouses; a couple living common-law and the children, if any, of either or both partners; or, a lone parent of any marital status with at least one child living in the same dwelling and that child or those children. All members of a particular census family live in the same dwelling. A couple may be of opposite or same sex. Children may be children by birth, marriage or adoption regardless of their age or marital status as long as they live in the dwelling and do not have their own spouse or child living in the dwelling. Grandchildren living with their grandparent(s) but with no parents present also constitute a census family. (Para. 1)

Conceptualization is essential since it helps us understand what is or is not being examined in a study. For example, based on the conceptualization provided above, children being raised by their grandparents or living in homes headed up by single parents would be included in the study, but might have otherwise been missed if a more traditional definition of family was employed.

© Betsy Streeter. www.Cartoonstock.com

Constructs Intangible ideas that do not exist independent of our thinking.

The term *concept* is often used interchangeably with a similar term, *construct*. Both refer to abstractions, however concepts derive from tangible or factual observations (e.g., a family actually exists), while **constructs** are more hypothetical or "constructed" ideas that are part of our thinking but do not exist in readily observable forms (e.g., love, honesty, intelligence, motivation). Although we can readily measure and observe crime through different acts that are deemed criminal (the concept of crime), we have to infer intelligence through measures such as test scores (the construct of intelligence). Both concepts and constructs are the basis of theories and are integral components underlying social science research. Similar to concepts, constructs undergo a process of conceptualization when they are used in research. Suppose a researcher is interested in studying social inequality, which we commonly understand to mean differences among groups of people in terms of their access to resources such as education or health care. We know some people can afford private schools while others cannot. We understand that health care benefits differ depending on factors such as how old a person is, how much one pays for a health plan, what type of job one has, and where one lives. Similar to the concept of family, social inequality is a construct that conjures up a wide range of examples and notions. To examine social inequality in a specific study, a

Indicator A measurable quantity that in some sense stands for or substitutes for something less readily measurable.

researcher might opt to use personal finances as an **indicator** of social inequality. An indicator is "a measurable quantity which 'stands in' or substitutes, in some sense, for something less readily measurable" (Sapsford, 2006, para. 1). Personal finances can be further specified as employment income, since most of the working population is able to state how much they earn in dollars.

Note that in the case of employment income, people earn a particular amount (i.e., gross pay), but they actually receive a very different amount as their take-home pay after taxes and various deductions come off their pay cheque (i.e., net pay). The process we use to examine with precision the progression of taking an abstract construct, such as social inequality, and conceptualizing it into something tangible, such as net income in the real world, is known as operationalization. **Operationalization** is the process whereby a concept or construct is defined so precisely that it can be measured. In this example, financial wealth was operationalized as net yearly employment income in dollars. Note that once an abstract construct such as social inequality has been clarified as financial wealth and then measured by way of net yearly income dollars, we are now working with a variable, since net yearly income is something that can change and differ between people. Quantitative social science researchers examine variables. A researcher interested in some of the implications of social inequality might test the hypothesis that among individuals who work full time, those with low net yearly incomes will report poorer health compared to people with

Operationalization
The process whereby a concept is defined so precisely that it can be measured.

Research in Action

Online Dating for Variables

In the case of a quantitative design, students routinely have difficulty understanding what variables are, let alone how to create testable hypotheses that contain them. A starting point is to examine what is contained in a typical profile posted on any Internet dating site, such as lavalife®, PlentyofFish(POF)™, eHarmony®, or Match.com®. Registered members list certain attributes they feel best describe themselves and that may also be helpful in attracting a compatible potential dating partner, such as their age, physical features, and certain personality traits. For example, someone might advertise as a single, male, 29 years of age, 5'11" tall, in great shape, with a good sense of humour, seeking a female between the ages of 20 and 30 for friendship. These attributes are variables; many are routinely used in social science research! Variables are often defined using categories. For example, "single" refers to a category of the variable "marital status." Marital status is a variable since it is a property that can differ between individuals and change over time, as in single, common-law, married, separated, widowed,

Personal profiles on dating sites are largely made up of variables.

or divorced. Other variables listed on dating sites include age (in years), sex (male or female), height (in feet and inches), body type (fit, slim, or average), eye colour (e.g., green, blue, or brown), astrological sign (e.g., Virgo, Libra, Scorpio, etc.), and whether the person has children (yes/no). Even the purpose or intent of the posting constitutes a variable, since a person may state whether they are seeking fun, friendship, dating, or a long-term relationship.

high net yearly incomes. In this example, health (the second variable) might be operationalized into the self-reported ratings of very poor, poor, fair, good, or very good.

In contrast, qualitative researchers tend to define concepts based on the users' own frameworks. Qualitative researchers are less concerned with proving that certain variables affect the individual. Instead, they are more concerned with *how* the individual makes sense of his or her own social situations and *what* the broader social factors are for such framing.

Test Yourself

- What is a concept? Provide an example of one that is of interest to social researchers.
- Why is conceptualization important to researchers?
- What is an indicator? Provide an example of one that could be used in a study on aggression.
- What are three variables you would want to examine in a study of online dating relationships?

Measuring Variables

LO3

Now that you better appreciate what is meant by a variable, you can also start to see how variables are operationalized in different ways. Some variables are numerical, such as age or income, while others pertain more to categories and descriptors, such as marital status or perceived health status. Decisions made about how to clarify a construct such as health have important implications for other stages of the research process, including determining what kind of analyses are possible and what kind of interpretations can be made. For example, the categories for the self-reported health variable described above can tell us whether someone perceives his or her health to be better or worse than someone else's (e.g., "very good" is better than "good," while "fair" is worse than "good" but better than "poor"). However, from how this particular variable is measured, we are unable to ascertain how much worse or how much better someone's health is relative to another.

Levels of Measurement

Nominal level A level of measurement used to classify cases.

Variables mean different things and can be used in different ways depending upon on how they are measured. At the lowest level of measurement, called the **nominal level**, we can classify or label cases, such as persons according to marital status, eye colour, religion, or the presence of children. These are all qualitative variables. Even if we assign numbers to the categories of the variable marital status, where 1 = single, 2 = common-law, 3 = married, 4 = separated, 5 = widowed, and 6 = divorced, we have not quantified the variable. This is because the numbers serve only to identify or name the categories so that a "6" now represents anyone who is currently "divorced." The numbers themselves are arbitrary; however, they serve the function of classification, which simply indicates that members of a particular category are different from one another.

Ordinal level A level of measurement used to order cases along some dimension of interest.

At the next level of measurement, called the **ordinal level**, we can classify and order categories of the variables of interest for particular cases, such as people's perceived health into levels, job satisfaction into ratings, or prestige into rankings. Note that these variables are measured according to whether there is more or less or higher or lower of some dimension of interest. The variable health, then, measured as very good, good, fair, poor, and very poor, is an ordered variable since we know that very good is higher than good and therefore indicates better health. However, as noted earlier, we cannot determine precisely what that means in terms of how much healthier someone is who reports very good health. Ordinal variables are also qualitative in nature.

Interval level A level of measurement in which the distance between categories of the variable of interest is meaningful.

At the next highest level of measurement, called the **interval level**, we can classify, order, and examine differences between the categories of the variables of interest. This is possible because the assigned scores include equal intervals between categories. For example, with temperature as a main variable, we know that 28°C is exactly one degree higher than 27°C, which is 7 degrees higher than 20°C, and so on.

Ratio level An interval level of measurement with an absolute zero.

Statisticians sometimes make a further distinction between an interval and **ratio level** of measurement. Both levels include meaningful distance between categories, as well as the properties from the lower levels. However, a true zero only exists at the ratio level of measurement constituting the additional property. In the case of temperature, 0°C cannot be taken to mean the absence of temperature (an absolute or true zero). At the ratio level, however, there is a true zero in the case of time, where a stop watch can count down from two minutes to zero and zero indicates no time left. Most variables that include the property of score assignment have a true zero. One way to determine if a variable is measured at the ratio level is to consider if its categories can adhere to the logic of "twice as." For example, an assessment variable where a person can achieve twice the score of someone else, or a net employment income variable where one employee can earn twice that of another are both measured at the ratio level. Interval and ratio level variables are quantitative and readily amenable to various types of statistical tests discussed in more detail in a later chapter. The properties of each level of measurement are summarized in Figure 4.2.

Indexes Versus Scales

Index A composite measure of a construct comprising several different indicators that produce a shared outcome.

Instead of using the response to a single statement as a measure of some construct, indexes and scales combine several responses together to create what is called a composite measure of a construct of interest. An **index** is a composite measure of a construct comprising several different indicators that produce a shared outcome (DeVellis, 2012). For example, in study on gambling, Wood and Williams (2007) examined the extent to which Internet gamblers manifest a "propensity for problem gambling" (the outcome). The propensity for problem gambling was

FIGURE 4.2 **Properties and Functions of Levels of Measurement**

Nominal	Ordinal	Interval	Ratio
• Identifies differences/attributes	• Makes greater vs. less than and higher vs. lower distinctions	• Makes precise comparisons (e.g., how much or how many more)	• Has a true zero
• Examples: gender, religion, ethnicity, hair colour, shoe brand, marital status, blood type, employment status, eye colour, favourite television show, presence of children, gun ownership, smoker, type of dwelling, political orientation, and pet preference	• Can order attributes	• Lacks a true zero (e.g., zero degrees is not the absence of temperature)	• Can use ratios
	• Examples: educational level, health status, job satisfaction, fitness level, hotel ratings (out of 5 stars), prestige ratings, student ratings of instruction, and customer service ratings	• Examples: intelligence (IQ), temperature in Celsius	• Examples: test scores, net yearly income (in dollars), age, height, weight, and employment service in years

Nominal: **Classify**

Ordinal: **Order** / **Classify**

Interval: **Equal Intervals** / **Order** / **Classify**

Ratio: **Uses Ratios** / **Equal Intervals** / **Order** / **Classify**

assessed using the Canadian Problem Gambling Index (CPGI). The CPGI consists of a series of nine questions that follow prompts to consider only the preceding 12 months, including: "Thinking about the last 12 months . . . Have you bet more than you could really afford to lose?"; "Still thinking about the last 12 months, have you needed to gamble with larger amounts of money to get the same feeling of excitement?"; and "When you gambled, did you go back another day to try and win back the money you lost?" The response categories for all nine items are sometimes (awarded a score of 1), most of the time (scored as 2), almost always (scored as 3), or don't know (scored as zero). The scores are added up for the nine items, generating an overall score for propensity for problem gambling that ranges between 0 and 27, where 0 = non-problem gamblers, 1–2 = a low risk for problem gambling, 3–7 = a moderate risk, and 8 or more = problem gamblers (Ferris & Wynne, 2001). Although an index has several items or indicators, they all independently measure the same thing, the propensity to become a problem gambler. Although there are expected relationships between the items, such as spending more than one can afford to lose is assumed to be associated with needing to gamble with larger amounts of money to get the same feeling of excitement, the indicators are not derived from a single cause (DeVellis, 2012). That is, a person may gamble more than he or she can afford to lose due to a belief in luck, while the same person might need to gamble larger amounts due to a thrill-seeking tendency. Regardless of their origins, the indicators result in a common outcome: the tendency to become a problem gambler. The higher the overall score on an index, the more of that trait or propensity the respondent has or displays.

Scale A composite measure of a construct consisting of several different indicators that stem from a common cause.

In contrast, a **scale** is a composite measure of construct consisting of several different indicators that stem from a common cause (DeVellis, 2012). For example, the Eysenck Personality Questionnaire-Revised (EPQR) is a 48-item questionnaire designed to measure an individual's personality (the construct) via extroversion and neuroticism (Eysenck, Eysenck, & Barrett, 1985). Extroversion and neuroticism are two underlying potential causes for particular behavioural tendencies. Extroversion is the propensity to direct one's attention outward toward the environment. Thus, extroverts tend to be people who are outgoing or talkative. Sample yes/no forced-choice items on the EPQR measuring extroversion include the statements: "Are you a talkative person?"; "Do you usually take the initiative in making new friends?"; and "Do other people think of you as being very lively?" Neuroticism refers to emotional stability. For example, a neurotic person is someone who worries excessively or who might be described as moody. Sample questions include: "Does your mood often go up and down?"; "Are you an irritable person?"; and "Are you a worrier?"

Note that there are some similarities between indexes and scales, and be aware that these terms are often used interchangeably (albeit incorrectly) in research! Both indexes and scales measure constructs—for example, dimensions of personality or risk for problem gambling—using nominal variables with categories such as yes/no and presence/absence, or ordinal-level variables depicting intensity such as very dissatisfied or dissatisfied. In addition, both are composite measures, meaning they are made up of multiple items. However, there are also some important differences (see Figure 4.3).

While an index is always an accumulation of individual scores based on items that have no expected common cause, a scale is based on the assignment of scores to items that are believed to derive from a common cause. In addition, scales often comprise items that have logical relationships or expected patterns between them. Namely, someone who indicates on EPQR that he or she "always takes the

FIGURE 4.3
Comparing Indexes and Scales

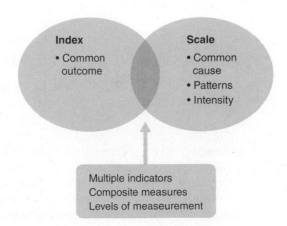

initiative in making new friends" and "always gets a party going" is also very likely to "enjoy meeting new people," but is very unlikely to be "mostly quiet when with other people." In addition, specific items in a scale can indicate varying intensity or magnitude of a particular construct in a manner that is taken into account by the scoring. For example, the Bogardus Social Distance Scale measures respondents' willingness to participate with members of other racial and ethnic groups (Bogardus, 1933). The items in the scale have different intensity, meaning certain items are more indicative of an unwillingness to participate with members of other groups than others. For example, an affirmative response to the item "I would be willing to marry outside group members" indicates very low social distance (akin to low prejudice) and would receive a score of 1, whereas an affirmative response to "I would have (outside group members) merely as speaking acquaintances" would receive a score of 5, indicating more prejudice. A scale is able to take advantage of differences in intensity or the magnitude between indictors of a construct and weight them accordingly when it comes to scoring. In contrast, an index assumes that all of the items are different but of equal importance.

In some cases it can be very difficult to determine if an instrument is better classified as a scale or an index. For example, the Eating Attitudes Test (EAT-26) was developed by Garner and Garkfinkel (1979) as a self-report measure designed to help identify those at risk for an eating disorder such as anorexia nervosa. Taken together, it can be considered an index since it is based on items that do not have a single underlying cause since eating disorders can result from many different individual causes. Importantly, as required by an index, the indicators are used to derive a composite score for a common outcome (risk of anorexia) by summing up the scores obtained for all 26 independent items. However, the EAT-26 also contains three sub-scales, where particular items can be used to examine three separate dimensions of anorexia that are believed to be the result of dieting, bulimia and food preoccupation, and oral control (common causes).

Test Yourself

- What property distinguishes the ordinal level of measurement from the nominal?
- What are the main properties and functions of the interval level of measurement?
- What special property does the ratio level have that distinguishes it from the interval level of measurement?
- In what ways are indexes and scales similar and different?

Criteria for Assessing Measurement: Reliability and Validity

LO4

To study a given social issue, a researcher may ask people for their opinions, similar to how a restaurant owner might survey customers for their views on the service. Measurement often involves obtaining answers to questions posed by researchers. In some cases, the answers to questions might be very straightforward, as would be your response to the question, "How old are you?" But what if you were instead asked, "What is your ethnicity?" Would your answer be singular or plural? Would your answer reflect the country you were born in and/or the one you currently reside in? Did you consider the origin of your biological father, mother, or both parents' ancestors (e.g., grandparents or great-grandparents)? Did you take into account languages you speak other than English or certain cultural practices or ceremonies you engage in? Ethnicity is a difficult concept to measure because it has different dimensions; it reflects ancestry in terms of family origin as well as identity in the case of more current personal practices. According to Statistics Canada (2013b), if the intent of the study is to examine identity, then a question such as "With which ethnic group do you identify?" is probably the best choice, since it will steer respondents to that dimension by having them focus on how they perceive themselves. To assess whether particular measures are "good" ones, you must evaluate their reliability and validity.

Reliability

Reliability
Consistency in measurement.

As a quantitative term, **reliability** refers to the consistency in measurement. A measurement procedure is reliable if it provides the same data at different points in time, assuming there has been no change in the variable under consideration. For example, a weigh scale is generally considered to be a reliable measure for weight. That is, if a person steps on a scale and records a weight, the person could step off and back on the scale and it should indicate the same weight a second time. Similarly a watch or a clock—barring the occasional power outage or worn-out battery—is a dependable measure for keeping track of time on a 24-hour cycle (e.g., your alarm wakes you up for work at precisely 6:38 a.m. on weekdays). Finally, a specialized test can provide a reliable measure of a child's intelligence in the form of an intelligence quotient (IQ). IQ is a numerical score determined using an instrument such as the Wechsler Intelligence Scale for Children—Fourth Edition (WISC-IV). The WISC-IV consists of a number of questions asked of a child by a trained psychologist who records the child's individual answers and then calculates scores to determine an overall IQ (Weschler, 2003). IQ is considered to be a reliable indicator of intelligence because it is stable over time. A boy who obtained an IQ score of 147 on the WISC-IV at age 8 would be classified as highly gifted. If that same person took an IQ test several years later, the results should also place the person in the highly gifted range. While a child could certainly have a "bad test" day if he felt ill, was distracted, and so on, it is not reasonable to assume that the boy originally fluked or guessed his way to a score of 147! Four ways to determine if a measure is reliable or unreliable are discussed below, including test-retest, split-half, inter-rater, and inter-item reliability.

Test-retest reliability
Consistency between the same measures for a variable of interest taken at two different points in time.

Test-Retest Reliablity

Demonstrating that a measure of some phenomenon such as intelligence does not change when the same instrument is administered at two different points in time is known as **test-retest reliability**. Test-retest reliability is usually assessed using a correlation coefficient called the Pearson product-moment correlation coefficient (represented by the symbol r). The correlation ranges between zero and $+1.00$ or -1.00, representing the degree of association between two variables. The closer the value of r is to 1.00, the greater the degree or strength of the association between the variables. For example, an r of $+.80$ is higher than one that is $+.64$, zero indicates no relationship between the two variables, and 1.00 indicates a perfect relationship. The positive or negative sign indicates the *direction* of a relationship between variables. A plus sign indicates a positive relationship where both variables go in the same direction. For example, an r of $+.60$ for the relationship between education and income tells us that as education increases, so does income. In 2006, persons with a high school diploma earned about $30,116 per year, those with a university degree (e.g., Bachelor's) earned $58,767, and those with a higher university degree made $69,230 (Statistics Canada, 2009). In the case of negative correlations, the variables go in opposite directions, such as $r = -.54$ for education and prejudice. With increased education, we can expect decreased prejudice.

To evaluate test-retest reliability, the correlation coefficient denotes the relationship between the same variable measured at Time 1 and Time 2. The correlation coefficient (also called a reliability coefficient) should have a value of .80 or greater to indicate good reliability (Cozby, 2012). Test-retest reliability is especially important for demonstrating the accuracy of new measurement instruments. The identification of gifted children, for example, is not as common as you might presume, and this is largely due to the lack of means for screening them. Currently, identification is largely restricted to outcomes determined by standardized IQ tests administered by psychologists (Pfeiffer, Petscher, & Kumtepe, 2008). Expensive IQ tests are only funded by the school system for a small fraction of students, usually identified early on as having some kind of special needs. This means most students are never tested and many gifted children are never identified as such. A new instrument for identifying gifted children called the Gifted Rating Scales (GRS), published by PsychCorp/Harcourt Assessment, is based on teacher ratings of various abilities, such as student intellectual ability, academic ability, artistic talent, leadership ability, and motivation. Test-retest reliability coefficients for the various scales on this new assessment tool were high as reported in the test manual. For example, the coefficient for the Academic Ability scale used by teachers on a sample of 160 children aged 12.0–13.11 years old and reapplied approximately a week later was .97 (Pfeiffer, Petscher, & Kumtepe, 2008).

Split-Half Reliablity

Split-half reliability
Consistency between both halves of the measures for a variable of interest.

An obvious critique of test-retest reliability concerns the fact that since participants receive the same test twice or observers provide ratings of the same phenomenon at fairly close intervals in time, the similarity in results could have more to do with memory for the items than truly measuring the construct of interest. One alternative to the test-retest method that provides a more independent assessment of reliability is the **split-half reliability** approach. Using this method, a researcher would provide exactly half of the items at Time 1 (e.g., only the odd-numbered items or a random sample of the questions on a survey or multi-item index) and the remaining half at Time 2. In this case, the researcher compares the two halves for their degree of association.

Inter-rater Reliability

Inter-rater reliability

Consistency between the same measures for a variable of interest provided by two independent raters.

Another way to test for the reliability of a measure is by comparing the results obtained on one instrument provided by two different observers (or raters). This is called **inter-rater reliability** (and interchangeably inter-judge, inter-coder, or inter-observer reliability). Inter-rater reliability can be thought of as the overall percentage of times two raters agree after examining each pair of results. Using the IQ example above, two different teachers would provide assessments of the students on the various indicators of giftedness and then the two sets of responses would be compared to see if they rate the children very similarly. If two different teachers agree most of the time that particular children exhibit signs of giftedness, we can be more confident that the scales are identifying gifted children as opposed to showing the biases of a particular teacher toward his or her students.

A statistical test called Cohen's Kappa is usually used to test inter-rater reliability because it takes into account the percentage of agreement as well as the number of times raters could be expected to agree just by chance alone (Cohen, 1960).[2] Given the conservative nature of this test, Landis and Koch (1977) recommend considering coefficients of between .61–.80 as substantial and .81 and over as indicative of near-to-perfect agreement. Building on the earlier example, the test manual for the GRS reported an inter-rater reliability of .79 for the academic ability of children aged 6–9.11 years old based on the ratings of two different teachers for 152 students (Pfeiffer, Petscher, & Kumtepe, 2008).

Inter-item Reliability

Inter-item reliability

Demonstrated associations among multiple items representing a single concept.

Lastly, when researchers use instruments that contain multiple indicators of a single concept, it is also possible to assess **inter-item reliability**. Inter-item reliability (also called internal consistency reliability) refers to demonstrated associations among multiple items representing a single concept. First, there should be close correspondence between items evaluating a single dimension. For example, students who score well above average on one item indicating intellectual ability (e.g., verbal comprehension) should also score well above average on other items making up the intellectual ability scale (e.g., memory, abstract reasoning). This is usually measured using Cronbach's alpha, which gives an overall correlation (i.e., an average correlation), taking into account how one particular item correlates with all of the other items and how many items there are in total.

In addition, since giftedness is a broad-ranging, multi-dimensional concept that is usually defined to mean more than just intellectual ability, students who score high on the dimension of intellectual ability should also score high on other dimensions of giftedness, such as academic ability (e.g., math and reading proficiency) and creativity (e.g., novel problem solving). Pfeiffer, Petscher, and Kumtepe (2008) reported a correlation coefficient of .95 between intellectual ability and academic ability, and one of .88 between intellectual ability and creativity using the GRS. The four approaches for assessing reliability discussed in this section are summarized in Figure 4.4.

FIGURE 4.4   **Distinguishing Among Techniques Used to Assess Reliability**

Test-retest	Split-half	Inter-rater	Inter-item
• renders the same findings at **two different times** using the same instrument	• renders the same findings as provided by **two halves** of the same instrument	• renders the same findings as provided by **two different observers**	• renders the same findings as provided by **two or more indicators**

Research on the Net

Assessing Inter-coder Reliability

Matthew Lombard, along with Jennifer Snyder-Duch and Cheryl Campanella Bracken (2002), created a web resource to help researchers and students better understand inter-rater reliability. The authors apply inter-coder (i.e., inter-rater) reliability to a specific research technique called

content analysis and provide step-by-step instructions alongside screenshots to illustrate how to calculate the measures using software. The site named "Practical resources for assessing and reporting inter-coder reliability in content analysis research projects" can be accessed at http://matthewlombard.com/reliability.

Test Yourself

- What is reliability? Provide an example of a reliable measure used in everyday life.
- What is the main difference between test-retest reliability and split-half reliability?
- What type of reliability renders the same findings provided by two different observers?
- What type of reliability refers to demonstrated associations among multiple items representing a single concept?

Measurement Validity

Validity The extent to which a study examines what it intends to.

Perhaps even more important than consistency in measurement, we need to be certain that we are in fact measuring the intended concept of interest. **Validity** is a term used by quantitative researchers to refer to the extent to which a study examines what it intends to. Not all reliable measures are valid. We might reliably weigh ourselves with a scale that consistency tells us the wrong weight because the dial was accidently bumped and it is now set 2 kilograms too high. Similarly, we may depend upon an alarm clock that is consistently ahead of schedule by a few minutes because it was incorrectly programmed after it was purchased or following a change due to daylight savings. In this section, you will learn about four methods for evaluating the extent to which a given measure is measuring what it is intended to using face validity, content validity, construct validity, and criterion validity.

Face Validity

Face validity The extent to which an instrument appears to be a good measure of the intended concept.

First, in trying to determine if a measure is a good indicator of an intended concept, we can assess the measure's face validity. **Face validity** refers to the extent to which an instrument or variable appears on the surface or "face" to be a good measure of the intended construct. Grade point average, for example, appears to be a pretty good measure of a student's scholastic ability, just as net yearly income seems like a valid measure of financial wealth. Your criteria for determining whether something has face validity is an assessment of whether the operationalization used is logical. For example, in the case of giftedness, would most teachers agree that children who exhibit very superior intellectual ability (i.e., the ability to reason at high levels) also tend to exhibit very superior academic ability (e.g., can function at higher than normal levels in specific academic areas such as math or reading)?

Content Validity

Content validity The extent to which an instrument contains the full range of content pertaining to the intended concept.

Content validity refers to the extent which a measure includes the full range or meaning of the intended concept. Suppose you were writing a final examination for a course in introductory psychology. To adequately assess your knowledge of the general field of psychology, the test should include a broad range of topics that cover the full spectrum of introductory psychology, such as how psychologists conduct research, the brain and mental states, sensation, perception, and learning. While a person might not score evenly across all areas of psychology (e.g., a particular student might score 20 out of 20 on the questions related to sensation and perception and only 15 out of 20 on items about research methods), the test result (35/40) should provide a more general measure of knowledge regarding introductory psychology. Similarly, the Gifted Rating Scale discussed earlier is an example of an instrument designed to identify giftedness, which includes not only items related to intellectual ability, but also content pertaining to the dimensions of academic ability, creativity, leadership, and motivation. This is not to say that a person scoring in the gifted range will achieve the same ratings on all items. For example, it is possible for a gifted child to score in the very superior range for intellectual and academic ability as well as creativity, but only superior for motivation and average for leadership. However, when taken together, the overall (full-scale) IQ score is 130 or greater for a gifted individual.

Construct Validity

Construct validity The extent to which an instrument is associated with other logically related measures of the intended concept.

Another way to assess validity is through **construct validity**, which examines how closely a measure is associated with other measures that are expected to be related based on prior theory. For example, Gottfredson and Hirschi's (1990) general theory of crime rests on the assumption that a failure to develop self-control is at the root of most impulsive and even criminal behaviours. Impulsivity, as measured by school records such as report cards, should then correspond with other impulsive behaviours, such as deviant and/or criminal acts. If a study fails to show the expected association (e.g., perhaps children who fail to complete assignments or follow rules in school as noted on report cards do not engage in higher levels of criminal or deviant acts relative to children who appear to have more self-control in the classroom), then the measures of missed assignments and inability to follow rules may not be valid indicators of the construct. That is, the items stated on a report card, for example incomplete assignments, may be measuring something other than impulsivity, such as academic aptitude, health issues, or attention deficit problems. In this case, a better school indicator of impulsivity might be self-reported ratings of disruptive behaviour by the students themselves or teachers' ratings of student impulsivity rather than the behavioural measures listed on a report card. Alternatively, behavioural measures from other areas of a person's life, such as a history of unstable relationships or a lack of perseverance in employment, may be better arenas for assessing low self-control than the highly monitored and structured early school environment.

Criterion Validity

Criterion validity
The extent to which an instrument holds up to an external standard, such as the ability to predict future events.

Finally, a measure of some construct of interest can be assessed against an external standard or benchmark to determine its worth using what is called **criterion validity**. There are a number of types of criterion-based validity. For example, predictive validity refers to the extent to which a measure predicts logically related future events. We can readily anticipate that students who are excelling are also more likely to achieve academic awards, such as scholarships, honours, or distinction, and go on to higher levels. Academic ability as measured in grades is predictive of future school and scholastic success. Similarly, consider how most research methods courses at a university or college have a prerequisite, such as a minimum grade of C– in a 200-level course. The prerequisite indicates basic achievement in the course. It is the cut-off for predicting future success in higher-level courses in the same discipline. The prerequisite has criterion validity if most students with it are able to successfully navigate their way through research methods. All four types of validity are summarized in Figure 4.5.

Test Yourself

- Are all reliable measures valid? Explain your answer.
- What does it mean to say a measure has face validity?
- What does content validity assess?
- Predictive validity is a form of which main type of validity?

FIGURE 4.5
Distinguishing Among Techniques Used to Assess Validity

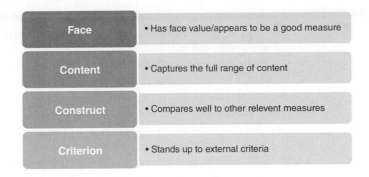

Face	• Has face value/appears to be a good measure
Content	• Captures the full range of content
Construct	• Compares well to other relevent measures
Criterion	• Stands up to external criteria

Random and Systematic Errors

LO5

In research involving humans, both researchers and research participants are potential sources of measurement error. Think about the last time you took a multiple-choice test and accidently entered a response of "d" when you intended to put "e," or when you rushed to finish the last couple of questions and missed including one of the items in your answer because you didn't have time to re-read the instructions or your answers before handing in the test. Also, errors occur in research when participants forget things, accidently miss responses, and otherwise make mistakes completing research tasks. Also, researchers can produce inconsistencies in any number of ways, including by giving varied instructions to participants, by missing something relevant during an observation, and by entering data incorrectly into a computer program (where a 1 might become an 11). Errors that result in unpredictable mistakes often due to carelessness are called **random errors**. Random errors made by participants can be reduced by simplifying the procedures (e.g., participants make fewer mistakes if instructions are clear and easy to follow and if the task is fairly short and simple). Even researchers and observers' unintentional mistakes can be reduced through the use of standardized procedures, such as using scripts to ensure that identical instructions are given, simplifying the task as much as possible, training observers, and using recording devices or other apparatus other than people to collect first-hand data (e.g., replaying an audio recording for verification following an interview). Random errors mostly influence reliability since they work against consistency in measurement.

Random errors
Measurement miscalculation due to unpredictable mistakes.

In contrast to random errors, **systematic errors** refer to ongoing inaccuracies in measurement that sometimes come about through deliberate effort. For example, due to researcher bias, a quantitative researcher who expects or wants a particular finding might behave in a manner that encourages such a response in his or her participants. Expecting a treatment group to have a better performance than a control group, a researcher might interpret certain responses more favourably in the treatment group and unjustifiably rate them higher. The use of standardized procedures, such as scripts and more objective measures that are less open to interpretation, can help reduce researcher bias. In addition, it might

Systematic errors
Miscalculation due to consistently inaccurate measures or intentional bias.

be possible to divide the participants into two groups without the researcher being aware of which group a particular participant ended up in until after the performance scores are recorded.

Study participants make other types of intentional errors, including ones resulting from a social desirability bias. Respondents sometimes provide untruthful answers to present themselves in a more favourable way. Just as people sometimes underestimate the number of cigarettes they smoke when asked by a family physician at an annual physical examination, survey respondents are likely to exaggerate the extent to which they engage in socially desirable practices (e.g., exercising, healthy eating), and minimize the extent to which they engage in unhealthy practices (e.g., overuse of non-prescription pain medicine, binge drinking). Researchers using a questionnaire to measure a concept of interest sometimes build in a lie scale along with the other dimensions of interest. For example, the Eysenck Personality Questionnaire-Revised (EPQR) contains 12 lie detection items, including the statements: "If you say you will do something, do you always keep your promise no matter how inconvenient it might be?"; "Are all your habits good and desirable ones?" and "Have you ever said anything bad or nasty about anyone?" A score of 5 or more indicates social desirability bias (Eysenck, Eysenck, & Barrett, 1985).

Similarly, participants in experimental research sometimes follow what Martin Orne (1962) called demand characteristics or environmental cues, meaning they pick up on hints about what a study is about and then try to help the researchers and the study by behaving in ways that support the hypothesis. Systematic errors influence validity since they reduce the odds that a measure is gauging what it is truly intended to.

Test Yourself

- Who is a potential source of error in measurement?
- Which main form of errors can be reduced by simplifying the procedures in a study?
- What is the term for the bias that results when respondents try to answer in the manner that makes them look the most favourable?

Rigour in Qualitative Research

While it is important for anyone learning about research to understand the centrality of reliability and validity criteria for assessing measurement instruments, it is also imperative to note that much of what has been discussed in this chapter pertains mainly to quantitative research that is based in the positivist paradigm. Qualitative research, largely based in the interpretative and critical paradigms, is aimed at understanding socially constructed phenomenon in the context in which it occurs at a specific point in time, and is therefore less concerned with the systematic reproducibility of data. In many cases, statements provided or processes and interactions studied cannot be replicated to assess reliability. Similarly, if we are to understand events from the point of view of those experiencing them, validity is really in the eyes of the individual actor for whom that understanding is real. That is not to say reliability and validity are not relevant in qualitative research; in fact, if we conclude that these constructs are not applicable to qualitative research, then we run the risk of suggesting that qualitative inquiry is without **rigour**. As defined by Gerard A. Tobin and Cecily M. Begley (2004) "rigour is the means by which we show integrity and competence; it is about ethics and politics, regardless of the paradigm" (p. 390). This helps to legitimize a qualitative research process.

Rigour A means for demonstrating integrity and competence in qualitative research.

Just as various forms of reliability and validity are used to gauge the merit of quantitative research, other criteria such as rigour, credibility, and dependability can be used to establish the trustworthiness of qualitative research. **Credibility** (comparable to validity) has to do with how well the research tells the story it is designed to. For example, in the case of interview data, this pertains to the goodness of fit between a respondent's actual views of reality and a researcher's representations of it (Tobin & Begley, 2004). Credibility can be enhanced through the thoroughness of a literature review and open coding of data. For example, in the case of a qualitative interview, the researcher should provide evidence of how he or she came to the conclusions reached. **Dependability** is a qualitative replacement for reliability and "is achieved through a process of auditing" (Tobin & Begley, 2004, p. 392). Qualitative researchers ensure their research processes, decisions, and interpretation can be examined and verified by other interested researchers through **audit trails**. Audit trails are carefully documented paper trails of an entire research process, including research decisions such as theoretical clarifications made along the way. Transparency, detailed rationale, and justifications all help to establish the later reliability and dependability of findings (Liamputtong, 2009).

Credibility An assessment of the goodness of fit between the respondent's view of reality and a researcher's representation of it.

Dependability An assessment of the researcher's process as well documented and verifiable.

Audit trails Attempts made by a researcher to carefully document the research process in its entirety.

Similarly, while questions of measurement and the operationalization of variables may not apply to qualitative research, questions concerning how the research process was undertaken are essential. For example, in a study using in-depth interviews, were the questions posed to the respondents in a culturally sensitive manner that was readily understood by them? Did the interview continue until all of the important issues were fully examined (i.e., saturation was reached)? Were the researchers appropriately reflective in considering their own subjectivity and how it may have influenced the questions asked, the impressions they formed of the respondents, and the conclusions they reached from the findings (Hennick, Hutter, & Bailey, 2011)? Qualitative researchers acknowledge subjectivity and accept researcher bias as an unavoidable aspect of social science research. Certain topics are examined specifically because they interest the researchers! To reconcile biases with empirical methods, qualitative researchers openly acknowledge their biases and remain transparent and reflective about the manner in which their own views may influence research processes.

Achieving Rigour Through Triangulation

Triangulation
The use of multiple methods or sources to help establish rigour.

One of the main ways rigour is achieved in qualitative research is through the use of **triangulation**. Triangulation is the use of multiple methods to establish what can be considered the qualitative equivalent of reliability and validity (Willis, 2007). For example, we can be more confident in data collected on aggressive behavioural displays in children if data obtained from field notes taken during observations closely corresponds with interview statements made by the children themselves. We can also be more confident in the findings when multiple sources converge (i.e., **data triangulation**), as might be the case if children, teachers, and parents all say similar things about the behaviour of particular children. Since the data comes from various sources with different perspectives, the data itself can also exist in a variety of forms, from comments made by parents and teachers, to actions undertaken by children, to school records and other documents such as report cards.

Data triangulation
The reliance on multiple data sources in a single study.

Other Means for Establishing Rigour

Various alternative strategies to triangulation that help to establish rigour in qualitative studies include the use of member checks, prolonged time spent with research participants in a research setting, peer debriefing, and audit checking (Liamputtong, 2009; Willis, 2007). **Member checks** are attempts by a researcher to validate emerging findings by testing out their accuracy with the originators of that data while still in the field. For example, researchers might share observational findings with the group being studied to see if the participants concur with what is being said. It helps to validate the data if the participants agree that their perspective is being appropriately conveyed by the data. Whenever I conduct interviews with small groups (called focus groups, as discussed in Chapter 9), I share the preliminary findings with the group and ask them whether the views I am expressing capture what they feel is important and relevant given my research interests. I also ask whether the statements I've provided are missing any information that they feel should be included to more fully explain their views or address their concerns about the topic.

Member checks
Attempts made by a researcher to validate findings by testing them with the original sources of the data.

Qualitative researchers also gain a more informed understanding of the individuals, processes, or cultures they are studying if they spend prolonged periods of time in the field. Consider how much more you know about your fellow classmates at the end of term compared to what you know about the group on the first day of classes. Similarly, over time, qualitative researchers learn more and more about the individuals and processes of interest once they gain entry to a group, establish relationships, build trust, and so on. Time also helps in triangulation as researchers are better able to verify information provided as converging sources of evidence are established.

In addition to spending long periods of time in the field and testing findings via their originating sources, qualitative researchers also substantiate their research by opening it up to the scrutiny of others in their field. **Peer debriefing** involves attempts to authenticate the research process and findings through an external review provided by another qualitative researcher who is not directly involved in the study (Creswell, 2014). This process helps to verify the procedures undertaken

Peer debriefing
Attempts made by a researcher to authenticate the research process and findings through an external review provided by an independent researcher.

and substantiate the findings, lending overall credibility to the study. Note reflexivity and other features underlying ethnographic research are discussed in detail in Chapter 10, while multiple methods and mixed-methods approaches are the subject matter of Chapter 11.

Test Yourself

- What is the qualitative term for validity?
- How do qualitative researchers ensure their research process and conclusions reached can be verified by other researchers?

Chapter Summary

LO1 **Describe the main components of a research design.**

A research design details the main components of a study, including who (the unit of analysis), what (the attitudes or behaviours under investigation), where (the location), when (at one or multiple points in time), why (to explain), and how (the specific research method used).

LO2 **Explain what conceptualization and operationalization processes entail.**

Conceptualization is the process whereby a researcher explains what a concept such as family or social inequality means within a particular research project. Operationalization is the process whereby a concept or construct is defined so precisely that it can be measured in a study. For example, financial wealth can be operationalized as net yearly income in dollars.

LO3 **Explain how the purpose of a variable is directly related to how it is measured in research.**

Variables are measured at the nominal, ordinal, interval, and ratio level. The nominal level of measurement is used to classify cases, while the ordinal level has the property of classification and rank order. The interval level of measurement provides the ability to classify, order, and make precise comparisons as a function of equal intervals. The ratio level includes all of the previous properties and a true zero. An index is a composite measure of a construct comprising several different indicators that produce a shared outcome, while a scale is a composite measure of construct consisting of several different indicators that stem from a common cause.

LO4 **Outline the main techniques used to assess reliability and validity.**

Reliability refers to consistency in measurement. *Test-retest* reliability examines consistency between the same measures for a variable at two different times using a correlation coefficient. *Inter-rater* reliability examines consistency between the same measures for a variable of interest provided by two different raters, often using Cohen's Kappa. *Split-half* reliability examines consistency between both halves of the measures for a variable of interest. *Inter-item* reliability involves demonstrated associations among multiple items representing a single concept. Validity refers to the extent to which a measure is a good indicator of the intended concept. *Face* validity refers to the extent to which an instrument appears to be a good measure of the intended concept. *Content* validity assesses the extent to which an instrument contains full range of content pertaining to the intended concept. *Construct* validity assesses the extent to which an instrument is associated with other logically related measures of the intended concept. *Criterion* validity assesses the extent to which an instrument holds up to an external standard, such as the ability to predict future events.

LO5 **Distinguish between random and systematic errors.**

Random errors are unintentional and usually result from careless mistakes, while systematic errors result from intentional bias. Sources of both types of errors include participants, researchers, and observers in a study. Errors can be reduced through training, the use of standardized procedures, and by simplifying tasks.

LO6 **Explain how rigour is achieved in qualitative research.**

Rigour refers to means for demonstrating integrity and competence in qualitative research. Rigour can be achieved through the use of triangulation, member checks, extended experience in an environment, peer review, and audit trails.

Research Reflection

1. Suppose you want to conduct a quantitative study on the success of students at your post-secondary institution. List five variables that you think would be relevant for inclusion in the study. Generate one hypothesis you could test using two of the variables you listed. Operationalize the variables you included in your proposed hypothesis.

2. Studies on the health of individuals often operationalize health as self-reported health using these five fixed response categories: poor, fair, good, very good, and excellent. What level of measurement is this? Provide an example of health operationalized into two categories measured at the nominal level and three categories at the ordinal level. Is it possible to measure health at the interval level? Justify your answer.

3. Consider some of the variables that can be used to examine the construct of scholastic ability (e.g., grades, awards, and overall grade point average). Which measure do you think best represents scholastic ability? Is the measure reliable and/or valid? Defend your answer with examples that reflect student experiences.

4. Define the concept of honesty and come up with an indicator that could be used to gauge honesty. Compare your definition and indicator with those of at least three other students in the class. Are the definitions similar? Consider how each definition reflects a prior conceptualization process.

Learning Through Practice

Objective: To construct an index for students at risk for degree incompletion. Directions:

1. Item selection: Try to come up with ten statements that can be answered with a forced-choice response of yes or no, where yes responses receive 1 point and no responses are awarded 0 points. Select items that would serve as good indicators of students at risk for failing to complete their program of study. Think of behaviours or events that would put a student at risk for dropping out or being asked to leave a program of study, such as failing a required course. Make sure your items are one-dimensional (i.e., they only measure one behaviour or attitude).

2. Try out your index on a few of your classmates to see what scores you obtain for them. Is there any variability in the responses? Do some students score higher or lower than others?

3. Come up with a range of scores you feel represents no risk, low risk, moderate risk, and high risk. Justify your numerical scoring.

Research Resources

1. For more information on the cohort-based longitudinal National Population Health Survey (NPHS) discussed in the Research in Action box, use the general search term "National Population Health Survey" on Statistics Canada's home page: statcan.gc.ca.

2. To learn more about the longitudinal panel study on cancer called *The Tomorrow Project* discussed near the start of this chapter, visit the website in4tomorrow.ca.

3. For an in-depth look at scale development, I recommend: DeVellis, R. F. (2012). *Scale development: Theory and applications* (3rd ed.). Thousand Oaks, CA: Sage Publications.

4. For a good discussion of the distinction between reliability and validity as used within the positivist (or quantitative) paradigm versus the interpretative (qualitative) realm, I recommend: Golafshani, N. (2003). Understanding reliability and validity in qualitative research. *The Qualitative Report, 8*(4), 596–607, which you can access at nova.edu/ssss/QR/QR8-4/golafshani.pdf.

5. To learn more about how rigour is achieved in qualitative research, see: Tobin, G. A., & Begley, C. M. (2004). Methodological rigour within a qualitative framework. *Journal of Advanced Nursing, 48*(4), 388–396.

 For more information on the resources available from McGraw-Hill Ryerson, go to www.mcgrawhill.ca/he/solutions.

References

Bogardus, E. S. (1933). A social distance scale. *Sociology and Social Research, 17,* 265–271.

Cohen, J. (1960). A coefficient of agreement for nominal scales. *Educational and Psychological Measurement, 20,* 37–46.

Cozby, P. C. (2012). *Methods in behavioral research* (11th ed.). New York, NY: McGraw-Hill.

Creswell, J. W. (2014). *Research design: Qualitative, quantitative, and mixed method approaches* (4th ed.). Thousand Oaks, CA: Sage Publications.

DeVellis, R. F. (2012). *Scale development: Theory and applications* (3rd ed.). Thousand Oaks, CA: Sage Publications.

Eysenck, S. B. G., Eysenck, H. J., & Barrett, P. (1985). A revised version of the psychoticism scale. *Personality and Individual Differences, 6*(1), 21–29.

Ferris, J., & Wynne, H. (2001). *The Canadian Problem Gambling Index: Final report.* Ottawa: Canadian Centre on Substance Abuse.

Garner, D. M., & Garfinkel, P. E. (1979). The Eating Attitudes Test: An index of the symptoms of anorexia nervosa. *Psychological Medicine, 9,* 273–279.

Golafshani, N. (2003). Understanding reliability and validity in qualitative research. *The Qualitative Report, 8*(4), 596–607.

Gottfredson, M. R., & Hirschi, T. (1990). *A general theory of crime.* Stanford, CT: Stanford University Press.

Hagan, F. E. (2010). *Research methods in criminal justice and criminology* (8th ed.). Upper Saddle River, NJ: Pearson Education.

Hennick, M., Hutter, I., & Bailey, A. (2011). *Qualitative research methods.* Thousand Oaks, CA: Sage Publications.

Landis, J. R., & Koch, G. G. (1977). The measurement of observer agreement for categorical data. *Biometrics, 33*(1), 159–174.

Liamputtong, P. (2009). *Qualitative research methods* (3rd ed.). Toronto, ON: Oxford University Press.

Lombard, M., Snyder-Duch, J., & Bracken, C. C. (2002). Content analyses in communication: Assessment and reporting of intercoder reliability. *Human Communications Research, 28,* 587–604.

Orne, M. T. (1962). On the social psychology of the psychological experiment: With particular reference to demand characteristics and their implications. *American Psychologist, 17,* 776–783.

Pfeiffer, S. I., Petscher, Y., & Kumtepe, A. (2008). The gifted ratings scales-school form: A validation study based on age, gender, and race. *Roeper Review, 30,* 140–146.

Sapsford, R. (2006). Indicator. In V. Jupp (ed.), *The Sage dictionary of social research methods.* DOI: 10.4135/9780857020116. Retrieved from www.srmo.sagepub.com/view/the-sage-dictionary-of-social-research-methods/n98.xml

Shooshtari, S., Menec, V., & Tate, R. (2007). Comparing predictors of positive and negative self-rated health between younger (25–54) and older (55+)

Canadian adults: A longitudinal study of well-being. *Research on Aging, 29*(6), 512–554.

Statistics Canada. (2013a). Concept: Census family. In *Definitions, data sources, and methods.* Ottawa, ON: Author. Retrieved from www.statcan.gc.ca/concepts/definitions/cfamily-rfamille-eng.htm

Statistics Canada. (2013b). Previous standard—ethnicity. In *Definitions, data sources, and methods.* Ottawa, ON: Author. Retrieved from www.statcan.gc.ca/concepts/definitions/previous-anterieures/ethnicity-ethnicite2-eng.htm

Statistics Canada. (2009). Average earnings of the population 15 years and over by highest level of schooling, by province and territory (2006 Census). Ottawa, ON: Author. Retrieved from www.statcan.gc.ca/tables-tableaux/sum-som/l01/cst01/labor50a-eng.htm

Tobin, G. A., & Begley, C. M. (2004). Methodological rigour within a qualitative framework. *Journal of Advanced Nursing, 48*(4), 388–96.

(The) Tomorrow Project (2013). *The Tomorrow Project.* Calgary, AB: Alberta Health Services. Retrieved from: http://in4tomorrow.ca

Weschler, D. (2003). *Weschler Intelligence Scale for Children (WISC-IV)* (4th ed.). Toronto: Pearson Education.

Willis, J. W. (2007). *Foundations of qualitative research: Interpretive and critical approaches.* Thousand Oaks, CA: Sage Publications.

Wood, R. T., & Williams, R. J. (2007). Problem gambling on the Internet: Implications for Internet gambling policy in North America. *New Media Society, 9,* 520–542.

Endnotes

[1] Bachrach, C. (2007). In S. L. Hofferth & L. M. Casper (Eds.), *Handbook of measurement issues in family research.* Mahwah, NJ: Lawrence Erlbaum Associates.

[2] Cohen's Kappa is generally used only with nominal level variables. If the variables of interest are at the ordinal or interval/ratio level, Krippendorff's alpha is recommended (Lombard, Snyder-Duch, & Bracken, 2002).

5

Sampling

Learning Objectives

After reading this chapter, students should be able to do the following:

LO1 Define sampling and differentiate between a population and a sample.

LO2 Explain why a researcher might choose a probability-based sampling method and distinguish between simple random, systematic, stratified, and cluster sampling techniques.

LO3 Identify the main advantages and disadvantages of probability-based sampling techniques.

LO4 Explain why a researcher might choose a non-probability sampling method and distinguish between convenience, snowball, purposive, and quota sampling techniques.

LO5 Identify the main advantages and disadvantages of non-probability-based techniques.

LO6 Explain how theoretical sampling differs from non-probability-based sampling techniques.

"The national census collects information about every person living in Canada, including age, sex and language. Unlike a census, a sample survey collects information from only part—a 'sample'—of the total population being studied. The results are then used to draw conclusions about the whole group. For example, you could collect data from ten of the 30 students in a class to estimate the average age of the 30 students. On a larger scale, Statistics Canada's Labour Force Survey questions over 50,000 households across Canada every month to estimate the total number of unemployed Canadians." (Statistics Canada, 2012, para. 1)[1]

Introduction

LO1

Sampling The technique or process used to acquire the unit of analysis from a population of interest.

Recall from Chapter 4 how a research design details the overall plan for a study, beginning with whom the study is about. In addition to identifying the unit of analysis—such as individuals, groups, or organizations—a design also provides details on how the particular unit of analysis was chosen to be included in a particular study. **Sampling** is the technique used to acquire the unit of analysis from a population of interest. You already use sampling in everyday life on a regular basis as you "sample" a grape or a cherry at a local supermarket before buying the entire bunch. Similarly, you might try a couple of food samples offered to you at a local food market before choosing a particular item to purchase in greater quantity. If you are a parent, perhaps you have tried out or sampled several babysitters for short periods of time before settling on one that you feel is best suited for looking after your child for an extended period of time. Finally, you probably hang out with a select group of friends as opposed to everyone in your class, and you invite only certain people over from your place of work because those particular individuals resonate with you. In social research, an investigator sometimes selects a sample of individuals, or chooses a group or an organization to study, in hopes of generalizing the findings to a wider population of interest. In other cases, a sample is chosen because that particular group best suits the research problem, interest, and/or needs of the investigator. In this chapter you will learn why it is important to sample, what the relationship is between samples and populations, and how to conduct probability- and non-probability-based sampling.

A couple tries a food sample at a local market.

Populations and Samples

Population The complete set of individuals, objects, or scores that the investigator is interested in studying.

A **population** is "the complete set of individuals, objects, or scores that the investigator is interested in studying" (Pagano, 2013, p. 6). As noted in the opening quote, Statistics Canada's Census population is every single person living in Canada, while another population of interest to Statistics Canada researchers is all unemployed Canadians. Similarly, all undergraduate students taking classes at the University of Toronto, (i.e., the study body at the U of T) might make up a population of interest to a researcher interested in views on tuition costs and perceived educational benefits. Universities keep various records on registered students, including whether they are taking classes full-time or part-time, their

FIGURE 5.1 A Sample Is a Subset of the Population

A researcher draws a sample from a population of interest and then generalizes findings from research on that sample back to the population.

home mailing addresses and phone numbers, and so on. In 2008–2009, the U of T had 55 352 undergraduate students (University of Toronto, 2012). However, while the population is "known," it is unlikely that you could locate all of those students because even though they are officially on record, many students move to another residence and/or change their phone number without updating their contact information at the school. In addition, some of the students who can be located may be too busy or otherwise uninterested in participating in the study. Finally, it could take several years to complete a study with tens of thousands of participants and it might be too costly to do so. An important, question, then, is whether it is really necessary to include all students in a study looking at student views on some issue of interest. The short answer is "no." Using techniques discussed in this section, a smaller **sample** of students can be obtained for use in a study and their views can still be considered indicative of the larger population (see Figure 5.1).

Sample A subset of the population of interest that represents the unit of analysis in a study.

As another example, Toronto's homeless might constitute a population of interest to a sociologist from the University of Toronto interested in the daily challenges faced by individuals who are living on the street. It is generally not possible to identify or locate all of the homeless people living in and around Toronto, therefore it would be very difficult to even determine who comprises the population of interest. Instead, a researcher could examine homelessness using

Probability sampling
A method in which every individual or element in the population has a known chance of being selected.

secondary resources, such reports from local agencies that deal directly with homeless individuals in the area or interviews with employees of agencies that work with homeless people. Alternatively, the researcher might opt to speak with a small number of homeless individuals who agree to participate in the study. While likely not representative of the entire population of interest, such a sample is likely available for inclusion in a study and it will still constitute an important unit of analysis, especially as a starting point, to learn about challenges facing homeless individuals.

Selecting a Sample

Non-probability sampling A method in which the chance of selection of an individual or element in the population is unknown.

Researchers use two main types of procedures to obtain a sample: **probability sampling** and **non-probability sampling**. Probability sampling is a method in which every individual or element in the population has a known chance of being selected. Non-probability sampling is a method in which the chance of selection of an individual or element in the population is unknown.

Test Yourself

- What is sampling and when might you use this in everyday life?
- What is the relationship between a sample and a population?
- What is the difference between probability and non-probability sampling?

Probability Sampling

LO2

Representative sample A sample with the same distribution of characteristics as the population from which it was selected.

Probability sampling is used when a researcher wants a **representative sample** or one with "the same distribution of characteristics as the population from which it was selected" (Babbie & Benaquisto, 2014, p. 169). For example, if a population consists of students who are mainly enrolled full-time and taking classes during the day, then those students who end up in the sample should also be mostly full-time students who attend day classes. To the extent that this is true, the findings obtained from the sample will generalize to the larger population. This is very important when the researcher wants to accurately capture the views of the entire population, but the population is so large it would difficult if not impossible to include every member in a study. A survey on the views of people living in the province of Ontario or a survey on the views of all Canadians are examples of projects that are best carried out with probability sampling. Most surveys conducted by Statistics Canada use probability sampling (Statistics Canada, 2013a). Probability sampling relies upon known probabilities concerning the proportion of times an event will occur. For example, when you roll a die and you hope for a "5," the probability of obtaining a 5 is one chance in six since there are six possibilities on the die (1, 2, 3, 4, 5, 6). Similarly, when you flip a coin and you hope for "heads," the probability of obtaining heads is one out of two (or 0.5) since there are two possible outcomes

Sampling frame
The complete list of individuals or elements making up the population.

(heads and tails). With probability sampling, the population must be known (i.e., every member must be identifiable to the researcher). In the example used earlier on, it is possible to identify all 55 352 students attending the University of Toronto via a list that could be generated by the registrar's office. The complete list of 55 352 students making up the population of undergraduate students is called a **sampling frame**. If a sampling frame can be made available, then the researcher can calculate probabilities and probability sampling is possible. Four types of probability-based sampling techniques are described below.

Simple Random Sampling

Simple random sampling A probability-based method used to obtain individuals or cases that make up a sample on the basis of chance alone.

Simple random sampling is a method used to obtain individuals (or cases) that make up a sample on the basis of chance alone. For example, if we randomly selected one student from the U of T sampling frame, this means that student, like any other student at the U of T, has a 1 in 55 352 chance of being selected. Note that the term "random" is not to be confused with "haphazard," as in any method will work. Random only means that chance alone determines the selection based on probability. For example, imagine ten people attend a meeting and all ten people write their names on slips of paper of the same size, which are then put into a hat and mixed around, and one is randomly drawn for a prize. Each person in attendance has an equal chance of winning with a probability of one out of ten. But what if two or three prizes were to be given out? "Sampling with replacement" means the first person drawn would be put back into the hat for another try at a prize, keeping the odds at 1:10 for all members in attendance, including the person who already won a prize. However, research in the social sciences (like many door prize raffles) is usually carried out using "sampling without replacement." This means that after the first person wins the prize, he or she is taken out of the draw. The odds for the next prize winner then change to one out of nine, and for a third prize to 1:8. While the probability of selection for each case (or element) from the population is always known, the probability of selection for each case is not always identical.

"Do you really care about my opinion or am I just a random sample?"

© Patrick Hardin. www.Cartoonstock.com

To obtain a random sample without replacement, a researcher follows these steps:

1. Generate a complete list of all of individuals in the population.
2. Number each individual in the sampling frame.
3. Use a random numbers table to randomly select the sample of a specific size as described below.

A random numbers table is a computer-generated listing of random numbers. A random numbers table is included in the back of most statistics textbooks,[2] and there are various Internet sites that contain tools for generating random number tables (e.g., stattrek.com). Random numbers table generators at Internet sites are the most straightforward since you can enter the size of sample you wish to include in your study (e.g., 100), which numbers represent the sampling frame (e.g., for the University of Toronto example above, the minimum possible value is 1 and the maximum value is 55 352), and that you wish to use sampling without replacement. When the table is generated, it will include *only* 100 randomly selected non-repeating numbers within that range. For example, the first number might be "09081," meaning the first person included in the sample will be the student whose name is beside the number 9081 on the sampling frame. Going across the first row, the second number listed is "50835," indicating that the second person included in the sample would be whoever was numbered 50 835, and so on, until the 100th person, who corresponds to whoever is listed as 8490 in the sampling frame (see Figure 5.2).

Systematic Random Sampling

Systematic random sampling A probability-based method used to obtain a sample on the basis of a fixed interval representing every *n*th case listed.

As a potentially more efficient alternative to simple random sampling, some researchers opt for **systematic random sampling**. Systematic random sampling is a straightforward method used to obtain a sample on the basis of a fixed interval representing every *n*th listed case. For example, using an interval of size 5, a random starting point is selected between 1 and 5, and then every fifth person listed in the sampling frame is selected to be included in the sample. The fixed interval

FIGURE 5.2   **A Random Numbers Table Generated Using Stat Trek**

100 Random Numbers												
09081	50835	36278	09897	33689	32363	06940	42558	05758	46105	50468	22680	50692
07308	00804	20315	17135	41375	09305	35463	27042	22904	35320	53424	13811	36646
23495	33546	03393	53200	29183	31181	10488	31916	37685	46329	35096	13444	23047
23638	21865	27186	51874	03760	11446	43740	02211	01395	18541	22456	25412	16544
43149	03984	51426	34505	15218	17726	39602	14626	19500	34281	30590	12262	26595
53648	53791	27410	36502	49877	24454	45371	23271	48918	12629	40193	12853	24821
18317	37828	19948	44188	26818	38276	44555	40417	52833	15585	31324	39458	41008
51059	20906	15361	46696	48694	28001	34728	55198	08490				

Source: Stat Trek (2012).

Sampling interval
The fixed interval used to select every *n*th case listed after a random starting point is obtained.

is called a **sampling interval** and is calculated by dividing the population size by the desired sample size. Using our earlier example, 55 352 ÷ 100 = 553.52, or rounded to the nearest whole number, every 553rd student would be chosen. The steps are summarized below:

1. Generate a complete list of all of individuals in the population.
2. Number each individual in the sampling frame.
3. Calculate the sampling interval by dividing the population by the desired sample size.
4. Randomly select the first case. It should be a number between one and the size of the sampling interval. For the example above, it would involve randomly selecting a number between 1 and 553, such as 10.
5. Use every *n*th number after that (as denoted by the sampling interval) until the number of cases selected reaches the desired sample size. In this example, the sampling interval is 553. The first person included in the sample would be whoever is listed at 10, then 653, then 1116, 1669, and so on until the desired sample size is reached.

Stratified Random Sampling

Stratified random sampling A probability-based method used to obtain a sample on the basis of known population characteristics.

Stratified random sampling is a method used to obtain a sample on the basis of known population characteristics. Researchers using stratified random sampling are trying to ensure that certain characteristics of the population, such as age, sex, ethnicity, education, location, or any other attribute deemed especially relevant to a given study, end up in the sample. To accomplish this, researchers divide the population into subgroups based on known characteristics and then randomly (or systematically) sample for a certain number of cases from each group. For example, a researcher interested in the views of 1200 instructional faculty toward publishing student ratings of instruction at a university might want to ensure that he or she ends up with a sample that includes full-time continuing instructors, as well as those who teach on a part-time basis (often called sessional or term instructors). In this example, the instructors would first be grouped on the basis of their teaching appointment status (full-time or part-time). Each of the two groups is considered a "strata." If the goal is to end up with a sample size of 100 instructors, 50 can be randomly selected from the part-time strata and 50 can be randomly selected from the full-time strata. While even subgroups are desirable for some statistical tests, this practice can detract from representativeness depending on how the characteristic of interest is distributed in the original population. For example, there are likely to be more part-time instructors overall, meaning that the sample obtained through the stratified sampling technique is now somewhat less representative than what was obtained through simple and systematic random sampling. Researchers can, however, opt for a "proportionate" sample that includes an equivalent ratio of relevant characteristics in the sample as exist in the population. For example, if 750 of the 1200 instructors teach part-time, then 62.5 percent of the sample would also need to be made up of instructors who teach on a part-time basis. This can be achieved if the researcher randomly selects 63 part-time and 37 full-time instructors.

Finally, in some instances, a researcher may wish to specifically examine certain characteristics of importance in a study and might purposely oversample for these traits. For example, if part-time instructors are known to have more reservations about publishing student ratings of instruction because they hold only limited appointment contracts without job security, a researcher might intentionally oversample for part-time instructors to learn as much as possible about their concerns, especially if plans are being developed to implement published ratings at that institution. **Disproportionate sampling** is the term used to describe a sampling method used deliberately to obtain a different ratio of relevant characteristics than what exists in the population.

Disproportionate sampling A sampling method used deliberately to obtain a different ratio of relevant characteristics than what exists in the population.

Research in Action

Statistics Canada Sampling Methods

Most of the national surveys conducted by researchers at Statistics Canada include representative samples based on one or more of the probability-based sampling techniques discussed in this section. For example, the Canadian Community Health Survey—Mental Health (CCHS), designed to assess the mental health and well-being of Canadians through a series of questions on mental health functioning and use of various health services (Statistics Canada, 2013b), targets everyone 15 years of age and over living in the ten provinces. Although the survey excludes a few groups, such as people who are living on reserves, people serving in the Canadian Forces, and institutionalized populations, the sample ends up including about 27 000 respondents and represents more than 97 percent of the Canadian population. The CCHS is based on a cross-sectional design and uses

multi-stage stratified cluster sampling. First, clusters are selected based on geographic location, and then they are adjusted for the population size to ensure adequate representation from individuals of various ages. Finally, systematic sampling is used to obtain dwellings within the clusters (Statistics Canada, 2013b). The data collected by the survey is used by various organizations and individuals, including Health Canada, mental health services, and universities. It is also used by researchers who wish to conduct additional analyses. For example, Piran and Gadalla (2007) examined the correspondence between eating disorders and substance abuse among adult Canadian women through a secondary analysis of data collected using the CCHS from 2002. The researchers reported significant associations between alcohol dependence and alcohol interference and the risk for eating disorders among women of all ages (Piran & Gadalla, 2007).

Cluster Sampling

Cluster sampling A probability-based method for selecting groups for a sample, usually on the basis of their geographic location.

In contrast to random, systematic, and stratified sampling methods, which all rely on the selection of cases one individual at a time, **cluster sampling** is a method for selecting groups for a sample, usually on the basis of their geographic location. Sometimes it is not possible to identify a sampling frame for a population of interest, or even with a list it might not be feasible to reach the entire sample, as might be the case if it is thinly spread across a huge geographic area. For example, a researcher wishing to interview people about their permanent summer vacation spots by lakes in Alberta would be unable to obtain a complete sampling frame of individuals who maintain campers and trailers or have cabins near lakes anywhere in Alberta. Even if it was possible to create such a listing, it would probably not be feasible for a researcher to try and reach the sample, which would span a vast area including Peace River, Grand Prairie, Hinton, Red Deer, Canmore, Jasper, Wainwright, and Lethbridge. Instead, the population of interest can be divided into a number of mutually exclusive clusters based on geographic location. As a fishing guide, Barry Mitchell (2012) divides Alberta lakes into 11 main geographic areas (e.g., Area 1 includes Peace River and High Level; Area 2 includes Grand Prairie and Grande Cache; Area 3 includes Edmonton, Whitecourt, and Hinton). Within each of the 11 areas (or clusters), there are several lakes (e.g., Area 1 contains Bistcho Lake, Caribou Lake, and Rainbow Lake). A researcher can randomly sample one lake from each cluster and then attempt to conduct interviews with everyone in the 11 particular lake communities. If every person or instance from a cluster is included in the sample, the overall process is called "one-stage cluster sampling." Even though the researcher in the example above limited the study to only 11 lake communities, there might be several hundred lake dwellers within each lake community, resulting in a sample size into the tens of thousands. To decrease the sample size, a researcher might use random or systematic sampling within each lake community. For example, the researcher might randomly sample for 20 members within each of the lakes chosen, for a total sample size of 220. Further random sampling within clusters is more officially known as "two-stage cluster sampling." For an overview of the four probability-based sampling techniques, refer to Figure 5.3.

FIGURE 5.3   **Overview of Probability-Based Sampling Techniques**

Simple Random	Systematic	Stratified	Cluster
• used when there is a known sampling frame	• used when there is a known sampling frame	• used when there is a known sampling frame	• used when the complete sampling frame is not readily available or accessible
• based on an equal chance of selection (unbiased)	• based on choosing every n^{th} element after a random start	• based on subgroups that contain important attributes	• considered practical when there are readily identifable subgroups spread across diverse geographic locations
• considered the ideal since the sample will be highly representative of the population	• considered more straightforward to carry out than simple random sampling	• used with simple or systematic sampling to ensure certain strata are represented in the sample	• can occur in stages
• could still have some sampling error, but this can be reduced by increasing the sample size	• could be problematic if there is any special order to the sampling frame	• may not be representative depending on the distribution of the strata in the population	• could be costly to study since it results in a fairly large overall sample size

Research in Action

Cluster Sampling

For a very user-friendly lesson that walks you through the process of cluster sampling and helps to distinguish this method from stratified sampling,

I recommend the short "Cluster Sampling" video uploaded by Steve Mays to YouTube on August 26, 2011. You can access this video at youtube.com by searching for "Cluster Sampling by Steve Mays."

Test Yourself

- When is probability sampling used in research?
- What is a sampling frame?
- Is sampling usually carried out with or without replacement in the social sciences?
- Which sampling method relies upon a fixed sampling interval?
- Which sampling method is used to try and mirror particular population characteristics?

Advantages and Disadvantages of Probability Sampling

LO3

Representativeness

The biggest advantage of a probability-based sampling method is that the sample generated is a fair representation of the population of interest. This means information obtained from the sample, often in the form of opinions of respondents who complete a survey or provide answers during an interview, is generalizable to the larger population of interest. As a result, when a sample of students expresses their desire for published instructor ratings, we can be reasonably assured that the points raised are relevant to the wider population of students at that particular post-secondary institution. For example, if students in the sample noted that they want ratings published so they can be used in the selection of courses and instructors, we can be fairly certain that most students would identify the same benefits stemming from the disclosure of student ratings of instruction (Howell & Symbaluk, 2001). A population that has very little variability, as would be the case if members of a population hold similar views or have similar characteristics, is considered to be "homogenous." The more homogenous a population is, the more confident we can be that a sample drawn from it represents that population of interest. For example, if the vast majority of students believe student ratings of instruction accurately measure teaching effectiveness and the vast majority support the public disclosure of ratings, then it doesn't really matter if our sample contains 100 or 500 students, since their responses are likely to repeatedly express the same position. Alternatively, if there is variation in views toward student ratings of instruction as is the case with instructors—where some consider student ratings to be valid measures of teaching excellence, while others perceive them to be biased measures of teaching that are highly influenced by things like grades or level of course difficulty—a larger sample of instructors would be necessary to ensure that the appropriate variation was similarly captured in the study.

Sampling Error and Sample Size

Although the overall purpose of using a probability-based sampling method is to obtain a sample that is representative of the population, a sample generally does not contain the exact same parameters as the population of interest. For example, imagine your methods class of 30 students constitutes a population of interest and your teacher randomly selects a group of five students from the class list. While the class or population average on a midterm might be 78 percent, with a range of marks from 48 percent to 100 percent, the average for a sample of only five students might be quite different depending on the exact students selected. If one of the top students ends up in the sample, even if the remaining four are "average," the mean for the sample is likely to be quite a bit higher than 78 percent. Similarly, if even just one student is quite a bit below average, the sample mean will be substantially lower than what exists for the population. The difference between the sample mean ($\bar{x}$) and the population mean (μ) is called **sampling error**. When researchers rely upon a sample to tell them about a population, they take into account the likely amount of measurement error using what is called a **confidence interval**. A confidence interval is an estimated range that is likely to contain the true population value based on the sample value. A confidence level tells you how sure you can be that the results obtained using the sample are accurate. For example, an analyst might report that a survey's findings are accurate within 4 percentage points (the confidence interval) with 95 percent accuracy (the confidence level). If the survey found that 56 percent of the Canadians sampled support raising the Goods and Services Tax (GST) back to the pre-2006 level (from 5 percent to 7 percent), this means that the analyst is 95 percent sure that between 52 percent and 60 percent of all Canadians support the tax increase.

One way to be more confident in the findings based on a sample by reducing sampling error is to increase the size of the sample used. That is, the larger the sample, the more confident we can be that it will contain the same features as the population. Clearly, selecting only two students from a methods class is less likely to give you an accurate sense of how 30 students are doing than if the sample contained ten students. But does a larger sample always increase accuracy? In other words, how big is big enough? The answer is determined by calculating the needed sample size using a statistical formula based on probability theory that takes into account the confidence level, the size of the confidence interval, and the population size. While such calculations are beyond this course, most introductory statistics textbooks include the formula in a chapter on sampling distributions. See Table 5.1 for sample sizes generated using a 95 percent confidence level and accuracy within 3, 5, and 10 percentage points. Examining Table 5.1,

Sampling error The difference between the sample statistic and the population parameter.

Confidence interval An estimated range that is likely to contain the true population value based on the sample value.

Research on the Net

Random Sampling and Sampling Error

To help make the notion of sampling error clear, complete the quick interactive activity that is part of a math tutorial provided by Annenberg Learner at learner.org/courses/learningmath/data/swfs/1d_circles.swf.

Goal: To select five circles (a sample) to accurately represent all 60 circles (the population). Instructions:

1. Click on the start button.

2. Read the instructions under "Your Selection" where you are invited to select five circles from a population of 60 circles of various diameters. The goal is to select circles that you think taken together would represent the average size of the circles in the population. When you are ready to begin, click on the "Make a Selection" button.

3. Note the average diameter for your selection.

4. Now click on the "Random Selection" tab. Note any differences between the randomly selected diameter and the one that was generated when you "eye-balled" the data. Also note that if you redo steps 2 or 4, you will get different values.

5. Finally, select the "All 60 Circles" tab to discover the true diameter of the 60 circles.

6. If the sample size was increased from 5 to 15, how do you think it might influence the average diameter for the sample?

Source: Annenberg Learner (2013). Random sampling. In *Data Analysis, Statistics, & Probability.* Session 1, Part D: Bias in Sampling. Annenberg Foundation.

note that if you wish to use a smaller confidence interval for greater precision with less of a margin of error, then you need to increase your sample size. For example, if you have a population of size 2000, you only need 92 in your sample to be within 10 percentage points of accuracy, but you will need 322 in the sample to be within 5 points, and 696 in the same sample to be within 3 points. Also note that as your sample size gets quite large, the needed sample size does not continue to increase at the same rate.

TABLE 5.1   Sample Size and Precision of Population Estimates (95 Percent Confidence Level)

	Precision of Estimate		
Size of Population	± 3%	± 5%	± 10%
2000	696	322	92
5000	879	357	94
10 000	964	370	95
50 000	1045	381	96
100 000	1056	383	96
Over 100 000	1067	384	96

Note: The sample sizes were calculated using conservative assumptions about the nature of the true population values.
Source: Cozby, 2009, p. 137.

Test Yourself

- What is the main advantage of using probability-based sampling methods?
- What does sampling error refer to?
- Does increasing a sample size always lead to improved accuracy?

Non-probability Sampling

LO4

Thus far I have discussed techniques based on probability or the known chance of being selected. All sampling that is not based on known probabilities is a form of non-probability sampling. In non-probability sampling, the likelihood of selection of an individual or element in the population is unknown. This is usually because the sampling frame cannot be readily identified, such as the opening example of homeless individuals in Toronto. Members of many subgroups of interest to researchers are often difficult to accurately identify or locate, including survivors of natural disasters or people living in remote communities, while others may wish to avoid detection for any number of reasons, such as families living in non-traditional arrangements (e.g., gay and lesbian unions, or polygamous marriages where a person has two or more spouses). Those who are identifiable and willing to participate in a study are very important and relevant contributors to our understanding of the subgroup, disaster, or community of interest. Four common non-probability sampling techniques are discussed in more detail below, including availability, snowball, purposive, and quota sampling.

Convenience sampling A non-probability method used to obtain a sample on the basis of availability alone.

Convenience Sampling

Convenience sampling is a non-probability method used to obtain individuals or cases that make up a sample on the basis of availability alone. A newspaper reporter who is developing a story about a fire in an apartment building might ask anyone who is present outside the apartment building if they have any information on the fire. Similarly, a researcher interested in community responses to fire evacuations after a state of emergency is declared might interview anyone who can be reached from the community of interest. In both cases, the sample will not be representative of the entire population of interest; however, the reporter is likely to find out something about the fire in the apartment building and about select resident concerns, just as the researcher will find out how particular members of the community are faring following the fire-related evacuation. Convenience sampling is sometimes called "haphazard sampling" and "accidental sampling" due to the manner in which the sample is obtained. However, I prefer convenience sampling since the other terms imply disorganized research practices. In reality, the nature of a research question or the characteristics of a population of interest may necessitate the use of a sample that was obtained on the basis of its availability. In this sense, availability only means potential accessibility or obtainability, not an easy route to acquiring a sample.

Convenience sampling is often used in exploratory qualitative research where it is possible to examine one particular group of interest as a starting point for learning more about an area that is less well established. For example, Globerman (1996) conducted a study to learn more about the motivations of family members caring for relatives with Alzheimer's disease, a form of dementia. Specifically, she was interested in the question: How do in-laws take responsibility for their spouses' parents? To obtain the sample, Globerman sent a letter to family contacts for patients diagnosed with Alzheimer's who were residing in the community and were registered with a particular geriatric psychiatric clinic. The letter of request specified that Globerman wanted to interview at least three members of the family, all of whom would need to be living within 60 miles of the city. Of the 60 requests she sent out, 38 families agreed to participate in the study. Although likely not generalizable to all Canadian caregivers of elderly family members with Alzheimer's, Globerman (1996) identified various patterns of interaction that could be explored in future research, including one in which son-in-laws tended to act as "performers" who help out when needed or directed to do so by their wives, and daughters-in-law who act more as "directors," taking more of the initiative to get things done.

Snowball Sampling

Snowball sampling A non-probability method used to obtain a sample on the basis of one available case, followed by associated referrals.

Another type of convenience sampling is **snowball sampling**. Snowball sampling, also called chain sampling and referral sampling, is a non-probability method used to obtain a sample on the basis of one or two available cases, followed by referrals that come from the original cases. For example, a researcher identifies one person who is suitable for the study, and that individual refers the researcher to another suitable individual, usually based on shared group membership. The next recruited participant then introduces the researcher to other potential participants, who then also provide contacts. The process continues until a large enough sample is secured, similar to how a snowball collects surrounding snow and grows larger as it is moved along.

This technique is often used by researchers studying deviant or "hidden" populations. For example, as part of a larger study on drug-using street-involved youth in Vancouver, Stoltz et al. (2007) identified associations between early forms of child abuse and later involvement in sex work. Clearly, a sampling frame for homeless youth who are drug addicts is non-existent. The starting point for such a sample is usually whoever can be obtained through a convenience strategy, in this case involving what the researchers refer to as "extensive street-based outreach." Willing participants are eventually located and recruited into the study, often with the help of social workers or members of agencies that already have an established rapport with members of the hidden population. For example, outreach organizations provide free condoms and clean needles to homeless individuals in an effort to reduce the transmission of diseases, and through their interactions, workers come to know some of the individuals living on the street. The snowball aspect of sampling comes into play through efforts to get initial participants to recruit their drug-using homeless peers and friends into the study (Stoltz et al., 2007).

Purposive Sampling

Purposive sampling
A non-probability method in which a researcher uses a combination of techniques to obtain all possible cases that possess the desired characteristics of the population of interest.

Purposive sampling involves a combination of sampling techniques used to obtain all possible cases that possess elements or characteristics of particular interest to the researchers. For example, McIntyre et al. (2003) were interested in finding out why disadvantaged women in Canada had lower than required dietary intakes but their children did not. The researchers used purposive sampling to obtain a sample of mothers living in Atlantic Canada who were lone parents of at least two children and whose income was at or below Statistics Canada's low-income cut-off. With this sampling technique, the goal is to obtain a certain type of sample using a combination of strategies. To locate as many cases as possible of the desired population, the researchers first developed community clusters based on geographical representation and community size (similar to cluster sampling). Then, within each cluster, the researchers tried to recruit participants via referrals from personnel working for parent resource centres, public health units, and community organizations who could identify low-income families headed by lone females (sampling by convenience). Finally, the researchers relied on snowball sampling to obtain additional participants once they had some initial recruits, until they achieved a final sample of 141 families. In case you are curious, results indicated that mothers' dietary intakes were consistently poorer than their children's. Further, the differences in dietary adequacy and intake between mothers and children widened as money for food dwindled, suggesting that mothers compromise their own nutritional needs to better provide for their children (McIntyre et al., 2003).

Quota Sampling

Quota sampling A non-probability method used to obtain a similar proportion of some characteristic of interest in a sample as exists in the population.

Finally, **quota sampling** is a method in which cases are selected on the basis of specified characteristics believed to represent the population of interest. Quota sampling is similar to stratified random sampling, except that the sampling frame is unknown. As a result, the population is not first divided into the groups or strata of interest, and the actual sampling method rests with the individual researcher. For example, a researcher might post an online survey, choose a sample size (e.g., 100), and then select for inclusion in the study the first 50 part-time faculty and the first 50 full-time faculty who complete the survey. While this method is an improvement over convenience sampling since an expected population characteristic is being replicated, the end result still might bear little resemblance to the population of interest due to the non-random selection process. For example, what if the 50 part-time faculty are all mainly from Biology, while the 50 full-time faculty are mainly from Psychology? In this case, any differences found between the full- and part-time faculty members might more accurately reflect differences in views based on the discipline of study rather than their employment status.

Research in Action

RCMP Use Quota Sampling in Affirmative Action Hiring

In an attempt to overcome disproportionate white male police officer prevalence in the workforce, the Royal Canadian Mounted Police (RCMP) endorses affirmative action practices in their recruitment of new officers. The underlying principle is that a modern and effective police force should be representative of the population it serves (RCMP, 2012). Using a method similar to quota sampling, certain characteristics of the population are over-emphasized in hiring, including women, visible minorities, and Aboriginal peoples. One of the current priorities of the RCMP is Aboriginal policing since it is considered to be beneficial to have a number of Aboriginal and Inuit police officers posted on reserves and in Aboriginal and Inuit communities that the RCMP serves throughout Canada. In an effort to recruit potential members, the RCMP sponsors an Aboriginal Police Studies Program and an Aboriginal Pre-Cadet Training Program. To further assist policing efforts, the

Royal Canadian Mounted Police.

RCMP also offers a paid special constable position for qualifying First Nations, Métis, and Inuit Canadians in Manitoba, Saskatchewan, Northwest Territories, and Nunavut to train alongside RCMP posted in Aboriginal communities. For more information, see "RM Recruitment" on the RCMP home page at www. rcmp-grc.gc.ca.

Test Yourself

- When might a researcher choose to use non-probability-based sampling?
- What is the main difference between convenience and snowball sampling?
- What does purposive sampling entail?
- Which non-probability sampling method is most similar to stratified random sampling?

Advantages and Disadvantages of Non-probability Sampling

LO5

Practicality

The main advantages of using non-probability-based sampling techniques include the fact that they are generally convenient, inexpensive, and are often efficient for getting access to a sample needed to carry out research on a topic of interest. Non-probability sampling is important because from a practical standpoint, it can enable a researcher to carry out a study in cases where probability sampling is not possible. A population can be hidden or difficult to reach, as might be the case if a researcher is interested in illegal drug users, homeless individuals, HIV-positive people, outlaw motorcycle gang members, street prostitutes, same-sex couples, families living in poverty, and/or individuals with an abusive family history. Non-probability sampling is especially effective for qualitative forms of exploratory research aimed at an in-depth understanding of small groups (Chambliss & Schutt, 2013).

Generalizability

One of the main challenges non-probability-based sampling poses is that the techniques produce samples that are not representative of the population. This means the findings generated by the sample, such as responses given on a survey, answers provided during an interview, or observations made on the group, pertain only to that particular group. In addition, samples obtained through non-probability methods are prone to errors such as bias because they are not random samples. It is impossible to even ascertain how the sample is biased because it is unclear which characteristics of the population ended up or did not end up in the sample (Bouma, Ling, & Wilkinson, 2012). Think about what would happen if you only included your closest friends in a study on matters of interest to you. It is likely that you and your friends share common interests such that any findings obtained from the sample will closely correspond to your personal views but may not represent the views of other individuals in your class, your city, or your home province.

While it is true that qualitative research poses issues for generalizability, it is just as important to note that qualitative research is not conducted for this explicit purpose. Instead, qualitative researchers examine a specific group or process at a particular time and location to learn more about it or to explain what is going on in that particular setting. That is not to say the findings cannot extend beyond that group. Scott and Garner (2013) suggest it may be more appropriate to use the term "relevance" in place of generalizability. They use an example of a researcher who studies episodes of violence carried out by members of a gang and concludes that there is more violence enacted toward fellow gang members (intra-gang victimization) than against rival gang members (inter-gang violence). If the goal is to understand a more generic process, "a study (or scientific story) of a specific set of gang members might not be generalizable to all gang members in all cities across the planet, but it might have relevance to the way many or most or a significant number of gangs operate" (Scott & Garner, 2013, p. 35). Similarly, Robert Yin (2003) argues that the logic that pertains to the kind of probability sampling discussed earlier on is suited to survey research but does not apply in the same way to case study designs. However, he also claims if it is possible to isolate what is happening in one particular case, then a researcher can later examine other cases to see if the findings extend. Yin (2003) calls this "replication logic," similar to experimental designs where additional case studies are used to test theories developed in the initial one.

Test Yourself

- What type of population is especially suited for non-probability sampling methods?
- What is the main disadvantage of using a non-probability sampling technique?

Theoretical Sampling

LO6

Theoretical sampling A concept-driven method for obtaining data used in qualitative research.

In concluding this chapter, I want to note that sampling is not just a technique that is decided upon prior to beginning a study. In certain forms of qualitative research, sampling can be an ongoing process that occurs largely at the data collection and analysis stage. In fact, sampling can produce findings that prompt additional and even different sampling techniques. This special type of sampling, called **theoretical sampling**, is a concept-driven method for obtaining data used in qualitative research (Corbin & Strauss, 2008). Theoretical sampling occurs as data gathering processes uncover important concepts, which then dictate how subsequent data gathering will take place to develop the emerging theory (Corbin & Strauss, 2008). For example, while conducting interviews with Vietnam war veterans, Corbin noted that one participant (a nurse) identified the war experience as "not too bad," leading the researcher to ask "How come?" The vet indicated he was not a "combatant" (p. 147). The concept "combatant" then prompted the researchers to immediately seek out a combatant who might offer a different perspective on what the war experience was like. The second interviewee brought up the centrality of "survival" and a "lack of healing"—issues that were part of the combatant experience and were still evident more than thirty years after the original ordeal. These findings then prompted the researcher to read memoirs written by combatants for more information on the "war experience" that was shared by combatants, and the process continued to unfold from there (Corbin & Strauss, 2008, p. 147). In theoretical sampling, the population and its central features are not known in advance. Instead, the sampling criteria are defined or created with each new step involving data collection and analysis. The process ends once an in-depth exploration and understanding of the main concepts is achieved. This is called "theoretical saturation" (Corbin & Strauss, 2008; Flick, 2009). Table 5.2 summarizes the sampling methods.

TABLE 5.2 **Comparing Sampling Methods**

Probability	Non-probability	Theoretical
• Sampling frame is generally known	• Sampling frame is unknown	• Sampling frame is unknown
• Certain characteristics of the population are known	• Certain characteristics of the population may be anticipated	• Population characteristics are unknown
• Probability of selection is known	• Probability of selection is unknown	• Probability of selection is unknown
• Sample size is known and is calculated for representativeness	• Sample size is defined on the basis of convenience	• Sample size is not defined in advance
• Sampling occurs prior to data collection and analysis	• Sampling occurs prior to data collection and analysis	• Sampling occurs during data collection and following data analysis
• Sampling ends when the sample size is met	• Sampling ends when a sufficient sample size is located	• Sampling ends when theoretical saturation is achieved
• Sample may be representative of the population	• Sample is not representative of the population	• Sample is not representative of the population

Test Yourself

• What is theoretical sampling?

Chapter Summary

LO1 **Define sampling and differentiate between a population and a sample.**

Sampling is a technique used to acquire the unit of analysis from a population of interest. The sample is a subset of the population, which contains the complete set of individuals, objects, or scores of interest to a researcher.

LO2 **Explain why a researcher might choose a probability-based sampling method and distinguish between simple random, systematic, stratified, and cluster sampling techniques.**

A researcher will likely employ a probability-based sampling method when he or she desires a representative sample and when a sampling frame can be made available. *Simple random sampling* is used to obtain a sample on the basis of chance alone. A random sample is usually obtained using a random numbers table after a sampling frame is identified. *Systematic* random sampling is also based on probability, except the sample is selected on the basis of a fixed interval. First the sampling frame is identified and a sampling interval is determined. After randomly selecting the first case, every *n*th case is chosen after that until the desired sample size is reached. *Stratified* sampling relies upon known population characteristics of interest. A researcher divides the population into groups based on particular features such as age, employment status, or location and then randomly samples for a certain number of cases from each group. For example, a

researcher might divide a population of workers into full-time, part-time, a
dent employment categories before randomly sampling from each group. F
cluster sampling involves selected groups rather than individual cases, often to
accommodate a population that is spread over a vast geographic area from which
it is not feasible to randomly sample individual cases. For example, to obtain
a sample of individuals living in remote communities, a researcher might first
create a sampling frame of remote community clusters based on geographic area,
and then randomly select clusters that will be included in the sample.

LO3   Identify the main advantages and disadvantages of probability-based sampling techniques.

The advantage of probability-based techniques is that they produce representative
samples that closely resemble populations of interest. This means generalizations
or inferences can be more readily made from samples to populations of interest. However, since samples are not exact replicas of populations, generalizations
need to be made with caution as there are still differences that result from measurement error. Larger samples help to increase accuracy and confidence that the
sample will contain the relevant population parameters.

LO4   Explain why a researcher might choose a non-probability sampling method and distinguish between convenience, snowball, purposive, and quota sampling techniques.

In some cases populations are hard to locate or are hidden, making it impossible
to identify the needed sampling frame used in probability-based techniques. In
such cases, researchers often elect to use non-probability techniques. *Convenience* sampling is a non-probability method in which individuals (or cases) are
selected on the basis of availability alone. For example, a researcher might interview the first few individuals who are present at a scene of interest. *Snowball*
sampling is a non-probability method that begins with a few cases selected by
convenience, followed by referrals resulting from the original cases. *Purposive*
sampling involves a combination of techniques used to obtain all possible cases
that possess particular characteristics of interest to researcher. For example, a
researcher interested in low-income families headed by a lone female will use
various strategies to try and locate families that fit the criteria. Finally, *quota*
sampling is a method in which certain individuals are selected to try and replicate
particular characteristics that are known to exist in the population of interest. For
example, a researcher might sample for a particular ratio of men to women or a
particular proportion of individuals of a certain ethnicity.

LO5   Identify the main advantages and disadvantages of non-probability-based techniques.

Overall, non-probability sampling methods are practical in many cases as they are
less costly and less time-consuming than probability-based techniques. It is also
not always possible or even desirable to use probability sampling. In some cases,
a sampling frame is unknown and therefore a non-probability method must be
employed to study a hidden or hard to reach population. The main disadvantage

is that the sample is not representative of the population. This means findings are generally limited to the sample itself.

LO6 **Explain how theoretical sampling differs from probability- and non-probability-based sampling techniques.**

Theoretical sampling is a concept-driven method for obtaining data in qualitative research. Data collection and analysis sometimes uncovers important concepts that warrant further exploration in a process that leads to eventual theory development. To learn more about the concepts, additional research is necessary, which entails additional sampling methods to acquire new participants or cases. Since the sampling emerges out of data analysis, the population is not identified ahead of time, as is the case with probability-based techniques. There is also no prior intent to obtain a sample of a certain size or with particular features.

Research Reflection

1. Think of a topic of interest that would be suitable to examine if students at your university constituted the population under investigation. Write three questions that would help you learn more about your topic of interest. Interview a couple of students in class to obtain information on your topic. Did the sample of students you talked to make up a suitable sample? Why or why not? Given your specific topic and interests, which sampling method would be ideal? Defend your answer.

2. Identify a practice in everyday life that involves simple random sampling. Explain your answer.

3. Suppose your post-secondary institution has 2400 academic faculty. The president decides to systematically sample 200 faculty members for suggestions on how to improve office space and working conditions.

   a. What would be the sampling interval?

   b. If the number 6 was randomly drawn for a starting point, what would be the next five numbers for inclusion in the sample?

Learning Through Practice

Objective: to review sampling concepts in an applied context.
Directions:

1. Locate Statistics Canada's 2010–2011 Survey of Young Canadians released on April 16, 2012. To find the survey, go to Statistics Canada's home page at statcan.gc.ca and type in the search term "survey of young Canadians." You will see a listing of links related to the survey. Select the link that says "Survey of Young Canadians (SYC)" dated 2010-01-01.

2. Read the description of the target population, instrument design, sampling, and estimation and then answer the following questions:

   a. Who is the target population?

   b. Was a probability- or non-probability-based sampling method used?

    c. Which specific sampling technique was used?

    d. What was the sample size?

3. Why do you suppose this sampling technique was used?

4. What are some of the potential challenges Statistics Canada researchers likely encountered using this technique?

Research Resources

1. The process for generating a simple random sample using a "stand-alone" random numbers table is much more complex than using a web-based statistics calculator, and it can be quite tedious in the case of large samples. For step-by-step instructions and illustrations, I recommend you read pages 188–193 on simple random sampling in Wolfer, L. (2007). *Real research: Conducting and evaluating research in the social sciences.* Toronto, ON: Pearson Education.

2. To learn more about probability-based sampling techniques and sampling issues that go beyond the scope of this chapter (e.g., ratio estimation), I recommend Levy, P. S., & Lemeshow, S. (2008). *Sampling of populations: Methods and applications* (4th ed.). Hoboken, NJ: John Wiley & Sons.

3. For a detailed discussion on theoretical sampling, see Chapter 7 in Corbin, J., & Strauss, A. (2008). *Basics of qualitative research* (3rd ed.). Thousand Oaks, CA: Sage Publications.

 For more information on the resources available from McGraw-Hill Ryerson, go to www.mcgrawhill.ca/he/solutions.

References

Annenberg Learner. (2013). Random sampling. In *data analysis, statistics, & probability.* Session 1, Part D: Bias in Sampling. Annenberg Foundation. Retrieved from www.learner.org/courses/learningmath/data/swfs/1d_circles.swf

Babbie, E., & Benaquisto, L. (2014). *Fundamentals of social research* (3rd Can. ed.). Belmont, CA: Wadsworth.

Bouma, G. D., Ling, R., & Wilkinson, L. (2012). *The research process* (2nd ed.). Don Mills, ON: Oxford University Press.

Chambliss, D. F., & Schutt, R. K. (2013). *Making sense of the social world* (4th ed.). Thousand Oaks, CA: Sage Publications.

Corbin, J., & Strauss, A. (2008). *Basics of qualitative research* (3rd ed.). Thousand Oaks, CA: Sage Publications.

Cozby, P. C. (2009). *Methods in behavioral research* (10th ed.). New York, NY: McGraw-Hill.

Flick, U. (2009). *An introduction to qualitative research* (4th ed.). Thousand Oaks, CA: Sage Publications.

Globerman, J. (1996). Motivations to care: Daughters and sons-in-law caring for relatives with Alzheimer's disease. *Family Relations, 45,* 37–45.

Howell, A. J., & Symbaluk, D. G. (2001). Published student ratings: Reconciling the views of students and faculty. *Journal of Educational Psychology, 93,* 790–796.

Levy, P. S., & Lemeshow, S. (2008). *Sampling of populations: Methods and applications* (4th ed.). Hoboken, NJ: John Wiley & Sons.

McIntyre, L. Glanville, N. T., Raine, K. D., Dayle, J. B., Anderson, B., & Battaglia, N. (2003). Do low-income lone mothers compromise their nutrition to feed their children? *Canadian Medical Association Journal, 168*(6), 686–691.

Mitchell, Barry J. (2012). *Alberta fishing guide (Vol. 42).* Red Deer, AB: Barry Mitchell Publications.

Pagano, R. R. (2013). *Understanding statistics in the behavioral sciences* (10th ed.). Belmont, CA: Wadsworth.

Piran, N., & Gadalla, T. (2007). Eating disorders and substance abuse in Canadian women: A national study. *Addiction, 102,* 105–113. doi:10.1111/j.1360-0443.2006.01633.x

Royal Canadian Mounted Police. (2012, Nov. 9). Gender-based assessment. In *Resources.* Ottawa, ON: Author. Retrieved from www.rcmp-grc.gc.ca/aud-ver/reports-rapports/gba-eces/gba-eces-eng.htm

Scott, G., & Garner, R. (2013). *Doing qualitative research: Designs, methods, and techniques.* Upper Saddle River, NJ: Pearson Education.

Statistics Canada. (2013a). Non-probability sampling. In *Sampling methods.* Ottawa, ON: Author. Retrieved from www.statcan.gc.ca/edu/power-pouvoir/ch13/nonprob/5214898-eng.htm

Statistics Canada. (2013b). Canadian Community Health Survey—Mental Health. In *Definitions, data sources, and methods.* Ottawa, ON: Author. Retrieved from www23.statcan.gc.ca/imdb/p2SV.pl?Function=getSurvey&SDDS=5015&lang=en&db=imdb&adm=8&dis=2

StatTrek. (2012). *Random number generator.* StatTrek.com. Retrieved from http://stattrek.com/statistics/random-number-generator.aspx

Stoltz, J. M., Shannon, K., Kerr, T., Zhang, R., Montaner, J. S., & Wood, E. (2007). Associations between childhood maltreatment and sex work in a cohort of drug-using youth. *Social Science and Medicine, 65,* 1214–1221.

University of Toronto. (2012). *Quick facts.* Toronto, ON: Author. Retrieved from www.utoronto.ca/about-uoft/quickfacts.htm

Wolfer, L. (2007). *Real research: Conducting and evaluating research in the social sciences.* Toronto, ON: Pearson Education.

Yin, R. K. (2003). *Case study research: Design and methods* (3rd ed.). Thousand Oaks, CA: Sage Publications.

Endnotes

[1] Statistics Canada (2012). *The Census of Canada.* Ottawa, ON: Author. Retrieved from www19.statcan.gc.ca/11/11_000-eng.htm

[2] If you use a random numbers table from the back of a statistics book (or one that includes more numbers than what you need to include in your sample), you will first need to randomly select a starting spot. For example, you can close your eyes and stick your finger on the page and whatever number is underneath your finger can be the starting number. Note that most lists contain five-digit numbers. If you want a sample of size 100, and your sampling frame is 55 352 students, then you will be selecting for any numbers that range from 1 through 55 352. Begin with the number under your finger (e.g., 49 421). Use this as your starting number and then read across the table to the next set of numbers (e.g., 18 442) and take that number as your second one included in the sample. Keep going across, including all numbers that are 55 352 or less. Skip numbers that exceed 55 352. Continue in this fashion until you reach the end of a row and then start over one row down, beginning with the first column on the left, until you have 100 numbers in your sample.

Experiments

6

Learning Objectives

After reading this chapter, students should be able to do the following:

LO1 Describe the rationale underlying an experimental method.

LO2 Identify the criteria needed to establish causality and explain which features of an experiment support the testing of cause-effect relationships.

LO3 Differentiate between and define the different types of research designs, including experimental, between- and within-subjects, factorial, and quasi-experimental.

LO4 Define internal and external validity.

LO5 Identify and describe potential threats to internal validity.

LO6 Identify and describe potential threats to external validity.

"Doubt the conventional wisdom unless you can verify it with reason and experiment." (Steve Albini)[1]

Introduction

LO1

Experiment A research method in which a researcher manipulates an independent variable to examine its effects on a dependent variable.

Independent variable The variable that is manipulated in an experiment and is presumed to be the cause of some outcome.

Dependent variable The variable that is measured in an experiment and is the outcome.

In Chapter 4, you learned that a research design is a template for a study detailing who, what, where, when, why, and how an investigation will take place. In addition to distinguishing between designs on the basis of "when" a study takes place, such as a cross-sectional study at one point in time versus a longitudinal design conducted at multiple points in time, researchers in the social sciences sometimes classify designs as "experimental" or "non-experimental" on the basis of their ability to determine causality. Also recall from Chapter 1 how explanatory research is conducted with the aim of answering the question of "why" something occurs the way it does or to clarify why there is variation between groups on some dimension of interest. Experimental methods provide a means for testing causal relationships through the manipulation and measurement of variables. In an **experiment**, at least one **independent variable** is manipulated by a researcher to measure its effects (if any) on a **dependent variable**. For example, a researcher interested in the effects of sleep deprivation on scholastic performance might manipulate the amount of sleep obtained by participants. Half of the participants in the experiment might be allowed only three hours of sleep. In other words, half of the participants experience the treatment (independent variable), which in this example is sleep deprivation. The other half might be allowed to experience a normal night's sleep of about eight to nine hours with no sleep deprivation. The independent variable is the presumed cause of some outcome. In this example, the researcher might hypothesize that sleep deprivation will lower academic performance on a memory-based word task. In this case, participants who experience sleep deprivation should remember fewer words than participants with normal amounts of sleep, since sleep deprivation is believed to cause impaired performance. The measured performance on the memory task is the dependent variable, or the outcome.

Research on the Net

Web Experiment List

If you would like to participate in an experiment that is currently being conducted over the Internet, visit the home page for the Web Experiment List at wexlist.net. This site provides a comprehensive list of current and past web-based experiments in psychology. Try using the search tab for "old experiments" to see the titles and descriptions of a range of studies that have already been conducted in the areas of cognitive psychology, Internet science, social psychology, perception, and methodology, among other categories.

Causality, Control, and Random Assignment

LO2

The study of cause-effect relationships rests on the assumption that one variable of interest is the cause of another; that is, changes in one variable produce changes in another. To establish a causal relationship, three criteria must exist. First, the variables must be related in a logical way. For example, education and income are associated as people with higher levels of education also tend to earn more. This is sometimes referred to as the "covariance" rule (Beins, 2009). Second, the cause must precede the effect in time establishing "temporal order." A person acquires an education and then enters the workforce to earn an income. Finally, the presumed cause should be the most plausible one and rival explanations should be ruled out. Although education contributes to income, there are a number of factors that help to explain one's income, including age, years of experience, family socioeconomic status (i.e., how well off a person's family of origin is), and type of employment. These factors cannot be completely ruled out from this example. While we have established an association, we have yet to prove causation. This can only be done by conducting an experiment.

Experimental methods common to the natural sciences are also regularly employed by psychologists and are used to a lesser extent by sociologists such as social psychologists and criminologists. Although experiments often conjure up images of scientists wearing white lab coats working with beakers in research laboratories, they can be conducted anywhere a researcher has control over the environment. Just as an instructor can close a classroom door and lock it, thereby preventing people from entering the room during a lecture, a researcher can follow standardized procedures, use scripts, and take precautions to turn a classroom, office, and/or some other area on campus into a carefully controlled laboratory setting.

Experiments constitute the only method that can demonstrate causation due to the strict environmental control and the random assignment of cases to the treatment. **Random assignment** is a method for assigning cases to the experimental group (the one that receives the independent variable) on the basis of chance alone. This is important because going back to the original example on sleep deprivation, some individuals require more or less sleep than others, some have better working memories than others, and some have higher overall scholastic aptitude than others—all of which can influence performance on the word task, as can mood, time of the day, and whether the person has recently eaten. If participants are randomly assigned to a sleep deprivation group or a normal sleep group, then any existing individual differences will also be randomly assigned across the groups, making them equivalent at the start of the study. The group exposed to the independent variable is called the **experimental group** and the group that does not experience the independent variable is called a **control group**. The control group provides a measure of what would "normally" happen in the absence of the experimental manipulation. In the example used earlier, the control group tells us how many words on average people can recall during a word task. We can then compare the results for the sleep-deprived experimental group to the control group to see if the experimental group fares worse, as hypothesized.

Therefore, with random assignment and strict control over the environment, where both groups receive identical instructions and undergo the exact same experience with the exception of the independent variable, we can be reasonably sure that any differences found between the two groups on some measure result solely from the manipulation. Using the example above, if the sleep-deprived group performs worse on the word task, we can attribute the difference to the independent variable.

Students routinely confuse random sampling (discussed in Chapter 5) with random assignment. Try to remember that random sampling has to do with how a sample is selected from a population of interest. This process permits a researcher to generalize from the sample to the population. For example, one of the probability-based sampling methods is simple random sampling, where a sample of a particular size is obtained using a random numbers table. This means chance alone determines who is selected to take part in a study. Random assignment, on the other hand, has to do with how participants are put into groups in experimental research. In this case, chance alone determines who from the collection of sample subjects ends up receiving the manipulation (see Figure 6.1). Random assignment helps ensure the experimental and control group are identical before the experimental manipulation.

Since the hallmark of an experiment is the manipulation of an independent variable presumed to be the cause of a change in the dependent variable, researchers often incorporate a "manipulation check" into their study procedures

Random assignment A method for assigning cases in which chance alone determines receipt of the experimental manipulation.

Experimental group The group that experiences the independent variable in an experiment.

Control group The group that does not experience the independent variable in an experiment.

FIGURE 6.1 **Random Sampling and Random Assignment**

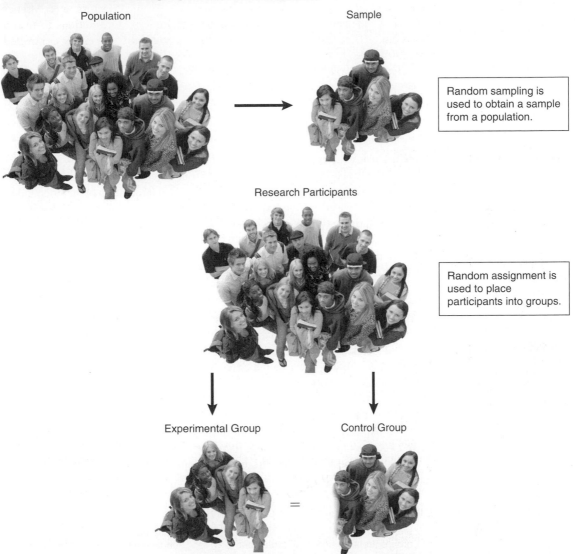

Population

Sample

Random sampling is used to obtain a sample from a population.

Research Participants

Random assignment is used to place participants into groups.

Experimental Group

Control Group

=

to be certain the experimental group experienced the independent variable as intended. For example, participants might be asked to report on how much sleep they received. Those in the experimental group should say they received about three hours of sleep, while those in the control condition should indicate about 8.5 hours on average. Similarly, an experimenter studying the effects of watching a video on subsequent attitudes might ask participants a question or two about the video to gauge whether they actually watched it. This is an important check to see that the procedures of the experiment unfolded as intended.

Test Yourself

- Which variable is manipulated in an experiment?
- What three criteria must exist to establish a causal relationship?
- How can random assignment be distinguished from random sampling?

Types of Experimental Designs

LO3

Basic experimental design An experimental design that includes random assignment, an experimental and control group, the manipulation of an independent variable, and a post-test measurement of the dependent variable.

Classic experimental design An experimental design that includes random assignment, an experimental and control group, a pre-test measure of a dependent variable, the manipulation of an independent variable, and a post-test measure of the same dependent variable.

There are many different types of experimental designs. What makes any experiment a "true" experiment is the presence of four core features: 1) random assignment, 2) an experimental and control group, 3) the manipulation of an independent variable experienced by the experimental group, and 4) the measurement of a dependent variable (i.e., the outcome) to see what (if any) effect the independent variable had. This is usually referred to as a "post-test." An experimental design that includes these four features and only these four features is referred to as a **basic experimental design** (see Figure 6.2).

Classic Experimental Design

A **classic experimental design** includes the four basic features from the basic design (random assignment, an experimental and control group, the manipulation of an independent variable, and a post-test measurement of the dependent variable), along with a pre-test of the dependent measure. This design is also commonly called a pre-test–post-test design. Even when random assignment is used to place participants into groups, there may be differences between the groups starting out. For example, perhaps some of participants who end up in the experimental group have exceptional memories or are really good at word tasks. If a basic experimental design is used, then the dependent variable is measured at only one time following exposure to the independent variable, during the post-test. Due to the exceptional qualities of the participants in the experimental group,

FIGURE 6.2   Steps in a Basic Experimental Design

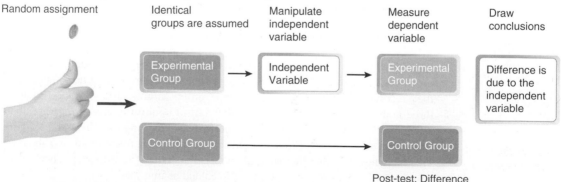

FIGURE 6.3   **Steps in a Classic Experimental Design**

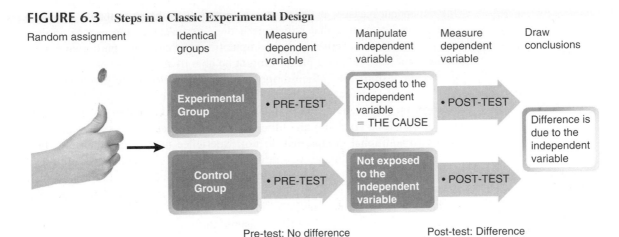

Pre-test: No difference   Post-test: Difference

the researcher might find no differences in word recall between the experimental and control group. In this case it would appear that the independent variable, sleep deprivation, had no impairing effect on performance. But what if the experimental group would have done even better had they not been sleep-deprived? With only one measure of the dependent variable, an experimenter will never know the answer. However, if performance is measured before and after exposure to the independent variable, we can see how much performance is impaired by sleep deprivation. In a classic experimental design, participants are randomly assigned to an experimental and control group and then given a pre-test where the dependent variable is measured prior to exposure to the manipulation (i.e., the independent variable). The participants in the experimental group then receive the manipulation (i.e., are sleep-deprived), and both groups are reassessed (i.e., given a post-test) on the dependent variable, as outlined in Figure 6.3.

Experimental designs are sometimes shown using standard notation symbols, where random assignment is represented by an "R," measurement of the dependent variable is represented by "O" for "observation," and exposure to the independent variable is represented as "X" for "treatment" (i.e., the experimental manipulation). Figure 6.4 shows a classic experimental design in notation.

Solomon Four-Group Design

With each added feature of an experimental design, additional questions can be answered, and more comparisons can be made. For example, an experimenter might be concerned that a pre-test will give the participants a sense of what

FIGURE 6.4
Notation for a Classic Experimental Design

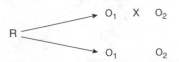

the dependent measure is and in doing so may help the participants acquire a skill or understanding that will benefit their performance the next time they are measured, irrespective of the manipulation. For example, participants who complete a word task as a pre-test might be able to develop memory strategies during the task that help them improve the next time they are given the same task during the post-test. To check this, an experimenter can employ a **Solomon four-group design**, named after its originator, Richard L. Solomon. A Solomon four-group design includes all of the features of the classic experimental design plus two additional groups that do not experience the pre-test measure. Following random assignment to conditions, Group 1 is measured at the pre-test, is exposed to the independent variable, and is then reassessed at the post-test; Group 2 is measured at the pre-test, is not exposed to the independent variable, and is assessed at the post-test; Group 3 does not get a pre-test, is exposed to the independent variable, and is then measured at the post-test; and Group 4 does not get a pre-test, is not exposed to the independent variable, but is measured at the post-test. The Solomon four-group design is a basic true experimental design plus a classic experimental design, as shown in Figure 6.5, where the rows represent the groups.

Using the earlier example for this design, an experimenter would randomly assign participants into one of four groups. The experimenter then pre-tests how well two of the groups do on a word recall task (the dependent variable). One of the groups that performed the pre-test and one of the groups that did not perform the pre-test are then exposed to the experimental manipulation (i.e., are sleep-deprived), and then all four groups are assessed using the word task (post-test). Several comparisons are possible using this design. Recall that the experimental groups are the ones exposed to the independent variable (refer to the Xs shown in Figure 6.5). If the independent variable has an effect as hypothesized, both experimental groups (shown in rows 1 and 3 in Figure 6.5) should perform worse than both control groups (rows 2 and 4) on the post-test since sleep deprivation is expected to impair performance. Note that one experimental group had a pre-test and one did not (see row 1 versus 3). If the experimental groups perform differently on the word task, the difference in outcome is likely the result of the pre-test, which may have helped the participants gain an edge in performance due to familiarity with the task.

Solomon four-group design An experimental design that includes random assignments to one of four groups: an experimental group with a pre-test, the manipulation of an independent variable, and a post-test measure of the dependent variable; a control group with a pre-test, no manipulation, and a post-test measure; an experimental group with no pre-test, a manipulation, and a post-test measure; or a control group consisting of a post-test measure only.

FIGURE 6.5
Notation for a Solomon Four-Group Design

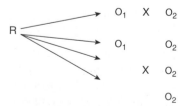

"Well, I guess we're the control group."

© Loren Fishman. www.Cartoonstock.com

Between-Subjects and Within-Subjects Designs

Between-subjects design A type of design in which the experimental group is exposed to only one level of the independent variable.

In all of the designs discussed thus far, the experimental group is exposed to an independent variable and the control group is not. The experimental group can experience an independent variable in two ways: it can be assigned either to one or to all of the levels of the independent variable. In a **between-subjects design**, participants in the experimental group are exposed to only one level of the independent variable. For example, in an experiment on the effects of music on personality, undergraduates at a Canadian university were randomly assigned to one of three possible conditions where they 1) listened to a classical song while reading the English translation of the lyrics; 2) listened to a classical song and followed along with the text provided in German; or 3) listened to an English translation of the lyrics (Djikic, 2011). This is called a between-subjects design because there are differences between participants (also known as subjects) in how they experience the independent variable. This type of design is also called an "independent groups design" since each fraction of the experimental group independently receives one treatment. One-third of the participants heard the song while reading the English translation (a music and lyrics condition), one-third listened to the song while looking at German lyrics (described as a music-only condition since no one in the study understood German), and one-third listened to the English translation (lyrics only without the music). In case you are curious, Djikic (2011) found that listening to classical music changed the participants' personalities for the better, leading to a self-reported enhanced variability in overall personality, while exposure to lyrics but no actual music produced a diminished variability in personality.

Within-subjects design A type of design in which the experimental group is exposed to all possible levels of the independent variable.

In a **within-subjects design**, the participants in the experimental group are exposed to all of the levels of the independent variable. For example, in an experiment on participants' willingness to endure a painful exercise for money, Cabanac

(1986) paid ten participants varying amounts of money to endure an isometric sitting exercise. Isometric sitting is like sitting without a chair, with one's legs at a ninety-degree angle, causing lactic acid to build up in the thigh muscles to produce a painful sensation. Using a within-subjects design, all participants were exposed to the six different levels of the independent variable where they were paid 0.2, 0.5, 1.25, 3.125, or 7.8125 French francs (Ff) per 20 seconds of exercise or a lump-sum amount presented in a random order. For example, participant number one attended his first session and might receive 0.2 Ff for every 20 seconds of exercise during that particular session, 1.25 on the next session, 7.8125 at his third session, 3.125 for the fourth session, a lump sum on the fifth session, and 0.5 for his last session. All participants experienced the same conditions; however, the order of presentation differed (e.g., participant number two might receive the lump sum during his first session and the highest pay amount during his second, etc.). In this case, the difference in how the independent variable occurs is within the participants themselves, who each receive the treatments in random order. Cabanac (1986) found that money motivated participants' willingness to endure pain up to a certain point: participants lasted longer for increasing amounts of money, but were eventually unable to continue the exercise due to physical limitations beyond their desire to continue to withstand the pain for money.

A within-subjects design is also called a repeated measures design since participants are exposed to the independent variable repeatedly at multiple points in time. In a within-subjects/repeated measures design, participants may receive exposure to the same condition repeatedly as opposed to encountering different levels of the independent variable at different times. For example, McConville and Virk's (2012) used a repeated measures design to examine the effectiveness of game playing training using the Sony PlayStation 2® and EyeToy® combination with the Harmonix AntiGrav™ game for improving postural balance. Participants were randomly assigned to either the control (no training) or the experimental group (attended nine scheduled training sessions over a period of three weeks). During each 30-minute training session, the participants played the game four times using the controls and incorporating necessary head, body, and arm movements. Participants who underwent game training showed significant improvement on two different facets of balance (McConville & Virk, 2012).

Order effects

Differences in the dependent variable that result from the order in which the independent variable is presented.

One potential drawback of this type of design is its tendency to create order effects. **Order effects** are differences in the dependent variable that result from the order in which the independent variable is presented (as opposed to the manipulation itself). For example, imagine you are interested in learning whether people state a preference for a particular brand of cola (e.g., Pepsi versus Coke) in a blind taste test. If, as the researcher, you always gave participants Coke first, it could be that the initial brand tasted lingered in a participant's mouth, confounding or interfering with the taste of the next cola; that is, effects from Trial 1 have carried over into Trial 2. To control for this, the researcher could increase the time between Trial 1 and 2 (to ensure the taste of the first cola has dissipated) or the experimenter could offer water in between trials to eliminate the traces left from Trial 1. Alternatively, the researcher could employ a technique called "counterbalancing," where all of the possible ways to order the independent variable are included in the design. For example, on half of the trials Coke would be presented first and on half of the trials Pepsi would be presented first.

Factorial Design

The designs discussed thus far only include the manipulation of one independent variable. In certain situations, a researcher may wish to examine more than one independent variable in the same study. For example, Symbaluk, Heth, Cameron, and Pierce's (1997) experiment was designed to investigate whether money *and* social modelling would motivate participants to withstand the pain of exercise. In their study, participants were paid zero (a control condition), $1.00 or $2.00 for every 20 seconds they endured a painful isometric sitting exercise. In addition, a second independent variable called social modelling was included to see whether prior observation of similar others who displayed signs of being either pain-tolerant (i.e., no moaning, rating pain as increasing slowly over time and lasting a long time) or pain-intolerant (i.e., moaning, rapid increase in pain ratings and lasting only a short time) would affect participants' own performance on the same exercise. Again, there was also a control condition in which participants received no feedback on how the models were experiencing pain or how long they lasted. A **factorial design** is one that includes two or more independent variables.

Factorial design An experimental design that includes two or more independent variables.

Not only can researchers examine the separate potential effects of two different independent variables, but they can look at how independent variables combine to produce an outcome. The effect of one independent variable on a dependent variable is called a main effect. The combined effect of two (or more) independent variables is called an interaction effect. In Symbaluk et al.'s (1997) study, the researchers hypothesized that money would have a main effect on participants' willingness to tolerate pain, anticipating that they would last longer at the isometric sitting exercise if they were paid money. They also hypothesized a main effect of social modelling, where exposure to a model would have an impact on subsequent performance. Since the two independent variables (money and social modelling) had more than one level (zero, $1.00 or $2.00 and pain unknown, pain-intolerant, or pain-tolerant), the researchers further hypothesized that higher amounts of money, such as $2.00 per 20 seconds of exercise, would cause participants to endure even longer than those paid less, such as $1.00 for every 20 seconds of exercise. For social modelling, the researchers hypothesized that exposure to tolerant models would improve performance while exposure to intolerant models would impair it. Finally, the researchers expected combined effects (interactions) such that participants who were in the highest pay conditions and exposed to tolerant social models should last the longest, while those who were not paid and exposed to intolerant social models should fair the worst. In reality, things did not go as anticipated, and this is the interesting part of research! The findings showed no effect of money—it was largely the intolerant condition that produced the outcome. That is, exposure to similar others who were intolerant of the pain of exercise had a negative effect on the participants' own ability to endure pain (Symbaluk et al., 1997).

Factorial designs are written and referred to in a mathematical notation that depicts the number of levels of each independent variable. Specifically, in the example used above, there were three levels of each independent variable, creating a 3 × 3 design. The first 3 indicates that one of the independent variables had three levels or possibilities (e.g., money was manipulated as zero, 1.00, and 2.00). The second 3 indicates that another independent variable was included that also contained three levels (e.g., social modelling as no model information, a tolerant model, and an intolerant model). When the two numbers are multiplied (3 × 3 = 9) you get the total number of possible combinations or conditions that were included in the study. In this example, 90 participants were randomly assigned to one of nine conditions (see Table 6.1). If the researchers had also hypothesized that being alone or being with other participants might influence how well a participant is able to endure pain, then the design would be a 2 × 3 × 3 factorial. In this case, the 2 would refer to a third variable such as accompaniment (alone versus accompanied by others), resulting in 18 possible combinations.

Quasi-experimental Designs

Although you might be inclined to infer that a more complicated design is always a better one, there are many instances in which even a basic experimental design cannot be used.

For instance, a counsellor who works with clients in a Manitoba-based treatment program for adolescents such as the Edgewood Program (for male sexual offenders) or the Mutchmor Program (for adolescent males with aggressive tendencies) might be interested in examining the effects of program completion on reoffending. It would be unethical and potentially unsafe to randomly offer treatment to certain offenders and not others to see if the treated group is less likely to reoffend than the untreated group at some point in the future. However, some offenders voluntarily enter treatment programs while others do not. And, similarly, some offenders who enter treatment programs complete treatment while

TABLE 6.1   A 3 × 3 **Factorial Design**

Condition 1 No money, no model N = 10	**Condition 2** No money, intolerant model N = 10	**Condition 3** No money, tolerant model N = 10
Condition 4 $1.00, no model N = 10	**Condition 5** $1.00, intolerant model N = 10	**Condition 6** $1.00, tolerant model N = 10
Condition 7 $2.00, no model N = 10	**Condition 8** $2.00, intolerant model N = 10	**Condition 9** $2.00, tolerant model N = 10

others fail to complete the full course of the treatment (e.g., they fail to comply with the rules and are asked to leave the program or they decide to quit the program). While random assignment to the independent variable (treatment) is not possible, naturally occurring groups sometimes become available for studying, such as treatment completers and non-completers. These groups might be compared to see if those who complete treatment have lower reoffending rates (the dependent variable) than those who fail to complete the treatment program.

Experimental designs lacking in one or more of the main features of a true experiment are commonly referred to as **quasi-experimental designs** (also called pre-experimental designs). Quasi-experimental designs are especially prevalent in research projects designed to examine the effectiveness of treatment programs in areas such as clinical psychology, sociology, and social work. One of the most common types of quasi-experimental designs is a **static group comparison** where there are two groups and a post-test measure, but random assignment was not an option for the placement of participants into the two groups. Instead, participants typically end up in the two groups as a function of self-selection (see Figure 6.6). For example, a static group comparison might be used to examine treatment completers versus non-completers in some kind of rehabilitative program for sexual offenders. Allowing a sufficient period of time for reoffending to occur following treatment (e.g., a period of up to five years), the research question of interest, then, could be: Is reoffending (called recidivism) lower in treatment completers compared to non-completers? A static group comparison is also useful for examining the differences between groups in situations where one group receives a novel treatment or when one group receives a placebo (or simulated treatment) while the other does not (Thayer, 2012). In evaluating the merit of a static group comparison, it is important to note that this design is often used in exploratory research that is more of a starting place for determining if a program or intervention appears to be effective. While static group comparisons are frequently employed to compare groups to see if a treatment helps, without random assignment, causal inferences are difficult to establish. For example, there could be important differences between offenders who complete treatment and those who do not which account for the lower recidivism, irrespective of what went on in a given treatment program.

Another common quasi-experimental design is a **one-shot case study** where a group receives exposure to an independent variable and then is measured on a dependent variable. This design lacks a control group. One-shot case studies are commonly employed in social work and educational research. In his book on quasi-experimental designs, Bruce Thayer (2012) notes that one-shot case studies play an especially important role in answering questions concerning the effectiveness of various interventions and programs, such as "What is the status of clients after they have received a given course of treatment?" and "Do clients improve after receiving a given course of treatment?"

Quasi-experimental design An experimental design that lacks one or more of the basic features of a true experiment, including random assignment or a control group.

Static group comparison A quasi-experimental design lacking random assignment in which two groups are compared following a treatment.

One-shot case study A quasi-experimental design lacking a control group in which one group is examined following a treatment.

FIGURE 6.6
Notation for a Static Group Comparison

Static group comparison

$$X \quad O_1$$
$$O_2$$

Research in Action

Impression Formation

In a classic study on impression formation, Solomon Asch (1946) read a list of peripheral character traits used to describe someone's general disposition—such as intelligent, skillful, practical, etc.—to a group of participants and then had participants describe the sort of person to whom the traits might apply. All of the participants heard the same list read with the various traits with the exception of one word. Half of the participants heard the word "warm" while the other half heard the word "cold" included among the descriptors. Results showed that participants exposed to the word "warm" created much more favourable impressions than those who were exposed to the word "cold." Asch (1946) explained that only certain words (such as warm and cold) are "central traits" that have an overall effect on impression formation as demonstrated in his early study.

In this example, only an experimental group was exposed to the independent variable (the warm or cold descriptor) and then measured on the dependent variable (their impression). This allowed the researcher to examine for an overall main effect, the difference between the warm and cold condition. However, without a control group it was not possible to say which of the conditions accounts for the effect. It could be that the warm descriptor produced a favourable impression and this alone accounted for the difference between the warm and cold condition, which might not have any effect. Conversely, it could be that the cold descriptor negatively impacted on the impression to create the difference between the cold and warm condition, which did not on its own produce an effect. Finally, it could be that the warm and cold descriptors produced separate main effects.

Test Yourself

- What four features underlie a true experimental design?
- What main feature distinguishes a classic experimental design from a basic design?
- What features constitute a Solomon four-group design?
- What does a factorial design contain?
- Which type of quasi-experimental design lacks a control group?

Internal and External Validty

LO4

Internal validity The capacity to demonstrate an experimental effect and to rule out rival explanations for that effect.

Recall how validity is an important consideration in evaluating whether a study is properly measuring/assessing the central concepts and constructs of interest to the researchers. In other words, is a study properly examining what it is supposed to? In an experiment, validity takes on an even greater level of importance as a researcher tries to prove causation and generalize the findings beyond the confines of that particular study. **Internal validity** refers to the capacity to demonstrate an experimental effect and to rule out rival explanations for that effect. Campbell and Stanley (1963) coined the term "internal validity," referring to it as "the basic minimum without which any experiment is uninterpretable: Did in fact the experimental treatments make a difference in this specific experimental instance?" (p. 5). In other words, internal validity pertains to whether or not a causal relationship has been established. A study has high internal validity if a researcher is able to demonstrate that it is highly likely an independent variable produced a particular outcome (i.e., the differences between groups observed on the dependent variable were due solely due to the independent variable) and it is highly unlikely that alternative explanations can account for the effect. Random assignment to an experimental and control group helps to establish internal validity by minimizing differences between the groups prior to the experimental manipulation.

External validity
The generalizability of an experimental effect.

External validity refers to the generalizability of the effect or outcome beyond that particular experiment. In other words, do the results generalize to other people in other settings at other times? Does sleep deprivation impair performance in general, such as other cognitive or behavioural areas of functioning in the real world for most people, or is it limited to the results found in this particular study measuring performance on a word task with a particular group of participants? Random sampling helps to establish external validity because it eliminates bias generalizing from the sample to the population (Dorsten & Hotchkiss, 2005).

Internal and external validity are related in a manner that is considered a trade-off in experimental research. With high internal validity, a researcher can be sure the independent variable is the cause of any differences found between the experimental and control group on the dependent measure. However, the greater the control over the environment, as is the case for most laboratory experiments, the more artificial and less lifelike the study becomes and the less likely the experiment will generalize to the real world (external validity). This can be countered

Field experiment A naturally occurring experiment that takes place in a real-life setting.

through the use of a **field experiment**, where the experiment occurs naturally in a real-life context. For example, the Smithsonian Tropical Research Institute conducts field experiments in different locations on the effects of global climate change on tropical plants, such as by looking at plant responses to various levels of carbon dioxide concentrations. Similarly, social researchers examine variations in the behaviour of groups that take place in actual social situations, such as performance on a sports team, shopping behaviour in a supermarket, motorist responses at busy intersections, and student engagement in a classroom. Although field experiments have higher generalizability because they take place in the real world, there is very little control over that environment and the isolation of variables can be quite problematic. As a result, high external validity corresponds to low internal validity and vice versa.

Test Yourself

- What is the term for the generalizability of an experimental effect?
- How are internal and external validity related?

Threats to Internal Validity

In their pioneering work on experimental design, Donald Campbell and Julian Stanley (1963) identify eight considerations they refer to as "classes of extraneous variables" that need to be carefully controlled for within an experiment design or ruled out as possibilities via careful consideration. Otherwise, these unintentional variables can confound or interfere with the effects of the independent variable and make it difficult to properly assess the findings. The eight classes of extraneous variables are now more commonly recognized as "threats to internal validity" and include: selection, history, maturation, selection by maturation interactions, experimental mortality, testing, instrumentation, and statistical regression.

Selection

Selection Methods used to obtain groups that can result in differences prior to the experimental manipulation.

As a threat to internal validity, **selection** refers to methods used to obtain groups that can result in differences prior to the experimental manipulation. Recall how true experimental designs rely upon random assignment to achieve identical groups at the onset of the study prior to exposure to an independent variable. The first threat to validity concerns any practices that can lead to a selection bias where the two groups are not identical at the beginning of the study. For example, allowing participants to self-select into groups can produce differences between the experimental and control groups since certain individuals opted for the treatment while others chose to avoid it (Mitchell & Jolley, 1996). Using my earlier example, if participants who normally need a lot of sleep opt to be in the control condition because they would prefer to avoid sleep deprivation and those who end up in the sleep deprivation treatment chose it because they do not feel they require the normal amount of sleep, the effects of the independent variable may be nullified. This is because those least impacted by sleep deprivation self-selected themselves into the study, while those likely to be most impacted opted out. A similar problem would occur if a researcher purposely assigned participants to the groups in a manner that appeared arbitrary but was in fact not, as would be the case if a teacher assigned students in the front of the class to one group and the back of the class to another (Mitchell & Jolley, 1996). To help assess whether selection is a threat to internal validity in a given study, ask yourself: "Can I be sure the experimental and control groups are identical at the onset of the study?" This threat can be prevented through the use of random assignment.

History

History Changes in the dependent measure attributed to external events outside of the experiment.

Another potential threat to internal validity concerns what is called **history**, which refers to changes in the dependent measure attributed to external events other than the independent variable that occurred between the first and second measurement. This threat pertains to classic experimental designs or other designs containing a pre-test and post-test measurement of the dependent variable. For example, suppose a researcher is interested in the effects of exposure to information on government cutbacks on students' attitudes toward tuition hikes. If large-scale student tuition protests take place during the testing periods, it is unclear whether changes in students' attitudes toward tuition from Time 1 to Time 2 result from learning about government cutbacks (the experimental manipulation) or the coinciding historical event. To help assess whether history is a threat to internal validity in a given study, ask yourself: "Is it possible that some other event outside of the study produced these findings?" This threat cannot be avoided, but random assignment will help ensure that both groups experience its effects similarly. In addition, the inclusion of a pre-test will indicate if a history effect may have occurred since there will be a difference between the pre-test and post-test for both groups, even the control group that did not experience the independent variable. Note that the difference will only indicate that history is a potential problem. The difference could also be the result of maturation, as discussed next.

Montreal riot police stand guard while students protest tuition fee increases.

Maturation

A third potential threat to internal validity pertaining to experimental designs containing a pre-test and post-test is maturation. In the context of experimental research, **maturation** refers to changes in the dependent measure that result from processes within the research participants themselves over the period of treatment, such as growing older, gaining experience, or growing fatigued. For example, Palys and Atchison (2014) provide a simplistic case of a researcher interested in whether the administration of pills will help children learn to walk. If the participants are one-year-olds and none of them are walking at Time 1 but all of them are walking at Time 2, it is impossible to determine if the pill administered on a monthly basis for a year (as the treatment or independent variable) facilitated walking, or if a natural biological process attributed to maturation resulted in all of the children walking at age two (p. 238).

Although none of the features of the designs discussed in this section protect against maturation, you can question whether this threat might be operating in studies showing a difference in the dependent measure at Time 1 and Time 2 for a control group. It cannot be the experimental manipulation that accounts for the unexpected change because this group is not exposed to the independent variable. To help assess whether maturation is a threat to the internal validity in a given study, ask yourself: "Is it possible that naturally occurring changes within the participants are responsible

Maturation Changes in the dependent measure that result from naturally occurring processes within the research participants themselves over the period of treatment.

for the findings?" Similar to history, this threat cannot be avoided, but random assign-ment will evenly distribute the effects across the experimental and control groups, and a pre-test will provide evidence of a difference that may be attributed to maturation.

Selection by Maturation Interaction

Selection by maturation interaction A combined effect of initial differences in the groups at the onset of the study and maturation.

The influence of maturation can sometimes be driven by the initial selection of the experimental and control groups. In a **selection by maturation interaction**, there is a combined effect of initial differences in the groups at the onset of the study alongside maturation effects. For example, suppose a researcher assigned six-year-old boys to an experimental group and six-year-old females to a control group for a study on spatial skills. The experimenter believes that he can design an exercise program that will improve spatial skills. Both groups are measured at Time 1, then the researcher then spends a few months designing his program and then places the boys in the exercise program where they do special drills once a week for a hour over the course of three weeks. Both groups are measured about a month after completing the program and the boys show marked improvement in spatial skills compared to the girls. In this example, several factors could account for the findings other than the exercise program. First, there could be differences in spatial skills between boys and girls to begin with. In addition, even if there are no initial differences between boys and girls, it could be that over a course of several months, the boys engaged in a variety of activities that the girls did not that inadvertently led to improvements in their spatial skills, irrespective of the specialized exercise program designed by the researchers. For example, some may have participated in organized sports such as baseball or soccer, while others perhaps played sports during their recess breaks and over the lunch hour.

To help assess whether a selection by maturation interaction is a threat to the internal validity in a given study, ask yourself: "Is it possible that the two groups would have eventually become different irrespective of the independent variable?" Again, random assignment helps to improve internal validity by elim-inating biases that could otherwise be present at the onset, and a pre-test for the control group helps to establish whether maturation is a possibility that could otherwise be mistaken for a treatment effect.

Experimental Mortality

Experimental mortality The course of participant drop-out over time.

A fifth potential threat to internal validity is **experimental mortality**, referring to the loss of participants due to a discontinuation of voluntary participation over time. Simply stated, the longer a study carries on, the greater the odds are that partici-pants will drop out of the study for any number of reasons (e.g., they move, they lose track of the study, they lose interest, etc.). Mortality, also called attrition, is an inherent problem in longitudinal studies, particularly ones that are conducted over many years and involve time-consuming and even unpleasant contributions from participants. For example, although highly important to our eventual understanding of the development of cancer among Canadians, the Tomorrow Project periodically requests that participants complete detailed documents on their food intake, activity levels, and body measurements. In addition, they are asked to go to a health centre to provide saliva samples, urine samples, and blood samples (Tomorrow Project, 2013). What if the participants who are most motivated or the healthiest choose to remain in the study and those who are least motivated or least healthy drop out? To help assess whether mortality is a threat to internal validity in a given study, ask yourself: "Did more participants drop out of the experimental compared to the control group (or vice versa)?" While mortality cannot be prevented by an experimental design feature, it can be reduced, where possible, by limiting the overall time frame for a study or by taking the pre-test and post-test measures at fairly close intervals in time. By examining the pre-test and post-test measures for the control group, a researcher can see if a change in the group size has potentially influenced the results of a study. Finally, it is especially important to monitor the number of participants in each group to see if more participants drop out of one group relative to the other.

Testing

Testing Changes in the dependent measure that result from experience gained on the pre-test.

Although a pre-test is very important for indicating the presence of potential threats such as mortality or maturation, **testing** itself can pose a threat to the internal validity of an experimental design. Just as students in a class sometimes perform better on a second midterm once they have gained familiarity with how a professor designs and words the questions on her exams, participants may improve from a first test to a second test regardless of the experimental manipulation. In this case, a researcher would expect both the experimental and control group to show improvement. If the independent variable has an effect, the change should be greater for participants in the experimental condition. To help assess whether testing is a threat to internal validity in a given study, ask yourself: "Is it possible that participants' test scores changed due to experience or familiarity gained from taking a pre-test?" The necessary feature for determining whether testing is a potential threat is the inclusion of a control group.

Practice tests help student improve their scores on the timed Law School Admission Test (LSAT).

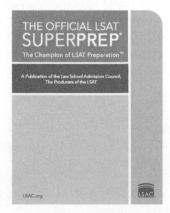

Instrumentation

Instrumentation Differences produced by changes in the manner in which the dependent variable is measured.

Instrumentation refers to any changes in the manner in which the dependent variable is measured that can lead to differences between Time 1 and Time 2. For example, a researcher might change a measuring instrument such as a scale or index because a newer or more improved version becomes available between Time 1 and Time 2. Alternatively, an observer or rater might fall ill or otherwise be unable to obtain measurements at both time periods, and there may be differences between how the first and second observer interpret events that influence the results. To help assess whether instrumentation is a threat to internal validity in a given study, ask yourself: "Were there any changes to the way the dependent variable was measured between the pretest and post-test that might account for the findings?"

Statistical Regression

Finally, as Mitchell and Jolley (1996) point out, "even if the measuring instrument is the same for both the pre- and post-test, the amount of chance measurement error may not be" (p. 143). Extreme scores are sometimes inflated by measurement error. That is, with increased measurement (as when testing someone at two points in time), extreme scores or outliers tend to level off to more accurately reflect the construct under investigation. In statistical terms, this is a phenomenon known as **regression** toward the mean. For example, researchers interested in helping people overcome phobias, obsessions, or behavioural disorders such as attention deficit might try to include participants likely to display extreme scores on a pre-test because extreme scores are indicative of those who are out of the range of normal and therefore have an actual disorder that needs to be managed. However, it is also likely that participants with extreme scores will show some improvement (their scores will go down from Time 1 to Time 2) regardless of the treatment, as they cannot really go any higher (since they are already extreme) and they are likely to have some good days and some bad days. There is a change in the dependent measure, but "the change is more apparent than real" (Palys & Atchison, 2008, p. 257). To help assess whether regression is a threat to internal validity in a given study, ask yourself: "Is it possible that participants were on the outlier or extreme end of scoring on the pre-test?" To help control for statistical regression, a researcher can try to avoid the use of participants with extreme scores.

Regression
Differences produced by the tendency for extreme scores to become less extreme.

Test Yourself

- Which threat to internal validity results from methods used to obtain participants that result in differences prior to the experimental manipulation?
- Which threat to internal validity results from external events that produce changes in the dependent measure irrespective of the independent variable?
- Which threat to internal validity results from processes occurring within the participants?
- Which threat results from the combined effect of initial differences in the groups at the onset of the study alongside maturation effects?
- Which threat is assessed by asking: "Were there any changes to the way the dependent variable was measured between the pre-test and post-test that might account for the findings?"
- What question should be asked to see if regression toward the mean is a threat to validity?

Threats to External Validity

LO6

Recall that external validity pertains to the ability to generalize beyond a given experiment. While a psychologist might rely upon a convenient sample of introductory psychology students who consent to participate in his study on jury deliberations, he is relying on the findings from his research to better inform him about how most Canadians jurors deliberate during trials. Just as there are threats to internal validity, there are features of experimental designs that can jeopardize the generalizability of findings beyond the particular experimental settings and the participants on which they were based. In this section, I discuss the three common threats to external validity: experimenter bias, participant reactivity, and unrepresentative samples.

Experimenter Bias

Experimenter bias
The tendency for researchers to influence the behaviour of research participants in a manner that favours the outcomes they anticipate.

In an earlier chapter you learned about sources of error in measurement and how a researcher might try to help along a study to get a desired outcome. **Experimenter bias** "exists when researchers inadvertently influence the behaviour of research participants in a way that favours the outcomes they anticipate" (Marczyk, DeMatteo, & Festinger, 2005, p. 69). For example, a researcher who expects sleep deprivation to hinder performance might distract participants in the experimental condition or fail to give them the full instructions for how to complete the task, whereas those in the control condition might receive additional cues that aid performance. Although experimenter bias is one of the most common and basic threats to external validity (Kintz, Delprato, Metteee, Persons, & Shappe, 1965), there are ways to minimize its occurrence. First, procedural control in an experiment can include the use of scripts to ensure a researcher reads the exact same instructions to each of the participants. Alternatively, control can even be removed from the researcher such that participants receive typed instructions, watch a video clip, or hear an audio recording that describes how to carry out the task that is being measured in the study. Anything that can be done to standardize the procedures to help ensure identical treatment for the control and experimental group (with the exception of the independent variable) will reduce the likelihood of experimental bias.

In addition to standardized instructions and procedures, where possible, experimenters should not be allowed access to the outcome measure while it is taking place. For example, in Symbaluk et al.'s (1997) pain experiment, the dependent variable was how long participants lasted at the isometric sitting exercise. Participants ended a session by sitting down on a box that contained a pressure plate that stopped a timer. The experimenter was not in the same room with the participants while they performed the exercise and therefore could not influence how long they lasted at the exercise. Further, a recording device (not the experimenter) indicated how long each participant lasted.

Finally, in some studies it is possible to keep an experimenter or research assistant "blind" to the important features of the study until after the dependent variable is measured. For example, in the pain experiment, an assistant was in the room with the participants while they performed the exercise. The assistant recorded pain ratings at regular intervals and noted when participants ended the exercise. The assistant was never informed about the hypothesis or the independent variable, or whether any given participant was in an experimental or control condition. As a result, the assistant had no reason to create an experimenter effect. It may even be possible to use a double-blind technique where both the researchers/assistants and the participants are unaware of which participants were assigned to the experimental and control conditions. In the pain experiment discussed above, participants were not informed about the other conditions until the completion of the study, so they could not form an expectation about whether they should or should not do well based on features of the study, such as the amount of money they were being paid relative to others. Participant bias is discussed in the next section.

Research in Action

Basic Instincts, Part 5: The Milgram Experiment Revisited

Recall the now classic experiments on obedience conducted by Stanley Milgram in the 1960s that were discussed in detail in Chapter 3 as an example of unethical research due to the prolonged psychological harm experienced by participants who believed they were giving painful electric shocks to a learner. Jerry Burger, a social psychologist at Santa Clara University, partially replicated Milgram's studies in an experiment that was broadcast on January 3, 2007 as part of an ABC News Primetime television program called *Basic Instincts.* Surprisingly, participants were almost as obedient in this study as they were in Milgram's original versions. To learn how Burger created a "safer" version of Milgram's procedures and to find out if there are differences in obedience between males and females, check out the video published by ABC News Productions. For more information on the video and Burger's (2009) article summarizing this study called "Replicating Milgram: Would People Still Obey Today?" published in *American Psychologist,* refer to scu.edu/cas/psychology/faculty/burger.cfm.

Participant Reactivity

Participant reactivity The tendency for research participants to act differently during a study simply because they are aware that they are participating in a research study.

A second source of bias rests with participants themselves. **Participant reactivity** refers to the tendency for research participants to act differently during a study simply because they are aware that they are participating in a research study. This sometimes occurs because participants try to "look good," suggesting a social desirability bias, or they pick up on what the study is about and try to help the researchers prove their hypothesis by following demand characteristics, as discussed in Chapter 4. One way to lessen participant reactivity is to withhold details regarding the hypothesis and/or experimental manipulation from the participants until after the dependent variable is measured. For example, suppose I was interested in whether or not students would help a fellow classmate get caught up on missed lecture notes. The dependent variable is whether students agree to lend their notes. Perhaps I hypothesize that students will be more willing to lend notes to someone who was sick from class versus someone who skipped class. I can manipulate the independent variable by sending one note to half of the class asking if anyone is willing to lend their notes to a fellow classmate who was recently ill and another note to half of the class asking if anyone is willing to lend their notes to a student who missed class to attend a Stanley Cup playoff game. If I told the class ahead of time that I was studying their willingness to help a classmate, they might react to my request to appear helpful irrespective of the independent variable.

Participant effects are also sometimes controlled for with the use of deception where participants are led to believe the experimenter is investigating something different than the true purpose of the study. In the example above, I might use a cover story in which I tell the students I am studying aspects of Internet usage and have them complete a short questionnaire asking about their familiarity with and time spent on a number of Internet sites, such Facebook and Twitter. As they complete the short survey, I might pass out the note with the request for help. The note might have a spot at the bottom where they can check off that they would lend notes and leave a contact number, or that they would be unwilling to lend notes and provide a contact number at this time. I could then collect the notes along with the completed questionnaires.

In cases where participants are not informed about the hypothesis under investigation or they are misled about the hypothesis, at the completion of the study the investigators may ask participants if they can guess the hypothesis under investigation. A participant who is able to accurately state the hypothesis under investigation despite the researcher's attempts to conceal it would be considered "suspicious" and the results for the experiment would be examined with and without suspicious cases as a further check to determine if reactivity was a problem in that particular study. Deception and the withholding of information is used only rarely in experimental research—typically involving social psychological processes that would be negated by full disclosure (e.g., willingness to help) because the practice goes against the participants' ethical rights to informed consent. In all cases where information is withheld from participants or they are deceived by a cover story or misled in any way by a procedure used in the experiment, a detailed debriefing must occur as soon as possible. The debriefing should include full disclosure of the nature and the purpose of any form of deception and allow the participant to seek further clarification on any aspect of the study.

Unrepresentative Samples

Researchers at universities across Canada regularly conduct studies using students enrolled in introductory psychology classes as a common pool of available research participants. In many cases, the students receive a small course credit as a direct incentive for their participation so that psychologists and graduate students can obtain the needed participants to further the interests of science, their own research agendas, and important degree requirements. To ensure voluntary participation from an ethical perspective, students who do agree to participate in research must be allowed to withdraw their participation at any time without penalty (i.e., they would still obtain the credit or be able to complete a comparable project for a course credit). While clearly a convenient sample, a group of psychology majors seeking a bachelor of arts or science degree is unlikely to represent the broader university population enrolled in any number of other programs, such as bachelor of commerce, bachelor of communication studies, or bachelor of music in jazz and contemporary popular music. Similarly, Canadian residents who volunteer as experimental research participants tend to be different in important ways from the wider, general-public population. Rosenthal and Rosnow (1975), for example, found that the typical volunteer in experimental research was more intelligent, more sociable, and from a higher social class.

Unrepresentative samples are especially problematic for claiming the effectiveness of programs for things like drug treatment since the participants who self-select into treatment tend to be the most motivated and are most likely to benefit from any treatment. Campbell and Stanley (1963) refer to this threat as a **selection by treatment interaction** effect since those most susceptible to the independent variable have placed themselves in the study. That is not to say that unwilling participants should be coerced into treatment just to balance out the sample. Research ethics aside, research has also shown that court-ordered participants are more resentful and less committed to the objectives of drug treatment programs (Sullivan, 2001).

Selection by treatment interaction A threat to external validity produced by the self-selection of participants susceptible to the independent variable.

Test Yourself

- What is experimenter bias and how can it be minimized in an experiment?
- What is participant reactivity and how can it be controlled for in an experiment?
- Why is a volunteer sample unlikely to be representative of the larger population from which it was drawn?

Chapter Summary

LO1 **Describe the rationale underlying an experimental method.**

In an experiment, at least one independent variable is manipulated by a researcher to measure its effects (if any) on a dependent variable.

LO2 **Identify the criteria needed to establish causality and explain which features of an experiment support the testing of cause-effect relationships.**

To establish causality, two variables must be related in a logical way, the presumed cause must precede the effect in time, and the cause should be the most plausible, ruling out rival explanations. Strict control over the environment and random assignment to the experimental and control group helps to ensure that the only difference between the two groups results from the independent variable.

LO3 **Differentiate between and define the different types of research designs, including experimental, between- and within-subjects, factorial, and quasi-experimental.**

A *basic experimental design* includes random assignment, an experimental and control group, the manipulation of an independent variable experienced by the experimental group, and the measurement of a dependent variable. A *classic experiment* includes these features along with a pre-test measure of the dependent variable prior to the manipulation of the independent variable. A *Solomon four-group design* combines the basic and classic designs to include four groups. Following random assignment, Group 1 is measured at the pre-test, is exposed to the independent variable, and then is reassessed at the post-test; Group 2 is measured at the pre-test, is not exposed to the independent variable, and is assessed at the post-test; Group 3 does not get a pre-test, is exposed to the independent variable, and then is measured at the post-test; and Group 4 does not get a pre-test, is not exposed to the independent variable, but is measured at the post-test. In a *between-subjects design,* participants in the experimental group are exposed to only one level of the independent variable. In a *within-subjects design,* participants in the experimental group are exposed to all levels of the independent variable. A *factorial design* includes two or more independent variables. A *quasi-experimental design* lacks one of the features of a true experiment, such as random assignment or a control group.

LO4   Define internal and external validity.

Internal validity is the capacity to demonstrate an experimental effect and to rule out rival explanations for that effect. External validity refers to the generalizability of the effect beyond a given experiment to other people in other settings at other times.

LO5   Identify and describe potential threats to internal validity.

This chapter discusses eight threats to internal validity: 1) *selection* refers to methods used to obtain groups that can result in differences prior to the experimental manipulation; 2) *history* refers to changes in the dependent variable attributed to external events occurring between the first and second measurement; 3) *maturation* refers to changes in the dependent measure that result from processes within the research participants; 4) *selection by maturation interaction* refers to a combined effect of initial differences in the groups and maturation; 5) *experimental mortality* refers to the course of participant drop-out over time; 6) *testing* refers to changes in the dependent variables that result from experience gained on the pre-test; 7) *instrumentation* refers to any changes in the manner in which the dependent variable is measured; 8) *statistical regression* refers to differences produced by the tendency for extreme scores to become less extreme.

LO6   Identify and describe potential threats to external validity.

This chapter discusses three threats to external validity: 1) *experimenter bias* exists when researchers influence the behaviour of research participants in a manner that favours the outcomes they anticipate; 2) *participant reactivity* refers to the tendency for research participants to act differently during a study simply because they are aware that they are participating in a research study; 3) *unrepresentative samples* such as introductory psychology students or other groups that self-select into experiments are likely different in important ways from the larger population of interest.

Research Reflection

1. Visit the home page for *Psychological Research on the Net* at psych.hanover. edu/research/exponnet.html. This website, maintained by John H. Krantz, Ph.D., lists ongoing web-based psychology experiments by general topic (e.g., health psychology, judgment and decision making, relationships, etc.). Select an experiment of interest to you and provide responses to the following:
   a. List the name of the study and the affiliated primary researcher(s).
   b. Describe the purpose of the study as identified in the associated consent form.
   c. Outline the procedures for potential participants.
   d. Based on details provided about the study, describe one potential threat to internal or external validity discussed in this chapter that could impact the results of your selected study.

2. Visit YouTube's official site at youtube.com. Search the title "Sheldon and Amy's Date Night Experiment—The Big Bang Theory" to locate and watch a short clip from the popular television series. In this clip, Amy sets up an experiment to test whether events associated with fond memories for Sheldon can be directed toward her so she can accelerate their intimate relationship.
   a. Does the experimental design used by Amy fit the criteria for a true experimental design? Why or why not?
   b. Why is it impossible to prove causality in this particular instance?
   c. What recommendations would you make to Amy to improve upon her design so she could be more confident that her manipulation is working?

3. Locate and read the following article: Morisano, D., Hirsch, J. B., Peterson, J. B., Pihl, R. O., & Shore, B. M. (2010). Setting, elaborating, and reflecting on personal goals improves academic performance. *Journal of Applied Psychology, 95*(2), 255–264. You can download a PDF version of the article at selfauthoring.com/JAPcomplete.pdf.
   a. Which type of experimental design discussed in this chapter was employed by the authors?
   b. What is the main independent variable and how was it manipulated?
   c. What is the main dependent variable and how was it measured?
   d. Does setting goals improve academic performance? What features of this study increase your confidence in the findings?
   e. Are there any potential threats to internal or external validity relevant to this particular study? Explain your response.

Learning Through Practice

Objective: To design an experimental taste test.
Directions:

1. Pair up with someone else in the class.
2. Discuss whether you believe people can accurately identify their favourite food or beverage brands from among a sample of competitors' brands.
3. Come up with two testable hypotheses of interest related to specific taste preferences. For example, H1: Participants will be able to identify their stated cola preference in a blind taste test between Pepsi and Coke.

4. Reflecting on threats to internal validity, identify factors that you think might influence taste and how you might control for these in your experimental design.

5. Write a detailed procedure section describing how you would design a study to test one of your hypotheses. Provide enough detail so that others could replicate it. Address these considerations in your procedures section:
   - What materials will you need to carry out this study?
   - How will you order the presentation of the beverages or food items?
   - What sort of instructions will you give participants?
   - How will you measure preference?

Research Resources

1. For an overview of the basic principles of experimental and non-experimental quantitative designs commonly used in the social sciences, refer to Spector, P. E. (1981). *Research designs.* Newbury Park, CA: Sage Publications.

2. For students and researchers with statistical proficiency who want to learn more about experimental designs, I recommend Montgomery, D. C. (2001). *Design and analysis of experiments.* New York, NY: John Wiley & Sons.

3. For an updated version of Campbell and Stanley's (1963) pioneering work on experimental design, I recommend Shadish, W. R., Cook, T. D., & Campbell, D. T. (2002). *Experimental and quasi-experimental designs for general causal inference.* Boston, MA: Houghton Mifflin.

4. For an overview of 19 issues that can potentially jeopardize the strength of causal claims and the interpretation of experimental findings, check out Peter Norvig's (2012). *Warning signs in experimental design and interpretation* page at norvig.com/experiment-design.html.

5. For practical advice on how to conduct behavioural research over the Internet, I recommend Gosling, S. D., & Johnson, J. A. (2010). *Advanced methods for conducting online behavioral research.* Washington, DC: American Psychological Association.

For more information on the resources available from McGraw-Hill Ryerson, go to www.mcgrawhill.ca/he/solutions.

References

Asch, S. E. (1946). Forming impressions of personality. *Journal of Abnormal Social Psychology, 41*, 258–290.

Beins, B. C. (2009). *Research methods: A tool for life* (2nd ed.). Toronto, ON: Pearson Education.

Burger, J. M. (2009). Replicating Milgram: Would people still obey today? *American Psychologist, 64*, 1–11.

Cabanac, M. (1986). Money versus pain: Experimental study of a conflict in humans. *Journal of the Experimental Analysis of Behavior, 46*(1), 37–44.

Campbell, D. T., & Stanley, J. C. (1963). *Experimental and quasi-experimental designs for research.* Chicago, IL: Rand McNally.

Djikic, M. (2011). The effect of music and lyrics on personality. *Psychology of Aesthetics, Creativity, and the Arts, 5*(3), 237–240.

Dorsten, L. E., & Hotchkiss, L. (2005). *Research methods and society: Foundations of social inquiry.* Upper Saddle River, NJ: Pearson Education.

Kintz, B. L., Delprato, D. J., Mettee, D. R., Persons, C. E., & Shappe, R. H. (1965). The experimenter effect. *Psychological Bulletin, 63,* 223–232.

Marczyk, G., DeMatteo, D., & Festinger, D. (2005). *Essentials of research design and methodology.* Hoboken, NJ: John Wiley & Sons.

McConville, K. M. V., & Virk, S. (2012). Evaluation of an electronic video game for improvement of balance. *Virtual Reality.* DOI 10.1007/s10055-012-0212-7

Mitchell, M., & Jolley, J. (1996). *Research design explained* (3rd ed.). Orlando, FL: Harcourt Brace & Company.

Montgomery, D. C. (2001). *Design and analysis of experiments.* New York, NY: John Wiley & Sons.

Morisano, D., Hirsch, J. B., Peterson, J. B., Pihl, R. O., & Shore, B. M. (2010). Setting, elaborating, and reflecting on personal goals improves academic performance. *Journal of Applied Psychology, 95*(2), 255–264.

Norvig, P. (2012). *Warning signs in experimental design and interpretation.* Retrieved from http://norvig.com/experiment-design.html

Palys, T., & Atchison, C. (2014). *Research decisions: Quantitative and qualitative perspectives* (5th ed.). Toronto, ON: Thomson Canada Limited.

Palys, T., & Atchison, C. (2008). *Research decisions: Quantitative and qualitative perspectives* (4th ed.). Toronto, ON: Thomson Canada Limited.

Rosenthal, R., & Rosnow. R. L. (1975). *The volunteer subject.* New York, NY: John Wiley & Sons.

Shadish, W. R., Cook, T. D., & Campbell, D. T. (2002). *Experimental and quasi-experimental designs for general causal inference.* Boston, MA: Houghton Mifflin.

Spector, P. E. (1981). *Research designs.* Newbury Park, CA: Sage Publications.

Sullivan, T. J. (2001). *Methods of social research.* Orlando, FL: Harcourt.

Symbaluk, D., Heth, C. D., Cameron, J., & Pierce, W. D. (1997). Social modeling, monetary incentives, and pain endurance: The role of self-efficacy and pain perception. *Personality and Social Psychology Bulletin, 23*(3), 258–269.

Thayer, Bruce, A. (2012). *Quasi-experimental research designs.* Oxford Scholarship Online: DOI:10.1093/acprof:oso/9780195387384.003.0001. Retrieved from www.oxfordscholarship.com.ezproxy.macewan.ca/view/10.1093/acprof :oso/9780195387384.001.0001/acprof-9780195387384-chapter-001

(The) Tomorrow Project. (2013). *Join the study.* Calgary, AB: Alberta Health Services. Retrieved from http://in4tomorrow.ca

Endnote

[1] Opening quote retrieved May 31, 2012 from www.brainyquote.com.

Surveys

"Users of surveys require solid, reliable data. The cliché 'garbage in, garbage out' applies to surveys. If a survey contains the wrong questions, good decisions cannot be based on the information." (Gray & Guppy, 1994, p. 7) [1]

Introduction

Survey An information-collection method used to describe, compare, or explain individual and societal knowledge, feelings, values, preferences, and behaviour.

From customer satisfaction surveys to public opinion polls to market research, a wealth of information can be obtained by asking questions. Surveys outnumber other data collection methods in the leading journals of various disciplines including economics, sociology, political science, and social psychology (Saris & Gallhofer, 2007). A **survey** is an "information-collection method used to describe, compare, or explain individual and societal knowledge, feelings, values, preferences, and behaviour" (Fink, 2009, p. 1). Statistics Canada's Census surveys the entire population in an effort to describe Canadians by asking questions on housing (e.g., whether people rent versus own their own dwelling), personal attributes (e.g., age and marital status), and economic characteristics (e.g., yearly income and employment status), among other topics (Statistics Canada, 2013a). Because the data is collected every five years, comparisons can be made to gauge trends over time such as population growth or changes to the employment rate. Census data is also grouped in particular ways so we can note, for example, the percentage of those 14 years of age and under, 15 to 64 years, and 65 years and older for Canada, as a whole as well as within and between provinces and territories.

The Purpose of Surveys

LO1

Simply put, the purpose of a survey is to find things out by asking questions. Researchers use survey methods to describe individuals and groups and to learn more about their existing knowledge, their thoughts about certain issues, their feelings toward particular phenomenon, and their actions—what they do, why they do it, or how they are likely to behave under specific circumstances. Similarly, surveys are routinely employed by psychologists, social workers, and health care professionals in the identification, assessment, and treatment of people for various conditions and disorders, such as anxiety, depression, attention-deficit, and anger management. Importantly, survey methods enable researchers to describe populations and examine relationships among and between variables of interest.

Asking Questions

One of the more common types of information collected through surveys is demographic. **Demographic questions** help describe a population by collecting "facts about a respondent's age, race/ethnicity, education, job, gender, marital status, geographic place of residence, type of residence, size of family, and so on" (Fink, 2003, p. 79). Demographic information helps us better understand the population and it can serve as an indicator for why people think or behave the way they do or why they experience events as they do. For example, we know that certain groups such as Aboriginal peoples, single-parent females, children, individuals with work-limiting disabilities, and recent immigrants are at greatest risk for poverty and unemployment in Canada (Hay, 2009; Statistics Canada, 2010).

In addition to demographic questions, most surveys include questions that measure knowledge, attitudes, and/or behaviours. **Knowledge questions** gauge whether respondents can retrieve and correctly report on factual information. Political knowledge, for example, can be assessed through questions pertaining to respondents' understanding of election procedures and the rights and responsibilities of Canadian citizens, Canada's social and cultural history, and/or Canada's political system (Citizenship and Immigration Canada, 2012). In an Institute for Research on Public Policy survey conducted in 2006, Henry Milner found that Canadians are relatively lacking in their knowledge of the politics and government of Canada and the United States. Ten questions were used to assess political knowledge, including: "Which of the following best describes who is entitled to vote in federal elections?" Response options included the fixed categories: "residents," "taxpayers," "legal residents," "citizens," and "don't know." Respondents were also asked open-ended questions, including "Please name two members of the President's [Federal] Cabinet and identify the department they represent [are in charge of]." Results showed that the average number correct for the 1354 respondents was 2.57 for those aged 15 to 25 years (N = 877), and 2.93 for those 26 years of age and older (Milner, 2007).

Attitude questions measure respondents' views toward a person, event, institution, or whatever the attitude object happens to be, such as "Are you in favour of abortion?"; "Do you consider yourself to be healthy?"; or "Is your instructor

Demographic questions Questions designed to collect facts about a respondent's age, race/ethnicity, education, job, gender, marital status, geographic place of residence, type of residence, size of family, and so on.

Knowledge questions Questions designed to gauge whether respondents can retrieve and correctly report on factual information about some area of interest.

Attitude questions Questions designed to measure points of view toward an attitude object such as a person or an event.

effective?" Attitudes are believed to consist of cognitive, affective, and behavioural components (Aronson, Wilson, Akert, & Fehr, 2013). The cognitive component has to do with what people think about the attitude object (e.g., "I think that political candidate is honest"). The affective component has to do with one's feelings toward the object (e.g., "I like that political candidate"), and the behavioural component involves a person's intended actions based on the attitude (e.g., "I plan to vote for that candidate"). Any or all of the attitude components might be assessed in a survey. Surveys are also used to compare the attitudes and opinions of various subgroups. For example, are students in business as satisfied with their educational outcomes as students in health and community studies, and if not, why might this be the case?

Behaviour questions Questions designed to find out more about the respondent's activities.

Finally, **behaviour questions** ask about respondents' actions or experiences and they are typically stated in reference to "time, duration, or frequency" (Fink, 2003, p. 71). For example, "Which of the following radio stations do you usually listen to?"; "How often do you eat out at restaurants?"; "When was the last time you had a physical examination by a medical doctor?"; or "In the last year, have you been a victim of an identity theft?" Behaviour questions often measure the central concepts or dependent variables (i.e., outcomes) in a study. For example, researchers might examine whether respondents do particular things or experience certain events because of other characteristics they possess, such as demographic variables or attitude measures that serve as independent variables (i.e., the presumed causes). Figuring out what type of questions to include and which specific concepts need to be measured in a survey becomes possible only after a researcher has clarified the overall purpose of the study.

Research on the Net

Institute for Research on Public Policy

The Institute for Research on Public Policy (IRPP) is an independent, non-profit organization dedicated to research aimed at helping Canadians and government make informed public policy decisions. An online survey of issues important to Canadians conducted by the IRPP in partnership with Nanos Research showed that the leading concerns of Canadians were 1) keeping our health care system strong and 2) job creation (Nanos, 2012). To learn more about public opinion toward issues facing Canadians, check out the home page for the IRPP (irpp.org/en). For more information on the survey discussed above, visit the IRPP home page, click on IRPP archive, and search for "Canadians rate highly the issues close to their day-to-day lives."

Test Yourself

- What is the purpose of a survey?
- What are the main types of questions typically included in surveys?

Preparing for Survey Research

LO2

The first step in any survey project is clarifying the research objectives. The research objectives are the underlying aims of the study, or what the study is about. The objectives provide direction for how to create the questions that will provide relevant information on the topic of interest. Otherwise, as noted in the opening quote, a researcher may ask questions that are the wrong ones, making the data meaningless. Guppy and Gray (2008, p. 13) offer five essentials questions a researcher can ask to help clarify a study's objectives *before* designing or beginning to carry out a study:

1. What needs to be known?
2. Why does it need to be known?
3. What else needs to be known? Why?
4. What will the results of the survey accomplish? What decisions will be based on the results of the survey?
5. Is a survey the best method?

Once the research objectives are clarified and a survey method is decided upon, a researcher can begin designing a survey instrument to collect the information to answer the main research question of interest. However, several decisions still need to be made and various steps will need to be followed before a survey gets to the data collection stage.

LO3

Methodological Considerations

In addition to clarifying the main research question, a researcher also needs to decide whether to employ a longitudinal or cross-sectional design, which sampling method is most appropriate, who or what will make up the units of analysis, and how the central variables are to be measured. In other words, how should the researcher design survey questions that will produce the relevant answers given the overall purpose and more specific objectives of the study? In addition, a researcher needs to determine if the survey will be administered using a questionnaire or interview format, how relevant ethical concerns will be addressed, and the best means for administering the survey (in person, by mail, over the Internet, or by telephone).

Choosing a Design

In Chapter 4, you learned that some studies are conducted at a single point in time while others take place at multiple points over time. A survey researcher is likely to choose a cross-sectional design when describing a phenomenon of interest as it currently exists. For example, a researcher might want to know how Canadians feel about the oil sands mining projects being carried out in Fort McMurray, Alberta. A cross-sectional design is especially suitable for revealing differences in views based on respondent attributes such as occupation, educational level, ethnicity, political affiliation, and/or the province a respondent resides in.

In contrast, a researcher is likely to choose a longitudinal design for studies concerned with changes in variables of interest over time. For example, do people's views toward the Athabasca oil sands mining projects change after learning about the greenhouse emissions and the destruction of ecosystems as identified by environmentalists? Using a longitudinal design, a researcher could measure views before and after exposure to environmental campaigns to see if attitudes change. Note that this follows the same logic as experimental designs with a pre- and post-test measure enabling researchers to identify influences on attitudes and explain how and why they change over time.

Sampling Considerations

After settling on the time dimension for the design, a researcher also needs to consider which of the sampling techniques discussed in Chapter 5 is most suitable for obtaining an appropriate sample. Remember that if one of the aims is to have a sample representative of the larger population from which it was drawn, then a probability-based method such as simple random sampling is likely to be employed. However, if the sampling frame cannot be readily identified or certain characteristics of the population are of particular interest, then a researcher is more apt to rely on one of the non-probability sampling techniques, such as purposive sampling. While survey research is most often associated with the quantitative realm and an aim of describing a population of interest with a representative sample using statistical or numerical terms such as percentages, qualitative surveys do exist and are used to examine diversity in a population through more open-ended questioning (Jansen, 2010).

Finally, a researcher needs to consider the size of the sample to be included in the survey. Time and cost permitting, a quantitative researcher may wish to include a fairly large sample to maximize generalizability while minimizing error. For example, a random sample of 15 519 respondents was included in the Canadian Financial Capability Survey conducted in 2009 to represent the financial knowledge, savings, and debt patterns of all Canadians aged 18 years of age and older (Chawla & Uppal, 2012). In contrast, a relatively small sample might be sufficient for certain research purposes. For example, Hägelli (2005) surveyed only 75 people to learn about winter backcountry use in Western Canada. In this case, the sample consisted of carefully selected avalanche professionals who were included because of their highly specialized experience and knowledge of non-commercial backcountry recreation in the study area.

Rate of response
The percentage of those sampled for whom data are actually collected.

Note that a requirement or preference for a particular sample size does not in any way guarantee the size of or even the quality of the sample that actually ends up taking part in the study. The **rate of response** for a survey refers to "the percentage of those sampled for whom data are actually collected" (Fowler, 2009, p. 7). The rate of response is calculated by dividing the number of completed questionnaires (or interviews) by the intended sample size (i.e., those initially targeted for inclusion). In general, the higher the response rate, the more likely the respondent sample will be representative of the population. However, perfect response rates are unlikely, and what is considered a "good" response rate is dropping all the time as individuals become more difficult to locate (e.g., some people have a cell phone but no land line, others have an unlisted telephone number), and even if reached are often unwilling to participate. This is partly because potential respondents are becoming increasingly mistrustful of surveys—particularly ones conducted over the telephone—due to the prevalence of computer-generated telemarketing efforts, repeated callbacks at various times of the day, and other unsolicited telephone requests (Dillman, Smyth, & Christian, 2009). As a rule of thumb, a response rate of at least 50 percent is deemed adequate for analysis and reporting, 60 percent is good, and 70 percent or higher is considered very good (Babbie, 1990). However, as Babbie (1990) notes, "these are only rough guides; they have no statistical basis, and a demonstrated lack of response bias is far more important than a high response rate" (p. 182). Hence, while the rate of response for the Canadian Financial Capability Survey conducted from February to May, 2009 was only 56.3 percent (Statistics Canada, 2013b), the data can be considered reasonably accurate because several efforts were undertaken to reduce errors at every stage in the data collection and analysis processes, such as extensive interviewer training and checks on interviewers while inputting data. In other words, we can be more confident that the main findings appropriately represent Canadians, including the fact that 76 percent of those aged 19 to 64 lived in a household that carried debt (averaging $119 000), and that people aged 19 to 34 were especially likely to be in debt, carrying $1800 worth of debt for every $1000 worth of earnings (Statistics Canada, 2011).

"This is interesting, 70% of the respondents to our survey said they don't respond to surveys."

© Larry Lambert. www.Cartoonstock.com

Measurement Errors

In addition to design and sampling considerations, a researcher needs to be mindful of errors that can affect the reliability and validity of the information obtained by a survey. Groves (1989) identifies the following four main types of errors that pose problems for survey research: coverage error, sampling error, non-response error, and measurement error.

Coverage error A type of error that results when not all members of the population have a known, non-zero chance of being included in the sample for the survey and when those who are excluded are different from those who are included on measures of interest.

1. **Coverage error**: Coverage error "occurs when not all members of the population have a known, non-zero chance of being included in the sample for the survey and when those who are excluded are different from those who are included on measures of interest" (Dillman, Smyth, & Christian, 2009, p. 17). For example, coverage error occurs when researchers surveying Canadians interview residents of the ten provinces while excluding those living in the three territories. Coverage error can also be a problem if a sampling frame is constructed from a telephone directory, since it will not include residents with cell phones but no land line, those who have an unlisted telephone number and people who have moved recently or recently acquired a telephone listing.

2. *Sampling error:* As described in Chapter 5, sampling error is the difference between the sample statistic and population parameter. Generally speaking, the larger the sample size, the lower the sampling error or the better a sample statistic will approximate the true population value.

Non-response error A type of error that results when the people selected for the survey who do not respond are different from those who do respond in a way that is important to the study.

3. **Non-response error**: Non-response error results from inaccuracies stemming from a failure to get everyone sampled to complete the survey as intended. Specifically, non-response error "occurs when the people selected for the survey who do not respond are different from those who do respond in a way that is important to the study" (Dillman, Smyth, & Christian, 2009, p. 17). To try and minimize this, survey researchers may employ a number of strategies to increase overall response rates, including the use of reminders, personalized contacts, and various incentives (Smyth & Pearson, 2011).

4. *Measurement error:* Systematic errors in measurement occur when a questionnaire contains poorly worded instructions, questions, and/or response categories. For example, suppose a survey on criminal activity includes items that ask respondents how often they have done something, such as carry a concealed weapon or steal from a department store. If the response options are: never, two to three times, and more than three times, someone who has carried out an act only once will either have to leave that item blank, resulting in a missing response, or provide an inaccurate response. In this case, the respondent is much more likely to choose zero since there is a greater tendency for respondents to skew estimates of infrequent behaviours toward zero (Bradburn, Sudman, & Wansink, 2004). This is highly problematic since respondents who commit a criminal offence once are likely to be different from respondents who never commit the act.

Test Yourself

- Why is a cross-sectional design especially suitable for survey research?
- How is the rate of response for a survey calculated?
- What are the four main types of errors that pose problems for survey research?

Survey Methods

Questionnaire A survey data collection instrument consisting of a series of questions or items to which a respondent provides responses containing the information of interest to the researcher.

Survey interview A highly structured data collection method consisting of a series of prescribed questions or items asked by an interviewer who records the answers provided by the respondent.

A respondent provides answers to survey questions posed by an interviewer.

Quantitative researchers use two main survey methods: questionnaires and structured interviews. A **questionnaire** is a survey data collection tool in the form of a series of questions, items, and/or prompts to which a respondent provides the information of interest to the researcher. A respondent may complete the instrument entirely on his or her own, called a self-administered questionnaire, or a respondent may complete an assisted questionnaire where a researcher or other trained staff member guides the respondent through it. The questionnaire itself can be in hard-copy (paper) format, or if it is administered online, it can be in a soft copy (screen image) that is accessed using a survey software program. Surveys can also take the form of highly structured **interviews** where respondents answer a series of prescribed (i.e., prearranged) questions posed directly by researchers or trained research assistants who record the responses. This can be done in person, over the telephone, or as an email exchange. Note that interviews can also be open-ended, unstructured, and highly intensive. These are designed to learn more about events from the perspective of participants. Such interviews are discussed in detail in Chapter 9 on qualitative interviewing. This chapter is dedicated to the more quantitative forms.

Surveys are popular methods for describing groups of interest and finding out more about their knowledge, attitudes, and behaviours. As a method, surveys are an efficient means for collecting a huge amount of information from large samples. Every question is potentially a different variable, except in the case of indexes and scales where multiple questions measure the same construct. This means researchers can examine relationships among variables and look at numerous social issues at one time. Unfortunately, survey methods also raise a number of validity concerns since responses are obtained from respondents who provide information that may or may not be accurate. Respondents make mistakes, forget relevant information, distort information, and give false answers. As noted in an earlier chapter, a social desirability bias, for example, can prompt respondents to give "good" answers as opposed to accurate ones. There are also ethical concerns raised by survey data collection methods.

Ethical Concerns

All survey methods pose ethical concerns. Respondents provide informed consent prior to participating in a survey based on a detailed description about the study, including information on the objectives and the type of questions they can expect to be asked. However, they need to be reminded that their participation is voluntary, they are free to refrain from answering any given question, and they may withdraw altogether at any time without penalty. Asking questions of any nature can produce potentially harmful psychological outcomes for respondents, who may feel bad about characteristics they possess or about actions that they are being asked to report on. In addition, respondents may feel uneasy about providing information that is requested, particularly if it involves highly personal issues or deals with sensitive topics. Respondents may even become upset by what they learn about themselves as a result of providing answers to the questions posed by researchers.

In addition to the ongoing potential for harm, anonymity can rarely be achieved in survey research. For example, in a face-to-face interview, the interviewer clearly knows who is providing the responses. Even for telephone, mailout, or Internet-based surveys, the number, address, or email account can be used by the researcher to identify the respondent. Identifying information is generally important only for sampling purposes. A researcher usually does not need to link up individual answers to a given respondent, and can therefore code the responses under an assigned number (e.g., Respondent #1, #2, etc.) rather than an actual identity to help protect respondents' privacy. Also, while anonymity cannot always be guaranteed, confidentiality usually can. A researcher can uphold confidentiality by never revealing identifying information publicly. A more detailed comparison of the specific data collection formats is provided next.

Face-to-Face Interviews

Prior to the 1960s most quantitative surveys were conducted in person by an interviewer who usually visited respondents at their place of residence. One of the main advantages of this method is that sought-after potential respondents are highly likely to agree to participate in the study, producing high response rates. This is also beneficial for reducing response bias since all types of respondents are equally likely to participate at high rates (Czaja & Blair, 1996). In an in-person interview, a trained interviewer asks questions and the respondent provides answers, which are recorded by the interviewer. Skilled interviewers are able to establish rapport and trust while remaining neutral so they do not influence the respondents' answers in any way. Interviewers carefully manage the conversation such that the respondent follows the instructions, does most of the talking, and provides appropriate answers to the questions of interest. Interviewers can assist in clarifying questions and explaining response categories to aid in the validity of responses obtained. In addition, interviewers can probe for responses and prompt respondents to provide additional details for increased accuracy in reporting. This also enables the researcher to explore topics in a bit more depth and complexity than is possible through a self-administered questionnaire.

While face-to-face interviews are still conducted today because they yield such high-quality data and they have the highest response rates of the survey methods, in-person surveys are rarely used for quantitative research purposes largely due to their inherent drawbacks. Face-to-face interviews are the most expensive and time-consuming form of data collection (Czaja & Blair, 1996). Imagine interviewing 1000 of the more than 660 000 people who live in the city of Winnipeg, Manitoba. There are 280 489 private dwellings spanning an area of about 464 square kilometres (Statistics Canada, 2013c). It would take a very long time—likely in excess of 2000 hours—for one researcher to complete all of the interviews. Even assuming the assistance of multiple trained interviewers who can conduct interviews simultaneously, if each interviewer conducted 50 interviews, the research project would require 20 interviewers. Each interviewer would need to travel to the location of his or her randomly assigned respondents and then spend an hour or so interviewing each person individually. Estimating a time of two hours per interview including travel, at a rate of $25 per hour, each interviewer would be paid $2500, amounting to $50 000 for data collection alone. And this is for a survey conducted only within the city of Winnipeg. A cross-national survey involving cities throughout Canada would be considerably more costly and time-consuming.

In addition to cost, in-person surveys also run the risk of interviewer bias (Wolfer, 2007). There are many ways in which the interviewer can influence the information collected. First, despite efforts to remain neutral, how an interviewer behaves toward the respondent, intentionally or unintentionally, can affect the respondent's willingness to answer any given question. In addition, the interviewer is the person asking the questions; therefore, how a question is asked might affect how it is interpreted and subsequently answered by the respondent. Also, how an actual response is recorded is determined by the interviewer, who may "interpret" responses in a manner that is more consistent with his or her own views rather than those of the respondent. Again note how this discussion is about interviewing for quantitative research purposes. While interviews pose many difficulties for quantitative researchers, they are especially beneficial to qualitative researchers seeking in-depth understanding with small samples (see Chapter 9).

Mail-Out Questionnaires

Beginning in the 1960s and 1970s, researchers routinely mailed out questionnaires to intended respondents at their place of residence. A mail-out survey is a self-report questionnaire containing a series of items to be completed by the respondent and then sent back to the researcher. One main advantage of this method lies in its efficiency since all of the questionnaires can be sent out at the same time, to be completed by respondents on their own without having to pay interviewers. In a few short hours, all of the envelope can be filled, labelled, and stamped accordingly. Although they are less expensive overall when compared to interviews, there are still substantial costs associated with mail-out surveys. For example, a researcher has to pay for paper, questionnaire printing, envelopes, and postage at two or three times the usual rate since most questionnaires exceed the size and weight of a regular letter. These costs are incurred even for surveys that fail to be returned or are returned unopened due to inaccurate mailing addresses. To increase the likelihood that a respondent will return a completed questionnaire, it is practical to also include return postage with an envelope addressed to the researcher.

One of the main advantages of a mail-out questionnaire is the absence of potential for interviewer bias. Another advantage afforded by the absence of an interviewer is anonymity. Respondents generally feel more comfortable and are therefore more inclined to answer sensitive questions and give accurate answers while completing a questionnaire alone than while being interviewed by a stranger (Fowler, 2009). Mail-out questionnaires can also include visual aids such as maps, charts, or other examples built into the design of the questionnaire. Visual aids help to explain instructions, can be used to illustrate points, and can provide additional guidance on how to answer questions using the response format provided for greater clarity and accuracy. In addition, respondents completing mail-out questionnaires can take the time to think about and even verify their answers before providing them.

As a disadvantage, mail-out questionnaires are easy to ignore or forget about, so they have a much lower rate of return than surveys involving some form of personal contact. Without additional follow-up, mail-out surveys are likely to yield a return rate of less than 50 percent (Heberlein & Baumgartner, 1978). Researchers relying on mail-out surveys, then, need to consider ways to increase response rates. Fowler (2009) notes that anything researchers can do to make a questionnaire appear more personalized, professional, and attractive will increase response rates. It is also important to make sure the questionnaire has very clear instructions and layout for how to complete it; is formatted in an attractive, easy-to-read manner; and consists of relatively simple response tasks (Fowler, 2009). This means, where possible, it is better to use closed-ended questions where a respondent can readily choose an answer from a small number of selections, rather than have them try to generate more effortful answers to open-ended items. Although open-ended responses are rich in detail, more often than not respondents will leave open-ended questions blank (Dillman, Smyth, & Christian, 2009). In addition, the response categories need to be straightforward and easy to complete without making errors, such as using large boxes the respondent can check off to indicate a choice or numbers that a respondent can easily circle as an answer. Aside from the design of the instrument, researchers can increase response rates through the use of incentives provided in advance, such as an enclosed gift card, as well as mailed out reminders sent more than once to those who have failed to respond (Fowler, 2009).

Telephone Surveys

Random digit dialling A technique used to create a sampling frame based on a computer-generated list of random phone numbers.

One way to retain most of the advantages of face-to-face interviews but reduce costs is through the use of telephone surveys. Gaining popularity in the 1980s and 1990s, telephone-based surveys are interviews conducted over the phone. Because many people today have unlisted phone numbers, researchers often substitute the use of phone directories for a sampling method called **random digit dialling**. Random digit dialling is a process where a computer randomly creates a sampling frame of phone numbers using the area codes for a given location. The interviewer can make the telephone calls to the prospective respondents, or a computer can make the calls and transfer the call to an interviewer only if someone answers. Many phone surveys take the form of **computer-assisted telephone interviews (CATI)**. In a CATI, the interviewer wears a headset and sits in front of a computer. The computer screen displays the question or item, which is read according to a script to the respondent. The respondent's answers are then directly inputted as they are provided. Note that computer-assisted methods are also used in face-to-face interviews, called computer-assisted personal interviewing (CAPI). In this case, responses are input into laptops or other mobile devices during the in-person interview (Dillman, Smyth, & Christian, 2009).

Computer-assisted telephone interviews (CATI) A telephone-based interview method in which the interviewer inputs survey responses directly into a software program.

An interviewer inputs responses during a computer-assisted telephone interview.

In a telephone survey, a trained interviewer reads questions to a respondent and records his or her answers. As in the case of in-person surveys, telephone interviewers can clarify instructions and questions for greater validity of responses. In addition, telephone surveys permit more anonymity than face-to-face interviews, which helps to increase the likelihood of providing truthful answers and decrease response bias, and allows for the inclusion of more sensitive topics.

Telephone surveys are generally less time-consuming and more cost-efficient than in-person surveys. However, trust and credibility are difficult to establish over the phone. As a result, respondents are less likely to agree to participate in a telephone survey than one that is conducted face to face. It is also easier to ignore a phone call, especially when call display indicates an unrecognized phone number. Nonetheless, with repeated callbacks—which are relatively cost-effective when using telephone surveys—response rates can eventually reach as high as 90 percent (Neuman & Robson, 2012). However, more and more people are opting for cell phones over land lines, and new technologies will continue to enable end users to block and screen unwanted calls—including those from unknown sources such as computers—thereby limiting the future viability of telephone surveys.

Research in Action

Population Research Lab

Every year the Population Research Lab at the University of Alberta surveys 1200 Albertans on a wide range of social issues, such as health care, social networking, and retirement, using a random-sample computer-assisted telephone interview method. Researchers at universities and other interested parties such as organizations or businesses can pay to include questions on the shared survey. For more information, visit the home page for the Alberta Survey at prl.ualberta.ca/AlbertaSurvey.aspx.

Internet Surveys

From 2000 to present, Internet surveys have become an increasingly popular data collection tool. Internet surveys can be conducted in one of two ways: A respondent is sent a questionnaire as an email attachment to save, complete, and return, or, more typically today, a respondent is asked to visit a website where a questionnaire is made available for completion (Dillman, Smyth, & Christian, 2009). Various web-based companies offer survey support to individuals and organizations wishing to develop and administer online surveys. User-friendly templates make formatting and question construction relatively straightforward, even for novice researchers and those with less-than-ideal computer programming skills. For only a modest monthly fee for a software license or subscription, Internet surveys can be readily developed and sent out. Most everyone today has access to the Internet, and respondents can reply almost immediately. Feedback provided to open-ended questions on Internet surveys is much more detailed than what is given through more traditional data collection formats (Dillman, Smyth, & Christian, 2009). Moreover, the results for closed-ended items are often tabulated with the software program, making this the most efficient and inexpensive form of survey data collection compared to the other methods that require ever-increasing expenses related to travel, postage, printing, and/or long-distance telephone bills, followed by data coding, data entering, data analysis, and then data interpretation.

Unfortunately the many advantages are overshadowed by some of the drawbacks. One of biggest drawbacks unique to this form of survey is the lack of a random sample. The people who choose to complete an Internet survey are generally not determined from a sampling frame, and even in cases where they are, those who respond are not likely to constitute a representative sample due to high rates of non-response. Internet surveys have the greatest variance in response rate. Some studies obtain a very low response rate, while other can secure a modest response rate. They also have a lower overall rate of response compared to the other data collection methods (Smyth & Pearson, 2011). Given the lack of personal contact and connection, Internet surveys are the easiest to delete or otherwise ignore. Dillman, Smyth, and Christian (2009) recommend using highly tailored Internet survey approaches that increase response rates through a careful consideration of all aspects of the survey process, from the targeted sample, to the form of initial contact, to the benefits of participation, to the sampling procedures, as well as the many features of the questionnaire design. For a summary of the advantage and disadvantages of the methods, see Figure 7.1.

FIGURE 7.1   **Advantages and Disadvantages of Survey Data Collection Methods**

Face-to-Face	Mail-Out	Telephone	Internet
Advantages	**Advantages**	**Advantages**	**Advantages**
High response rate	Efficiency	Modest time and cost	Inexpensive and efficient
Good rapport	Sensitive topics	Computer-assisted	Software can aid data coding and analyses
Ability to clarify questions	No interviewer bias	Ability to clarify instructions and questions	Detailed responses to open-ended questions
Detailed responses	Ability to include visual aids	Likely to answer sensitive questions	
	Anonymity		
Disadvantages	**Disadvantages**	**Disadvantages**	**Disadvantages**
Expensive	Slow and modest return rate	Trust is lacking	Low response rate
Time-consuming	Expensive	Unlisted numbers and blocked calls	Not a random sample
Interviewer bias	Inability to clarify questions or instructions		Requires Internet access
Not great for sensitive topics			

Test Yourself

- What is the overarching limitation of data collected from survey respondents?
- Under what circumstances might it be preferable to use a self-report questionnaire rather than a face-to-face interview?
- Which of the survey data collection methods produces the highest response rate?

Research on the Net

Survey Monkey

One of the more well-established survey software programs is Survey Monkey, an Internet-based company. The program helps users create their own surveys, such as Facebook surveys or telephone surveys, using a variety of question formats, such as multiple-choice, open-ended, etc. Survey Monkey also provides support for data collection and analysis. At the home page for the site, you can find all kinds of survey templates (e.g., customer satisfaction surveys, market research surveys, student feedback) that will help you design survey questions. You can also create your own survey for free using an expert template. While you can create good questions with this software, there are some limitations to how you can ask certain types of questions and how you can set up the response formats. Visit the site at surveymonkey.com.

Survey Construction

LO5

A survey is only as good as the questions asked. Keeping in mind the overall purpose and objectives of the study, a researcher aims to develop valid and reliable measures of the sought-after concepts or constructs. While the exact wording of questions will differ from survey to survey, good questions are "clear, short, unbiased, [current] and relevant to the target respondents" (Sue & Ritter, 2007, p. 29). In addition, effective surveys avoid the pitfalls associated with the use of double-barrelled items, negative questions, and certain kinds of terminology such as slang words and abbreviations. In this section I discuss established practices that can be considered the essential "dos" and "don'ts" of survey construction, including aspects of question wording, response formats, and design layout. Note that although I keep discussing questions, in many surveys respondents are asked in statement form for their opinions about items, rather than in the form of actual questions.

Question Wording

Be Clear

First and foremost, survey questions need to be clear so that respondents readily understand what is being asked of them. If the goal is to find out what students think of courses and instructors, the evaluation tool should include items focused specifically on aspects of the course, such as course content, assignments and tests, and level of difficulty, as well as aspects of the instructor, such as communication style, clarity, and knowledge. One way to help make the objectives of questions clear is to state items in complete-sentence form. For example, course evaluation surveys prompt students to rate their level of agreement with a number of statements, such as: "The course met my learning objectives" and "Overall, my instructor was effective." Note that an item such as "office hours" on its own is vague and therefore inadequately worded since a respondent cannot tell whether he or she is being asked to comment on whether there were office hours, whether the office hours attended were helpful, or something else entirely. A much better item, stated in a complete sentence, makes the point clear: "My instructor was available during regularly scheduled office hours."

Another way to make questions clear is to define central concepts and constructs so that respondents similarly interpret items as intended before they provide an answer. For example, rating "health" can entail aspects of well-being (e.g., social, physical, mental), as well as the absence of illness or disease (Statistics Canada, 2013d). Similarly, asking respondents if they have experienced "aggressive driving" from other motorists necessitates a common understanding of the sorts of actions that constitute aggressive driving, such as aggressive tailgating, lights flashed at them because the other motorist was annoyed, rude gestures, and/or being deliberately obstructed or prevented from moving their vehicle (Neuman, Pfefer, Slack, Hardy, Raub, Lucke, & Wark, 2003).

Finally, one way to be sure you are writing clear questions is to assume a lack of knowledge about the subject matter. For example, a criminologist interested in public opinion toward crimes and associated penalties should not assume that respondents understand anything about crime from a legal perspective (e.g., how Canada's legal system originated), or how specific crimes are categorized in Canada (e.g., based on their perceived seriousness and depending on the intended victim of harm). All relevant background information should be provided, along with definitions for all crime-related terminology that would not be considered general public knowledge.

Keep It Short

Words, questions, and the survey itself should all be kept relatively short. In most cases, word concepts should be stated at the most basic level possible. For example, the term "job" or where you "work" is more straightforward than "employer" or "place of employment," and a prompt for the "city where you live" is much easier to interpret than the "locality where you currently reside." Similarly, long questions are more difficult to interpret since they may raise several points or include multiple concepts, and this increases the likelihood that different respondents will hear or read different things into the question being asked. Even the overall length of the survey itself is a concern. The longer it takes to complete a questionnaire or interview, the greater the likelihood that respondents will lose interest, potentially leading to more errors. For example, respondents may give inaccurate answers because they are no longer paying close attention to what is being asked or are rushing to finish. In addition, length can contribute to a greater tendency for respondents to leave items blank or choose to end their participation before completing the survey.

Minimize Bias

Minimizing bias is also an important goal in the creation of good survey questions. Bias exists when a question is worded in such a way that a particular response or opinion appears to be the most appropriate one or is favoured in some way. For example, it would be difficult for a respondent to disagree with an item stating "To ensure the highest-quality education for Canadian children, a greater portion of tax dollars must be spent on education." From a social desirability standpoint, few respondents would admit that they fail to endorse a practice tied to quality education. Similarly, an item stating "As a proud Canadian, do you plan to vote in the next federal election?" implies that only those who are ashamed to be Canadian would respond in anything but the affirmative. A question is considered leading if it suggests the appropriate answer. Instead, questions should be worded in a neutral, value-free manner, as in "Do you support giving more tax dollars to education?" and "Do you plan to vote in the next federal election?" or "Did you vote in the last federal election?"

A question can also be biased by the inclusion of endorsements by high-ranking individuals. For example, knowing the president or senior manager of a company supports a particular position makes employees more likely to provide similar opinions. Similarly, a question can be biased by references to prestigious institutions, organizations, or professions, such as "Do you agree or disagree with the Canadian Medical Association's decision?" or "Do you agree or disagree with the proposed solutions suggested by researchers at McGill University?" While there is no guarantee of an endorsement, in all of these examples, the prestige of the person or organization biases the likelihood that respondents will provide support (Babbie, 1990).

Ensure Relevancy and Currency

Surveys also need to be relevant to most participants. That is, if a researcher is interested in attitudes toward some topic, it should be a topic that the respondents know about and are likely to have an informed opinion on. Most students, for example, can tell a researcher about the quality of instruction they received in a course they have taken. Course evaluation surveys are especially relevant to students more so than to administrators, who may know something about the class and instructor based on the course outline, a peer review, or the instructor's employment history, but who lack the overall knowledge of what actually occurs in the classroom on a regular basis. Similarly, a student resource centre looking for ways to improve its services to students with disabilities should ask its client base, not the more general student body, for direction.

Even with a carefully selected sample, not all questions on a survey will apply equally to all participants. Consider the case of a criminologist who is interested in learning more about variables associated with particular aggressive driving behaviours. Rather than ask a series of questions about each aggressive form of driving that may only apply to a very small fraction of the respondents, the researcher can include **contingency questions**. Contingency questions are special questions that are answered only if a particular issue is relevant to the respondent. This is usually determined by an affirmative response to a main question on the issue. If the issue does not apply, the respondent is supposed to skip over to another part of the survey. If the issue applies, the respondent is prompted to answer one or more subsequent questions. Figure 7.2 shows how a main question about one particular form of aggressive driving with a contingency question could appear on a questionnaire.

Contingency question A question prompting additional information about a previous item identified as relevant for the respondent.

FIGURE 7.2
A Contingency Question Based on a Previous Item

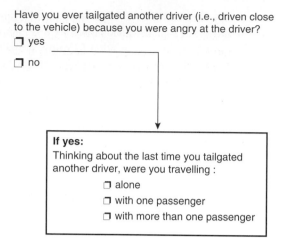

Have you ever tailgated another driver (i.e., driven close to the vehicle) because you were angry at the driver?

❒ yes

❒ no

If yes:
Thinking about the last time you tailgated another driver, were you travelling :

❒ alone

❒ with one passenger

❒ with more than one passenger

Finally, to help increase accuracy, survey questions should be limited to events occurring now or events that will happen or happened in the not-too-distant future or past. For example, if I asked you what classes you plan to enroll in next semester, I would obtain more reliable results than if I asked you what you plan to enroll in two years from now. Similarly, asking respondents about daily events, such as what they had to eat or drink in the last 24 hours, is likely to produce a much more accurate recollection than asking them what they did last month, or even last week. This is why course evaluations occur near the end of the term while students are still in the classes they are evaluating. Imagine rating a class you took several years ago. How many details can you recall pertaining to how the instructor organized the class or whether course materials were appropriately reflected on exams? An exception to this rule is rare but highly salient events, which are likely to be recalled for a much longer period of time. For example, people can readily recall victimization experiences: "Within the last year, were you the victim of a motor vehicle theft?" However, significant experiences are also likely to be inaccurately reported by respondents who tend to bring important events forward in time, a survey response error known as "telescoping." That is, a respondent might say "yes" to victimization involving a motor vehicle theft even though the person's car was stolen three years ago, not within the last year. This occurs because the event is salient to the respondent, not because the respondent is intentionally fabricating his or her response.

Avoid Double-Barrelled Questions

Double-barrelled question A question prompting a single answer to a combination of questions.

In addition to suggestions for what researchers should do, there are also practices to avoid in question construction. First, researchers should always avoid the use of double-barrelled questions. A **double-barrelled question** is a question prompting a "single answer to a combination of questions" (Babbie, 1990, p. 128). The question contains more than one idea, often identified by the use of the joiner "and." For example, an item asking respondents to agree or disagree with the following statement, "The Canadian Government should spend more money on health care *and* the environment" contains two separate opinions, one related to health care and one about the environment. What if the respondent feels more money should go to health care but not the environment (or vice versa)? In either case, a respondent would likely provide a neutral response to reflect a combination of agreement and disagreement, even though his or her response is not neutral toward either item.

Avoid Negative Questions

Negative question A question made up of the negative form of a statement.

Researchers should also try to avoid the use of negative questions. A **negative question** is a question made up of the negative or opposing form of a statement. In everyday usage, a negative question generally prompts a favourable response: "Don't you hate it when it rains on golf night?" "Yes, I do hate it." "Aren't you going to accept your award in person?" "Yes, I am." "Isn't this cheesecake excellent?" "Yes, it is." If you encountered one of these questions on a multiple-choice exam, it likely took the form of an item asking you to pick out the exception: "All of the following statements are part of this theory except. . ." or "Which of the following is not part of this theory. . ." Although commonly used in the English language, negative questions on surveys are difficult to understand and should be reworked into the affirmative form. Consider the case of motorists in Ontario who are caught texting, typing, emailing, dialling" or chatting while using a hand-held device such as cell phone and fined $155 (Ontario Transportation Ministry, 2012). A negative question on a survey by the transportation ministry might be: "Don't you support the new distracted driving law?" In the positive format, it is much easier to understand as: "Do you support the new distracted driving law?"

Avoid Technical Terms, Abbreviations, and Other Jargon

Researchers should also steer clear of highly technical or specialized terms, abbreviations, and informal jargon. Every group, organization, profession, culture, and subculture develops its own specialized language over time. At a Canadian university, students might know how to become an RPN (Registered Psychiatric Nurse), find out about a BCS degree (Bachelor of Communications Studies), attend a meeting of the AGC (Academic Governance Council), apply to an REB (Research Ethics Board), and see what the SIFE club is up to (Students in Free Enterprise). While convenient for those directly involved in such groups at a particular university, abbreviations are meaningless to those outside the group and/or can be readily misinterpreted. For example, AGC also stands for Associated Gospel Churches of Canada, and it is the name of a Canadian automotive glass assembly company. Researchers should always include the full name the first time an identifying term is used, and when necessary explain what the term refers to.

Slang terms, sometimes called idioms or jargon, are words or phrases that are widely used and understood within the culture or group in which they originated. For example, an anger scale that asks about a respondent's tendency to "fly off the handle," meaning "lose one's temper," is unlikely to be understood by someone whose first language is anything but English. Similarly, regular users of marijuana may refer to their drug of choice as pot or weed. Pot smokers understand how to roll a joint and inhale by taking a toke. They might also save the roach (i.e., the butt left from a joint) if they are running low on supply. If a survey is directed at a particular subgroup, the slang for that subgroup might be relevant to incorporate. However, if the survey is aimed at a more general population, avoid slang terms.

Developing Response Formats

In some cases a survey respondent is asked to provide any answer that comes to mind, while in other cases a respondent is asked to choose a response that best approximates his or her view.

Open- and Closed-Ended Questions

Open-ended question A question prompting any response deemed appropriate in the participant's own words.

Open-ended questions prompt any response a participant deems appropriate in his or her own words, such as: "In your opinion, what are the advantages of published ratings of instruction?" This could be answered in an infinite number of ways. One student might answer that question by noting something like: "I would use them to help me choose courses," while another student might respond with: "They help students match their learning styles with particular instructors." Open-ended questions are advantageous for obtaining highly detailed responses, learning about unanticipated views, and finding out how respondents think about certain issues (i.e., their thought processes). Open-ended questions are used most often in cases where the response categories are not well known in advance, as might be the case in a more exploratory study. For example, in looking for effective ways to reduce prostitution, a criminologist might ask prostitution offenders if there are any potential consequences for their actions that would lead them to stop using the services of prostitutes.

Closed-ended question A question prompting an answer selected from a pre-determined set of responses provided.

Closed-ended questions prompt a participant to respond using a pre-determined or a fixed-choice set of responses, usually consisting of two, four, five, or seven choices. Closed-ended questions often require carefully worded instructions that help the participant understand how to respond, much like you might be instructed to choose the one best option from a set of four potentially correct responses on a multiple-choice test. By using the same response choices and by limiting the number of possible responses across participants, researchers can readily code, analyze, and compare the answers provided. A drawback is that respondents can select answers to questions they know little or nothing about (much like a student might guess on a multiple-choice exam). In addition, the answer a respondent wishes to provide may or may not be included in the provided set of response choices.

The most commonly used response format for questionnaires are closed-ended ordinal categories because they are easy to complete, they allow for range of intensity in responses, and they lend themselves well to the measurement of attitudes and behaviours (Dillman, Smyth, & Christian, 2009). For example, Howell and Symbaluk (2001) asked students to provide views on potential outcomes of published ratings of instruction. One question asked if instructor evaluations were made accessible to students, how likely is it that this practice would: "Increase the likelihood that students will participate in student ratings of instruction?" Students were asked to rate the likelihood using an ordinal measure ranging from not at all likely, to slightly likely, to moderately likely, to very likely, to extremely likely.

Another especially popular response category arrangement is the use of a Likert format depicting levels of agreement with the ratings: strongly disagree, disagree, neutral, agree, and strongly agree. For example, a student might be asked to indicate his or her level of agreement pertaining to the statement "Overall, my instructor is effective" by checking off the appropriate response box:

❐ strongly disagree   ❐ disagree   ❐ neutral   ❐ agree   ❐ strongly agree

Survey respondents are frequently asked to rate their opinions using closed-ended ordinal response categories.

Exhaustive
Comprehensive enough to include all likely responses.

Mutually exclusive Response categories are separate and distinct from each other.

Response categories for closed-ended questions should always be **exhaustive** and **mutually exclusive**. Exhaustive signifies that the choices are comprehensive enough to cover the range of all possible responses. For example, asking participants in an Internet survey to select their age from a set of age categories—for example, 19 and under, 20 to 29, 30 to 39, 40 to 49, 50 to 59, and 60 to 69—doesn't allow for the appropriate selection by individuals who are 70 years of age and older. To remedy this so the categories are exhaustive, the researcher should add additional categories and/or include an open-ended final category, such as 70 and over. Mutually exclusive indicates that all of the response categories are separate and distinct from each other. Age responses are not mutually exclusive if one category includes "20 and under" while the next category is "20 to 30" because the categories overlap. A respondent's age should correspond to one and only one response category. Due to the limited number of responses, closed-ended items are much easier to code for and interpret than open-ended items when it gets to the data analysis stage of research.

In addition to the wording of questions and response categories, a survey researcher needs to think through a few other considerations before finalizing a survey instrument.

Appealing Format and Design

Every effort should be made to make a questionnaire as professional-looking and appealing as possible to the potential respondent. This can include decisions about the type of font used, the size of the lettering, the arrangement of the questions, the style of the question numbering, and the format of the responses. While there is no exact formula for what works and doesn't work, the objective is to strike a balance between design appeal and ease of completion. Respondents are more apt to complete a questionnaire that is easy to navigate. This means the questions should be well spaced (uncluttered), and the response formats should be clearly laid out and be relatively easy to complete.

Perhaps the questionnaire can be divided into three or four sections with ten questions in each. This seems less daunting than answering 30 questions in a row. Related questions on the same topic should generally be grouped together. Also, by using the same response formats for a series of questions or items, respondents can provide answers quite quickly and will be less discouraged by survey length. That said, there should also be some variation in question and response formats to prevent respondents from developing the tendency to provide the same answer throughout, regardless of the specific question. For example, if a person agrees with one item, that person may agree with most items without reading them carefully.

Clear Instructions

Whether in questionnaire or interview format, a respondent completing a survey needs to be provided with clear instructions for how to provide responses. Are respondents supposed to indicate their opinion by checking off a box, circling a number, or providing a written response? Are respondents supposed to choose all of the responses that apply to a given question or only the one that most closely approximates their view? In the case of an interview, are the respondents supposed to choose from a range of answers provided or say anything that comes to mind? Even trained interviewers need carefully laid out instructions for how to proceed with the survey and how to give standardized responses to potential questions raised by the respondents.

Question Order

Researchers also need to be careful about the order in which specific questions are included. It is a good idea to include a few relatively simple, non-threatening questions at the beginning of a survey, such as demographic questions designed to describe the respondent like: "Are you a full- or part-time student? and "On which campus do you mainly attend classes?" Threatening questions tend to be ones that involve sensitive or personal issues (e.g., income, ethnicity, relationships), private behaviour (e.g., sexual behaviour, alcohol consumption), or socially undesirable practices (e.g., aggressive driving, racism)—all of which are likely to form the basis of research in the social sciences. Non-threatening questions are especially important at the start of interviews where developing a good rapport with the respondent can be critical to securing participation.

Sensitive questions should be left to near-end of a survey because by this po[...]
the respondent has already developed a rapport with the interviewer or has
already invested time on the questionnaire and will be more likely to provide
answers. Also, placing threatening questions near the end helps to ensure that
most of the survey will be completed even if respondents choose not to respond
to these items (Rea & Parker, 2005).

Pre-testing the Instrument

The best way to obtain feedback about the design, length, wording, formatting,
instructions, or any other survey feature is to pre-test it. A pre-test is a trial run
using a different group of respondents than those who will be included in the
final sample. Just as having someone proofread a paper before you turn it in to
your professor can identify errors, a pre-test can help identify problems with the
survey. At the minimum, a pre-test will help determine if respondents can readily follow the instructions as intended, if the questions are worded clearly, if the
responses are appropriate, if there are any obvious errors, and how long it takes
to complete the survey.

Research on the Net

WebSM

Today, owners of smart phones and users of
popular social media such as Facebook are the
latest sought-after population of potential survey respondents (Blair, Czaja, & Blair, 2014). Of
course, with most advantages come drawbacks,
including response and non-response biases based
on attributes of cell phone and social media users,
such as they tend to be younger. To learn more

the advantages and disadvantages of conducting
surveys over the Internet as well as how new media
can be used in research, I highly recommend the
WebSurveyMethodology website at websm.org.
The site is maintained by the University of Ljub-
ljana, Faculty of Social Science, Centre for Methodology and Informatics, in Slovenia. It contains a
current bibliography of more than 6000 articles on
methodological issues related to web surveys.

Test Yourself

- What features make for good survey questions?
- What practices need to be avoided in the construction of good survey questions?
- When would it be appropriate to use an open-ended question?
- Why is the question order important in the creation of a survey?

Chapter Summary

LO1 **Describe the purpose of a survey and the kinds of questions surveys ask.**

The purpose of a survey is to find things out by asking questions. A researcher might choose this method to describe a population, to learn more about people's feelings about some issue, to determine the frequency of certain behaviours, and/ or to examine ways in which various variables are related. Common types of questions include demographic questions that help describe a population's features, knowledge questions about factual information, attitude questions made up of opinions about people and events, and behaviour questions about respondents' actions and experiences.

LO2 **Explain why research objectives need to be clarified prior to the onset of research.**

The research objectives outline what the study is about and they provide direction for the creation of appropriate questions for obtaining answers on the topic of interest. Questions that help facilitate this process include: "What needs to be known?"; "Why does it need to be known?"; "What else needs to be known?"; "What will the results of the survey accomplish?"; "What decisions will be based on the results of the survey?"; and "Is a survey the best method?"

LO3 **Outline key methodological considerations that precede survey research.**

A researcher needs to decide upon the type of design for the survey (e.g., a longitudinal or cross-sectional design), which sampling method is most appropriate (e.g., a probability- or non-probability-based technique), who will be included in the sample, and how the central variables are to be measured or how to design the survey. In addition, a researcher needs to determine if the survey will be administered using a questionnaire or interview format, how relevant ethical concerns will be addressed, and how the survey will be administered, such as in person, by mail, over the Internet, or by telephone.

LO4 **Compare and contrast questionnaires and interviews.**

A *questionnaire* is a data collection tool consisting of a series of questions or items to which a respondent provides answers. An *interview* is also a structured data collection method, but in this case an interviewer asks the questions and records the answers provided by the respondent. *Face-to-face interviews* produce the highest response rate and result in rich, detailed information, but also constitute the most expensive and time-consuming survey data collection method. Interviewer bias is also problematic in the case of in-person interviews and is alleviated through the use of mail-out questionnaires. *Mail-out surveys* also afford greater anonymity to the respondent, who is more likely to provide answers to sensitive questions but less likely to complete or send back the survey. *Telephone surveys* are good for establishing rapport (like face-to-face interviews), they are less costly than in-person surveys, and they take less time to conduct. However, sampling frames are likely to be incomplete and it is difficult to establish trust and credibility over the phone. *Internet surveys* can reach a vast number of respondents and collect information inexpensively in a short period of time. The greatest drawback to Internet surveys is their lack of a random sample and their low overall response rate compared to the other data collection formats.

LO5 **Identify recommended "dos" and "don'ts" in the construction of surveys.**

Good survey questions are clear, short, free from bias, relevant, and time-sensitive. Poor questions that need to be avoided contain terms and phrases that are double-barrelled, negative, highly technical, abbreviated, or full of jargon. Open-ended questions prompt any response deemed appropriate by the participant, whereas closed-ended questions force the respondent to choose an answer from a fixed set of responses. Surveys should also have appealing designs and clear instructions, be carefully ordered, and undergo pre-testing.

Research Reflection

1. For each statement listed below, indicate why it is not suitable as a survey question and then rewrite it to correct the error. Assume that students were instructed to rate their level of agreement with the following statements.

   1. The instructor was helpful and organized.
   2. The instructor posted lectures notes on BB for students to access online.
   3. The instructor didn't always start class on time.
   4. The instructor used effective pedagogy to facilitate student engagement.
   5. The dean's offer of full-time employment to this instructor is a good decision.

2. Suppose a researcher wished to describe the prevalence of dangerous driving behaviours among motorists in Ontario. Design five closed-ended survey questions that could help meet this research objective.

3. Duff, Michelow, Chow, Ivsins, and Stockwell (2010) conducted a survey on drug use in Victoria and Vancouver. Why do you suppose the researchers targeted the following three groups for inclusion in their sample: 1) club and rave party attendees, 2) street-involved youth aged 15 to 19 years, and 3) street-entrenched drug users aged 19 years and older?

4. Fidelis Ifedi (2008)'s longitudinal study of Canadian involvement in sports based on Statistics Canada's General Social Survey data from 1992, 1998, and 2005 showed a decline in sports participation over time for all age groups.
   a. What do you think might account for the decline?
   b. In each study, respondents were asked: "Did you regularly participate in any sports over the last 12 months?" If this was your study, how would you define "sports"? Would an activity such as jogging fit into your definition? Why or why not?
   c. How would you define "regular participation"? To read the full report and/or to learn how these terms are defined by Statistics Canada, go to: statcan.gc.ca/pub/81-595-m/81-595-m2008060-eng.pdf.

5. In 2010, the Conservative government decided to replace what was formerly a mandatory census conducted every five years with a voluntary one. From a methodological standpoint, what are some of the potential implications of this change? Note that the voluntary 2011 National Household Survey had a response rate of 68.6 percent compared to 93.5 percent for the mandatory one in 2006 (Fekete, 2013).

Learning Through Practice

Objective: To evaluate a service provider on campus.
Directions:

1. Pair up with someone in the class.
2. Identify various service providers on campus, such as the library, a lunch vendor, the computer help desk, etc.
3. Select one of the service providers and discuss ways in which the service provider could be evaluated (e.g., speed of service, quality of service).
4. Design a questionnaire consisting of four closed-ended questions and one open-ended question that could be used to evaluate different aspects of the services provided.
5. Pre-test the five questions with another pair from the class. Make any necessary revisions to the questionnaire based on information provided during the test. For example, are you measuring what you intend to? Were the questions clear to the pre-testers?

Research Resources

1. To learn more about framing research questions and developing them into high-quality survey questions, I recommend Guppy, N., & Gray, G. (2008). *Successful surveys: Research methods and practice* (4th ed.). Toronto, ON: Nelson.
2. To learn more about sampling considerations in survey research and for more information on questionnaire development, see Blair, J., Czaja, R. F., & Blair, E. A. (2014). *Designing surveys: A guide to decisions and procedures.* Thousand Oaks, CA: Sage Publications.
3. For assistance in questionnaire layout and design, please refer to Dillman, D. A., Smyth, J. D., & Christian, L. M. (2009). *Internet, mail, and mixed-mode surveys: The tailored design method* (3rd ed.). New York, NY: John Wiley & Sons.
4. To explore the scientific context of survey research and to learn more about the underlying logic of survey sampling, refer to Babbie, E. (1990). *Survey research methods* (2nd ed.). Belmont, CA: Wadsworth Publishing Company.
5. For a step-by-step guide on how to conduct surveys, including how to analyze and organize survey data, I recommend Fink, A. (2009). *How to conduct surveys: A step-by-step guide* (4th ed.). Thousand Oaks, CA: Sage Publications.

References

Aronson, E., Wilson, T. D., Akert, R. M., & Fehr, B. (2013). *Social psychology* (5th Can. ed.). Toronto, ON: Pearson Education Canada.

Babbie, E. (1990). *Survey research methods* (2nd ed.). Belmont, CA: Wadsworth Publishing Company.

Blair, J., Czaja, R. F., & Blair, E. A. (2014). *Designing surveys: A guide to decisions and procedures.* Thousand Oaks, CA: Sage Publications.

Bradburn, N., Sudman, S., & Wansink, B. (2004). *Asking questions: The definitive guide to questionnaire design.* San Francisco, CA: John Wiley & Sons.

Chawla, R. K., & Uppal, S. (2012). *Household debt in Canada.* Ottawa, ON: Statistics Canada. Retrieved from www.statcan.gc.ca/pub/75-001-x/2012002/article/11636-eng.htm

Citizenship and Immigration Canada. (2012). *The citizenship test.* Ottawa, ON: Author. Retrieved from: www.cic.gc.ca/english/citizenship/cit-test.asp

Czaja, R., & Blair, J. (1996). *Designing surveys: A guide to decisions and procedures.* Thousand Oaks, CA: Pine Forge Press.

Dillman, D. A., Smyth, J. D., & Christian, L. M. (2009). *Internet, mail, and mixed-mode surveys: The tailored design method* (3rd ed.). Hoboken, NJ: John Wiley & Sons.

Duff, C., Michelow, W., Chow, C., Ivsins, A., & Stockwell, T. (2009). The Canadian recreational drug use survey: Aims, methods, and first results. *Contemporary Drug Problems, 36* (Fall/Winter), 517–539.

Fekete, J. (2013, May 4). Making sense of the census: The National Household Survey comes with a few caveats. *Postmedia News.* Don Mills, ON: Canada. com. Retrieved from www.canada.com/technology/Making+sense+census+National+Household+Survey+comes+with+caveats/8333345/story.html

Fink, A. (2003). *How to ask survey questions* (2nd ed.). Thousand Oaks, CA: Sage Publications.

Fink, A. (2009). *How to conduct surveys: A step-by-step guide* (4th ed.). Thousand Oaks, CA: Sage Publications.

Fowler, F. J. (2009). *Survey research methods* (4th ed.). Thousand Oaks, CA: Sage Publications.

Groves, R. M. (1989). *Survey errors and survey costs.* Hoboken, NJ: John Wiley & Sons.

Guppy, N., & Gray, G. (2008). *Successful surveys: Research methods and practice* (4th ed.). Toronto, ON: Nelson.

Hägelli, P. (2005). *Winter backcountry use trend estimates for Western Canada.* Revelstoke, BC: Canadian Avalanche Association.

Hay, D. I. (2009). *Poverty reduction policies and programs in Canada* [electronic book]. Canadian Council on Social Development. Retrieved from: http://site.ebrary.com.ezproxy.macewan.ca/lib/macewanpubpolicy/docDetail.action?docID=10330319

Heberlein, T. A., & Baumgartner, R. (1978). Factors affecting response rates to mailed questionnaires: A quantitative analysis of the published literature. *American Sociological Review, 43,* 447–462.

Howell, A. J., & Symbaluk, D. G. (2001). Published student ratings: Reconciling the views of students and faculty. *Journal of Educational Psychology, 93,* 790–796.

Ifedi, F. (2008). Sport participation in Canada, 2005. *Research paper.* Ottawa, ON: Statistics Canada: Culture, Tourism, and the Centre for Education Statistics. Catalogue no. 81-595-MIE—No. 060. Retrieved from www.statcan.gc.ca/pub/81-595-m/81-595-m2008060-eng.pdf

Jansen, H. (2010). The logic of qualitative survey research and its position in the field of social research methods. *Forum Qualitative Sozialforschung/Forum: Qualitative Social Research, 11*(2), Art. 11. Retrieved from http://nbn-resolving.de/urn:nbn:de:0114-fqs1002110

Milner, H. (2007). Political knowledge and participation among young Canadians and Americans. *IRPP Working Paper number 2007-01.* Montreal, QC: IRPP, November 2007. Retrieved from www.irpp.org/en/research/strengthening-canadian-democracy/political-knowledge-and-participation-among-young-canadians-and-americans

Nanos, N. (2012). Canadians rate highly the issues close to their day-to-day lives. Policy Challenges for 2012. *Policy Options, 2012, August.* Montreal, QC: Institute for Research on Public Policy. Retrieved from www.irpp.org/en/po/policy-challenges-for-2020/canadians-rate-highly-the-issues-close-to-their-day-to-day-lives

Neuman, W. L., & Robson, K. (2012). *Basics of social research: Qualitative and quantitative approaches* (2nd Can. ed.). Toronto, ON: Pearson Canada.

Neuman, T. R., Pfefer, R., Slack, K. L., Hardy, K. K., Raub, R., Lucke, R., & Wark, R. (2003). *National cooperative highway research program report 500: Guidance for implementation of the AASHTO Strategic Highways Safety Plan. Volume 1: A guide for addressing aggressive-driving collisions.* Washington, DC: Transportation Research Board.

Ontario Ministry of Transportation. (2012). Driving requires your full attention. *Road safety: Distracted driving.* Ottawa, ON: Queen's Printer for Ontario. Retrieved from www.mto.gov.on.ca/english/safety/distracted-driving/index.shtml

Rea, L. M., & Parker, R. A. (2005). *Designing and conducting survey research: A comprehensive guide* (3rd ed). San Francisco, CA: Jossey-Bass.

Saris, W. E., & Gallhofer, I. N. (2007). *Design, evaluation, and analysis of questionnaires for survey research.* Hoboken, NJ: John Wiley & Sons.

Smyth, J. D., & Pearson, J. E. (2011). Internet survey methods: A review of strengths, weaknesses, and innovations. In M. Das, P. Ester, & L. Kaczmirek (Eds.), *Social and behavioral research and the Internet* (pp. 11–44). New York, NY: Routledge.

Statistics Canada. (2013a). *About us.* Ottawa, ON: Author. Retrieved from www.statcan.gc.ca/survey-enquete/subject-list-sujet-eng.htm

Statistics Canada. (2013b). *Canadian financial capability survey.* Ottawa, ON: Author. Retrieved from www23.statcan.gc.ca:81/imdb/p2SV.pl?Function=getSurvey&SDDS=5159&lang=en&db=imdb&adm=8&dis=2#a3

Statistics Canada. (2013c). Winnipeg, Manitoba (Code 4611040) and Division No. 11, Manitoba (Code 4611) (table). *Census profile. 2011 Census.* Statistics Canada Catalogue no. 98-316-XWE. Ottawa. Released October 24, 2012. Retrieved from www12.statcan.gc.ca/census-recensement/2011/dp-pd/prof/index.cfm?Lang=E

Statistics Canada. (2013d). Health profile: Definitions, sources and symbols. In *Health in Canada.* Ottawa, ON: Author. Retrieved from www12.statcan.gc.ca/health-sante/82-228/help-aide/DQ-QD04.cfm?Lang=E

Statistics Canada. (2011, April 21). Study: Debt and family type. *The daily.* Ottawa, ON: Author. Retrieved from www.statcan.gc.ca/daily-quotidien/110421/dq110421b-eng.htm

Statistics Canada. (2010). *Persons in low income after tax.* Ottawa, ON: Author. Retrieved from www.statcan.gc.ca/tables-tableaux/sum-som/l01/cst01/famil19a-eng.htm

Sue, V. M., & Ritter, L. A. (2007). *Conducting online surveys.* Thousand Oaks, CA: Sage Publications.

Wolfer, L. (2007). *Real research: Conducting and evaluating research in the social sciences.* Toronto, ON: Pearson Education.

Endnote

[1]Gray, G., & Guppy, N. (1994). *Successful surveys: Research methods and practice.* Toronto, ON: Harcourt Brace & Company, Canada.

Unobtrusive Methods

8

Learning Objectives

After reading this chapter, students should be able to do the following:

LO1 Define unobtrusive methods and explain what is meant by reactive and non-reactive research methods.

LO2 Explain what physical trace analysis is used for and differentiate between erosion and accretion measures.

LO3 Differentiate between public and private archives and note a main advantage and disadvantage of archival analysis.

LO4 Define content analysis and outline the steps for conducting a content analysis.

LO5 Explain what secondary analysis of existing data entails, identify key sources for secondary data analysis, and note a main advantage and disadvantage of secondary data analysis.

"A major confounding factor in social research is eliminated in nonreaction studies because the observed person or group is not able to react to the measurement process—that is, is not able to manipulate presentation-of-self for the researcher." (Jackson & Verberg, 2007, p. 143)[1]

Introduction

LO1

Unobtrusive research methods
Strategies in which the researcher examines evidence of people's behaviour or attitudes, rather than interacting directly with those being studied.

Most methods rely on participants who provide the data of interest to researchers through their actions or words, such as experiments, surveys, ethnographic studies, or qualitative interviews. These methods are considered obtrusive because they necessitate an intrusion into the lives of participants to obtain the data. They are also considered to be reactive because participants are responding or reacting to the research instrument (e.g., the questions posed on a questionnaire or an experimental manipulation), the researcher (e.g., a qualitative interviewer), and/or to the study itself (e.g., demand characteristics). In contrast, non-reactive methods, called **unobtrusive research methods**, are ones in which "the researcher examines evidence of people's behaviour or attitudes, rather than interacting directly with those being studied" (Strand & Weiss, 2005, p. 161). This evidence takes the form of a variety of sources of information created by and for people (e.g., government statistics, official documents, newspaper stories, personal diaries, song lyrics, and television scripts), and it can also include things left behind by people (e.g. litter, belongings, patterns of erosion). Notably, the information may be originally produced for a particular purpose (e.g., song lyrics might be designed to express an artist's creativity and to make money for producers), but it is later examined by social science researchers for an entirely different purpose (e.g., to determine the prevalence of gender stereotypes in a particular music genre), thereby circumventing issues of reactivity since the song is already written and produced.

As early as 1966, Gene Webb and Don Campbell (joined by Richard Schwartz and Lee Sechrest in 1981) wrote about the need for innovative, non-conventional means for finding things out that they originally dubbed "oddball research" and "oddball measures." For example, they noted how the careful examination of children's drawings, library withdrawals, and worn floor tiles could be used to inform researchers about children's interests, the potential effects of new forms of media, and the popularity of museum exhibits (Webb, Campbell, Schwartz, & Sechrest, 2000). Unobtrusive methods include any number of non-reactive measures or techniques. This chapter examines four types of unobtrusive measures that are classified based on characteristics of the data studied, including: 1) forms of physical evidence examined using physical trace analysis, 2) public and private records observed using archival analysis, 3) written, spoken, or visual messages examined using a technique called content analysis, and 4) official statistics and other forms of existing data studied through secondary analysis. This chapter explains how physical trace analysis, archival analysis, content analysis, and secondary analysis can be used to examine data unobtrusively; that is, in a manner that is independent of the original processes that produced it (Berg & Lune, 2012).

Physical Trace Analysis

LO2

Physical traces The remnants, fragments, and products of past behaviour.

Erosion measures Patterns of selective use based on wear.

Physical traces are the "remnants, fragments, and products of past behaviour" (Shaughnessy, Zechmeister, & Zechmeister, 2009, p. 183). Just as a criminal investigator might examine a crime scene for remaining clues such as fingerprints, blood stains, or clothing fibres, researchers can examine locations for physical evidence that helps them to better understand humans as a result of their past behaviour. This is not unlike what archeologists and anthropologists have been doing for centuries as they study bones, artifacts, and other aspects of material culture left behind by humans to learn more about earlier civilizations. Physical traces are usually one of two types. First, physical traces can take the form of **erosion measures** or use traces "where the degree of selective wear on some material yields the measure" (Webb, Campbell, Schwartz, & Sechrest, 2000, p. 36). Erosion measures indicate patterns of human use, as in the case of heavily worn and dirty carpets or flooring in high traffic areas on a university campus. Similarly, pathways woven through the grass between buildings can indicate frequently used routes or desired walkways.

Erosion measures, such as well-worn paths, reveal what people actually do, not what they are expected to do.

Accretion measures Patterns of selective use and non-use based on accumulation.

Physical traces can also take the form of **accretion measures,** "where the research evidence is some deposit of materials" (Webb, Campbell, Schwartz & Sechrest, 2000, p. 36). Accretion measures are products left behind as a result of prior activity, such as waste or graffiti. For example, the accumulation of empty beer, liquor, and wine bottles in a recycling bin can help to establish the level of alcohol consumption in a given household. The analysis of waste in trash bins can reveal information about people's habits, such as their nutrition and dietary practices, material use and misuse, and waste disposal and recycling behaviours.

Garbology

Garbology The study of behaviour practices based on the analysis of waste.

The term **garbology** is frequently used today to refer to the study of behavioural practices based on the analysis of waste. Garbology as an academic pursuit can be traced to William Rathje (1945–2012), an archeologist at the University of Arizona, who founded the Garbage Project that lasted from 1973 to 2005. In an earlier independent studies project, two of Rathje's students examined the correspondence between stereotypes and "physical realities" through a comparison of the trash collected from two affluent and two poor families (Humes, 2012). Results showed that all four homes consumed similarly, with the same amounts and types of foods and drinks. However, the poorer households spent more on educational items for their children and they bought more household cleaners than the affluent ones (Rathje & Murphy, 2001). Although questionable due to the very small sample size and the limited time frame for analysis, the findings nevertheless sparked an interest in Rathje that resulted in a career-long exploration into the assumptions and potential misconceptions related more generally to consumption and waste disposal.

Instead of taking his students out on archeological "digs," Rathje and his students excavated carefully sampled garbage that was re-routed by the sanitation department and dumped at the University of Arizona (Humes, 2012). For more than three decades, Rathje and his students surveyed, itemized, counted, and weighed garbage, dispelling popular myths about what is most commonly thrown away and what happens to trash after it gets thrown away. For example, while the American public believed that the most common form of solid waste was things like diapers and take-out food containers, more prevalent forms of waste turned out to be newspaper and building materials. Another interesting finding was that consumption increased, as opposed to decreased, during food shortages, especially when red meat was scarce. The Garbage Project also showed how many forms of organic waste were unexpectedly preserved by plastics rather than broken down over time in landfills. Finally, how people actually behave is very different from how they claim to behave, as evident in the under-reporting of unhealthy consumption (e.g., chips, bacon, and alcoholic beverages) and the over-reporting of healthy intake (e.g., cottage cheese, high fibre cereals, and skim milk) (Rathje & Murphy, 2001).

Garbology helps us learn about human consumption, excess, and waste management.

Graffiti

Graffiti A form of visual communication, usually illegal, involving the unauthorized marking of public space by an individual or group.

Graffiti is a special kind of accretion measure that takes various forms and is interpreted in just as many ways. For example, the Encyclopaedia Britannica Online (2013) defines graffiti as a "form of visual communication, usually illegal involving the unauthorized marking of public space by an individual or group. Although the common image of graffiti is a stylistic symbol or phrase spray-painted on a wall by a member of a street gang, some graffiti is not gang-related. Graffiti can be understood as antisocial behaviour performed in order to gain attention or as a form of thrill seeking, but it can also be understood as an expressive art form." As a means of self-expression, graffiti commonly takes the form of "tagging," which involves personalized signatures, or "piecing" and "bombing," which include much more highly specialized forms of artwork created with spray cans to embody names and symbolize particular subcultures (Alonso, 1998). Graffiti also consists of written phrases and statements that express particular viewpoints and positions (Abel & Buckley, 1977). For example, predominant themes tend to be gang graffiti denoting territories, political-based graffiti, or derogatory forms of graffiti directed at particular groups (Alonso, 1998). Graffiti can also take the form of ongoing dialogue as one graffiti writer responds to what another has written, as in the case of bathroom graffiti. The graffiti that appears on the stalls inside bathrooms is usually referred to as "latrinala" (Abel & Buckley, 1977; Melhorn & Romig, 1985).

Graffiti also occurs within particular subcultures and in response to particular events. Rawlinson and Farrell (2010), for example, examined construction site graffiti at ten large-scale construction projects. They identified various common subcultures of graffiti producers (e.g., subcontractors, trades, and football fans), as well as various predominant themes within the graffiti itself, such as celebrations of ownership and personal immortalization. Hagen, Ender, Tiemann, and Hagen (2005) studied disaster graffiti following a major flood that they coined "catastroffiti." The Red River Valley flood of 1997 took place along the Red River in North Dakota, Minnesota, and Southern Manitoba. The most dominant theme in the graffiti following the flood was humour as a coping mechanism. Even within the humorous graffiti, several themes emerged, including jocular humour (e.g., "1-800-big-mess"), sarcasm (e.g., "Are we having fun yet? Keep it up!"), and satirical humour (e.g., "49 FEET MY ASS") in response to a nearby dike that was supposed to be fortified to 52 feet (Hagen, Ender, Tiemann, & Hagen, 2005).

Graffiti can be considered a criminal act, a form of art, or an accretion measure that provides important insight into subcultures.

Research in Action

Bomb It

Bomb It 1 (2007) is an award-winning documentary about graffiti directed by John Reiss. This film documents the history of graffiti and street art and highlights the work of modern artists, including graffiti writers Taki 183, Cornbread, Stay High 149, T-Kid, Cope 2, and Shepard Fairey. Filmed on five different continents, the documentary tracks current controversies around the definition and use of public space in various major cities, including Los Angeles, New York, Tijuana, London, Paris, Cape Town, and Tokyo. Bomb It 2 (2010) broadens Jon Reiss's investigation of graffiti to previously unexplored areas of Asia, South East Asia, the Middle East, Europe, the United States, and Australia. For more information on these films, go to bombit-themovie.com.

Advantages and Disadvantages of Physical Trace Analysis

The biggest advantage of using physical trace analysis pertains to the use of non-reactive measures. Because the traces already exist, they are not subject to the problems inherent in surveys and experiments where participants may alter their responses or behaviour as a function of being studied, such as trying to please the researcher or appear as socially desirable as possible. In most cases, the originators of the physical evidence will never even know it was examined for social scientific purposes. This means the physical traces are likely to have occurred naturally. As a result, the garbologist studying what was thrown out can be reasonably sure that the data reflect true habits versus what would or would not be thrown away if people knew ahead of time that their waste was going to be examined, perhaps to see how many items could have been diverted from a landfill through recycling efforts. In addition, with the exception of graffiti deliberately designed in some instances to identify its authors, physical traces are anonymous because the originators are long gone from the scene when researchers arrive to examine the remaining evidence.

Although free from participant biases common to reactive measures, physical trace measures raise questions concerning the validity of the inferences drawn from the measures. For example, does the presence of lots of cleaning products in a trash bin indicate that a residence is likely to be clean or dirty? Similarly, does the absence of cleaning products mean little cleaning is taking place or something else, such as hired house cleaners bringing in and taking away supplies with them? In addition, since the researcher cannot determine who the originator of the data is, it is difficult to generalize with certainty the findings to any given group or subculture. This is compounded by the fact that only certain kinds of traces are likely to persist long enough to make it into a study (e.g., worn carpets get cleaned or replaced, floors can be polished, rain can wash away footprints, and graffiti can be painted over). Webb, Campbell, Schwartz, & Sechrest (2000) point out that

Selective deposit A bias resulting from the greater likelihood of establishing certain physical traces over others.

Selective survival A bias resulting from the greater likelihood of certain physical traces persisting over time.

especially in the case of accretion measures, some physical traces have a higher probability of being established in the first place while others have a higher probability of surviving over time. They refer to these drawbacks as **selective deposit** and **selective survival** biases. Thus, while physical trace measures can constitute a novel means for studying past behaviours, researchers need to be aware of the potential for biases. One way to help establish the validity of the measures as true indicators of behaviour is to combine physical trace analysis with other methods to see if they all point to similar conclusions, thereby demonstrating convergent validity of the measures.

Test Yourself

- Physical traces usually take the form of which two measures?
- What can we learn through an analysis of waste?
- Which type of physical trace measure is graffiti?
- Which two biases are of particular concern to researchers using physical trace measures?

Archival Analysis

Archives Historical documents, records, or collections detailing the activities of businesses, agencies, institutions, governments, groups, or individuals.

Archives are historical documents, records, or collections of information that detail the activities of businesses, agencies, institutions, governments, groups, or individuals. To help you understand what archives consist of, consider the various organizations or institutions that can be considered archival sources for information pertaining to you, such as the current school you attend as well as any previous school you attended, employers, creditors, doctor's offices, and perhaps even a hospital or police agency. Now think of all of the different ways that information about you and others can be collected and stored, such as in files, in stacks, as journal entries, as taped transcripts, and in electronic format. Finally, consider that archival data can be public or private in nature.

Public and Private Archives

LO3

Public archives Public records that are prepared specifically to be examined by others.

Public archives are public records that are prepared specifically to be examined by others. Public archives tend to be continuous and ongoing, as in the case of running records such as monthly budgets or annual reports, official documents such as school attendance records or hospital intake records, and library collections such as periodicals and books. Public records are also prepared, collected, or organized in standard ways, such as arranged alphabetically, organized by date, indexed, and so on.

Research on the Net

Library and Archives Canada

The largest collection of Canadian public archives is Library and Archives Canada. As of 2004, the collection brings together what used to be the National Archives of Canada (established in 1872) and the National Library of Canada (founded in 1953). The vast collection includes Canadian films and documentaries; architectural drawings, maps, and plans; periodicals and books; photographic images; video and sound recordings; works of art, including watercolours, sketches, miniatures, oil paintings, and caricatures; sheet music; postal archives; medals, seals, posters, and coats of arms; textual archives; national, provincial, and territorial newspapers; periodicals, microfilms, and theses; and portraits of Canadians (Library and Archives Canada, 2013). To conduct an archives search, visit collectionscanada.gc.ca.

Researchers sometimes further categorize public archival data based on characteristics of the data itself. For example, Berg and Lune (2012) modernized the original archival categories first described by Webb and his colleagues into three main groups: commercial media accounts, actuarial records, and official documentary records. Commercial media accounts "represent any written, drawn, or recorded (video or audio) material produced for general or mass consumption" (Berg & Lune, 2012, pp. 283–284). These public archives can include books, newspapers, periodicals or magazines, television program transcripts, film scripts, photographs, music lyrics, radio broadcasts, Twitter posts, YouTube videos, website information, and so on. Actuarial records are "produced for special or limited audiences but they are typically available to the public under certain circumstances" (Berg & Lune, 2012, p. 285). Examples of actuarial records include birth, death, marriage, and divorce records, as well as things like land titles and credit histories. Official documentary records are those "originally produced for some special limited audiences, even if they eventually find their way into the public domain" (Berg & Lune, 2012, p. 287). Official documentary records include school, hospital, dentist, or medical records, as well as court documents, police records, minutes from meetings, annual reports, sales records, and so on.

Actuarial records include birth, death, marriage, and divorce records.

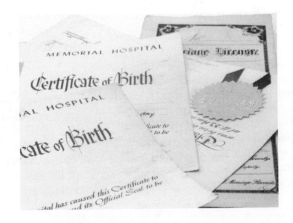

Researchers may later examine public archives, such as official records collected for one purpose, for a completely different purpose. For example, Moulden, Firestone, Kingston, and Wexler (2010) from the University of Ottawa in Ontario, examined official documentary records collected on convicted sexual offenders to learn more about patterns of sexual offending involving teachers. Specifically, the researchers analyzed Archival Violent Crime Linkage Analysis System Reports obtained from the Royal Canadian Mounted Police to describe the cases of 113 Canadian teachers who committed a sexual offence against a child in their care between 1995 and 2002. Archival analysis indicated that most offenders abused a position of trust to initiate contact with the victim (84 percent). In addition, many of the offenders befriended the victim (40 percent), offered assistance to the victim (16 percent), or offered the victim money, treats, toys, or work (14 percent). In addition, findings showed that many of the offences occurred at school (44 percent), the offender's residence (41 percent), the victim's residence (19 percent), in a religious facility (14 percent), or in another residence (12 percent).

> **Private archives** Personal records that are usually directed at a small known target or are produced only for use by the originating author.

Private archives, in contrast, are personal records created for use mainly by the originating author. These are sometimes directed at a small known target, such a friend or loved one. Examples of private archives include personal items such as diaries, letters, or journal entries. The Internet is now changing what would traditionally be considered a private archive into what is probably better considered a **social domain personal archive**. For example, some people post videos depicting their (otherwise) private personal events on YouTube, while others post highly personal information on websites such as Facebook.

> **Social domain personal archive** Personal information that is posted to public arenas using social media such as Facebook or Twitter.

Research in Action

Online Dream Diary

As a further illustration of a social domain personal archive, one young man posted a detailed description of his dreams on a personal website. Psychologist Jayne Gackenbach and her research team a studied this video game player's 13 year-long online dream diary (consisting of 831 dreams), as well as his daily activity blogs, to see if the reported dream content was consistent over time and whether it corresponded to what is already known about dreams in video game players. In addition, the researchers examined the correspondence between daily blog activity and subsequent dreams to see if prior everyday events were incorporated into dreams. Results for the 447 dreams included in the analysis from the archive showed that the dream content was consistent over time (e.g., similar characters appeared, similar social interactions took place), and there was some incorporation of elements of the daily blog into subsequent dreams. The video game player's dreams also contained themes consistent with other gamers, including the prevalence of dead and imaginary characters (Gackenbach, Sample, Mandel, & Tomashewsky, 2011).

Advantages and Disadvantages of Archival Analysis

Similar to trace measures, archives are beneficial to researchers largely because they are non-reactive. In addition, archives often provide a low-cost means for researchers to access a multitude of existing records. Since archives can be collected indefinitely, archival analysis is especially suited for longitudinal analysis where pattern and trends can be examined over time.

The main drawback of archival analysis relates to validity because, as with trace measures, selective deposit and selective survival biases may determine who or what ends up in the records and which records have a better chance of persisting over time (Webb, Campbell, Schwartz, & Sechrest, 2000). For example, because records are sometimes created for the benefit of a particular agency or organization or on behalf of a particular agency (e.g., sales records, annual reports), biases may be built in to how the data was collected in the first place. In addition, records may be incomplete, they may get lost, and/or certain records may be destroyed over time. One way to increase validity and lessen the likelihood of errors due to missing data is to use archival analysis in combination with other data collection methods.

Finally, since unobtrusive methods involve means of obtaining evidence indirectly, people are usually unaware that data about them has been used for research purposes and therefore informed consent was never obtained.[2] While we may learn important insights and historical facts through the analysis of private records, such as diaries and letters often found only after people pass on, should this knowledge come at the expense of the privacy of the originator? Finally, in many cases it is difficult to establish the accuracy of existing documents—especially personal ones such as biographies.

Test Yourself

- What kinds of records are accessible as public archives?
- What are the main advantages and drawbacks of archival analysis?

Content Analysis

Content analysis A repertoire of methods that allow researchers to make inferences from all kinds of verbal, pictorial, symbolic, and communication data.

Another main source of non-reactive data comes from visual and print-based forms of media, such as television shows, films, photographs, books, and newspapers, which contain messages studied by social scientists about race, class, violence, and gender, for example. **Content analysis** refers to "any technique that allows researchers to make inferences based on specific characteristics they objectively identify in messages" (Shaughnessy, Zechmeister, & Zechmeister, 2009, p. 193). Although content analysis can be traced to propaganda techniques employed by the media (e.g., see Lasswell, 1927), it has also been used to examine messages in a variety of archival records, including messages delivered by the words, phrases, and passages in books, articles, and news stories, in song lyrics, in information found on websites, in representations shown in magazines, and in character portrayals as shown in television commercials, television programs, and major motion pictures. Similarly, while some researchers view content analysis as an objective, quantitative means for looking at message characteristics (e.g., see Neuendorf, 2002), others view interpretations of text as largely an interpretive, qualitative endeavour involving a technique called discourse analysis (e.g., see Van Dijk, 1997). At this point, it is probably most accurate to "say that content analysis has evolved into a repertoire of methods of research that promise to yield inferences from all kinds of verbal, pictorial, symbolic, and communication data" (Krippendorff, 2013, p. 23).

Conducting a Content Analysis

Any number of topics can be studied using content analysis. Popular topics that students in my research methods courses have studied using this method include:

- gender stereotypes
- use of humour in advertising
- use of sex in advertising
- violence in the mass media
- themes in children's books
- sports injuries
- negative portrayals of men and women
- representations of groups in the media

As is the case with any research method, the first step in a content analysis is to clarify the research objectives (see Figure 8.1).

FIGURE 8.1   **Main Steps for Conducting a Content Analysis**

Clarify research objectives → Identify an appropriate archival source → Employ sampling procedures → Code the data as guided by the conceptual framework → Summarize and disseminate the findings

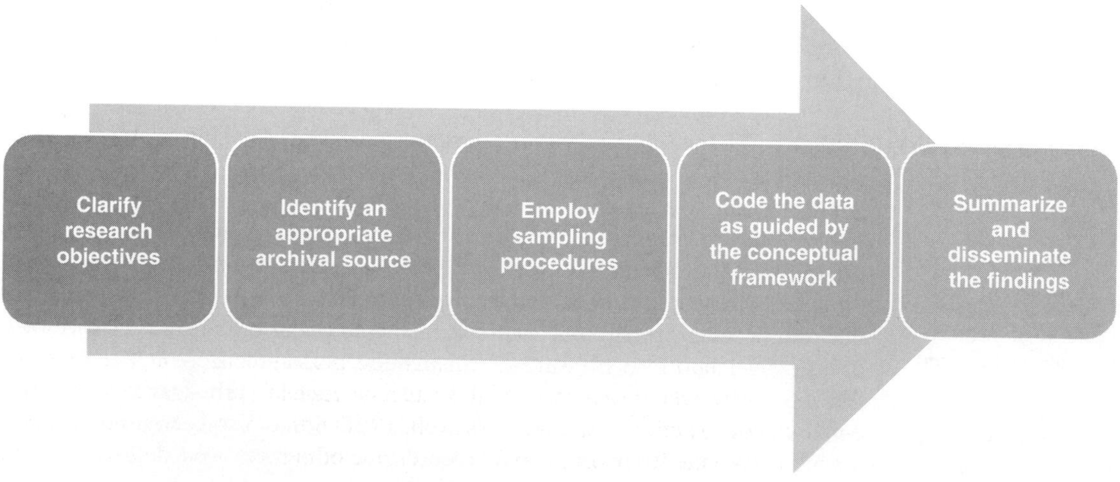

Once the researcher is clear about what he or she wishes to study and has determined content analysis is the most appropriate method for obtaining the data of interest, the next step is to determine the most relevant archival source. For example, a researcher interested in the representation of Aboriginal people in the mass media might narrow his or her focus to an exploration of whether Aboriginals are over- or under-represented in media stories involving Canadian crime. Similarly, a researcher might compare how more or less liberal news outlets report on stories involving crimes committed by Aboriginal youth. My students have selected a range of archival sources for research projects involving content analyses, including local newspapers, national newspapers, prime time television shows, television shows aimed at preschool children, television commercials for children's products, car magazines directed at young and older audiences, and songs within particular genres such as hip hop. The appropriateness of any given archival source is largely determined by the specific research questions and objectives. For example, one student examined National Football League (NFL) injury records to describe where injuries are most likely to occur in football players and which team members are mostly likely to suffer them (MacIntosh, 2012). In case you are curious, in the 2010 NFL regular season, knee injuries were the most prevalent, followed by head and ankle injuries. Players in the cornerback position were most likely to incur injuries, with wide receivers taking second place (MacIntosh, 2012).

After locating an appropriate source, a researcher needs to employ a sampling procedure. Will the study include all available records, a sample obtained using a probability-based technique, or a sample obtained using a non-probability-based technique? Again, it will depend on what the specific study is about. A researcher interested in the portrayal of gender in magazine advertisements might begin by examining a random sample of ten magazines from the 100 top-selling Canadian magazines, such as *What's Cooking, Reader's Digest, Chatelaine,* and *Maclean's.* Within the selected magazines, another simple random sample of advertisements could be obtained. Although magazines constitute the more general unit of analysis for the study, the actual observations centre on the advertisements. As noted in Chapter 4, it is sometimes helpful to distinguish between units of analysis (the magazines) and the more precise units of observation (the advertisements). Once sampling procedures have been worked through, a researcher can begin to code the data.

Coding The process of transforming raw data into a standardized form.

Coding is the "process of transforming raw data into a standardized form" (Babbie, 2013, p. 361) and is used to help make sense of the data collected. If a researcher takes a quantitative approach, he or she develops hypotheses and establishes a precise coding scheme according to some conceptual framework in advance of data collection. The researcher defines specific variables for use in analyzing the content of the particular message to test the hypotheses. For example, a researcher might code the advertisements in magazines to test a hypothesis that females will be more likely than males to be portrayed in gender-stereotyped ways for particular products. The literature is replete with established coding schemes for examining gender portrayals in advertisements. A coding scheme might include the following variables: sex, type of product sold, role depicted by the main character, and type of portrayal depicted by the main character. Each one of these variables would be precisely defined, such as operationalizing sex as male or female, and type of product as food, clothing, service, and so on. Using the coding scheme, the researcher codes each advertisement for each variable and then examines the data collected to see if females are portrayed in gender-stereotyped roles for particular products, for example as traditional housewives to sell cleaning products. Quantitative content analysis usually involves coding the presence or absence of some event, determining the frequency of a variable, or counting the number of times a word or theme appears in text as described in numbers 1 through 3 below. In each of these cases, the researcher is most likely recording the **manifest**, or more obvious, stated content in the message, such as words or phrases actually contained in the message.

Manifest content Stated content in the message itself.

Qualitative content analysis, in contrast, is directed more at understanding the underlying meaning or **latent** content of a message. It is therefore more likely to involve coding text or images for implied themes and the repetition of particular constructs, as explained in numbers 4 and 5 below. From a qualitative approach, the researcher begins with a research question (as opposed to a hypothesis) and looks for themes to emerge from the data that are then reinterpreted using theory, as opposed to coding for specific variables at the onset. For example, in an exploratory study, Mezzana, Lorenz, and Kelman (2012) were interested in learning more about how rock music lyrics portray islands. Theory is still important for developing a conceptual framework that informs the data collection. In this case, the researchers examined what previous research had to say about the constructs of "islands," "islandness," and "island features" in rock music. However, the purpose was not to test theories, but to try and uncover the meaning of islands in reference to the rest of the lyrics within rock songs. The researchers looked at five decades of rock music—412 songs containing island references—to see how island references were used in the songs. They ended up identifying broader categories (themes) that could be used to help qualify the more specific observations. The 24 themes included the notions of loneliness and despair, seclusion, fear, depression, spirituality, love and romance, adventure, and intimacy, among others. The 24 individual themes that were adapted from the data and corresponding literature were then further coded under five main meta-themes of space (e.g., seclusion), lifestyle (e.g., adventure), emotions/psychology (e.g., fear), symbolism (e.g., spirituality), and social-political relations (e.g., dominance) (Mezzana, Lorenz, & Kelman, 2012).

Latent content Implied meaning inferred by the message.

To summarize, in content analysis, researchers examine messages contained in visual and print media for measurable indicators of more abstract constructs and ideas such as aggression, love, "islandness," or gender stereotyping. According to Krippendorf (2013, pp. 62–63), these five indexes are typically employed in content analyses:

1. The *presence or absence* of a reference or concept as an indication of some phenomenon of interest. For example, DeJean, Giacomini, Schwartz, and Miller (2009) examined 608 Canadian health technology assessment reports produced from 1997 to 2006 for the presence or absence of ethics content. They found that only a minority incorporated any form of ethical consideration into the documents.

2. The *frequency* with which a symbol, idea, reference, or topic occurs generally as an indicator of a concept's importance or emphasis. A content analysis on 150 top-selling video games, for example, revealed a high frequency of the use of profanity (Ivory, Williams, Martins, & Consalvo, 2009).

3. The *number of* favourable or unfavourable characteristics attributed to a symbol, idea, or reference that indicates an attitude toward some phenomenon of interest. For example, in Symbaluk and Howell's (2010) study, students' posted ratings of instructor attributes at Ratemyprofessors.com were coded as positive or negative depending on the nature of the actual comment. For example, "knows nothing" would be considered a negative comment about intelligence, while "really knows his stuff" would be positive. The study showed that teaching-award winners receive more positive ratings than research-award winners.

4. The *kinds of* qualifications used in statements about a symbol, idea, or reference that are indicative of the intensity associated with the belief signified by the symbol, idea, or reference. Weitzer and Kubrin's (2009) content analysis of rap music revealed five prevalent kinds of misogyny, including: derogatory naming and shaming of women; sexual objectification of women; distrust of women; legitimization of violence against women; and a celebration of prostitution and pimping.

5. The repeated *co-occurrence* of two concepts that indicates the strength of association between them. Singer's (1982) employed a content analysis of Ontario newspaper coverage of Aboriginal peoples to reveal an association between "Indian identification" and words depicting conflict, especially in relation to unresolved land claims.

Research in Action

Disclosure of Personal Information on Facebook

Researchers from the Cyprus Neuroscience & Technology Institute and Eastern Mediterranean University studied how young people manage privacy issues through an examination of posted member profiles on Facebook. More specifically, the researchers were interested in whether there were gender differences in the amount and type of personal information disclosed in Facebook profiles (Taraszow, Aristodemou, Shitta, Laouris, & Arsoy, 2010). Profiles of 131 males (N = 63) and females (N = 68) aged 14 through 29 years were coded for type of profile, profile name, profile picture, birth date, email address, instant message (IM) screen name, mobile phone number, other phone number, and home address. Results showed that while most profiles (76.3 percent) were not for public use and were only accessible by friends, almost everyone published a profile picture that could be used to determine sex or approximate age. In addition, the vast majority of members published their real names and their full birth dates, and many publicly revealed an email address and listed their home town. Only a small portion of Facebook users posted their IM screen name, mobile number, home number, or home address. While there were no differences between males and females in their tendencies to have a public or private profile, males were more likely to disclose their IM screen name, home address, and mobile phone number (Taraszow et al., 2010).

Advantages and Disadvantages of Content Analysis

Content analysis, like the other unobtrusive measures, is a great economical and non-reactive means for learning more about the messages conveyed in print and visual forms. Content analysis is free from biases that can lead to distortion in the data when it is obtained from participants, such as in a carefully controlled laboratory experiment or through the use of a highly structured survey. It is also beneficial because it takes into account how the data was originally conceived. The songwriter did not write the lyrics for a content analysis, nor did an author write a book for such purposes. As content analysis expert Klaus Krippendorff (2013) puts it, "the chief advantage of the unstructuredness of content analysis data is that it preserves the conceptions of the data's sources, which structured methods largely ignore" (p. 41). While it may be more difficult to examine text and messages that come in a range of unstandardized formats and types, the structure is not imposed and therefore exists as envisioned by the originator. As a related point, this also means that the context-sensitive nature of the data can be taken into account during content analysis (Krippendorff, 2013).

Content analysis is also beneficial because it can be applied to a multitude of topics and it can also manage large amounts of data. For example, recall how Gackenbach et al. (2011) analyzed the content of 447 dreams and DeJean et al. (2009) examined 608 health technology assessment reports. Since the data for content analysis is archival in nature, there is also the potential for longitudinal analyses (e.g., are there fewer gender stereotypes portrayed in children's books that were written in the last twenty years compared to books from the 1970s and 1980s?). In addition, since the records already exist, they can be examined and re-examined to increase coder reliability.

A main limitation of content analysis is that the data originated for other purposes and therefore it may be biased toward a particular viewpoint or perspective, as in the case of information contained in the mass media that is produced for profit. Also, it may be incomplete for examining certain hypotheses or questions of interest. Disadvantages of content analysis often relate to questions of validity. Once a coding scheme has been developed and the constructs are operationalized into variables that can be readily measured by trained observers, will observers be able to use it properly? Manifest content is much more straightforward to code than latent content since manifest coding generally only involves counting the number of times a word appears or noting the presence or absence of a particular theme. However, the way in which a message is understood by a coder may not be the way in which the original producer intended the message to be interpreted (Richardson, 2007). Moreover, especially in the case of latent content, different coders are likely to interpret the same message in different ways, resulting in disagreements over what is or is not identified as a major theme in the message and a low inter-rater reliability.

Test Yourself

- What are the main steps for conducting a content analysis?
- How does manifest content differ from latent content?
- Which indexes are usually employed in qualitative content analysis?

Secondary Analysis

LO5

Secondary analysis of existing data Examination of data originally collected by someone other than the researcher for a different purpose.

As an alternative to collecting data first hand directly from participants—as in the case of surveys and experiments—or indirectly—as in the case of trace, archival, and content analysis—researchers can also re-examine existing data using a method called **secondary analysis of existing data.** Secondary analysis involves the examination of data originally collected by someone other than the researcher for a different purpose. Secondary data can be quantitative or qualitative in nature, such as archived survey data or interview transcripts.

Locating Secondary Sources

Examples of existing Canadian data include official census data and data obtained through national surveys, such as the General Social Survey and the National Population Health Survey. Various government departments and agencies (e.g., Environment Canada, the Correctional Service of Canada), institutes (e.g., Canadian Research Institute for Law and the Family, First Nations Statistical Institute), and universities throughout Canada (e.g., the Institute for Social Research at York University, the Canadian Plains Research Centre at the University of Regina, and the Quebec Interuniversity Centre for Social Statistics) also collect a wealth of information.

Research in Action

Access to Health Care in Canadian Immigrants

Using existing data from the National Population Health Survey (NHPS), researchers from McGill University, the School of Health Sciences, and the University of Bristol conducted a longitudinal study on access to health care experienced by Canadian immigrants (Setia, Quesnel-Vallee, Abrahamowicz, Tousignant, & Lynch, 2011). Since the NHPS

is conducted annually (beginning in 1994), the researchers were able to examine findings for 30 181 males and 4187 females over a 12-year period. Despite widespread beliefs that immigrants are at a disadvantage in a new country, results showed that immigrants had similarly high odds to Canadian-born individuals (around 95 percent) when it came to having access to a regular doctor (Setia et al., 2011).

Determining the Appropriateness of a Source

It is one thing to know of potential sources of secondary data and quite a different thing to locate one that can be of specific use for a particular study. The starting point is always the narrowed research focus. For example, one of my students was interested in a phenomenon in sports known as the "Myth of the Contract Year" where professional athletes purportedly play harder in their final contract year to secure more lucrative future contracts. To determine whether this is the case in hockey, the student examined statistics for hockey players made available by the National Hockey League (NHL). By comparing production measured in points per game (goals, assists) for well-known NHL players averaged over their contract year versus non-contract years, Janke (2012) showed that some players were as productive or even more productive in non-contract years, helping to dispel the myth.

Some sources may appear to be appropriate but may not actually contain the variables needed to answer a specific research question, and sometimes information exists in a format other than what an individual researcher requires for a specific study. For example, suppose a researcher wanted to test the applicability of Gottfredson and Hirschi's (1990) general theory of crime for explaining differences in treatment completion rates for sexual offenders using indicators of self-control. In this case, offenders with higher levels of self-control are expected to be more likely to complete treatment, while those with lower levels are less likely to complete treatment. After gaining the necessary ethical and institutional permissions to access what would appear to be an appropriate secondary source (e.g., a data set on Canadian offenders who underwent treatment for sexual offending at a minimum security institution), the researcher might discover that the data set only contains minimal information collected on patients at the beginning and end of treatment. The information the researcher is actually interested in, such as background characteristics pertaining to early school years and the stability of relationships and job histories that would serve as indicators for self-control, might still exist, but it may be contained in individual patient files as notes from various sources (e.g., the head psychiatrist, therapists who regularly interact with the client, etc.). How then can a researcher determine if a data set will be appropriate in advance of carrying out the research?

In most instances, a researcher can assess the merit a potential secondary data set through its accompanying **codebook** that details the methodology underlying the data set and lists the variables contained in the data set. Also included in a codebook is information on how the variables were operationalized for the purposes of the original study or source, such as the exact question wording for items on a questionnaire along with the response categories, as well as information on how each variable is labelled and coded in the data set. For example, the first variable in a data set might be "Sex" and it could refer to the respondent's sex which might be coded as 1 = male and 2 = female; a variable such as "offence" might refer to the type of offence committed by the persons included in the data set. A codebook also includes details on how any scales and indexes were constructed, how missing data was dealt with, and so on. Note that for a qualitative study, a researcher may be able to access journal notes, audit trails, and other documents that detail the process by which the available data was transformed into its current format, which could be in the form of words, images, or even artifacts.

In addition to the codebook, a researcher also needs to pay special attention to the format and structure of the data. The **data format** usually refers to "the statistical format in which data are saved or stored" (Pienta, McFarland O'Rourke, & Franks, 2011, p. 18). For example, quantitative data is likely to be in a numerical format amenable to statistical analysis using a software package designed

Codebook A detailed listing of how each variable is coded in the data set along with information on the methodology underlying the original study.

Data format The statistical format in which data are saved or stored.

especially for the social sciences, such as IBM SPSS Statistics. Qualitative data is more apt to be a collection of visual or written statements (see Chapter 9 for more information on how verbal information collected in interviews is turned into data). The **data structure** refers to "the number and organizational nature of distinct files that compose a data collection and the relationship among those data" (Pienta et al., 2011, p. 18). For example, secondary data is often contained in a single file in a table with a number of rows of information. Note any number of variables could be contained within that file and they are usually labelled and listed across the first row as shown in Table 8.1. Each row except for the first row corresponds to the information from one case.

Data structure The number and organizational nature of distinct files that compose a data collection and the relationship among those data.

TABLE 8.1
Sample Data Structure

Case	Sex	Age	Offence	Risk
1	1	23	1	2
2	2	21	4	1
3	1	20	2	4
4	2	19	3	5
5	2	20	2	3
6	1	19	2	3

Research on the Net

Finding Canadian Statistics

The University of Toronto Map and Data Library is an amazing resource with links to directory sites that house Canadian statistics located in print and in electronic publications. Here you can find information on general Canadian statistical sources with emphasis on data provided by Statistics Canada (e.g., Canadian Statistics, Canadian Economic Observer, Statistics Canada Daily), as well as Canadian statistics on special topics such as Aboriginal peoples, cities, aging, crime, and justice. This resource is available at data.library.utoronto.ca.

Statistics Canada as a Leading Data Source

Statistics Canada regularly collects data on virtually all aspects of Canadian life that are of interest to federal government agencies. For example, in terms of the area of criminal justice alone, Statistics Canada conducts various annual surveys such as the Adult Correctional Services Survey, the Adult Criminal Court Survey, and the Uniform Crime Reporting Survey, among others (Statistics Canada, 2012a). The Adult Correctional Services Survey collects data from all institutions in the provincial and federal correctional systems on new admissions, conditional releases, and financial/human resources. The Adult Criminal Court Survey collects information on criminal court appearances and charges (Statistics Canada, 2012a). The Uniform Crime Reporting Survey is managed by the Canadian Centre for Justice Statistics, a division of Statistics Canada responsible for collecting national data on crime.

Police agencies throughout the country use the Uniform Crime Reporting Survey (UCR) to report statistics in a standard way for criminal offences. Since 1962, the UCR has collected information on the number of criminal incidents, the clearance status of those incidents, and on the persons charged. In 1988, a second survey was created (called the UCR2) to obtain additional details on the characteristics of the incidents, victims, and accused (Statistics Canada, 2012b). The UCR and UCR2 provide available data on close to 100 difference offences. See Table 8.2 for summary information on the number and type of homicides committed in Canada between 2007 and 2011. Crime data can be re-examined to test theories, look for patterns and trends, and explore relationships among variables.

TABLE 8.2
Homicides by Method, 2007–2011

	2007	2008	2009	2010	2011
All methods	594	611	610	554	598
Shooting	188	201	182	171	158
Stabbing	190	201	210	165	204
Beating	118	123	118	116	125
Strangulation	52	45	46	41	40
Fire (burns/suffocation)	4	7	12	11	21
Other methods*	19	20	28	31	29
Not known	23	14	14	19	21

Notes: Homicide includes *Criminal Code* offences of murder, manslaughter, and infanticide. If multiple methods against one victim are used, only the leading method causing the death is counted. Thus, only one method is scored per victim.
* Other methods include poisoning, exposure, shaken baby syndrome, deaths caused by vehicles, and heart attacks.
Source: Statistics Canada, CANSIM, Table 253-0002 and Homicide Survey, Canadian Centre for Justice Statistics.

It is important to note that Canadian crime data is the end-result of crimes that were recorded by the police, as opposed to a "true" measure of the amount of crime committed since many crimes go undetected, many go unreported, and many are not classified as crimes after being reported. Furthermore, there are concerns about how particular crimes are counted. For example, in the case of multiple offences committed at the same time, only the most serious offence is recorded. In addition, some of the categories are fairly broad and contain more than one type of offence, such as attempted theft and actual theft which are recorded in the same category (Evans & Himelfarb, 2009). To try and gain a more accurate estimate of the true amount of crime, criminologists and other interested parties typically supplement official crime statistics with other measures, such as information obtained on surveys completed by offenders and/or victims of crime.

Advantages and Disadvantages of Secondary Analysis

Secondary analysis is a very inexpensive and time saving method for looking at patterns and trends in official data, such as the information collected through surveys conducted by Statistics Canada. In addition to being non-reactive, secondary analysis may have built-in safeguards, including the protection of privacy pertaining to how the data was collected in the first place. Information collected by Statistics Canada through surveys, for example, is confidential. That is, Statistics

Canada will not release information (even to the Royal Canadian Mounted Police) that would identify individuals who provided particular responses. Furthermore, the collected data is reported and released in aggregate form as grouped data. Secondary analysis is especially suited to longitudinal research since the data from multiple surveys can be examined and compared over time.

One of the main drawback of secondary analysis is the data was collected for purposes other than the present research study. This means the data may be incomplete or not contain the essential variables of interest for the secondary analysis. Moreover, with the exception of sources such as Statistics Canada, there may be no way to determine how the data was originally collected, calling into question whether ethical safeguards were put into place and whether the measures are reliable and valid.

Research on the Net

Open Data Pilot Project

In an effort to make Canadian data more available for commercial and non-commercial purposes, the Government of Canada recently launched the Open Data Pilot Project. Open Data allows access to a catalogue of federal government data sets freely available to users for secondary analysis. Tens of thousands of data sets can be accessed using key word search terms, such as roads, immigration, law, or health. You can access the home page at data.gc.ca.

Test Yourself

- What is secondary data analysis?
- Which agency serves as the main source of secondary data on virtually all aspects of Canadian life?
- Why does secondary data analysis pose ethical concerns?

Chapter Summary

LO1 Define unobtrusive methods and explain what is meant by reactive and non-reactive research methods.

Unobtrusive methods are strategies in which the researcher examines evidence of people's behaviour or attitudes, rather than interacting directly with those being studied. A reactive method is one that directly involves a research participant who may react to being in a study as a result of how questions are asked (e.g., in a survey) or due to the presence of a researcher (e.g., in an experiment). Non-reactive methods are unobtrusive because the data is obtained without participant involvement.

LO2 Explain what physical trace analysis is used for and differentiate between erosion and accretion measures.

Physical trace analysis is the study of products of past behaviour that provide insight into patterns and trends. Erosion measures are signs of selective wear and tear that tell us about human use and non-use (e.g., worn paths that denote desired walkways). Accretion measures are product deposits left behind as a result of prior activity, such as garbage or graffiti.

LO3   **Differentiate between public and private archives and note a main advantage and disadvantage of archival analysis.**

Public archives are public records prepared specifically to be examined by others, such as annual reports or attendance records. Private archives are created for personal use and include letters and diaries. As with all unobtrusive methods, archival measures are beneficial because they are non-reactive. In addition, archival records are economical and lend themselves well to longitudinal analysis. Drawbacks to this method include selective deposit and selective survival biases, as well as a potential lack of informed consent.

LO4   **Define content analysis and outline the steps for conducting a content analysis.**

Content analysis is a repertoire of methods that allow researchers to make inferences from all kinds of verbal, pictorial, symbolic, and communication data. Steps for carrying out a content analysis include clarifying research objectives, identifying relevant archival sources, employing sampling procedures, coding data in accord with conceptual frameworks, and summarizing and reporting on the findings.

LO5   **Explain what secondary analysis of existing data entails, identify key sources for secondary data analysis, and note a main advantage and disadvantage of secondary data analysis.**

Secondary analysis of existing data involves an examination of data originally collected by someone other than the researcher for a different purpose. Key sources for secondary data analysis include official census data and data obtained through national surveys, as well as data collected in research centres and institutes. Statistics Canada is the main federal government source for secondary data on most topics involving Canadians. One advantage of using data from Statistics Canada is that it includes built in privacy and informed-consent safeguards from when the data was collected. However, the data was collected for particular purposes and may therefore be incomplete for the purposes of the current study.

| **Research Reflection** | 1. Suggest a physical trace measure that could be employed as one of the main variables for each of the following research topics: |

  • Students' use of food service providers on campus.
  • Students' typical commute patterns on campus.
  • Students' food consumption on campus.
  • Students' preferred study space on campus.

2. Suggest an appropriate archival or secondary data source for each of the following research topics:

  • Popular vacation spots
  • Fashion trends

- Crime statistics
- Canadian documentaries

3. Suppose you wanted to conduct a content analysis on the portrayal of gender in popular G-rated movies.

   a. First, list ten movies that are rated G for a general audience and are suitable for younger children (e.g., *Planes*, *The Smurfs 2*, *The Little Mermaid*, *Tarzan*, *Benji*).

   b. Now consider who or what is likely to constitute the main character in one of these movies. If you had to categorize the main character as one of only five different "types," what would the types consist of to ensure that your categories were mutually exclusive and exhaustive? For example, would all animals of any kind, such as mammals, birds, and fish, all be classified as the category "animal"?

   c. Come up with one research question on gender that you could examine in a content analysis of popular G-rated movies.

If you would like to learn how gender was assessed and how the main character type was operationalized and formulated in a study on gender-related portrayals in top-grossing G-rated films, refer to: Smith, S. L., Pieper, K. M., Granados, A., & Choueiti, M. (2010). Assessing gender-related portrayals in top-grossing G-rated films. *Sex Roles, 62,* 774–786.

Learning Through Practice

Objective: Learning how to code data for a content analysis.
Directions:

1. Locate and examine several advertisements for a dating service in the personal section of the classified ads in a local newspaper or visit a free online dating site such as DateaCanadian.ca, POF.com, or eHarmony.ca.

2. Write down several variables located on the site, such as smoking, height, hobbies, and occupation.

3. Develop three research questions you could examine based on the information provided at the site. For example, how do women describe themselves on the site DateaCanadian.ca?

4. What exactly would you need to code to explore your research questions?

5. Choose one research question, make up a coding sheet that lists the central variables, and then try coding ten relevant profiles at the selected site.

6. Did you employ a sampling procedure to obtain relevant profiles? Explain.

7. Are your initial findings what you expected? Why or why not?

Research Resources

1. To learn more about the use of creative methods and the limitations of non-reactive measures, I recommend Webb, E. J., Campbell, D. T., Schwartz, R. D., & Sechrest, L. (2000). *Unobtrusive measures* (Rev. ed.). Thousand Oaks, CA: Sage Publications.

2. For an overview of strategies for navigating library archival data for use by social scientists, refer to Hill, M. R. (1993). *Archival strategies and techniques.* Newbury Park, CA: Sage Publications.

3. To learn more about the conceptual foundation of content analysis, content analysis designs, and how to record and code data, refer to Krippendorff, K. (2013). *Content analysis* (3rd ed.). Thousand Oaks, CA: Sage Publications.

4. For examples of content analyses on the mass media, including health, class, gender, and race in the press, the media, and the news, as well as various topics such as self-presentation and disaster communication on the Internet, refer to Franzosi, R. (2008). *Content analysis: Volume 3, Applications: A focus on mass media.* Thousand Oaks, CA: Sage Publications.

5. For an overview of secondary data analysis and content analysis framed within a Canadian context, I recommend Chapter 5 in Jackson, W., & Verberg, N. (2007). *Methods: Doing social research* (4th ed.). Toronto, ON: Pearson Education Canada.

 For more information on the resources available from McGraw-Hill Ryerson, go to www.mcgrawhill.ca/he/solutions.

References

Abel, E. L., & Buckley, B. E. (1977). *The handwriting on the wall: Toward a sociology and psychology of graffiti.* Westport, CT: Greenwood.

Alonso, A. (1998, February 14). Urban graffiti on the city landscape. Paper presented at the Western Geography Graduate Conference, San Diego State University. Retrieved from: www.streetgangs.com/academic/alonsograffiti.pdf

Babbie, E. (2013). *The practice of social research* (13th ed.). Belmont, CA: Wadsworth.

Berg, B. L., & Lune, H. (2012). *Qualitative research methods for the social sciences.* Upper Saddle River, NJ: Pearson Education.

DeJean, D., Giacomini, M., Schwartz, L., and Miller, F. A. (2009). Ethics in Canadian health technology assessment: A descriptive review. *International Journal of Technology Assessment in Health Care, 25*(4), 463–469.

Encyclopaedia Britannica Online. (2013). Graffiti. Chicago, IL: Encyclopaedia Britannica, Inc. Retrieved from www.britannica.com/EBchecked/topic/240670/graffiti

Evans, J., & Himelfarb, A. (2009). Counting crime. In R. Linden (Ed.), *Criminology: A Canadian perspective* (6th ed., pp. 103–136). Toronto, ON: Nelson Education.

Franzosi, R. (2008). *Content analysis: Volume 3, Applications: A focus on mass media.* Thousand Oaks, CA: Sage Publications.

Gackenbach, J., Sample, T., Mandel, G., & Tomashewsky, M. (2011). Dream and blog content analysis of a long term diary of a video game player with obsessive compulsive disorder. *Dreaming, 21*(2), 124–147.

Gottfredson, M. R., & Hirschi, T. (1990). *A general theory of crime.* Stanford, CA: Stanford University Press.

Hagen, C. A., Ender, M. G., Tiemann, K. A., & Hagen, C. O. (2005). Graffiti on the Great Plains: A social reaction to the Red River Valley flood of 1997. In K. J. Strand & G. L. Weiss (Eds.), *Experiencing social research: A reader* (pp. 181–190). Boston, MA: Pearson Education.

Hill, M. R. (1993). *Archival strategies and techniques*. Newbury Park, CA: Sage Publications.

Humes, E. (2012). *Garbology: Our dirty love affair with trash*. New York, NY: Avery.

Ivory, J. D., Williams, D., Martins, N., & Consalvo, M. (2009). Good clean fun? A content analysis of profanity in video games and its prevalence across game systems and ratings. *Cyberpsychology & Behavior, 12*(4), 457–460.

Jackson, W., & Verberg, N. (2007). *Methods: Doing social research* (4th ed.). Toronto, ON: Pearson Education Canada.

Janke, J. (2012). The contract year myth: Do NHL players produce at a higher level during the the final year of their contracts? Poster Session. Sociology Undergraduate Symposium. MacEwan University, Edmonton, Alberta, April 10.

Krippendorff, K. (2013). *Content analysis* (3rd ed.). Thousand Oaks, CA: Sage Publications.

Lasswell, H. (1927). *Propaganda techniques in the world war*. New York: Knopf.

Library and Archives Canada. (2013). About the collection. Overview. Ottawa, ON: Government of Canada. Retrieved from www.collectionscanada.gc.ca/collection/003-300-e.html

MacIntosh, C. (2012). Professional football injuries: Who is being injured and where? Poster Session. Sociology Undergraduate Symposium. MacEwan University, Edmonton, Alberta, April 10.

Melhorn, J. J., & Romig, R. J. (1985). Rest room graffiti: A descriptive study. *Emporia State Research Studies* (Fall), 29–45.

Mezzana, D., Lorenz, A., & Kelman, I. (2012). Islands and islandness in rock music lyrics. *Island Studies Journal*, 7(1), 69–98.

Moulden, H. M., Firestone, P., Kingston, D. A., & Wexler, A. F. (2010). A description of sexual offending committed by Canadian teachers. *Journal of Child Sexual Abuse, 19*, 403–418.

Neuendorf, K. A. (2002). *The content analysis guidebook*. Thousand Oaks, CA: Sage Publications.

Pienta, A. M., McFarland O'Rouke, J., & Franks, M. M. (2011). Getting started: Working with secondary data. In Kali H. Trzesniewski, M. Brent Donnellan and Richard E. Lucas (Eds.), *Secondary data analysis* [electronic resource]: An introduction for psychologists. Washington, DC: American Psychological Association. Retrieved from http://ehis.ebscohost.com.ezproxy.macewan.ca/ehost/detail?sid=0e86d55d-4979-4768-9935-383cdd4eb836%40sessionmgr198&vid=1&hid=105&bdata=JnNpdGU9ZWhvc3QtbGl2ZSZzY29wZT1zaXRl#db=pzh&jid=201009298

Rathje, W. & Murphy, C. (2001). *Rubbish: The archeology of garbage*. Tucson, AZ: The University of Arizona Press.

Rawlinson, F., & Farrell, P. (2010). Construction site graffiti: Discourse analysis as a window into construction site culture. In C. Egbu (Ed.), Proceedings of the 26th annual ARCOM conference (pp. 361–370), 6–8 September 2010, Leeds, UK, Association of Researchers in Construction Management.

Richardson, J. E. (2007). *Analysing newspapers: An approach from critical discourse analysis.* New York, NY: Palgrave MacMillan.

Setia, M. S., Quesnel-Vallee, A., Tousignant, P., & Lynch, J. (2011). Access to health-care in Canadian immigrants: A longitudinal study of the National Population Health Survey. *Health and Social Care in the Community, 19*(1), 70–79.

Shaughnessy, J. J., Zechmeister, E. B., & Zechmeister, J. S. (2009). *Research methods in psychology* (8th ed.). New York, NY: McGraw-Hill.

Singer, B. D. (1982). Minorities and the media: A content analysis of native Canadians in the daily press. *Canadian Review of Sociology and Anthropology, 19*(3), 348–360.

Smith, S. L., Pieper, K. M., Granados, A., & Choueiti, M. (2010). Assessing gender-related portrayals in top-grossing G-rated films. *Sex Roles, 62*, 774–786.

Statistics Canada. (2012a). *Data sources.* Ottawa, ON: Author. Retrieved from www.statcan.gc.ca/pub/85-002-x/2012001/sources-eng.htm

Statistics Canada. (2012b). *Uniform crime reporting survey.* Ottawa, ON: Author. Retrieved from www23.statcan.gc.ca/imdb/p2SV.pl?Function=getSurvey&SDDS=3302&lang=en&db=imdb&adm=8&dis=2

Strand, K. J., & Weiss, G. L. (2005). *Experiencing social research: A reader.* Boston, MA: Pearson Education.

Symbaluk, D. G., & Howell, A. J. (2010). Web-based student feedback: Comparing teaching-award and research-award winners. *Assessment and Evaluation in Higher Education, 35*(1), 71–82. First published on 15 May 2009 (iFirst).

Taraszow, T., Aristodemou, E., Shitta, G., Laouris, Y., & Arsoy, A. (2010). Disclosure of personal and contact information by young people in social networking sites: An analysis using Facebook™ profiles as an example. *International Journal of Media and Cultural Politics, 6*(1), 81–102.

Van Dijk, T. (Ed.). (1997). *Discourse studies: A multidisciplinary introduction (Volume 1: Discourse as structure and process; Volume 2: Discourse as social interaction).* London, UK: Sage Publications.

Webb, E. J., Campbell, D. T., Schwartz, R. D., & Sechrest, L. (2000). *Unobtrusive measures* (Rev. ed.). Thousand Oaks, CA: Sage Publications.

Weitzer, R., & Kubrin, C. (2009). Misogyny in rap music: A content analysis of prevalence and meanings. *Men and Masculinities, 12*(1), 13–29.

Endnotes

[1] Jackson, W. & Verberg, N. (2007). *Methods: Doing social research* (4th ed.). Toronto, ON: Pearson Education Canada.

[2] Note that in Gackenbach et al.'s (2011) study, informed consent was obtained from the young man who posted his dreams and daily activities.

Qualitative Interviewing

Learning Objectives

After reading this chapter, students should be able to do the following:

LO1 Explain what a qualitative interview is.

LO2 Describe the structure of qualitative interviews and explain why qualitative interviewing is considered to be "responsive."

LO3 Identify and explain important considerations that arise in the main steps for conducting a qualitative interview.

LO4 Define and differentiate between main question types.

LO5 Define focus group and compare focus groups to in-depth interviews.

LO6 Describe the main components of a focus group.

"Rather than stripping away context, needlessly reducing people's experiences to numbers, responsive interviewing approaches a problem in its natural setting, explores related and contradictory themes and concepts, and points out the missing and the subtle, as well as the explicit and the obvious." (Rubin & Rubin, 2005, p. viii)

Introduction

LO1

Qualitative interview A technique used to understand the world from the subjects' point of view, to unfold the meaning of their experiences, and to uncover the world prior to scientific explanations.

In Chapters 6 and 7 you learned about two quantitative approaches based on deductive logic stemming from the positivist paradigm and resting on objective conceptions of social reality (i.e., surveys and experiments). In this chapter will learn about a qualitative method known as qualitative interviewing which is grounded in the interpretive paradigm in its emphasis on naturalism and subjective understanding. A **qualitative interview**, also known as an intensive interview, an in-depth interview, or just depth interview, is an approach to research which "attempts to understand the world from the subjects' points of view, to unfold the meaning of their experiences, [and] to uncover their lived world prior to scientific explanations" (Kvale & Brinkmann, 2009, p. 1). You are already familiar with the many uses of interviews in the social world as evident in places of employment where they are regularly relied upon for hiring and promotional purposes. Interviews are an integral part of therapeutic and correctional processes used to assess, monitor and rehabilitate clients and offenders. Interviews are also employed in everyday life by reporters, historians, and authors who wish to learn more about a person of interest's life, career, or accomplishments. Similarly, qualitative interviewing is an especially popular method among researchers interested in understanding processes, organizations, and events from the perspective of those most knowledgeable about such phenomena—the people who directly experience the processes, who work within the organizations, and/or who undergo or are most impacted by the conditions of interest.

Beagan and Etowa (2011), for example, conducted in-depth interviews with African Canadian women living in Nova Scotia in order to understand the meaning and function of spiritually related practices they regularly engaged in. According to the women, spiritually related occupations such as attending church, participating in prayer, singing in a choir or teaching Sunday School provided an essential sense of community and support for them. The spiritual practices were especially important for providing moral direction and serving as a buffer against frequently experienced forms of racism. As another example, Cain, Jackson, Prentice, Mill, Collins, and Barlow (2011) used in-depth interviews to explore ways in which Aboriginal people living with HIV and AIDS experience feelings of depression. The researchers found that participants framed their discussions of depression in relation to disconnections from other people, their communities, and their culture. Depression was also closely linked to personal experiences involving racism, fostering and adoption, and childhood abuse.

Qualitative Interview Structure

LO2

Semi-structured interview A somewhat flexible interview format in which main questions are prepared ahead of time but the questions can be modified or clarified based on participant feedback.

Unstructured interview format A highly flexible interview format based on questions that develop during the interaction based on participant feedback.

While quantitative interviewing in the form of a survey tends to be a formal, direct, and highly structured data collection method, qualitative in-depth interviewing is based on informal and flexible approaches to data collection. Qualitative interviews can be **semi-structured** in format where some of the questions or an outline of potential questions are prepared ahead of time with room to clarify responses and probe for additional details. The format of qualitative interviews can also be completely **unstructured** where question wording develops in the moment more similar to a casual conversation consisting of a variety of friendly exchanges between the interviewer and interviewee with flexibility in choice of topics and issues explored. (See Figure 9.1 for a comparison of structured, semi-structured and unstructured approaches to interviewing.) Since qualitative interviewing relies on listening, understanding, and asking questions, it shares a number of features with everyday conversations including a fundamental social component. Like two friends sharing a private conversation, the qualitative interviewer needs to establish trust and rapport and even be able to "read" unspoken cues evident in non-verbal forms of communication such as facial expressions or tone of voice. However, a qualitative interview is not a casual conversation because unlike casual conversations, qualitative interviews have an established purpose, they tend to involve more questioning from the interviewer and more responding from the interviewee, and they deliver much more detail (Rubin & Rubin, 2005).

In addition, while a quantitative survey consists of mainly closed-ended items (see Chapter 7), a qualitative interview comprises open-ended questions wherein

FIGURE 9.1
A Comparison of
Interview Structures

Structured	Semi-structured	Unstructured
• Quantitative	• Quantitative or qualitative	• Qualitative
• Survey	• Survey or in-depth interview	• In-depth interview
• Questions are prepared ahead of time	• Main questions are prepared ahead of time	• Questions are developed based on respondent answers
• Standardized	• Some flexibility (i.e., questions can be clarified, additional questions can included or earlier items can be omitted)	• Highly flexible (i.e., there is no prearranged item wording)
• Often relies on closed-ended response formats		• Relies on open-ended questions
• No flexibility (i.e., re wording of questions or order of questions)	• Can include follow-up/probing questions designed to learn more about a topic raised by the respondent	• Questions can be clarified and modified by the interviewer
• No clarification or follow-up		• Incorporates follow-up questions that emerge as a function of reponses provided

participants are asked to describe their views and personal experiences, however they make might sense of those experiences in their own words. The order of the questions and even the content of any given question can vary from participant to participant although covering the same topics and even the same questions may be desirable for later comparing the responses across different interviewees. The central underlying feature of qualitative interviewing that makes it unique is its reliance on what Rubin and Rubin (2005) refer to as a "responsive approach." "The term responsive interviewing is intended to communicate that qualitative interviewing is a dynamic and iterative process, not a set of tools to be applied mechanically" (p. 15). The qualitative interviewer's main objective is to listen carefully to what the interviewee is saying in order to achieve a basic understanding and then dependent upon what the interviewer hears, subsequently probe the interviewee for verification and for additional details in order to achieve an even deeper and more thorough understanding. The flexibility of the design is what makes responsiveness possible rendering in-depth interviews ones of the only methods that can be used to truly "get inside a person's head" (Tuckman, 1972) so we can understand "the lived experience" of that person (Seidman, 2006).

Many exploratory topics that begin with the question "What's it like to . . .?" are especially suited to qualitative interviewing. Listed below are some examples that follow from: What's it like to:

• Undergo a transition from a two-year college to a four-year degree-granting university?

• Attend an all-girls school?

- Be a student teacher in a school for gifted children?
- Be a parent of a highly gifted child?
- Be a member of an outlaw motorcycle gang?
- Be a street prostitute?
- Be a professional hockey player?
- Grieve the loss of a loved one due to an unexpected accident or abduction?
- Live out a life sentence for murder while on parole?
- Stay at a shelter after leaving an abusive relationship?

Research on the Net

Forum: Qualitative Social Research (FQS)

FQS is a peer-reviewed multilingual online journal for qualitative research that was started in 1999. The journal publishes articles based on studies conducted using qualitative methods. Go to www.

qualitative-research.net to learn more about the use of biographies, in-depth interviews, participatory qualitative research, qualitative archives, visual methods, and much more!

Test Yourself

- In what ways does a qualitative interview differ from a quantitative survey?
- In what ways does a qualitative interview differ from a casual conversation?
- In what ways is qualitative interviewing considered to be a reflexive process?

Conducting a Qualitative Interview

After settling on a topic, narrowing the focus, and developing a research questions as is the case in any research project, main stages for conducting a qualitative interview include determining the type of format to use, selecting a sample, working through ethical considerations, establishing rapport, developing questions ahead of time and/or while carrying out the interview, coding and analyzing the interview data, and disseminating the findings. Special considerations are associated with some of these stages as discussed below.

Determining the Most Appropriate Structure

Deciding upon the structure for a qualitative interview depends in part on the nature of the research question and the overall purpose of the study, on the anticipated sample, and on various other considerations such as the amount of time and resources available to allocate to the particular project. First, it is important to consider what the interview is designed to accomplish. For example, if the purpose of an interview is to assess the needs and requirements of individuals so they can perhaps receive the most appropriate therapy or treatment, then a semi-structured interview is likely since specific kinds of information will be sought. Similarly, if the interview is designed to test an assumption or more fully explain a process, it is likely to be semi-structured since particular objectives are known in advance. In contrast, an interview that is designed to identify processes or relationships that will become the focus of a later study or an interview that is used to follow up from another method such as an experiment in order to learn more about why things happened the way they did would likely be unstructured. Unstructured interviews also work best for research designed to get at people's lived experiences. Ethnographic research that takes place in natural settings heavily relies upon unstructured in-depth interview techniques (see Chapter 10). In many cases, the decision about structure boils down to how much control the researcher needs to have over the type of responses provided by the interviewees (Bernard, 2011).

Sample considerations also impact on the overall structure selected for an interview. For instance, if the intended sample comprises a group whose responses will be compared for similarities and differences, the interview is likely to be more structured than would be the case if there was only going to be one person interviewed because he or she is perhaps considered to be the starting point, an usual case, or an extreme example of some topic of interest. Here, the issue is more one of whether the researcher wishes to obtain comparable responses suggesting more structure to the design versus a unique understanding warranting a less structured approach (Cohen, Manion & Morrison, 2011).

Overall, unstructured interviews are an excellent means for obtaining rich, detailed, information on a topic of interest from the point of view of the participant. Credibility is likely to be high because the unstructured approach of an in-depth interview is flexible enough to allow for clarification of questions and the use of prompts based directly on the responses provided by an interviewee. This helps ensure that the data obtained is a close approximation of the respondent's construction of reality. However, the researcher still needs to reconstruct or interpret the transcribed data in a manner that is consistent with the respondent's perspective in order to disseminate the findings. While reliability in the "quantitative" sense is likely to be low especially if the questions were tailored to a particular participant and may not lend well to replication with different participants, dependability can be high if the researcher is careful to document the research process including his or her interpretations of the findings and justification for the conclusions reached. See Chapter 4 for more information on how rigour is achieved in qualitative research.

Selecting a Sample

Qualitative research is usually more concerned with gaining an in-depth understanding of a particular phenomenon from those experiencing it than it is with obtaining results that generalize from a large representative sample to a population of interest. Hence, qualitative researchers carefully select for particular kinds of interviewees using techniques such as purposive sampling or snowball sampling in an effort to identify and locate appropriate participants (see Chapter 5 for a discussion of the various sampling techniques). Ideal interviewees are well informed about the research topic (i.e., they have first-hand experience with the event, process, condition, or issue being studied). As Rubin and Rubin (2005) note, finding knowledgeable participants is often not as easy as it first appears to be since "not everyone who *should* know about something is necessarily well informed" (emphasis in original, p. 65). In addition, researchers try to select for interviewees who can offer a diverse range of perspectives and opinions on the same topic. For example, to fully appreciate the collective experience of a two-year community college transitioning to a four-year undergraduate degree granting university, researchers might interview a small number of students, instructors, advisors, support staff, and administrators who were present at the educational institution prior to, during, and after the change in status.

Participants for in-depth interviews are selected for their unique experiences using purposive sampling.

Ethical Considerations

Ethical concerns need to be taken into consideration during the early planning stage of a study. Most social research projects entail at least a minimal risk of harm to participants and in-depth interviews are no exception. The difficulty with in-depth interviews for both researchers and research ethics review board members lies in anticipating in advance the kinds of risks likely to be experienced by participants since the questions that evoke emotion or otherwise affect interviewees develop within the research process itself. There are several ways to mitigate for potential risks. First, researchers should be qualified to carry out in-depth interviews. In order to obtain ethical approval for a study based on qualitative interviews, for example, researchers generally need to validate their qualifications by indicating their prior research experience, by demonstrating their familiarity with use of qualitative interview techniques, and by providing evidence of completion of the TriCouncil Policy Statement Tutorial (see Chapter 3 for a detailed discussion of the TriCouncil Policy Statement on research involving humans as participants). In addition, researchers may be required to provide a detailed project description, a literature review that establishes the scholarly context for the study, and a summary of the methodology including details about the recruitment of participants.

Anticipated risks and benefits to participants also have to be described in advance to an ethics review board (described in Chapter 3). Researchers detail potential sources of psychological harm that could result from the type of questions the researcher plans to ask. This is usually accomplished through the creation of an **interview guide.** An interview guide is similar to an outline, consisting of a series of key questions developed by the researcher after consulting the relevant academic and non-academic literature and taking into account any "hunches" about what might be relevant beyond what is already known (Rapley, 2007). An interview guide helps to frame the interview based on the overall objectives of the study. Although this will only be loosely followed during the actual interview, an interview guide or set of main questions helps to inform the ethics board and potential interviewees about what participation can be expected to entail as part of the informed consent process. Researchers also need to identify specific means for mitigating any of the potential risks posed by the study. For example, a researcher planning on interviewing students about their aggressive driving practices can note that questions about unsafe driving practices will be asked during the interview and can even provide a few sample potential questions. In addition, potential participants can be made aware that they may find some of the questions to be embarrassing or uncomfortable to answer. Finally, a researcher can debrief participants with information that helps them to address their emotions and/or actions beyond the study such as a listing of local driver education resources and/or anger management resources.

Maintaining privacy is another ethical consideration that necessitates special consideration when planning a study based on qualitative interviewing. Anonymity as in not knowing who the participant is (see Chapter 3) clearly cannot be achieved since an interviewer knows who is being interviewed. Moreover, since the sample size is relatively small for in-depth interview methods, the findings do not get reported as group data in a manner that would obscure the identity of participants as is the case with quantitative survey methods. Instead, the researcher is likely to note themes and use quotes from particular individuals to substantiate the findings. How, then, does a qualitative researcher protect the identity of his or her interviewees? There are several ways to protect the identity of interview subjects. First, a pseudonym or alias name can be attached to the interviewee's comments. In addition, identifying details can be removed or left out of the published findings. For example, in explaining how sociology student Kaitlin Fischer (original name) described her experience within one of the first graduating classes from the Bachelor of Arts program at Algoma University in Sault Ste. Marie, Ontario, the researchers might simply state "a female student taking sociology notes . . ." But what would happen if the researchers wanted to share information provided

Interview guide A series of key questions that provide the framework for an interview.

by the president of the University or one of the deans? When there are only a few individuals in a given role or the field of study is quite small, it is highly likely that even when names are left off, information made public could inadvertently identify the participant (e.g., there is only one president). Researchers could in this case conceal the role of the participant by generalizing the position to "an administrator" and broadening the description of the institution by noting "a president at a university in Eastern Canada."

Researchers even need to ensure that others outside of the study cannot compromise privacy by gaining access to the data including any identifying information. Since most interviews are recorded and that information is often stored on the computer of the principal researcher, privacy could be compromised if the researcher's computer was stolen or accessed by someone other than the principal researcher. This is why ethics review boards require information on how the data will be collected and stored and who will have access to the data. Password-protected software helps to alleviate concerns about unauthorized access but still might not resolve the issue of data being subpoenaed by the criminal justice system in cases involving interviews that expose criminal activity. Since this cannot always be anticipated ahead of time, researchers need to carefully think through how they will handle sensitive information they may become privy to. In extreme cases, qualitative researchers have even gone to jail in order to protect the confidentiality of their interview subjects (e.g., see Rubin & Rubin, 2005).

Researchers are especially likely to face ethical dilemmas regarding privacy while studying individuals who engage in criminal activities.

Establishing Rapport

In all forms of qualitative research, the researcher is the data gathering instrument. In the case of an in-depth interview this means the quality and amount of data collected largely rests with the interviewer's ability to establish and maintain rapport with the interviewee. Due to the personalized nature of any given in-depth interview, there are no guaranteed methods for establishing great rapport. An interviewer, however, should try to do whatever is possible given the circumstances to make an interviewee feel at ease and valued for whatever contributions may be forthcoming. After all, it is the views of the interviewee which are essential to the study itself. This is not an easy task as everything about the interviewer from how an interviewer looks, acts, and conducts the interview will have an impact, even if indirectly, on how successful that interview will be. Just as some instructors are more or less able to engage with their students, some interviewers will be more or less adept at developing rapport with interviewees. Think about what is likely to happen when a student offers up an incomplete or incorrect answer in class and the instructor's sharp rebuttal makes that student feel embarrassed or ashamed. The student will be less likely to speak up in the future. If instead, the instructor had thanked the student for responding, clarified the answer, and reassured the student, the same student might be just as willing to try again at another point in time. Similarly, an interviewer needs to create a safe climate in which a participant will be encouraged to offer up information with an implicit understanding that it will be appreciated not judged by the interviewer.

In the development of this climate, it is even important to consider the physical location in which the interview takes place. The location and setting for an interview should be one that is familiar to the participant and would make him or her feel at ease discussing personal issues. Many in-depth interviews take place in the home or work place of the interviewee or in a public location such as a restaurant or coffee shop that can offer privacy and is conveniently located near to where the participant lives or works. The important consideration in choosing a location for an interview is to make sure it is a place where the interviewee will feel comfortable and will be able to speak freely about the topics raised in the interview.

Berg and Lune (2012, pp. 148–150) identify three simple, yet crucial, techniques employed by interviewers to help build trust and establish rapport during interviews including tolerating uncomfortable silence, echoing the interviewee, and letting people talk. "Tolerating uncomfortable silence" means an interviewer should purposely build in long, silent pauses after asking an interviewee a question. Interviewees require time to consider the question, think about how it relates to them and the situation as they understand it, and then try to formulate an answer. As a teaching analogy, I regularly conduct peer reviews on probationary instructors who are new to the institution where I teach. During peer reviews, I often witness inexperienced instructors fail to give students enough time to digest a question posed before the nervous instructor answers it for them. Berg and Lune (2012) recommend waiting for up to 45 seconds before assuming an interviewee truly has nothing to say about a subject.

"Echoing the interviewee" involves acknowledging what the interviewee is saying by repeating back the main idea. This technique conveys interest and understanding. It also helps establish and maintain rapport because the interviewee is inadvertently encouraging the interviewer to continue (Berg & Lune,

2012). The key to this technique is to keep it brief and only echo back what the interviewee has said as demonstrated in the following exchange:

Interviewer: "Can you tell me what it was like when you learned your son was highly gifted?"

Interviewee: "When I initially read the results of the intelligence test, I was relieved. The findings gave us an explanation for Brant's disruptive behaviour at school."

Interviewer: "So you were relieved because you had a reason for the disruptive behaviour?"

Interviewee: "Yes. Brant's kindergarten teacher told us that Brant appeared to be low-functioning and easily distracted. Instead, he may have been highly capable but bored by the repetition."

Imagine instead, how the conversation might have gone if the interviewer was inexperienced and failed to use echoing correctly, inserting a personal viewpoint such as "I know what you mean, I was also a disruptive kid in school." The point of the interview is to obtain needed information from the interviewee, whose perspective needs to remain front and centre throughout the interview process. The underlying goal is to let the participant lead most of the discussion.

Just as the researcher needs to do everything possible in order to get the participant to feel at ease so he or she will be forthcoming in the discussion, it is also important to do everything possible to ensure that the participant does not feel he or she should stop talking. "Letting people talk" literally means the interviewer must be careful not to interject at the wrong times. The worst mistake an interviewer can make in this regard is to interrupt an interviewee's thought processing or react in some manner that interferes with an interviewee's response and cuts it short thereby losing potentially important data (Berg and Lune, 2012). Obviously it takes time to develop interviewer skills and one of the best ways to learn how to conduct great interviews is through first-hand experience and lots of practice. Just as we are apt to make mistakes in some of our exchanges with certain friends and family members, over time we also become more adept at reading cues and figuring out what is working and not working in any given discussion.

Active listening A technique in which the interviewer demonstrates an understanding of what is being said and expressed through appropriate feedback.

Accomplished interviewers are able to demonstrate **active listening**. Active listening is a technique in which the interviewer demonstrates an understanding of what is being said and expressed by the interviewee through feedback. Active listening is evident when an interviewer appropriately echoes the interviewee and uses emotional displays based on what the interviewee has expressed. For example, if a participant conveys a happy experience, the interviewer should appear happy by smiling and conversely, if the interviewee appears to be upset, the interviewer should acknowledge this, appear empathetic and possibly even try to console the person (Berg & Lune, 2012). A skilled interviewer is also able to steer an interviewee away from the tendency to answer with "monosyllabic" responses of "yes" or "no" by using a number of questioning techniques such as probes and pauses (Berg & Lune, 2012). Probes are defined and discussed in detail in the next section.

The quality of data collected during an interview rests largely with the interviewer's ability to establish and maintain rapport.

LO4

Types of Questions and Interview Sequencing

Various types of questions are routinely used in qualitative interviews. This section describes question types and outlines the order for the sequence of events in a typical interview.

Ice Breaker

Ice breaker An opening question that is used specifically in order to establish rapport.

An interview usually begins with an **ice breaker,** or opening question that is unrelated to the research topic and is used specifically in order to establish rapport. The ice breaker can pertain to anything the interviewer feels will be effective for getting that particular participant talking. For example, the interviewer might begin by asking the participant how he or she is enjoying the nice weather or if the interview takes place in the home of the participant, the interviewer might start by asking how long the participant has lived in the neighbourhood, or inquire about a picture that is prominently displayed in the home. The ice breaker should always be a question that is easy for the interviewee to answer.

Informed Consent for Participation

Following the ice breaker, the interviewer can introduce the study by reiterating the overall purpose (e.g., objectives) and procedures. In many cases, the study will consist of a tape-recorded interview that is carried out in the home or work place of the interviewee. Permission needs to be sought from the participant before starting the recording device. Additional details concerning responsibilities of the participant are also provided ahead of time (e.g., about how long the interview will take, what the questions will pertain to). In addition, as part of the consent process, the participant will need to be made aware of the benefits of the research (e.g., how the study contributes to our understanding of a particular condition experienced by the participant) and the potential risks of participation (e.g., that the participant might find some of the questions to be embarrassing or make the participant feel uncomfortable while answering them). Interviewees need to be made aware that participation is voluntary and that even if the interviewee agrees to participate he or she can refrain from answering questions and can withdraw from the study at any time without penalty. If an interviewee chooses to end the study early, the participant is free to decide whether views provided up to that point are to remain as part of the data or will need to be removed from the study. A participant also needs to be informed ahead of time about how privacy will be protected. For example, how will potentially identifying information be stored and who will have access to it? In addition, the participant needs to be informed about how long data will be kept and how records will be destroyed once the study is completed. Finally, the participant needs to know how the findings will be reported (e.g., direct quotes may be used) and what the plans are for dissemination of findings (e.g., findings may be reported at a conference and published in a peer-reviewed journal). All of these details should be contained in the consent form which is reviewed with the participant prior to the onset of the interview. Assuming the participant approves of the conditions, signs the consent form and agrees to be interviewed, the study can officially commence.

Transition Statements

Transition statements
Statements that move the conversation into the essential questions.

Having established informed consent, the researcher can lead the participant into the focus of the study through the use of a **transition statement.** Transition statements are designed to "move the conversation into the key questions that drive the study" (Krueger & Casey, 2009). For example, in a study on teaching I concluded the consent process with: "if you have no further questions or concerns about what the study entails, I'm now going to collect the consent form from you and begin the interview." To transition to the first question, I said: "Take a moment to think about the kinds of things you do to prepare for your classes." After waiting about 45 seconds I then asked, "What is one of the things you do in order to prepare for class?"

Essential Questions

Essential questions Questions that exclusively concern the central focus of the study.

Essential questions, also called key or main questions, "exclusively concern the central focus of the study" (Berg & Lune, 2012, p. 120). Essential questions are usually developed in advance of the interview and they form the basis of the interview guide. If demographic information is pertinent to the study, these items will generally be near the beginning of the interview (e.g., questions on age, marital status and occupational status). Questions that more directly relate to the study topic follow from here, beginning with the least sensitive questions and then moving into the more sensitive ones once rapport is flowing well. Sensitive questions are ones that are most likely to pose the greatest risk of psychological harm by evoking emotions (e.g., asking about the loss of a loved one, asking the participant to retell a painful event or asking about a private condition the interviewee is deeply affected by).

Probes

Probes Questions used to motivate an interviewee to continue speaking or to elaborate on a topic.

Probes are short questions and prompts designed to obtain additional information and details from a participant that will help to further understanding. Interviewees can be encouraged to elaborate on their responses through short prompts such as:

"And then what happened?"; "Anything else?"; "How come?"; "Hmm"; "I see"; "Why do you think that?"; "Could you tell me more about X?"; "What do you mean by X?"; or "How did that make you feel?" As cultural anthropologist H. Russell Bernard (2011) puts it, "the key to successful interviewing is learning how to probe effectively—that is, to stimulate a respondent to produce more information, without injecting yourself so much into the interaction that you only get a reflection of yourself in the data" (p. 161). For example, suppose an interviewee is asked: "Have you ever used illegal drugs while at work?" Assume the participant replies "Yes." The next question can be the probe: "Like what?" Note how this prompt enables the interviewee to choose the direction of the ensuing discussion (as opposed to the interviewer stating the name of some drug and waiting for the respondent to answer in the affirmative or negative thereby leading the creation of the data obtained).

Throw-Away Questions

In cases where it may be difficult for an interviewee to stay focused on a central topic for long periods of time (e.g., because it is stressful or painful to relive), an interviewer can help the interviewee take breaks by asking occasional **throw-away questions.** Throw-away questions are unessential questions that may be unrelated to the research. Berg and Lune (2012) highlight the importance of including throw-away questions while probing sensitive issues as a way to "cool out" the participant.

Throw-away questions Questions unrelated to the research topic that are used to take breaks in the conversation.

Extra Questions and Follow-up Questions

One way to examine the reliability and validity of the responses being provided by the interviewee is to include **extra questions** and **follow-up questions.** Extra questions "are those questions roughly equivalent to certain essential ones but worded slightly differently" (Berg & Lune, 2012, p. 121). Extra questions help to assess reliability in responding since the interviewee should discuss similar issues in a consistent manner. Follow-up questions are "specific to the comments that conversational partners have made" (Rubin & Rubin, 2005, p. 136). Follow-up questions help to clarify main ideas or themes that emerge during the interview to ensure that the interviewer has properly understood the intended meaning of the main idea (e.g., Can you tell me more about . . .?). Follow-up questions are similar to probes but they are usually asked in order to obtain clarification about an issue raised during the interview that is considered to be central to the overall research objectives. Follow-up questions help to establish validity since the aim of qualitative interviewing is to understand an issue from the viewpoint of the participant (Miller & Glassner, 2011). Follow-up questions may be asked within an initial interview or they may be asked in subsequent interviews, after a researcher has had an opportunity to explore the findings to identify themes or concepts that warrant further clarification.

Extra questions Questions roughly equivalent to essential ones that are used to assess reliability.

Follow-up questions Questions specific to comments made that are used to clarify main ideas.

Closing Questions

While there is no set length to a qualitative interview and the actual length will largely be determined by the objectives of the study, the interviewee, and the overall dynamics that develop within the interview process, you can plan as a general

Closing questions Questions used to bring closure to the interview by re-establishing distance between the interviewer and interviewee.

rule of thumb for an interview to be about 90 minutes in length. Since friendly rapport is established within a new social relationship, it is sometimes difficult for the interviewer to bring the interview to an end. **Closing questions** are questions designed to help bring closure to the interaction by re-establishing some of the original distance between the interviewer and interviewer (Hennink, Hutter, & Bailey, 2011). Closing questions often consist of slightly reworked earlier statements concerning data storage and plans for the dissemination of the findings since these topics reflect late stages of the study and are more technical than personal in nature. The **final question** in an interview is typically one that inquires if the participant has any questions of the interviewer about the research or anything else he or she would like to add before the interview concludes. At that point, the participants can be thanked for his or her time and contributions and reminded that the researcher has provided contact information should any questions about participation in this study arise at a later date. A follow-up interview can be scheduled at the end of the interview or the researcher can contact the participant at a later date to schedule a subsequent interview. In-depth interviews are generally not a one-time event. In most cases, the participants are interviewed at least on one other occasion. This is because the researcher needs time to analyze the information collected during the first interview (or round of interviews if multiple people are interviewed for the same project) to determine which of the findings warrant further exploration.

Final question The last interview question in the form of a general inquiry to determine if the participant has any questions about the study or further comments to make).

Coding and Analyzing Interview Data

Assuming the interview was properly recorded in some manner, the information obtained during the interview can now be transcribed so that data analysis can take place. **Transcription** is a data entry process in which the obtained verbal information is transferred verbatim (i.e., word for word), including where possible indications of mood, emotion, and pauses into a written (i.e., typed) format. Transcribing interview tapes or sound recordings into text is a very time-consuming process and the longer the time elapsed between the interview and the transcription, the less able a researcher is to capture gestures or indications of special emphasis that took place during an interview (e.g., perhaps the interviewee shrugged his or her shoulders or fidgeted nervously prior to answering certain questions). As an example, it took students in one of my advanced qualitative methods courses 6 to 8 hours, on average, to transcribe one 90-minute interview for a course assignment. Those who did their transcription right away were able to add in additional insights such as lengthy pauses and facial expressions used by the interviewee. A few opted to save time using voice-activated software which then transcribed the interview for them with minimal errors. However, the students who transcribed the data themselves benefited from listening repeatedly to what the interviewee was actually saying, thereby increasing the detail and authenticity of their interpretations of the responses provided by the interviewee. Reliability can be assessed at the transcription phase through the use of two transcribers, whose verbatim accounts of the interview should end up very similar provided the audio recording is of adequate quality. Once the data is transcribed it can be coded for themes, ideas, and main concepts.

Transcription A data entry process in which the obtained verbal information is transferred verbatim into text.

Coding was defined in Chapter 8 as means of standardizing data. Coding qualitative data involves "extracting concepts from raw data and developing them in terms of their properties and dimensions" (Corbin & Strauss, 2008, p. 159). Recall that the purpose of a qualitative interview is to gain an understanding of a topic from the perspective of someone who has experienced it first-hand. Thus, if you were studying what is it like for someone to parent a highly distracted ten-year-old boy, your research findings should help others understand what distractibility means as explained by one of his parents. As you read through the transcription, you need to underline passages that identify main ideas. For example, the parent might note that "the child rarely remembers to bring home his homework," that "teachers continuously indicate that the boy cannot complete school work independently," and that "it takes hours upon hours to complete a short piece of homework." These types of comments help to identify what distractibility means in terms of school-related behavioural indicators. The transcript might also contain other indicators of distractibility such as social implications. For example, the interview transcript might include a comment that "he never gets invited to birthday parties even by the children who attend his party" and "no one ever comes to door to call on him when the neighbourhood kids are going to the park." The researcher's task is to try and tell the story of distractibility from the perspective of the parent, highlighting main concepts and themes as reflected in the conversation.

Context The sets of conditions that give rise to problems or circumstances to which individuals respond by means of action/interaction/emotions.

In addition to the identification of key concepts, qualitative researchers pay particular attention to context. **Context** refers to "the sets of conditions that give rise to problems or circumstances to which individuals respond by means of action/interaction/emotions" (Corbin & Strauss, 2008, p. 229). In reference to the distracted child, you might be tempted to conclude that the child probably has something like an attention-deficit disorder. However, the researcher would try to make sense of the distractibility in relation to other issues that help to provide a context for understanding why it occurs. For example, the researcher might note that most of the problems are only evident at school and in relation to age-related peers. Careful consideration of the transcript might also reveal that the child has a few close friends who are several years older. In addition, there may be passages indicating that the child has an unusually advanced sense of humour, learns new things very quickly, and is able to retain large amounts of information. These behaviourial traits are associated with giftedness. As noted in an earlier chapter, gifted children are those whose intelligence (as measured by standard IQ tests) is well out of the range of normal (i.e., over 120). Gifted children have a very low tolerance for repetitive tasks, they tend to have what is called sensual and intellectual overexcitability wherein they easily become distracted in environments that are not interesting or highly challenging for them (Webb, Amend, Webb, Goerss, Beljan, & Olenchak, 2005). Trying to make sense of distractibility in the context of giftedness clearly paints a different picture than understanding distractibility in the context of an attention deficit disorder. Qualitative data analysis is discussed in further detail in the final chapter on report writing.

Test Yourself

- Why might a qualitative researcher choose an unstructured interview format?
- Why would a qualitative researcher opt for purposive sampling over a probability-based technique?
- Why is it difficult to anticipate the potential risks stemming from a qualitative interview?
- What three techniques are used during interviews to help establish trust and build rapport?
- What is the purpose of a "throw-away" question?
- What does transcription refer to?
- Why is context important to a qualitative researcher?

Focus Group Interviewing

LO5

Focus group A small discussion group led by skilled interviewer that is designed to obtain views and feelings about a particular topic of interest through group interaction.

A **focus group** is a small discussion group led by a skilled interviewer that is designed to obtain views and feelings about a particular topic of interest (Krueger & Casey, 2009). Similar to in-depth interviewing, a focus group is a method for collecting data about people's thoughts, feelings, and behaviours. What sets a focus group apart from an in-depth interview with multiple participants is the source of the data. In a group interview, multiple participants provide independent answers to questions posed by an interviewer. In contrast, in a focus group, a moderator creates a small group discussion and that interactive collaboration becomes the source of the data collected (Morgan, 1996). Most focus groups consist of between 5 and 10 participants who are selected because they possess certain characteristics in common or they are believed to have especially well-informed views on the topic of interest. For example, in advance of a residence being built at a university, focus groups could be conducted with student groups for applied research purposes in order to learn about the potential impact of a residence on existing campus services. Who better to ask than the primary users of services directed at students and those likely to live in residence? Focus groups can provide insight into how students' current patterns of service use might change if they lived in residence. For example, participants might indicate that if they lived in an adjacent residence, they would like to be able to access the library after regular hours since they tend to study at night. In addition, they could note that they might be less likely to purchase food to eat on campus, since it would be just as convenient and now cost saving to head home between classes to make lunches and snacks. Sometimes focus groups can be extremely beneficial for identifying unanticipated findings. In an actual focus group conducted on this topic at the university where I teach, participants identified the need for a special type of "quiet space" or "spiritual room" for prayer on campus. Note that as a group, the participants did not pin point any particular religion but explained that such a space would be especially important for students who are expected to pray several times a day.

The quality of data collected from focus groups rests largely with the skills of the moderator.

Like in-depth interviews, focus group topics span an infinite range. When I was seconded from my teaching role by the Office of the Vice-President of Resources to serve a two-year term as a resource development planner, I relied heavily upon focus groups to learn more about how students use existing resources and space on campus. I also used focus group studies to learn about the ideas and interests of recently retired and soon to be retired faculty and staff members to see whether and how they might wish to stay connected to their former place of employment. As part of the scholarship of teaching, I've led focus group studies with students as participants to learn about study strategies and to determine what they perceive to be effective learning practices. I have similarly interviewed instructors in focus groups to discern how they prepare for courses they are teaching for the first time. Focus groups are especially usefully for gaining insight into particular problems, issues, or processes. Some examples of issues that have been studied by other Canadian researchers using focus groups include:

- Challenges experienced by female university students with disabilities (Erten, 2011)
- The use of Web technologies to support group work outside of class (Vaughan, Nickle, Silovs, & Zimmer, 2011)
- Barriers to educating new immigrant groups about asthma (Poureslami, Rootman, Doyle-Waters, Nimmon, & FitzGerald, 2011)
- Perceptions of the barriers faced by health care providers working in on-reserve First Nation communities (Bhattacharyya, Rasooly, Naqshbandi, Estey, Esler, Toth, Macaulay, & Harris, 2011)
- Experiences of marginalized patients without a primary care provider (Crooks, Agarwal, & Harrison, 2012)

Similar to an in-depth qualitative interview, a focus group interview is initiated by a skilled interviewer typically referred to as a moderator or facilitator, who poses open-ended questions and attempts to steer the otherwise natural conversation toward the exploration of particular topics and themes. Because the interviewer stands out in a focus group especially in his or her semi-structured attempts to manage group dynamics and lead the group through specific issues and questions, a focus group is generally considered to be less natural and more "staged" compared to a one-on-one interview (Morgan, 2001). In addition, participants in focus groups are affected by the presence of others who say things and do things that shift the conversation in directions that might not have occurred had the participants been interviewed individually. This can have positive and negative implications on validity. For example, validity decreases as participants agree with other group members because they think this is the most appropriate response given demand characteristics created by the group. Or, similarly, participants may be unwilling to express divergent viewpoints they possess because they do not want to stand out as being different from the rest of the group (i.e., social desirability bias). Comments made by certain members of the group can also be distracting for other members since they take attention away from what any given individual might have originally stated had someone else not provided a response first. In other words, listening to one member's response can mean interrupting the thought pattern or potential response of everyone else. On the other hand, comments made by other group members may also trigger ideas for greater innovation or they may help a participant more fully clarify his or her own responses in manner that enhances validity.

Compared to in-depth interviews, focus groups can be a relatively inexpensive, time-efficient means for obtaining rich, detailed information from knowledgeable participants. Because group members share common characteristics and have specialized knowledge about the topic of interest, their feedback during the focused discussions can be very instrumental in producing novel insights for ways to solve important issues or create programs tailored to the needs of a specific group. However, much of the data obtained will largely depend on the skill set of the individual moderator, whose role it is to steer the discussion in such a way to produce and maintain group dynamics that yield the most relevant feedback from the participants. In summarizing the most important characteristics of good moderators, Krueger and Casey (2009) point out that the "right" kind of moderator shows his or her respect for participants, understands the purpose of the study and the topic, communicates clearly, is open and not defensive, and is able to bring about the most useful information from the group.

Research in Action

Focus Groups: Behind the Glass

Focus Groups: Behind the Glass is a short video recording produced and distributed by the Canadian Broadcasting Corporation. This video demonstrates the utility of focus groups in marketing for learning about consumer attitudes and views toward products. Using WorldCat Libraries, you can identify libraries near you that carry a copy of the video. Go to www.worldcat.org and search for "Focus Groups: Behind the Glass."

LO6

Focus Group Components

The three most essential elements of a successful focus group include: clear objectives, an appropriate group of participants, and a highly skilled moderator.

Clear Objectives

As with any study, a researcher first needs to be clear about the overall purpose and objectives of the study. Like in-depth interviews, a focus group is utilized in order to learn more about a topic of interest from the perspective of individuals who have first-hand knowledge regarding that process, event, or condition of interest. Beyond an in-depth interview, there is in assumption that through the ensuing discussion, group members will provide a range of views and ultimately information and details might emerge beyond what could be obtained in individual interviews.

Participant Groups

Although marketing-based focus groups investigating consumer views often include as many as twelve participants in a session, social science researchers recommend no more than ten participants (e.g., Krueger & Casey, 2009) and suggest the most appropriate size is 6 to 8 (e.g., Hennink, Hutter, & Bailey, 2011; Berg & Lune, 2012). Based on experience, I would prefer to break a larger group (e.g., of 12 or 10 members) into 2 separate focus groups (e.g., of 6 or 5 members). However, the actual size of a group is best determined by the overall research purpose and other design considerations such as the number of potential questions. Krueger and Casey (2009) offer a good rule of thumb by noting when "the purpose is to understand an issue or behaviour, invite fewer people" and when "the purpose is to pilot-test an idea or materials, invite more people" (p. 68). The key is to strike a balance in numbers of participants that will promote discussion and allow the researcher to fully cover off the main issues in a reasonable time frame anticipating that some of the members will talk more or less than others. A researcher typically runs about three or four different focus groups on the same topic in order to fully explore the issue (Krueger & Casey, 2009). A good indication that "enough" groups have been utilized is when the interviewer can reasonably anticipate what the next group is going to say about the issues during the ensuing discussion (Bryman, Bell, & Teevan, 2012).

In addition to size, a researcher needs to carefully consider the composition of focus groups. Ideally, the more diverse but homogenous (i.e., alike) a group is with respect to the relevant characteristic of interest, the better. For example, if a researcher is interested in how instructors prepare for courses they have never taught before, the shared characteristic is new course preparation but the group could include for diversity, instructors who teach full and part-time and those with more or less overall teaching experience. Alternatively, if a researcher is interested in how sessional (i.e., part-time) instructors teaching introductory-level courses prepare for classes, the common elements are instructors with limited-term appointments and introductory-level courses. In this case, diversity can be achieved by including instructors that meet the criteria and who are from a variety of social science disciplines (e.g., sociology, anthropology, and political science).

An email or paper copy letter of invite is often employed in order to recruit participants into a focus group. The letter of invite is usually less formal in tone than a consent form and it outlines who the researcher is, what the purpose of the study is, what the expectations are for participants, what the participation incentives are (if any), and what the eligibility criteria are (see Figure 9.2).

Moderator A trained facilitator used in focus group research who guides the focus group discussion.

A Skilled Moderator

A **moderator** "is a trained facilitator used in focus group research who guides the focus group discussion" (Neuman & Robson, 2012, p. 261). A moderator in a focus group is akin to an interviewer in an in-depth qualitative interview. First,

FIGURE 9.2
Sample Letter of Invite

Term Instructor Focus Group

Dear [term instructor's name],

You are invited to participate in a focus group on teaching preparations.

My name is X and I am an associate professor in the Department of X at X. I am conducting research on teaching introductory X. Since the majority of introductory X courses are taught by term instructors, I would like to learn more about how you go about preparing for your classes and what kinds of resources you find to be useful for instructional purposes.

The focus group will take approximately two hours. If you choose to participate, I will be asking you to comment, as part of an informal discussion with about 5 other term instructors, on a series of questions related to course preparation. For example, I will be asking you if you use any supplementary resources (e.g., an instructor's manual or test bank), what types of supplementary resources work well for you, and which ones are of little or no value to you. In addition, I will be asking you for any ideas or recommendations you have for resources that might better facilitate introductory-level teaching among term instructors.

Note: This study is considered institutional research and was approved by X's Research Ethics Board. You will be provided with a consent form and agreement to maintain confidentiality at the session.

Date and Time:
Location:

Light refreshments will be included, and as a token of appreciation you will receive a $50 gift certificate.

Eligible participants are individuals who are currently teaching at least one course at X and have taught an introductory-level course at least once within the last two years. If you are interested in participating in the focus group, please email me as soon as possible.

Sincerely,

X

X's email address

---

a moderator prepares ahead of time all of the technical and organizational de pertaining to the study. This can include setting up a meeting room (e.g., arrang the chairs so participants can see one another), bringing in refreshments for participants or at a minimum, providing water for the participants, distributing other necessary materials such as consent forms and pens, and bringing in and setting up some type of audio recording device. An assistant might be included in the session in order to take some back-up, "real-time" notes or to type comments during the session that can be later used to contextualize the transcribed discussion. The role of a moderator is to welcome the participants, obtain informed consent from the participants, explain the ground rules for the focus session, get the participants talking, and guide the discussion in a manner that elicits responses from the various participants while covering all of the essential questions (Krueger & Casey, 2009). In addition, the moderator helps to establish a positive group dynamic by encouraging equitable participation. For example, a moderator must be able to encourage participation by everyone, even the shy participants or people who seem more reluctant to speak out (e.g., by using prompts, by nodding, and by establishing turn-taking rules). Moreover, just as a skilled instructor leads his or her classroom discussions so that one student doesn't predominate, a moderator may also need to incorporate strategies to help foster equitable group dynamics.

Analyzing Focus Group Data

Similar to how in-depth interview transcripts are coded for themes using qualitative analysis and how messages in the media are coded for prevalent patterns using content analysis (see Chapter 8), focus group data is first transcribed and then examined and coded in stages. This process can be extremely time-consuming and complex especially in studies based on several different focus groups. For example, in a study on parents' and teachers' views on physical activity and beverage consumption in preschoolers, De Craemer et al. (2013) utilized 24 parent focus groups and 18 teacher focus groups from 6 different countries (i.e., Belgium, Bulgaria, Germany, Greece, Poland, and Spain). First, each audio-taped focus group discussion was made available in all six countries wherein the focus group discussions were transcribed into written text in the local language of each recipient country. Next, the transcriptions were independently coded using qualitative content analysis by local researchers. Following this, the main findings from all of the focus groups were then translated into English and forwarded to two principal researchers (who received a total of six versions of the original data). The principal researchers then further assessed and compiled the main findings using a qualitative software program called NVivio (see Chapter 12 for more information on this software). Finally, the principal researchers summarized the key findings along with illustrative quotes and excerpts from the original data into a report that "was reviewed and validated by all the focus group organizers" (De Craemer, De Decker, De Bourdeaudhuij, Deforche, Vereecken, Duvinage, Grammatikaki, Iotova, Fernández-Alvira, Zych, Manios, & Cardon, 2013).

One of the more interesting findings of this study pointed out by the researchers was a strong opinion by parents that their preschoolers were sufficiently physically active and that they had healthy beverage intakes (e.g., they drank enough water and only minimal amounts of sugar-laden drinks such as juices, pop, and chocolate-flavoured milk). The parental perspective was not consistent with the conclusions substantiated in the previous literature by more objective methods (e.g., dietary records) suggesting that parents may need more information about existing dietary practices if they are to be motivated to make changes in their own families.

Test Yourself

- What is a focus group?
- In what ways does a focus group differ from a qualitative interview?
- How might the presence of others increase validity in a focus group?
- Why would a researcher run multiple focus groups on the same topic?
- In what ways is focus group composition important?
- What is the role of a focus group moderator?

Chapter Summary

LO1 **Explain what a qualitative interview is.**

A qualitative interview is a technique that is designed to help a researcher understand aspects of the social world from the perspective of the participant who is experiencing them.

LO2 **Describe the structure of qualitative interviews and explain why qualitative interviewing is considered to be "responsive."**

A semi-structured interview is somewhat flexible since questions can be modified and clarified while an unstructured interview is highly flexible enabling questioning to develop as a function of exchanges within the interview itself. Qualitative interviewing is considered to be responsive because an interviewer asks questions and probes for details based upon what is being said during the interview, rather than just asking questions that are prepared in advance.

LO3 **Identify and explain important considerations that arise in the main steps for conducting a qualitative interview.**

First, a qualitative researcher needs to adopt the most appropriate interview format and try to obtain the most suitable interviewees. In addition, a researcher needs to anticipate potential risks to participants. Since the interviewee is not anonymous, a researcher needs to take special precautions to uphold confidentiality. The interviewer also plays an important role as he or she is the research instrument establishing trust, motivating the interviewee to provide detailed information, and carefully steering the interview in the desired direction.

LO4   **Define and differentiate between main question types.**

An *ice breaker* is an opening statement that is used specifically in order to establish rapport. An *essential question* is one that exclusively concerns the central focus of the study. *Probes* are used to motivate an interviewee to continue speaking. *Throw-away questions* are unrelated to the research and are used to give the interviewee a break. *Extra questions* are equivalent to essential questions and help to assess reliability. *Follow-up questions* are specific to comments and are used to clarify main ideas. *Closing questions* bring the interview to an end by re-establishing distance. The *final question* asks if the participant has any questions about the study or further comments to make.

LO5   **Define focus group and compare focus groups to in-depth interviews.**

A focus group is a small discussion group led by a skilled interviewer called a moderator. A focus group is more structured relative to an in-depth interview and group dynamics can influence individual responses so they are different from how someone would normally respond in a one-on-one interview. Focus groups are a relatively inexpensive and efficient means for gaining rich, detailed information from an informed group who likely has first-hand experience with the topic of interest. A disadvantage of a focus group is that the quality of information obtained can be negatively affected by an inexperienced or unskilled moderator.

LO6   **Describe the main components of a focus group.**

The three essential components of a focus group are clear objectives, an appropriate group of participants, and a skilled moderator.

Research Reflection	1. Suppose you are interested in conducting an exploratory study into what it would be like to be married to more than one spouse at the same time (called polygamous or plural marriage). Would an in-depth interview be the most suitable technique for this particular research question? Why or why not?
	2. Develop an interview guide that you could use if you were going to interview a sample of your classmates about their cell phone use.
	3. Identify a topic you think would be best addressed using a focus group. Explain your rationale. If you were the moderator for the focus group, what are 3 essential questions you would ask the group in order to explore the topic? Provide one example of an ice breaker you could use to start the session.
Learning Through Practice	Objective: Learning how to conduct a focus group.
	Directions:
	1. Suppose you wanted to learn more about effective study strategies using a focus group.
	a. First, enlist 5 or 6 of your classmates.
	b. Next, assign the role of moderator to one of the members of your group. Also ask one of the group members to take notes while the group discusses study strategies.

   c. Come up with 4 essential questions that would help us learn about study strategies.

   d. Identify strategies your group would use to establish rapport and maintain good group dynamics.

2. Try running a 20-minute focus group with the selected moderator as the facilitator.

3. Describe your main findings.

4. How would you improve upon the focus group if you were going to repeat this topic using a different group of participants?

Research Resources

1. To learn more about qualitative interviewing, I highly recommend Kvale, S., & Brinkmann, S. (2009). *Interviews: Learning the craft of qualitative research interviewing* (2nd ed.). Thousand Oaks, CA: Sage Publications.

2. For more information on responsive interviewing, I highly recommend Rubin, H. J., & Rubin, I. R. (2005). *Qualitative interviewing: The art of hearing data* (2nd ed.). Thousand Oaks, CA: Sage Publications.

3. For a description of feminist qualitative interviewing, refer to DeVault, M. L., & Gross, G. (2012). Feminist qualitative interviewing: experience, talk, and knowledge. In Hesse-Biber, S. N. (Ed.), *The Handbook of feminist research: Theory and praxis* (2nd ed., pp. 173–198). Thousand Oaks, CA: Sage Publications.

4. For more information on how to interview particular groups (e.g., children and adolescents, women, seniors) and how to conduct certain types of interviews (e.g., therapy interviewing, interviewing in education, internet interviewing), I recommend Gubrium, J. F., & Holstein, J. A. (2001). *Handbook of interview research: Context & method.* Thousand Oaks, CA: Sage Publications.

5. For detailed information on how to plan for and carry out focus group interviews as well as how to analyze focus group results, I highly recommend Krueger, R. A., & Casey, M. A. (2009). *Focus groups: A practical guide for applied research* (4th ed.). Thousand Oaks, CA: Sage Publications.

Mc Graw Hill Education connect®   For more information on the resources available from McGraw-Hill Ryerson, go to www.mcgrawhill.ca/he/solutions.

References

Beagan, B. L., & Etowa, J. B. (2011). The meaning and functions of occupations related to spirituality for African Nova Scotian women. *Journal of Occupational Science, 18*(3), 277–290.

Berg, B. L., & Lune, H. (2012). *Qualitative research methods for the social sciences* (8th ed.). Upper Saddle River, NJ: Pearson Education.

Bernard, H. R. (2011). *Research methods in anthropology: Qualitative and quantitative approaches* (5th ed.). Plymouth, UK: AltaMira Press.

Bhattacharyya, O. K., Rasooly, I. R., Naqshbandi, M., Estey, E. A., Esler, J., Toth, E., Macaulay, A. C., & Harris, S. B. (2011). Challenges to the provision of diabetes care in first nations communities: Results from a national survey of healthcare providers in Canada. *BMC Health Services Research, 11,* 283. Retrieved from http://www.biomedcentral.com/1472-6963/11/283

Bryman, A. Bell, E., & Teevan, J. J. (2012). *Social research methods* (3rd Can. ed). Don Mills, ON: Oxford University Press.

Cain, R., Jackson, R., Prentice, T., Mill, J., Collins, E., & Barlow, K. (2011). Depression among Aboriginal people living with HIV in Canada. *Canadian Journal of Mental Health, 30(1),* Spring, 105–120.

Cohen, L., Manion, L., & Morrison, K. (2011). *Research methods in education* (7th ed.). New York, NY: Routledge.

Corbin, J., & Strauss, A. (2008). *Basics of qualitative research: Techniques and procedures for developing grounded theory* (3rd ed.). Thousand Oaks, CA: Sage Publications.

Crooks, V. A., Agarwal, G., & Harrison, A. (2012). Chronically ill Canadians' experiences of being unattached to a family doctor: A qualitative study of marginalized patients in British Columbia. *BMC Family Practice,* doi:10.1186/1471-2296-13-69

David, M., & Sutton, C. D. (2011). *Social research: An introduction* (2nd ed.). Thousand Oaks, CA: Sage Publications.

De Craemer, M., De Decker, E., De Bourdeauhuij, I., Deforche, B., Vereecken, C., Duvinage, K., Grammatikaki, E., Iotova, V., Fernández-Alvira, J. M., Zych, K., Manios, Y., & Cardon, G. (2013). Physical activity and beverage consumption in preschoolers: Focus groups with parents and teachers. *BMC Public Health 2013, 13,* 278. Retrieved from http://www.biomedcentral.com/1471-2458/13/278

DeVault, M. L., & Gross, G. (2012). Feminist qualitative interviewing: Experience, talk, and knowledge. In Hesse-Biber, S. N. (Ed.). *The handbook of feminist research: Theory and praxis* (2nd ed.). Thousand Oaks, CA: Sage Publications.

Erten, O. (2011). Facing challenges: Experiences of young women with disabilities attending a Canadian university. *Journal of Postsecondary Education and Disability, 24*(2), 101–114.

Gubrium, J. F., & Holstein, J. A. (2001). *Handbook of interview research: Context & method.* Thousand Oaks, CA: Sage Publications.

Hennink, M., Hutter, I., & Bailey, A. (2011). *Qualitative research methods.* Thousand Oaks, CA: Sage Publications.

Krueger, R. A., & Casey, M. A. (2009). *Focus groups: A practical guide for applied research* (4th ed.). Thousand Oaks, CA: Sage Publications.

Kvale, S., & Brinkmann, S. (2009). *Interviews: Learning the craft of qualitative research interviewing* (2nd ed.). Thousand Oaks, CA: Sage Publications.

Miller, J., & Glassner, B. (2011). The "inside" and the "outside": Finding realities in interviews. In D. Silverman (Ed.). *Qualitative research: Issues of theory, method and practice* (3rd ed., pp. 131–148). Thousand Oaks, CA: Sage Publications.

Morgan, D. L. (1996). Focus groups. *Annual Review of Sociology, 22,* 129–152.

Morgan, D. L. (2001). Focus group interviewing. In J. F. Gubrium & J. A. Holstein (Eds.), *Handbook of interview research: Context & method* (pp. 141–159). Thousand Oaks, CA: Sage Publications.

Neuman, W. L., & Robson, K. (2012). *Basics of social research: Qualitative and quantitative approaches.* Toronto, ON: Pearson Canada.

Poureslami, I., Rootman, I., Doyle-Waters, M. M., Nimmon, L., & FitzGerald, J. M. (2011). Health literacy, language, and ethnicity-related factors in newcomer asthma patients to Canada: A qualitative study. *Journal of Immigrant Minority Health, 13,* 315–322.

Rapley, T. (2007). Interviews. In C. Seale, G. Gobo, J. F. Gubrium, & D. Silverman (Eds.), *Qualitative Research Practice* (pp. 15–33). Thousand Oaks, CA: Sage Publications.

Rubin, H. J., & Rubin, I. S. (2005). *Qualitative interviewing: The art of hearing data.* Thousand Oaks, CA: Sage Publications.

Seidman, R. (2006). *Interviewing as qualitative research: A guide for researchers in education and the social sciences* (3rd ed.). New York, NY: The Teacher's College Press.

Tuckman, B. W. (1972). *Conducting educational research.* New York, NY: Harcourt Brace Jovanovich.

Vaughan, N., Nickle, T., Silovs, J., & Zimmer, J. (2011). Moving to their own beat: Exploring how students use Web 2.0 technologies to support group work outside of class time. *Journal of Interactive Online Learning, 10*(3), 113–127.

Webb. J. T., Amend, E. R., Webb, N. E., Goerss, J., Beljan, P., & Olenchak, F. R. (2005). *Misdiagnosis and dual diagnosis of gifted children and adults: ADHD, bipolar, OCD, Asperger's, depression, and other disorders.* Scottsdale, AZ: Great Potential Press.

Ethnography

10

Learning Objectives

After reading this chapter, students should be able to do the following:

LO1 Define ethnography and describe the role of an ethnographer.

LO2 Outline the main features of ethnographic studies.

LO3 Differentiate between the four main roles of ethnographers engaged in fieldwork.

LO4 Describe the main stages of fieldwork.

LO5 Explain the techniques used by ethnographers to blend into a group.

LO6 Discuss ethical issues in fieldwork.

"From the standpoint of ethnography, the only plausible way to study social and cultural phenomenon is to study them in action." (Murchison, 2010, p. 4)[1]

Introduction

LO1

Ethnographers
Social scientists who undertake research and writing about groups of people by systematically observing and participating (to a greater or lesser degree) in the lives of the people they study.

Ethnography
A multi-method approach to field research that is used to study a social group or culture in its natural setting over time.

Ethnographers "are social scientists who undertake research and writing about groups of people by systematically observing and participating (to a greater or lesser degree) in the lives of the people they study" (Madden, 2010, p. 1). The historical origins of **ethnography** can be traced to naturalistic observation and fieldwork in social and cultural anthropology and later in the Chicago school of sociology (O'Reilly, 2009). Ethnographers share the assumption that to understand a group, researchers must engage in fieldwork that involves spending a considerable length of time with the group in its natural setting. This fieldwork includes watching, listening, taking notes, asking questions, and even perhaps directly participating in the activities and conversations as a member of the group being studied. While ethnography is often used interchangeably with the term "participant observation," ethnography is probably better understood as a multi-method approach to field research that may include any number of qualitative and quantitative data collection techniques undertaken to understand a social group or culture in its natural setting. Data collection in naturalistic settings can be accomplished using systematic observation, participant observation, in-depth interviewing, field notes, surveys, and even visual materials such as drawings and photographs. It is sometimes debated whether ethnography should even be considered a methodology in and of itself since the purpose of ethnography is intricately tied to the end product of fieldwork: the description of a group, culture, or process. From this perspective, "ethnography is about telling a credible, rigorous, and authentic story" (Fetterman, 2010, p. 1).

Research in Action

William Foote Whyte's (1943) Street Corner Society

As a pioneer in ethnography, William Foote Whyte spent three and half years in an inner city Italian district in Boston's North end dubbed Cornerville, living among, interacting with, and studying various groups, including a gang he referred to as the "corner boys" (Whyte, 1943). In a later book called *Participant Observer: An Autobiography* (1994), Whyte describes how he learned to conduct ethnographic research for his "slum study" through trial and error, beginning with an overly ambitious research topic in which he first hoped to study "the history of the North End, the economics (living standards, housing, marketing, distribution, and employment), the politics (the structure of the political organization and its relations to the rackets and the police), the patterns of education and recreation, the church, public health, and—of all things—social attitudes" (p. 64). Following the advice of his mentors, including L. J. Henderson and Talcott Parsons, Whyte narrowed his "ten-man" project into something more manageable for one person lacking in field experience, and then set out to gather information from residents.

As a researcher, Whyte encountered several false starts, beginning with knocking on doors in hopes of surveying tenants about their living conditions.

As he surmised: "it would have been hard to devise a more inappropriate way to begin the study I eventually made. I felt ill at ease and so did the people. I wound up the study of the block and wrote it off as a total loss" (pp. 65–66). Next, Whyte tried out a method shared by an economics instructor who claimed it was easy to learn about local women while purchasing drinks for them in a bar. This approach proved even worse for Whyte, who was nearly thrown out of a bar which he later learned was never frequented by any North Enders anyway (Whyte, 1994). It was only after Whyte met Ernest Pecci (whom he called Doc) that he understood the fundamental importance of getting to know someone from the community. Among many other insights, Whyte's (1943) early work teaches us that in order to study a group of interest, a researcher must first find a way to access that group. Knowing someone who is already a member of the group can be extremely helpful in this regard. In addition, the insider can also be of assistance in explaining what is going on and how to conduct oneself within that group to be accepted, to not stand out, and to not offend anyone. Finally, it is often through the establishment of relationships developed while in the field that a researcher begins to gain the insider perspective needed to better understand events from the perspective of those experiencing them.

Main Features of Ethnography

To help you understand what ethnography is and how it is distinct from other research methods used by social scientists, this section describes ten main features of ethnographic studies adapted from anthropologist Harry Wolcott's (2010, pp. 90–96) list of what he considers the "essence" of ethnography after more than 50 years of experience in the field.

1. Ethnography takes place in natural settings.
2. Ethnography is context-based.
3. Ethnography relies on participant observation.
4. Ethnography is undertaken by a single principal investigator.
5. Ethnography involves long-term acquaintances.
6. Ethnography is non-judgmental.
7. Ethnography is reflexive.
8. Ethnography is mostly descriptive.
9. Ethnography is case-specific.
10. Ethnography requires multiple techniques and data sources.

Ethnography Takes Place in Natural Settings

First, the research must be conducted in a natural setting. A natural setting is one that is not established for the purpose of research, such as a private home, a park, a shopping mall, a daycare, a library, or a lunchroom (Judd, Smith, & Kiddler, 1991). The underlying assumption is that behaviour examined in a natural setting is also natural and depicts people as they are in everyday life. In contrast, people's behaviour within the confined parameters of research contexts, such as experimental settings that may bear little resemblance to the participants' real lives, is assumed to be not natural. Moreover, any events or interactions that take place within natural settings are deemed to be the result of naturally occurring causes as opposed to manipulated or controlled independent variables. "Naturalness" in research is beneficial to validity since it is devoid of the participant biases common to survey and experimental methods. For example, "unobtrusively observed

Ethnography takes place in everyday, natural settings.

behaviours (such as racially integrated seating patterns in a lunchroom) are likely to reflect the desired construct (unprejudiced attitudes) to a greater extent than questionnaire or other responses obtained for obvious research purposes" (Judd et al., 1991, p. 272).

The Internet is rapidly changing the way we view natural settings, communities, and the manner in which ethnographers do research. People can be members of all sorts of virtual communities, from friends and followers on social networking sites such Facebook and Twitter, to various online support groups, to virtual worlds that are part of interactive games. **Virtual ethnography** is the term for "an in-depth study of a group or culture that exists in an online environment" (Van den Hoonaard, 2012, p. 161). In this case, ethnographic research is undertaken through participation on the Internet with other group members as part of a virtual community, such a discussion group.

Virtual ethnography An in-depth study of a group or culture that exists in an online environment.

Ethnography Is Context-Based

To understand social interactions and social processes, an ethnographer must also take into account the wider context in which the studied phenomena arise. The context often contains important conditions that help frame problems and can provide clues to why events unfold the way they do. For example, in an evaluation of an educational program, Fetterman (1987) noted that low school attendance should be interpreted within the environment in which the students and their program were situated. This particular context included insufficient materials within the classroom to meet impoverished students' needs. For examples, even basic supplies such as paper and pens were lacking, making it difficult for students to achieve. In addition, there were various competing distractions outside of the classroom, including high rates of prostitution, arson, sexual assault, and homicide, that posed special challenges for students.

Ethnographers try to understand behaviour within the wider context in which it occurs.

Ethnography Relies on Participant Observation

Participant observation A research method in which the researcher is actively involved with the group being observed over an extended period of time.

Ethnographers often employ a research strategy called **participant observation** or what anthropologist Clifford Geertz (1998) called "deep hanging out." In this strategy, the researcher joins a group of interest for an extended period of time to observe and study its members and functioning first-hand. Participant observation is also sometimes referred to as naturalistic observation and fieldwork, but there are differences between these terms. Fieldwork is the general term for any research conducted in a natural setting, such as a qualitative researcher conducting in-depth interviews with participants in their homes. Naturalistic observation is also a general term that is used to describe observations made in a "particular natural setting (the field) over an extended period of time, using a variety of techniques in order to collect information" (Cozby, 2009, p. 108). Participant observation is one of the techniques that may be used to carry out naturalistic observation. Participant observation as a data collection method requires a researcher to join a group of interest and actively participate in that group over time to study it. Not all observation entails direct participation with group members, as discussed in the following section.

LO3

An Ethnographer's Role During Fieldwork

An ethnographer's level of participation while engaged in fieldwork can range from complete observer with no active participation, through to complete participation as a member of that community or culture. Gold (1958) identified a continuum for participation as illustrated in four ethnographer roles: complete observer (no participation), observer as participant (minimal participation), participant as observer (increased participation), and complete participant (full participation), as shown in Figure 10.1.

Complete observer A participant observation role in which the researcher covertly observes a group but is not a group member and does not participate in any way.

Complete Observer   As a **complete observer**, the ethnographer's role is to unobtrusively observe a group as a non-member who does not participate with the group in any way. For example, an ethnographer might set up recording equipment in advance of classes to videotape students during class lessons to be examined as part of an exploration of class dynamics. This example illustrates a qualitative approach if the variables of interest emerge from the observations, such as patterns of interaction that become apparent from content analyses of the videotaped sessions. A complete observer role may also entail systematic observation using a quantitative approach called **structured observation**, which is behaviour observed "using categories devised before the observation begins" (Bryman, Bell, & Teevan, 2012, p. 102). For example, Zetou, Amprasi, Michalopoulou, and Aggelousis (2011) examined feedback provided by Greek National League volleyball coaches to athletes in practices during the 2010–11 championships. Researchers videotaped practices and then coded the frequency of the following 12 specific types of feedback according to a standard recording instrument called the Revised Coaching Behavior Recording Form: technical instructions, tactical instructions, general instructions, motivation, rewards and encouragement, comments, non-verbal punishment, criticism, demonstration,

Structured observation A quantitative approach in which behaviour is observed and coded using predetermined categories.

FIGURE 10.1
An Ethnographer's
Role During
Fieldwork

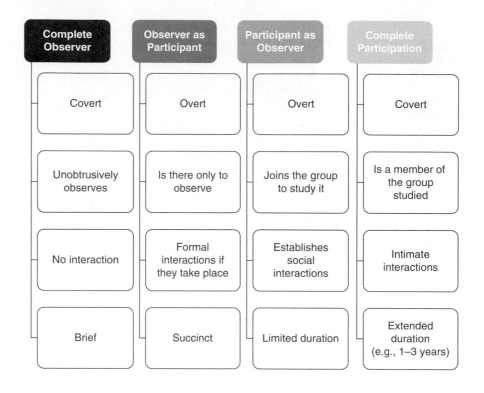

non-verbal reward, and humour. Results indicated that any given practice session included about 279 separate coaching behaviours, with tactical instructions being most prevalent (17.4 percent), followed by general instructions (15.9 percent) (Zetou et al., 2011).

Observer as participant An overt participant observation role in which the researcher systematically observes a group but is not a group member and only interacts indirectly with the group.

Observer as Participant   In an **observer as participant** role, the researcher's role is brief. For example, an ethnographer might sit in on one or two classes to observe and code student dynamics. During these observational periods, the students will be aware that the researcher is present, but the researcher's role does not entail direct involvement with the group members so it is minimally intrusive. After a few minutes, the students are likely to forget the novel researcher collecting data and behave as they usually do. In comparison, the complete observer role is wholly unobtrusive.

To carry out structured observations in a complete observer or an observer as participant role, a number of decisions must be made ahead of time with respect to the selection of the type of behaviour examined, the manner in which the behaviour will be recorded, and the format in which the data is to be collected and encoded (Judd et al., 1991). Beginning with the selection of the behaviour observed, a researcher might focus on any aspect of an interaction, event, or behaviour deemed to be relevant to the research interest. In the example used above, the volleyball coaches' verbal and non-verbal feedback provided to the athletes was selected for systematic observation. Next, it is important to determine who to sample for the behaviour of interest. In the coaching example, the researchers selected 12 coaches from the top divisions to observe as they were deemed to be "the most experienced and effective."

It is also important to determine how to observe the behaviour of interest and in what format. In this example, video recordings were made of each training session and the coaches wore wireless microphones so the researchers could examine verbal comments and non-verbal gestures. Each training session was recorded in its entirety for the 2010–11 season of play. The video/audio recordings were then systematically examined for coaching behaviours. Each and every separate instance of coaching feedback was considered a new event and was encoded into one of the predetermined categories (Zetou et al., 2011). This method of collecting observations is called **continuous real-time measurement** because every instance of the behaviour that occurs during a particular time frame (in this case a practice session) is included in the observations. When it is difficult to determine when a behaviour begins and ends or behaviour is going to be observed over long periods of time, researchers sometimes opt for **time-interval sampling** where observations are made "instantaneously at the end of set time periods, such as every ten seconds, or every sixth minute or every hour on the hour, with the number and spacing of points selected to be appropriate to the session length" (Judd et al., 1991, p. 279). In this case, only behaviour taking place at the end of the time interval ends up being included as part of the data collected.

Finally, it is important to decide upon a method for encoding the observations. Similar to the data-reduction coding schemes used in content analysis, **encoding** is a process used to simplify observations through the use of categorizations (Judd et al., 1991). Volleyball coach feedback was encoded into 1 of 12 coaching behaviour categories indicated earlier or it was labelled as "non-coding behaviour" in the few instances that did not fit the prescribed categories (Zetou et al., 2011).

Participant as Observer   If an ethnographer joins the group to study it over a more prolonged period of time and will interact with that group, then the researcher is engaged in a **participant as observer** role. For example, an ethnographer interested in a particular subculture such as a weekly poker session might join in, identifying him or herself as a researcher and as a card-playing member to become immersed in the group over the course of several weeks. In a participant as observer role, the ethnographer directly interacts with members of the group in a somewhat informal role that permits the establishment of communication and relationships while studying group members.

Complete Participant   Finally, in a **complete participation** role, an ethnographer fully immerses him or herself in the group as one of the members for a prolonged period of time to study the group. To lessen reactivity, the research usually takes place covertly in a concealed manner such that the researcher's true identity and purpose is not made known to the members. Recall Laud Humphreys's (1970) research on impersonal sexual exchanges in public restrooms discussed in Chapter 3. Humphreys pretended to be a "watchqueen" so that he would be

Continuous real-time measurement An observation-based data coding method in which every separate and distinct instance of a variable is recorded during an observation period.

Time-interval sampling An observation-based data coding method in which variables are recorded at the end of each set time interval throughout an observation period.

Encoding A data-reduction method used to simplify observations through the use of categorizations.

Participant as observer An overt participant observation role in which the researcher systematically observes a group by becoming a group member to establish relationships and interact directly with the group.

Complete participation A covert participant observation role in which the researcher systematically observes a group as a full member whose true identity and research purpose is unknown to the group members.

accepted into the group as a voyeur who could then study the sexual encounters taking place, but he would not be expected to actively participate in them.

Researchers engaged in participant as observer and complete participant roles are still interested in observing behaviour (both verbal and non-verbal), people, and patterns of interaction, but the emphasis is more on understanding the subjective meanings of the observed events for the actors themselves as opposed to coding for particular behaviours according to pre-established criteria. "Participant observation gives you an intuitive understanding of what's going on in a culture and allows to you speak with confidence about the meaning of the data" (Bernard, 2011, p. 266). For example, anthropologist and motorcyclist Daniel Wolf joined an outlaw motorcycle club called the Rebels to study the group dynamics and activities from within the group for his Ph.D. research while studying at the University of Alberta, in Edmonton (Wolf, 1991). As Wolf (1991) put it:

> In order to understand the biker subculture, or any culture for that matter, one must first try to understand it as it is experienced by the bikers themselves. Only then can one comprehend both the meaning of being an outlaw and how that meaning is constructed and comes to be shared by bikers. Only by first seeing the world through the eyes of the outlaws can we then go on to render intelligible the decisions that they make and the behaviours that they engage in. (P. 21)

Data collection *in situ* is very difficult to undertake since it involves finding creative ways to discretely observe, take notes, and record conversations and events in a manner that is not obvious to those who are present at the time. Imagine what would happen in a conversation with one of your friends if you suddenly pulled out a notebook and starting writing down things the person was saying to you. Field notes, however, are critical in ethnographic research since the notes ultimately become the data that is later used to describe and explain

Anthropologist Daniel Wolf used participant observation to study the Rebels outlaw motorcycle gang for his Ph.D. dissertation.

the setting, people, and relationships under investigation. As difficult as it may be to record notes, "*No* observation is complete until those notes have been done" (Palys & Atchison, 2014, p. 211). At a minimum, field notes should detail relevant people, conversations, and events and indicate the date, time, and location for each observation.

Ethnography Is Undertaken by a Single Principal Investigator

In most cases, ethnographic fieldwork is carried out by a single principal investigator, such as Laud Humphreys's ethnographic study of impersonal sex in public washrooms, Daniel Wolf's study on the Rebels, William Foote Whyte's study of an Italian slum, and cultural anthropologist Margaret Mead's research on adolescent girls in Samoa. Sociologist Fiona Martin (2011) from Dalhousie University in Halifax, Nova Scotia recently conducted interviews with 21 young women who were pregnant or were mothers who habitually used injection drugs. The interview project was part of a larger ethnographic study on injecting drug use that she carried out over a period of two years while in a placement at a hospital clinic for women with substance use issues. Martin (2011) found that while most of the addicts were trying to overcome their drug use, they faced various barriers including established drug identities and the absence of non-drug-using relationships.

Ethnography Involves Long-Term Acquaintances

Since the goal of ethnography is to provide an accurate account of a culture or group, it is important to be around that group long enough to establish relationships with members. The researcher needs to be in a position to begin to understand relationship dynamics and how members view the events and activities they engage in. Not surprisingly, ethnographers tend to spend long periods of time in the field studying groups of interest. How long is long enough? The amount of time largely depends on what the research interest entails, including the complexity of the study, how difficult it is to access the setting, how long it takes to get to know people in that setting, and how skilled the particular researcher is. A study could be carried out in a few weeks, or it could take several years to complete. It is common for field research to take place over a period of about 18 months to two years. During this time, the ethnographer will initiate and develop several contacts, form friendships, and establish intimate relationships. After all, who would you be more likely to disclose personal details of your life to, a stranger or a friend? Getting to know others takes time, so it is probably better to spend more rather than less time in a field setting for the sake of data quality. As H. Russell Bernard (2011) explains:

> It may sound silly, but just hanging out is a skill, and until you learn it you can't do your best work as a participant observer. . . . When you enter a new field situation, the temptation is to ask a lot of question to learn as much as possible

as quickly as possible. There are many things that people can't or won't tell you in answers to questions. If you ask people too quickly about the sources of their wealth, you are likely to get incomplete data. If you ask too quickly about sexual liaisons, you may get thoroughly unreliable responses. Hanging out builds trust, or rapport, and trust results in ordinary conversation and ordinary behaviour in your presence. Once you know, from hanging out, exactly what you want to know more about, and once people trust you not to betray their confidence, you'll be surprised at the direct questions you can ask. (P. 277)

Ethnography Is Non-judgmental

Cultural relativism The non-judgmental view that a society's customs and ideas should be described objectively and understood in the context of that society's problems and opportunities.

Although ethnographers can never be truly objective by being completely detached from the research process, and they may even be active, contributing members of a group, they still strive to be analytical and non-judgmental in their opinions and evaluations of groups and group behaviour. As Wolcott (2010) notes, "the ethnographer wants to see how things are, not to judge how they ought to be" (p. 92). Anthropologists Ember, Ember, and Peregrine (2009, p. 219) use the term **cultural relativism** to refer to this non-judgmental position where "a society's customs and ideas should be described objectively and understood in the context of that society's problems and opportunities." Researchers are still going to have their own opinions, and their views are not value-neutral. However, researchers strive to maintain a distinction between their personal views and their perceptions of what is going on in the observational setting. For example, an ethnographer may create several different kinds of field notes about the same event, including: quick short-form "jotted notes" taken in the moment; highly "detailed notes" that resemble interview transcriptions and include where possible direct quotes or words and expressions used by the group members; "analytical notes" where a researcher attempts to give meaning to what he or she has observed; and "personal notes" that are more like journal entries and can include information on a researcher's personal feelings toward members of the group (Wolfer, 2007).

Using cultural relativism, ethnographers are able to learn about diverse practices including Holi, a religious festival of colours celebrated by Hindus.

Ethnography Is Reflexive

In ethnographic research, the researcher is the data instrument—that is, the researcher observes, participates, listens, records, and otherwise takes notes of events as they are occurring within the research context. Just as siblings never remember the same event in exactly the same way, no two researchers are likely see, record, or interpret data in the exact same manner. As Juliet Corbin and Anselm Strauss (2008) explain:

> Qualitative data are inherently rich in substance and full of possibilities. It is impossible to say that there is only one story that can be constructed from the data. Though participants speak through data, the data themselves do not wave flags denoting what is important and what is not. Different analysts focus on different aspects of the data, interpret things differently, and identify different meanings. Also, different analysts arrive at different conclusions even about the same piece of data. For example, interviews with persons who have chronic illnesses can be examined from the angle of illness management (Corbin & Strauss, 1988), identity and self (Charmaz, 1983), and suffering (Morse, 2001; 2005; Riemann & Schütze, 1991). (P. 50)

Reflexivity A self-reflection process in which a researcher considers the ways in which his or her own subjectivities may have influenced the research outcomes.

Ethnography is considered to be reflexive because the product of the research is necessarily influenced by the perceptions of the researcher and the processes enacted by that particular researcher as part of the data-gathering fieldwork (Davies, 2008). **Reflexivity** is often described as "a turning back on oneself," "a process of self-reference," and/or a "self-reflection" in which an individual researcher considers the ways in which his or her own particular subjectivities and values may have influenced the research outcomes (Davies, 2008, p. 7). All qualitative research requires some degree of reflexivity since data on its own is devoid of meaning. Since it is through interpretive data analysis that researchers make sense of their observations, it is important for researchers to recognize their unique perspectives and acknowledge how such perspectives come to bear upon the research process and the meanings that result from it.

Ethnography Is Mostly Descriptive

"Descriptive notes are the meat and potatoes of field work" (Bernard, 2011). Most of the techniques used to collect field data generate enormous amounts of information. For example, interviews are transcribed into descriptive field notes. Overheard conversations may be jotted down as notes. Observed practices, customs, processes, and interactions are detailed in descriptive field notes. Wolcott (2010) advises ethnographers to err on the side of "thick" rather than "thin" description because one of the "best ways to be non-evaluative is to be intensively descriptive, to attend to what is, and what those in the setting think about it, rather than become preoccupied with what is wrong, or what ought to be" (p. 103). The goal of the ethnographer is to try and understand the meaning of this data for the participants. To achieve this, a researcher should begin to examine data as soon as it is collected, such as after an interview is completed or an initial observation is made. A "sequential approach to data collection and analysis allows a researcher to identify relevant concepts, follow through on subsequent questions, and listen and observe in more sensitive ways" (Corbin & Strauss, 2008, p. 57). This also prevents the researcher from being overwhelmed with data at the end of a study when it may be too late to further investigate particular themes or validate particular findings. As Fetterman (2010) argues, the very "success or failure of either report or full-blown ethnography depends on the degree to which it rings true to natives and colleagues in the field. These readers may disagree with the researcher's interpretations and conclusions, but they should recognize the details of the description as accurate" (p. 11).

Ethnography Is Case-Specific

Ethnographic research takes place at a particular time, in a particular place, with a particular group, within a particular setting. Purposive or theoretical sampling is usually used to obtain the most relevant case (group or setting) given a specific research interest. Alternatively, it could also be that only a particular group is accessible by a given researcher, and this would more closely approximate convenience or availability sampling. Either way, the group is not a representative sample and the results are unlikely to generalize beyond a given case. However, the specific focus on a single case or setting is precisely what facilitates an in-depth study that produces the rich, detailed, and authentic understanding that lies at the heart of ethnography (Hammersley & Atkinson, 2007).

Also, in ethnography, while a case generally refers to the group or setting studied, the researcher is most interested in what goes on within that setting. As a result, data is obtained on a number of individuals, activities, rituals, processes, and so forth, rather than one person as in a single case. To avoid confusion, Gobo (2011) suggests researchers use the terms "instance" or "occurrence" when describing various events that go on within a given setting.

Ethnography Requires Multiple Techniques and Data Sources

While ethnographic research primarily involves participant observation, details of the group and setting are obtained through any number and combination of specific techniques, including observational analysis, in-depth interviews, field notes, documents, photographs, and visual recordings. Observational analysis and field notes have already been discussed in detail in earlier sections of this chapter, while in-depth interviewing is the subject matter of Chapter 9 and documents are part of the unobtrusive measures reviewed in Chapter 8. Photographs are used in a number of ways in ethnographic research. A researcher might take a picture of a group, event, or setting to visually depict certain aspects of the stimuli that might not be captured as eloquently by descriptive notes, such as the implications of crowding, the extent of cultural diversity, or the elaborate detail on clothing. However, photographs are much more than visual aids, and anthropologists and other researchers rely upon visual ethnography as a means for understanding human behaviour and culture. For example, John Collier, Jr. and Malcolm Collier (1986) explain how photographs can used within data collection methods such as in-depth interviewing to help facilitate communication:

Psychologically, the photographs on the table performed as a third party in the interview session. We were asking questions of the photographs and the informants became our assistants in discovering the answers to the questions in the realities of the photographs. We were exploring the photographs *together*. Ordinarily, note taking during interviews can raise blocks to free-flowing information, making responses self-conscious and blunt. Tape recorders sometimes stop interviews cold. But in this case, making notes was totally ignored, probably because of the triangular relationship in which all questions were directed at the photographic content, not at the informants (emphasis in original). (Pp. 105–106)

Skilled ethnographers sometimes incorporate photographs into interviews as focal points to help establish rapport and to keep interviews on track, much in the same manner as transition questions and probes.

Visual ethnography
Representations of culture as depicted in photographs and film documentaries.

Visual ethnography is a term used to describe the visual representation of a culture as depicted in film. Ethnographers may use visual recordings for various types of observational analyses, such as structured observation in a complete observer role as discussed earlier. Video recordings can also be used to capture and represent a culture on film. Ethnographic documentaries are a popular means for portraying a culture or group in its natural setting through visual representations and participant accounts.

Research in Action

People of a Feather

People of a Feather, produced by Joel Heath and the community of Sanikiluaq (2011), is a multiple-award-winning documentary about the way of life of the Inuit peoples on the Belcher Islands in the Hudson Bay area. This visual ethnographic study of the Arctic takes place over seven winters. Learn how the residents live and survive challenges, especially those arising from the hydroelectric dams that have special implications for sea currents and the ecosystems tied intricately to them. You can find out more about this ethnography by visiting peopleofafeather.com.

People of a Feather is a visual ethnography of the way of life of Inuit peoples on the Belcher Islands.

Test Yourself

- What is the main assumption shared by ethnographers?
- What ten features exemplify an ethnographic study?
- Which of the four ethnographer roles identified by Gold (1958) involve the researcher as a member of the group?
- Why is ethnography considered to be reflexive?

Ethnographic Fieldwork

While ethnographic research will vary depending on the research interest, the group studied, and the methods used during fieldwork, the main stages of any ethnographic field project include: accessing the field, dealing with gatekeepers, establishing relations, becoming invisible, collecting data, and exiting the field.

Accessing the Field

First, a researcher must be able to gain entry into the group he or she wishes to study. Depending on the nature of a particular group or setting, as well as the researcher's own characteristics that may help him or her fit into or stand out in a group, access can be a relatively open, straightforward, and uneventful process, or it may be a highly restricted, difficult, and even dangerous process. Entering the field of study is crucial for the researcher to be able to examine the group in its natural setting and for the researcher to establish relationships needed to begin to acquire an insider's view of what is going on. Note that even before he ever posed as a watchqueen, Humphreys had to learn about homosexual men so that he would be able to later pass himself off as one. He notes that "homosexuals have developed defenses against outsiders" (Humphreys, 1970, p. 24) and he therefore underwent considerable preparation to learn about what was then considered to be a "deviant subculture" so that he would be able to gain entry into it. For example, while in clinical training at a psychiatric hospital, he got to know a number of homosexual patients, and while serving as a pastor in parishes in Oklahoma, Colorado, and Kansas, he counselled "hundreds of homosexuals of all sorts and conditions." He also visited "gay bars" and observed "pick-up operations in the parks and streets" (see Humphreys, 1970, pp. 23–26).

One of the more straightforward (and less time-consuming) means for accessing a group and navigating within it is through one of the existing group members. Fetterman (2010) claims an "introduction by a member is an ethnographer's best ticket into the community." Regardless of who the specific member is in terms of social standing or specific role, as long as the member has some "credibility with the group—either as a member or as an acknowledged friend or associate . . . the trust the group places in the intermediary will approximate the trust it extends to the ethnographer at the beginning of the study" (p. 36). This was the fortune of

William Foote Whyte who had an automatic entry into the group through Doc, as Doc explains:

> You won't have any trouble. You come in as my friend. When you come in like that, at first everybody will treat you with respect. You can take a lot of liberties, and nobody will kick. After a while, when they get to know you, they will treat you like anybody else—you know, they say familiarity breeds contempt. But you'll never have any trouble. (Whyte, 1994, p. 68)

In cases where it is not possible to first get to know an existing member of the group who can serve as an entrance guide, a researcher might need to assume a more covert role, pretending to be a full member to gain inside acceptance based on membership status (Berg & Lune, 2012).

Dealing with Gatekeepers

Gatekeepers People who have power to grant or deny permission to do a study in the field.

Most groups and research settings are formally or informally "policed" by **gatekeepers**. Gatekeepers refer to "people who have power to grant or deny permission to do a study in the field" (Bailey, 1996, p. 149). Gatekeepers can control access to a setting in a formal or informal capacity, and there may be a number of gatekeepers in any given setting. For example, when I conducted my dissertation research on low self-control among sex offenders as identified by information contained in patient files for inmates who had previously undergone treatment for sexual offending at Alberta Hospital Edmonton, formal gatekeepers included the institutional manager, the program supervisor, and the psychiatrist in charge of sex offender treatment. In addition, once I gained approval from the formal gatekeepers and was granted ethical approval from the hospital and the University of Alberta, I still had to negotiate access to the data from an informal gatekeeper who managed the research database containing variables I needed to include in my study, as well as an informal gatekeeper who managed the records department where I needed to verify information contained in the database against original documents.

Whenever possible, interactions with gatekeepers should be honest and overt. Even in the case of covert participation roles, gatekeepers are generally fully aware of who the ethnographer is and what the research objectives are. This is an important consideration as gatekeepers are in a position to vouch for the researcher's presence, which can actually aid in the establishment of relations within the field (Wolfer, 2007).

Establishing Relations

Even with an introduction into the community and the successful negotiation past gatekeepers, the intricacies of fieldwork have barely begun. To gain a true insider perspective, an ethnographer must spend a considerable amount of time in a setting and be fairly skilled at establishing and maintaining relations with various group members while living alongside or spending time in that setting. Gaining the acceptance of a group will depend on any number of considerations, including a researcher's personal characteristics such as age, sex, or ethnicity, as well as professional attributes such as experience, social skills, and/or demeanour.

Key insider A member of the setting who is willing to act as a guide or assistant within the setting.

Every culture and subculture tends to develop its own patterns, rituals, rules, and specialized language that may not be readily understood by an outsider, even by someone who is specifically attempting to learn the language and customs to gain an insider's view. **Key insiders**, also called sponsors, can be especially helpful to an ethnographer who is learning who people are and how things operate. A key insider is "a member of the setting who is willing to act as a guide or assistant within the setting" (Bailey, 1996, p. 55). Key insiders are often people who initially befriend the ethnographer and are willing to help him or her understand the nuances of the setting, such as informal norms and specialized jargon. Ernest Pecco, known as Doc, helped William Foote Whyte understand all of the intricacies of the world he was now immersed in as evident in his warning admonishment:

> Go easy on that 'who,' 'what,' 'why,' 'when,' 'where' stuff, Bill. You ask those questions and people will clam up on you. If people accept you, you can just hang around, and you'll learn the answers in the long run, without even having to ask the questions. (Whyte, 1994, p. 75)

Due to their existing status within the culture or group, insiders are invaluable for helping the ethnographer to better understand the setting and the roles of the individuals in it.

LO5

Becoming Invisible

The primary goal of the ethnographer is to observe and describe the setting and its participants without affecting them. To accomplish this, a researcher needs to find a way to blend in with the group he or she is studying so that members will act naturally around the researcher and view the researcher as an insider. Stoddart (1986) suggests the ethnographer immerse him or herself within the community using an invisible presence that is created through disattending or misrepresentation. Stoddart goes on to describe six potential ways to achieve invisibility while engaged in fieldwork (1986, pp. 109–13), adapted as follows:

1. *Disattending with time.* Recall that most field studies are carried out over a considerable length of time. When a researcher first joins a group, his or her presence is obvious and visible. However, over time, members will begin to accept the researcher's presence and will eventually habituate to his or her presence, failing to take special notice. When members fail to notice the researcher, we can say they are "disattending" and that the researcher now has invisible status within the community.

2. *Disattending by not standing out.* Stoddart (1986) claimed it was important for an ethnographer to fit in with the group members by making sure there was "no display of symbolic detachment" (pp. 109–110). This means an ethnographer needs to look, act, and sound like the rest of the group to fit in. An ethnographer wearing a suit is less likely to fit in with a group of children on a playground than someone who is dressed more appropriately for digging in the sand or playing soccer. Similarly, someone who wishes to study street

prostitutes would need to be familiar with the language, norms, and practices of the sex trade.

3. *Disattending by participating in the group.* In addition to trying not to stand out, an ethnographer can achieve invisibility by actively participating with the group members in their everyday routines. For example, an ethnographer studying school-aged children can become a playground supervisor during recess, a lunch hour classroom monitor, or an assistant for art projects.

4. *Disattending by establishing personal relationships.* In this case, ethnographers can elicit information and support from group members on a personal, rather than professional level. As Stoddart (1986) put it, "the ethnographer was invisible insofar as informants suspended concern with the research aspect of his or her identity and liked him or her as a person" (p. 111).

5. *Misrepresentation involving the research purpose.* Another way that researchers can achieve invisibility is through the use of deception. An ethnographer may, for example, identity him or herself as a researcher but fail to disclose all of the details of the study, or may misrepresent details about the true nature of the study.

6. *Misrepresentation involving the researcher's identity.* In some ethnographic studies, the researcher adopts a covert participant observation role, perhaps posing as a potential recruit to the group, a new hire to the organization, or a returning member of the existing community.

While becoming invisible supports an ethnographer's need to blend into the environment to better study the setting and its inhabitants, an ethnographer's role as an observer also warrants ongoing consideration while engaged in fieldwork. Recall the earlier discussion of the ethnographer as the data collection instrument and ethnography as a reflexive method. Reinharz (2011) suggests that there are three main selves operating simultaneously in the field, including a "research self," a "personal self," and a "situational self" (p. 5). The research self largely reflects the ethnographer role, which is focused on gathering data. The personal self consists of individual characteristics such as age, gender, and existing belief systems that the researcher brings to the setting that can influence the kinds of relationships that develop while in the setting, and can even affect how events and observations are interpreted by the ethnographer. The situational self is the insider or member position that develops in response to specific events and group interactions that take place while immersed in the setting. Reinharz (2011) notes that by recognizing these selves in her own field research on aging in a kibbutz (an agricultural-based community in Israel), she was also able to recognize who she was not: "For example, in this study of aging, I, myself, was not an elderly woman. This fact probably affected what I understood and how people related to me" (p. 205).

Data Collection

While the essence of ethnography is listening and observing in the field in an ongoing and extensive capacity to achieve understanding, the final product of ethnographic research is generally a written document. Hence, an ethnographer

Field notes Detailed records about what a researcher hears, sees, experiences, and thinks about while immersed in the social setting.

records detailed **field notes** at every available opportunity. Field notes are detailed records about what the researcher hears, sees, experiences, and thinks about while immersed in the social setting. To an ethnographer, "field notes are the qualitative equivalent to quantitative researchers' raw data" (Warren & Karner, 2010, p. 121). After taking the initial field notes, an ethnographer reviews the notes and records additional reflexive thoughts and observations on a regular basis using audio recordings as well as further journal entries, for example. To distinguish field notes from analytic notes that a researcher makes as he or she begins to interpret the data, Schatzman and Strauss (1973) recommend preparing three different kinds of notes: 1) observational notes, which are the highly detailed notes written about the actual events made while still in the field; 2) theoretical notes, which are based on the researcher's interpretation of events including hunches, analytical insights, and initial attempts to classify the information into concepts; and 3) methodological notes, which are procedural details about how observations were carried out.

Accompanying field notes, researchers may conduct various informal interviews that are later transcribed or summarized in a written format. While in the field, researchers may even supplement or substantiate information obtained in interviews with data gathered through other methods, such as focus groups or surveys. Ethnographers can also employ a number of visual aids—such as photographs, video recordings, sketches, and maps—to describe the setting and provide details of interactions, processes, and events going on in that setting.

Data analysis often begins while still in the field as an ethnographer examines and re-examines notes looking for ways to best describe processes, to locate ideas within existing theoretical frameworks, and to identify emerging ideas, patterns, and themes. Data analysis continues long after the ethnographer has exited the field.

Exiting the Field

Just as entering the field and establishing relationships has to be carefully negotiated, ending relationships and leaving the group is also a process that can be relatively smooth or highly problematic. An ethnographer will often plan for a

---

Research on the Net

The Journal for Undergraduate Ethnography

The Journal for Undergraduate Ethnography (JUE) is an online journal that publishes ethnographies carried out by undergraduate students in a variety of disciplines as part of their course work. The journal was started in 2011. In its first issue, you can learn about a community based on an ethnographic study of a historical cemetery, why people engage in "freeganism" where they eat and recycle garbage from dumpsters, how sex offenders view themselves, and how women in relationships with incarcerated men view the criminal justice system, among other interesting topics. Visit undergraduateethnography.org.

gradual disengagement or look for a natural ending to a process or project occurring within the community to provide closure to the various relationships involving the ethnographer. Warner and Karner (2010) suggest as a rule of thumb that it is time to leave the field when "your observations are no longer yielding new and interesting data" (p. 102). Although an ethnographer may realize from an objective, data-driven perspective that it is time to leave the field, disengaging from the setting and people with whom one has spent a great deal of time with can be difficult on a more personal and social level.

Test Yourself

- Why is it important to identify gatekeepers?
- How do key insiders help researchers establish relations?
- What four techniques can be used to achieve disattending?
- How does misrepresentation help a researcher to become invisible in the field?

Ethical Considerations

Informed Consent and Deception

In contrast to methods such as experiments and surveys where participants sign an informed consent statement outlining all of the main features of study, including expectations regarding the participants' role and the true purpose of the study, informed consent in ethnographic fieldwork is not always possible ahead of time. This poses special challenges for ethnographers and members of research ethics boards who need to weigh the potential risk to participants of withholding information against the need to use deception to establish natural relations with group members.

On the one hand, it can be argued that informed consent is not necessary or even desirable in the case of fieldwork. This is because fieldwork takes place in a natural setting and the behaviours and processes are going to take place irrespective of whether a researcher is studying them (Bailey, 1996). In addition, a covert approach may be preferable to lessen the potential for research-induced reactivity (Douglas, 1979). Finally, since deception exists in real-life interactions, it may also be necessary in research to study particular groups, especially ones engaged in illegitimate activities (Bailey, 1996).

On the other hand, we have to ask ourselves, is it ethical or morally acceptable to knowingly deceive participants in order to study them? Bailey (1996) notes that, for example, "a premise of a feminist ethical stance is that the process and outcomes of field research are greatly affected by the reciprocal relationships that develop between the field researcher and those in the setting" (p. 13). From this perspective, it would be unethical to use deception to achieve what a researcher hopes will become open and honest relationships with group members. Moreover, if a researcher is upfront about his or her position and objectives, it may be even more likely that a group will come to trust the researcher. Since outsider status is often obvious to group members, attempts to cover the newcomer's identity may lead to mistrust and could actually inhibit the establishment of relationships. A researcher's outsider status may even afford group members the additional liberty to ask stupid or blunt questions or provide highly insightful responses that would not be characteristic of insider relations (Bailey, 1996).

One way to resolve the dilemma of choosing between informed consent versus the need for deception in field research is to conceptualize consent as an ongoing process rather than an initial step or one-time document. In this case, there may be alternatives such as an **alteration of documentation of informed consent**, which refers to "an informed consent discussion with every subject" as opposed to a written, signed, statement of informed consent listing all of the risks and requirements of participation in a particular study (Scott & Garner, 2013, p. 61). Another option is a **step-wise consent process** in which you (as the researcher) "describe roughly how you're going to enter the community or group, how and when you're going to first describe what you're doing and what their involvement will consist of as subjects, and so forth" (Scott & Garner, 2013, p. 61).

Alteration of documentation of informed consent An informed consent discussion that takes place with each participant in the setting in lieu of a signed informed consent statement.

Step-wise consent process A consent process that takes place in stages following the establishment of relationships within a group.

Maintaining Privacy

Due to the personal nature of the insider information collected in the course of fieldwork, an ethnographer needs to carefully consider how issues of privacy relate to the research project in its entirety, and what the researcher's own accountability is when it comes to maintaining the privacy of respondents. First, while a researcher may attempt to maintain confidentiality by leaving out names or by using pseudonyms for information that will appear in print, the descriptions, quotes, or illustrations used may still identify participants or groups to others based on the nature of the information revealed. In such cases, researcher may have to take further measures to disguise the identity of participants by changing the age and sex of the participants or by modifying their roles to protect them from potential privacy violations and their subsequent harm.

In describing globalizing feminist research, Mendez (2009) points out that privacy and accountability issues can be especially problematic because "there is no single homogenous community to which the researcher is accountable, but rather multiple groups, communities, organizational and international levels, and conflicting interests. It is within these often intersecting and sometimes conflicting communities that the researcher and those she is studying must negotiate mechanisms of accountability" (p. 87). For example, while studying labour mobility, Mendez encountered women whose undocumented immigration status, if known, would result in incarceration or deportation. She also spoke with outreach workers who were highly sensitive about their lack of decision-making authority within the larger organizations, and higher-level administrators who were reluctant to share information that would negatively reflect on their own or other organizations. Given established relations at various levels within and between groups, an ethnographer has to be especially mindful of what information is obtained, how that information will be shared, how that information will be received, and what the repercussions might be as a result.

Risk of Harm to the Researcher

Field research, because of its inherent naturalness, presupposes a level of unpredictability that can pose risk of harm to researchers. An ethnographer who infiltrates an outlaw motorcycle club known for its reliance on violence as a means for resolving conflict is going to be at risk for physical danger. Similarly, an ethnographer who joins a travelling carnival to understand what life is like for members of that subgroup is likely entering a setting that contains many yet to be discovered illegal behaviours and questionable practices that may inadvertently pose risks to any insider. Then again, it is precisely the use of first-hand observation in a natural setting that produces highly valid representations and conclusions.

Research in Action

Why Not Dad?

Why Not Dad? (2009), produced and directed by Monique Derenia, is an ethnographic study of four stay-at-home dads in San Francisco. Find out how these men experience parenthood and gender stereotypes as they get together each week at the playground. You can learn more about this documentary and watch it by visiting whynotdad.com.

Test Yourself

- Why might an ethnographer oppose the need to obtain informed consent?
- What are the two alternatives to obtaining informed consent prior to the onset of fieldwork?

Chapter Summary

LO1 **Define ethnography and describe the role of an ethnographer.**

Ethnography is a methodology for studying a social group or culture based on observation. An ethnographer systematically studies a group by observing it and by participating in it.

LO2 **Outline the main features of ethnographic studies.**

Ethnographic studies usually include the following ten features:

1. Ethnography takes place in natural settings.
2. Ethnography is context-based.
3. Ethnography relies on participant observation.
4. Ethnography is undertaken by a single principal investigator.
5. Ethnography involves long-term acquaintances.

6. Ethnography is non-judgmental.

7. Ethnography is reflexive.

8. Ethnography is mostly descriptive.

9. Ethnography is case-specific.

10. Ethnography requires multiple techniques and data sources.

LO3   **Differentiate between the four main roles of ethnographers engaged in fieldwork.**

As a *complete observer,* an ethnographer observes a group but is not in the group and does not participate with the group in any way. In an *observer as participant* role, the researcher systematically observes a group but is not a group member and only interacts indirectly with the group. A researcher in a *participant as observer* role systematically observes a group by becoming a member to establish relationships and interact with group members. Finally, in *complete participation,* a researcher is already a group member at the onset of the research or becomes a group member to covertly study that group as a fully participating member over a prolonged period of time.

LO4   **Describe the main stages of fieldwork.**

To conduct fieldwork, ethnographers need to access the field, often through the introduction of existing members. In addition, ethnographers must identify and gain permission from gatekeepers, establish relations with group members, and become invisible so members stop viewing the ethnographer as a researcher and start accepting him or her as a group member. While in the field, researchers also collect data through a variety of techniques and eventually exit the field by disengaging from ongoing activities and relationships with group members.

LO5   **Explain the techniques used by ethnographers to blend into a group.**

The main method used to blend into a group is to achieve invisibility. This can occur in a number of ways. For example, if a researcher spends a considerable amount of time with a group, the members will habituate to the researcher's presence (i.e., disattending with time). In addition, a researcher can become invisible by not standing out, by participating in everyday routines, and by establishing personal relationships. A researcher may even use deception or adopt a covert participation role to achieve invisibility.

LO6   **Discuss ethical issues in fieldwork.**

Various ethical considerations arise in fieldwork, beginning with initial decisions pertaining to the need to obtain informed consent versus the use of deception to be accepted as a group member. Other ethical considerations relate to privacy and how to keep information provided by members confidential but still meet the research objectives and maintain accountability to various groups and individuals with sometimes competing or conflicting interests. Finally, researchers have to be aware of ongoing personal risks of harm incurred through participation in the group.

Research Reflection	1. Over the course of a week, keep a reflective journal to record entries that describe conversations you have with your close friends and family members. Try to jot down details of the conversation using "thick description" (adapted from Watt, 2010).

2. At the end of the week, go back over the journal entries and review the descriptions. Using reflexivity, identify several ways in which the conversations resulted from or show evidence of your own personal interests, values, and points of view (adapted from Watt, 2010).

3. Now suppose you are an ethnographer studying group dynamics. In what ways could you change your future behaviour during interactions with the individuals described in your reflective journal to be less directing and more neutral during the conversations?

Learning Through Practice

Objective: Learning how to conduct fieldwork.

Directions:

1. Choose a well-known service provider on campus (e.g., a food provider, a library service, computer help desk, etc.).

2. Visit the service provider to examine the setting from the perspective of an ethnographer planning to do a field study.

   a. Draw a map of the physical setting.

   b. Identify gatekeepers and describe the process you would need to go through to gain access to the setting for research purposes.

   c. Provide a description of any individuals you think might serve as key insiders. If you don't know anyone on the setting, indicate who might be a potential key insider. For example, if you were studying the library borrower services, one of the staff at the circulation desk would be a potential key insider.

3. Of the four roles ranging from complete observer to complete participation, which do you feel would be most appropriate given your selected site? Justify your response.

4. Describe a technique you think would help you become invisible in this environment.

5. Visit your selected service provider/location a total of four times on two different days and at two different times. Take notes each time you go and see if you can detect changes in the environment at different times or on particular days. Describe your observations.

6. What ethical issues are raised by observational studies? What can be done to address these considerations?

Research Resources

1. Senior lecturer Rachela Colosi's interest in women's roles in deviant and unregulated occupations informed her dissertation research on lap-dancing described in Colosi, R. (2010). *Dirty dancing? An ethnography of lap-dancing*. New York, NY: Willan Publishing.

2. Associate Professor Vincent Lyon-Callo describes his insider view of homeless sheltering in Lyon-Callo, V. (2008). *Inequality, poverty, and neoliberal governance: Activist ethnography in the homeless sheltering industry.* Toronto, ON: Higher Education University of Toronto Press.

3. Anthropologist and activist David Graeber details his ethnographic dissertation research on the emergence of a global justice movement that drove a protest against the Summit of the Americas in Quebec City in 2001 in Graeber, D. (2009). *Direct action: An ethnography.* Oakland, CA: AK Press.

4. For a comprehensive guide to ethnography, I recommend Atkinson, P., Coffey, A., Delamont, S., Loftland, J., & Loftland, L. (Eds.). (2007). *The Sage handbook of ethnography.* Thousand Oaks, CA: Sage Publications.

5. For a comprehensive guide to fieldwork, I recommend Hobbs, D., & Wright, R. (Eds.). (2006). *The Sage handbook of fieldwork.* Thousand Oaks, CA: Sage Publications.

connect For more information on the resources available from McGraw-Hill Ryerson, go to www.mcgrawhill.ca/he/solutions.

References

Atkinson, P., Coffey, A., Delamont, S., Loftland, J., & Loftland, L. (Eds.). (2007). *The Sage handbook of ethnography.* Thousand Oaks, CA: Sage Publications.

Bailey, C. A. (1996). *A guide to field research.* Thousand Oaks, CA: Pine Forge Press.

Berg, B. L., & Lune, H. (2012). *Qualitative methods for the social sciences.* Upper Saddle River, NJ: Pearson Education.

Bernard, H. R. (2011). *Research methods in anthropology: Qualitative and quantitative approaches* (5th ed.). Plymouth, UK: AltaMira Press.

Bryman, A., Bell, E., & Teevan, J. J. (2012). *Social research methods* (3rd Can. ed.). Don Mills, ON: Oxford University Press.

Charmaz, K. (1983). Loss of self: A fundamental form of suffering in the chronically ill. *Sociology of Health and Illness, 5,* 168–195.

Collier, J. Jr., & Collier, M. (1986). *Visual anthropology: Photography as a research method.* Albuquerque, NM: University of New Mexico Press.

Colosi, R. (2010). *Dirty dancing? An ethnography of lap-dancing.* New York, NY: Willan Publishing.

Corbin, J., & Strauss, A. (2008). *Basics of qualitative research* (3rd ed.). Thousand Oaks, CA: Sage Publications.

Corbin, J., & Strauss, A. (1988). *Unending work and care.* San Francisco, CA: Jossey-Bass.

Cozby, P. C. (2009). *Methods in behavioral research* (10th ed.). New York, NY: McGraw-Hill.

Davies, C. A. (2008). *Reflexive ethnography: A guide to researching selves and others* (2nd ed.). New York NY: Routledge.

Douglas, J. (1979). Living morality versus bureaucratic fiat. In C. B. Klockars and F. W. O'Connor (Eds.), *Deviance and decency* (pp. 13–33). Beverly Hills, CA: Sage Publications.

Ember, C. R., Ember, M., & Peregrine, P. N. (2009). *Human evolution and culture: Highlights of anthropology* (6th ed.). Upper Saddle River, NJ: Pearson Education.

Fetterman, D. M. (2010). *Ethnography* (3rd ed.). Thousand Oaks, CA: Sage Publications.

Fetterman, D., M. (1987). Ethnographic educational evaluation. In G. D., Spindler (Ed.), *Interpretative ethnography of education: At home and abroad.* Hillsdale, NJ: Lawrence-Erlbaum.

Geertz, C. (1998). Deep hanging out. *New York Review of Books, XLV, 16* (Oct. 22), 69–72.

Gobo, G. (2011). Ethnography. In David Silverman (Ed.). *Qualitative methods* (3rd ed., pp. 15–34). Thousand Oaks, CA: Sage Publications.

Gold, R. L. (1958). Roles in sociological field observations, *Social Forces, 36,* 217–23.

Graeber, D. (2009). *Direct action: An ethnography.* Oakland, CA: AK Press.

Hammersley, M., & Atkinson, P. (2007). *Ethnography: Principles and practice* (3rd ed.). New York, NY: Routledge.

Hobbs, D., & Wright, R. (Eds.) (2006). *The Sage handbook of fieldwork.* Thousand Oaks, CA: Sage Publications.

Humphreys, R. A. L. (1970). *Tearoom trade: Impersonal sex in public places.* Chicago, IL: Aldine Publishing Company.

Judd, C. M., Smith, E. R., & Kidder, L. H. (1991). *Research methods in social relations* (6th ed.). Fort Worth, TX: Harcourt Brace Jovanovich, Inc.

Lyon-Callo, V. (2008). *Inequality, poverty, and neoliberal governance: Activist ethnography in the homeless sheltering industry.* Toronto, ON: Higher Education University of Toronto Press.

Madden, R. (2010). *Being ethnographic: A guide to the theory and practice of ethnography.* Thousand Oaks, CA: Sage Publications.

Martin, F. S. (2011). Deep entanglements: The complexities of disengaging from drug use for young mothers. *Contemporary Drug Problems, 38,* 335–336.

Mendez, J. B. (2009). Globalizing feminist research. In M. K. Huggins & M. L. Glebbeek (Eds.), *Women fielding danger: Negotiating ethnographic identities in field research.* Plymouth, UK: Rowman & Littlefield Publishers.

Morse, J. M. (2005). Creating a qualitatively derived theory of suffering. In U. Zutler (Ed.), *Clinical practice and development in nursing* (pp. 83–91). Aarhus, Denmark: Centre for Innovation in Nurse Training.

Morse, J. M. (2001). Toward a praxis theory of suffering. *Advances in Nursing Science, 24*(1), 47–59.

O'Reilly, K. (2009). *Key concepts in ethnography.* Thousand Oaks, CA: Sage Publications.

Palys, T., & Atchison, C. (2014). *Research decisions: Quantitative and qualitative perspectives* (5th ed). Toronto, ON: Nelson Education.

Reinharz, S. (2011). *Observing the observer: Understanding ourselves in field research.* New York, NY: Oxford University Press.

Riemann, G., & Schütze, F. (1991). "Trajectory" as a basic theoretical concept for analyzing suffering disorderly social process. In D. R. Maines (Ed.), *Social organization and social process* (pp. 333–357). New York, NY: Aldine de Gruyter.

Schatzman, L., & Strauss, A. L. (1973). *Field research: Strategies for a natural sociology.* Englewood Cliffs, NJ: Prentice-Hall.

Scott, G., & Garner, R. (2013). *Doing qualitative research: Designs, methods, and techniques.* Upper Saddle River, NJ: Pearson Education.

Stoddart, K. (1986). The presentation of everyday life: Some textual strategies for adequate ethnography. *Urban Life, 15*(1), 103–121.

Van den Hoonaard, D. K. (2012). *Qualitative research in action: A Canadian primer.* Don Mills, ON: Oxford University Press.

Warren, C. A. B., & Karner, T. X. (2010). *Discovering qualitative methods: Field research, interviews, and analysis* (2nd ed.). New York, NY: Oxford University Press.

Watt, S. (2010). Leaving the field: A reflexive journey. In Jones, J. S., & Watt, S. (Eds.), *Ethnography in social science practice* (pp. 187–196). New York, NY: Routledge.

Whyte, W. F. (1994). *Participant observer: An autobiography.* Ithaca, NY: Cornell University.

Whyte, W. F. (1943). *Street corner society: The social structure of an Italian slum.* Chicago, IL: Chicago University Press.

Wolcott, H. F. (2010). *Ethnography lessons: A primer.* Walnut Creek, CA: Left Coast Press.

Wolf, D. (1991). *The Rebels: A brotherhood of outlaw bikers.* Toronto, ON: University of Toronto Press.

Wolfer, L. (2007). *Real research: Conducting and evaluating research in the social sciences.* Boston, MA: Pearson Education.

Zetou, E., Amprasi, E., Michalopoulou, M., & Aggelousis, N. (2011). Volleyball coaches' behavior assessment through systematic observation. *Journal of Human Sports Exercise, 6*(4), 585–593.

Endnote

[1] Murchison, J. M. (2010). *Ethnography essentials: Designing, conducting, and presenting your research.* San Francisco, CA: Jossey-Bass.

Mixed Methods and Multiple Methods

11

"Mixed methods research recognizes, and works with, the fact that the world is not exclusively quantitative, or qualitative; it is not an either/or world, but a mixed world." (Cohen, Manion, & Morrison, 2011, p. 22)[1]

Introduction

In earlier chapters, you learned to distinguish between qualitative and quantitative approaches to social research. In this chapter, you will learn about the merits of mixing qualitative and quantitative approaches for adding depth and breadth to your understanding of just about any social topic. In addition, you will learn about various ways to combine multiple methods in a single study.

How the Approaches Differ

Recall how quantitative approaches tend to stem from the positivist tradition that emphasizes objectivity and the search for causal explanations, while qualitative approaches can often be traced to a more interpretive framework with an emphasis on the socially constructed nature of reality. In addition, while quantitative approaches are usually rooted in deductive reasoning and include research questions framed into hypotheses with operationalized variables, qualitative methods often incorporate inductive reasoning and research questions that are broader or take the form of exploratory statements about concepts of interest. There are always exceptions to these patterns, as in the case of qualitative research that is designed to test theories or quantitative research that is inductive. However, it is fair to say that the methods used by quantitative researchers often consist of experiments, surveys, or unobtrusive measures such as the analysis of secondary data, while qualitative researchers are more apt to rely upon in-depth interviews, participant observational approaches, or ethnography to examine phenomenon in its natural setting.

Acknowledging differences between qualitative and quantitative approaches does not imply that there must be a division between them so much as it helps to illustrate the ways in which the approaches are complementary. That is, the strengths of one approach tend to be the weaknesses of the other and vice versa. For example, a survey in the form of a questionnaire can be used to obtain a great deal of data from a large representative sample, and the measures on the questionnaire might be considered highly reliable and valid using quantitative criteria such as inter-item reliability and construct validity. However, from a qualitative perspective, the findings still might not be genuine since they are based on pre-determined categories and highly structured questions—meaning respondents cannot provide additional details or explain the issue from their own perspective. In addition, respondents may choose not to answer certain items and may provide less truthful albeit socially desirable answers. Conversely, the rapport established in an in-depth qualitative interview can uncover a wealth of information from the perspective of an interviewee in his or her own words. The insightful discoveries are deemed to be credible because of the trustworthy processes used to obtain the data, as well as the rigour used to verify the findings, such as through member checks and peer debriefing. However, from a quantitative perspective, the same results are going to be viewed as having limited reliability due to the small sample size and a lack of generalizability. Figure 11.1 provides a highly simplified comparison of the key differences between quantitative and qualitative methods. For a more detailed discussion of the various ways to assess reliability and validity in qualitative and quantitative studies, please refer to Chapter 4.

How the Approaches Are Similar

Although it may appear that quantitative and qualitative approaches are polar opposites, there is one main similarity shared by the approaches when it comes to their overall orientation to research: both approaches rely on empirical methods. Both approaches are geared toward empirical observations even though they rely upon different techniques to obtain them. Although different methods are used, the processes undertaken follow systematic procedures that are recognized by other researchers. Qualitative researchers, for example, carry out in-depth interviews in standardized ways, by first obtaining ethical approval, by obtaining consent from the interviewee, by using opening remarks to break the ice and establish rapport, and by using various types of questions and prompts. Similarly, quantitative researchers administer a questionnaire in standardized ways, by first obtaining ethical approval, by obtaining consent from the participants, by including clear instructions for completing the questionnaire, and by developing a questionnaire instrument that avoids the use of jargon and technical language. In the same way, quantitative researchers carefully create their instruments so

FIGURE 11.1
Comparing
Quantitative
and Qualitative
Approaches

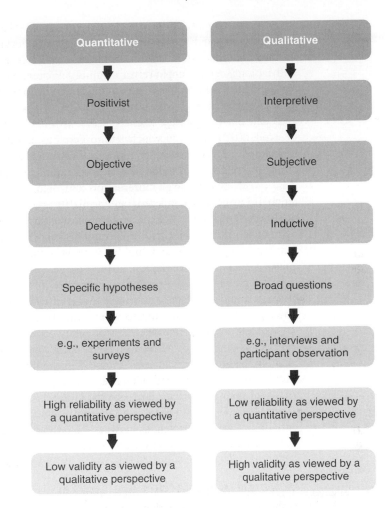

they constitute highly reliable and valid measures, while qualitative researchers go to great lengths to ensure their approaches to data collection are trustworthy and credible and that the data obtained is accurate. Moreover, when it comes to the dissemination or sharing of research findings, all researchers describe the procedures they followed to undertake the study in such detail that others can check and verify the processes, and in some cases even replicate the study based on how it was described. Thus, one approach is not better or worse, or more or less accurate—it is just different.

Combined Approaches Are Not New

Research in the social sciences is highly complex, particularly when the goal is to accurately describe a group, explain a process, or explore an experience. Relying on either qualitative or quantitative methods exclusively can be unnecessarily limiting. For example, Padgett (2012) points out that while "surveys supply much-needed aggregate information on individuals, households, neighborhoods, organizations, and entire nations....they fall short in assessing individuals as they live and work *within* their households, neighborhoods, organizations, and nations" (p. 9, emphasis in original). Wouldn't it make sense to combine approaches to achieve a more complete understanding? Research using combined approaches is common in a variety of disciplines, including education, health care and nursing, library science, political science, psychology, and sociology (Terrell, 2012). Some approaches to research are always based on a combination of methods. Ethnography, for example, is routinely carried out using a combination of qualitative methods of equal importance within the overall design of a study, such as participant observation and qualitative interviewing (see Chapter 10). Further, methods that are primarily quantitative sometimes include a qualitative component, such as structured questionnaires that include closed- and open-ended items (see Chapter 7). Some methods are conducive to both qualitative and quantitative approaches, such as content analysis and observational analysis. Finally, triangulation in qualitative research necessitates attempts to locate a point of convergence or agreement in findings as based on multiple observers, multiple data sources, or the use of multiple methods (see Chapter 4). There are endless possibilities for combining methods and approaches in a single study. Methods were introduced in singular forms in earlier chapters mainly for the sake of simplicity so you would first be able to understand their underlying logic and unique contributions. As noted in the opening quote, using a combination of approaches has the potential to describe and explain phenomenon more fully and completely than could be ever be the case if researchers limit themselves to only one quantitative or qualitative method.

Test Yourself

- Why are qualitative approaches considered to be empirical?
- In what ways are qualitative and quantitative approaches complementary?

Mixed-Methods Approaches

Mixed-methods approach A research design that includes an explicit combination of qualitative and quantitative methods as framed by the research objectives.

Distinct from the use of multiple methods of any kind, a **mixed-methods approach** always entails an explicit combination of qualitative and quantitative methods as framed by the research objectives. This can involve designing a study to include a qualitative and quantitative method undertaken at the same time, such as obtaining existing data for an organization for secondary analysis at the same time that members of that organization are interviewed and examining the findings from both methods concurrently. A mixed-methods approach can also include the use of two or more methods at different times, such as seeking participants for qualitative interviews based on the findings from the secondary analysis of existing data.

Why Researchers Mix Methods

Researchers combine qualitative and quantitative methods for any number of reasons. The most commonly cited reason for mixing methods pertains to the benefits that can only be obtained through a combination of different but complementary approaches. For example, after employing one method a researcher can elaborate upon or clarify the results obtained using the first method with a second one (Green, Caracelli, & Graham, 1989). For example, a researcher might employ a quantitative experiment and then later conduct in-depth qualitative interviews to better understand why the participants behaved the way they did as a result of the experimental manipulation. Likewise, a researcher might conduct a survey using a highly structured quantitative questionnaire and then conduct qualitative interviews to learn more about why the respondents hold particular views.

A second, related reason for combining approaches is to capitalize on the benefits of both approaches while minimizing or offsetting their associated drawbacks (Bryman, 2008). Recall that an experiment is conducted in a controlled environment that lends itself to high internal validity but may be so artificial that is not representative of a real-life setting. In-depth interviews with participants can help to determine whether the findings have external validity. Finally, a researcher might also use mixed methods for the purpose of development where the findings from one method (e.g., qualitative) are then used to inform the second method (e.g., quantitative) (Green et al., 1989). This kind of development usually takes place in what Creswell and Clark (2011) refer to as sequential designs, where one method is used in a particular phase of a study and the results then inform a different method that is used in a later phase as part of the overall plan. For example, a researcher may start off with a focus group or in-depth interviews to establish categories or to develop items that will be later used in a structured survey.

Mixed-Method Designs

There are various ways to mix methods within a research study based on the order or sequence in which the methods are employed and the point (or points) at which the data are combined. Three mixed-method designs are discussed in this section to illustrate customary ways to combine qualitative and quantitative methods within a single study.

Convergent Design

Convergent design A mixed-method design in which qualitative and quantitative methods are employed concurrently, with independent data collection and analysis compared in the final interpretation.

In a **convergent design** (also known as a convergent parallel design), both qualitative and quantitative methods are employed at the same time with equal priority (Creswell & Clark, 2011). For example, secondary analysis of existing data might coincide with interviews during the same phase of a research study. Using a convergent design, researchers carry out independent data collection and analyses where the secondary analysis is done separately from the interviews. Only at the end stage of the research are findings from the qualitative and qualitative components compared and integrated as part of the overall interpretation (see Figure 11.2). Note that convergent designs are used in triangulation strategies where more than one method is employed to see if the results converge. However, in such cases, the two methods are likely to both be qualitative as opposed to qualitative and quantitative.

Wilson et al. (2012) employed a mixed-methods convergent design to understand the implications of care setting transitions during the last year of life for rural Canadians. The researchers concurrently used a number of methods. They used quantitative secondary analysis to describe and compare health care transitions between rural and urban residents based on in-patient hospital and ambulatory care information on Albertans contained in databases. At the same time, the researchers used an online survey to collect information from individuals who could provide details on rural Canadians who had died in the last year. Respondents were asked to provide information on the number of moves, the location of the moves, and the impact of care moves undertaken by the deceased. Researchers also conducted qualitative interviews with bereaved family members located through notices posted in rural newspapers and in community service settings (e.g., grocery store billboards) to learn more about the moves and their experiences over the last year. Findings from the secondary data revealed that rural decedents underwent more health care setting transitions for in-patient hospital care than urban patients. Survey data indicated that the deceased underwent an average of eight moves in the last year of life, and that a great deal of travelling was required to take the now deceased individual to and from appointments, generally at different hospitals in various locations. The main themes that emerged from the interviews included the point that necessary care was scattered across many places, that travelling was difficult for the terminally ill and their caregivers, and that local services were minimal (Wilson et al., 2012).

FIGURE 11.2   Convergent Design

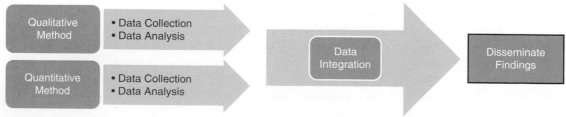

Explanatory Design

Explanatory design

A mixed-method design which a quantitative method is employed first and then the findings are followed up on using a qualitative method.

Recall that one of the main reasons for combining methods is to clarify the results of one method through the use of a second method. In an **explanatory design** (also known as an explanatory sequential design), a quantitative method is employed first and then the findings are followed up on using a qualitative method (see Figure 11.3). For example, a researcher might administer a survey to understand the general views of a sample on an issue of interest. After the survey data is collected and analyzed, researchers might conduct in-depth qualitative interviews with a few respondents to better understand and explain the results obtained in the earlier, prioritized quantitative phase.

In a study on the organizational performance of service-based companies, Al-Mawali and Al-Shbiel (2013) first surveyed the top management from 98 of the 192 Jordanian companies listed on the Amman stock exchange, such as companies in the insurance industry, banking industry, hotels and tourism industry, commercial services, and real estate. Management completed self-report questionnaires in which they compared the company they worked for with its major competitor on performance items rated on a seven-point scale ranging from (1) below average to (7) above average. Factor analysis, a statistical method for explaining the dimensionality of a set of variables, revealed three main dimensions to performance: financial performance, consisting of operating profit, return on investment, and return on equity; market performance, including new service success rate, market share rate, and sales growth rate; and customer-service performance, consisting of customer complaints and customer satisfaction rate. Overall, the quantitative findings indicated that companies had achieved moderate to slightly high levels of organizational performance, with the financial dimension coming out on top (Al-Mawali & Al-Shbiel, 2013).

In the next phase of the study, qualitative interviews were conducted with seven top managers to learn more about their views on organizational performance. Results from qualitative interviews generally supported the earlier quantitative findings, with all of the managers highlighting a prioritization of financial performance over market and customer-service measures and most of the interviewees emphasizing a perception that their company's performance was in an acceptable range. However, for those who cited less than satisfactory company performance, interviews helped to explain why. Specifically, managers pointed to a lack of attention placed on research and development and attributed this to

FIGURE 11.3 **Explanatory Design**

cost reduction measures taken to offset the negative implications of wider global market financial crises (Al-Mawali & Al-Shbiel, 2013).

Exploratory Design

Exploratory design
A mixed-method design in which a qualitative method is employed first and then the findings are used to help develop a subsequent quantitative method-based phase.

In an **exploratory design** (also known as an exploratory sequential design), a qualitative method is prioritized, and then based on the findings from the qualitative study, a quantitative method is developed and subsequently employed (see Figure 11.4). For example, themes emerging from transcribed data based on a small number of in-depth interviewees can help to create categories and constructs included in a questionnaire for use with a much larger, more representative sample of respondents.

Moubarac, Cargo, Receveur, and Daniel (2012) used a two-stage exploratory mixed-methods design to examine the situational context associated with the consumption of sweetened food and drink products in a Catholic Middle Eastern Canadian community living in Montreal. In Stage 1, the researchers conducted semi-structured interviews with 42 individuals to learn more about sweetened food and drink consumption. Specifically, the convenience sample was asked to think about their consumption of sweetened drinks and foods and they were provided with examples. Interviewees were then directed to comment on the last three times they consumed sweetened products, noting conditions and circumstances associated with consumption such as time of day and location. In addition, the interviewees were asked to name their favourite sweetened product and to note conditions and circumstances associated with it. Finally, they were asked about customary consumption of sweetened product in different locations, such as at work or at home. A content analysis of the transcribed interview data revealed 40 items and six main themes associated with consumption of sweet products including: energy (i.e., sweets provide energy); negative emotions, or the tendency to eat sweets when sad; positive emotions, such as a reward; social environment (e.g., offered at someone's house); physical environment or availability; and constraints (e.g., eating out at restaurants) (Moubarac et al., 2012).

Findings from Stage 1 were then used to construct the Situational Context Instrument for Sweetened Product Consumption (SCIPC), a self-report questionnaire used in Stage 2 of the study. Stage 2 consisted of a cross-sectional study in which 192 individuals (105 women and 87 men) completed the SCIPC. The participants also completed a food frequency questionnaire that included a listing of sweet products such as brownie, cake, candy, cookie, muffin, and soft drink along with the associated total sugar content, a questionnaire on socio-demographics,

FIGURE 11.4   Exploratory Design

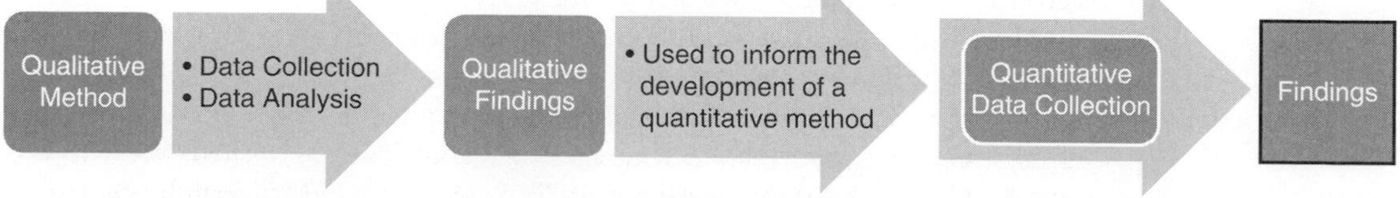

and items on self-reported weight and height. Quantitative analyses revealed seven situational factors related to the consumption of sweets, including emotional needs, snacking, socialization, visual stimuli, constraints, energy demands, and indulgence (Moubarac et al., 2012).

Test Yourself

- In what way is a qualitative approach similar to a quantitative one?
- What six core characteristics underlie true mixed-methods research?
- For what reasons might a researcher choose a mixed-methods design?
- In which kind of mixed-methods design does research begin with quantitative data collection and analysis?

Research Using Multiple Methods

Within the social sciences, certain types of studies are routinely carried out using multiple methods, such as ethnography as discussed in Chapter 10. In this section, I discuss three areas of research that have not been discussed thus far that typically employ multiple methods (but not necessarily mixed methods): case study research, evaluation research, and action research.

LO3

Case Study Research

Recall from Chapter 4 that a case study pertains to research on a small number of individuals or an organization carried out over an extended period of time. A case study is an intensive strategy that employs a combination of methods such as archival analysis, interviews, and/or direct observation to describe or explain a phenomenon of interest in the context within which it occurs. As Yin (2003) puts it, a case study is relevant when "a 'how' or 'why' question is being asked about a contemporary set of events, over which the investigator has little control" (p. 9). The focus of a case study can be a person, a social group, an institution, a setting, an event, a process, or even a decision. In addition, the scope of a case study can be narrow, as in an examination of one person's journey through a single round of chemotherapy treatments, or it can be broad, as in a case study of chemotherapy as an available treatment option for cancer patients. What sets case study research apart from other forms of research is that it is a strategy that intensively "investigates a contemporary phenomenon in its real-life context, especially when the boundaries between phenomenon and context are not clearly evident" (Yin, 2003, p. 13).

By holistically examining one person undergoing chemotherapy treatment, for example, a researcher can gain insight into the greater context of how other variables such as interactions with doctors and hospital staff, travel arrangements, family dynamics, and pain management all contribute in various ways to the overall experience for that particular individual. Case study research relies upon multiple methods of data collection with the goal of uncovering converging evidence that will help to explain or describe the phenomenon of interest. If the goal of a case study is to understand a person's experience while undergoing chemotherapy, a researcher is likely to interview that person on several occasions and speak to primary caregivers close to that person, such as a spouse, parent, sibling, and/or child. In addition, the researcher might examine archival documents, such as postings on Facebook or entries in a personal diary, to get a sense of what the experience means to the person undergoing treatment. While most often employing qualitative methods, case studies are not inherently qualitative in nature and can include quantitative methods or a combination of qualitative and quantitative data collection techniques.

Single Versus Multiple-Case Study Designs

Single-Case Design Case study research is based on either a single-case or a multiple-case design. A **single-case design** refers to case study research that focuses on only one person, organization, event, or program as the unit of analysis as emphasized by the research objectives. Yin (2003) offers five reasons why researchers might choose a single-case design. First, a single-case design might be selected by a researcher if the case represents a critical case that exemplifies all of the criteria that would be necessary for testing a theory of interest. A single-case design is also likely to be chosen if a case can be identified that is highly representative or typical among a larger range of phenomena. However, a single-case design might also be preferred if the case represented an extreme situation or event, since an outlier is likely to provide insights that are unanticipated. In addition to features of the case itself, a single-case design might be selected largely because of the unique opportunity it affords to investigate an area. For example, a case study of a patient with a rare disorder can help medical practitioners and families to more accurately describe the disorder, find appropriate interventions, and reveal new insights. This is usually called a revelatory case (Yin, 2003, p. 42). Finally, if the goal of a study is to determine how a person, organization, or process changes over time, a single-case study is a good choice as this design is especially suited to longitudinal analysis.

As an example of a single-case strategy focused on one person, Harr, Dunn, and Price (2011) examined the utility of household task participation for improving other activities such as work opportunities in a 20-year-old disabled male who was born with spina bifida. The study included a period of initial assessment, an intervention period designed to promote autonomy and independence as a function of successes experienced through the completion of household chores (e.g., doing the dishes on a regular basis), and a subsequent post-intervention reassessment. Quantitative measures included standardized assessment instruments such as a self-determination scale, a chores instrument, and an occupational performance measure. Separate qualitative interviews were also conducted with the young man and his father (the primary caregiver) at regular intervals over the period of study to gauge perceived progress. Results of this quasi-experiment showed that performance and satisfaction increased from pre- to post-assessment.

Single-case design
A case study strategy that focuses on only one person, organization, event, or program as the unit of analysis as emphasized by the research objectives.

The young man also demonstrated increased participation at home and in the community following the intervention. In addition, qualitative data highlighted additional benefits, including improved communication between father and son (Harr et al., 2011).

As another example, Hamm, MacLean, Kikulis, and Thibault (2008) focused their single case study research on a longstanding Canadian non-profit sports organization to examine value congruence between the employees and the organization. First, the researchers collected and examined existing documents, such as policy statements, meeting notes, and emails. The next phase of the study involved non-participant observation in meetings and activities. In the third phase, employees rated their personal employee values by completing the Rokeach Value Survey. Finally, employees identified as having the highest and lowest value congruence, based on the survey findings, were then interviewed to learn more about their opinions and experiences. Overall, the findings indicated a significant discrepancy or incongruence between organization and employee values. For example, while the organization emphasized "wisdom" and "equality," the employees rated "accomplishment" and "family security" as being much more important. Moreover, while the organization highly valued "equality," the employees did not feel that they were treated with equality. In addition, the organization heavily promoted their five core values (i.e., leadership, open, listen, responsive, and relevant), but none of interviewed employees mentioned these as values they felt they shared with the organization (Hamm et al., 2008).

Multiple-Case Design

Multiple-case design A case study strategy that focuses on two or more persons, organizations, events, or programs selected for the explicit purpose of comparison.

A **multiple-case design** is a case study strategy that involves more than one case studied concurrently for the explicit purpose of comparison. According to Yin (2003), a small number of cases are specifically chosen for use in multiple-case study designs because they are expected to produce similar findings akin to replication in experimental research. Alternatively, two or more cases might also be selected because they are expected to show contrasting findings as predicted by relevant theoretical assertions. It is important to note that the logic underlying the inclusion of additional cases cannot be likened to the sampling logic used in quantitative survey research to obtain representative samples or generalizable findings. However, it can approximate the control obtained in experimental research if the two selected cases are virtually identical with the exception of one feature that becomes the focus of a controlled comparison (George & Bennett, 2005).

As an example of a multiple-case design, Sussman et al. (2011) sought to identify factors associated with positive palliative care outcomes through a comparison of four health care systems from different regions of Ontario. In an attempt to identify factors contributing to positive outcomes, they used purposive extreme case sampling so that their unit of analysis would consist of the health care systems with the highest and lowest cancer-related acute care deaths and emergency department visits within the last two weeks of life. Based on qualitative and quantitative data analyses, findings revealed main differences between the regions on three measures: capacity, such as available funding for palliative care services;

access to after-hours service and mechanisms for palliative care identification; and coordination for things such as formalized reporting structure and location-of-death planning. Sussman et al. (2011) also identified the presence of various features in superior care systems, including 24/7 palliative care team access and the use of a common chart to facilitate care provider communication.

Research on the Net

Case Studies

An excellent overview of case studies is provided by LearningFrom WOeRK on YouTube. Here, you can learn more about four types of single-design case studies and how case study research is similar to and different from ethnography. You can find the video on youtube.com by searching for "Plymouth University LearningFrom WOeRK case studies."

LO4

Evaluation Research

Another form of research that relies upon the use of multiple methods for data collection and analysis is evaluation research. Recall from Chapter 1 that evaluation research is undertaken in order to assess whether a program or policy is effective in reaching its desired goals and objectives. Evaluation research includes "the application of empirical social science research to the process of judging the effectiveness of [. . .] policies, programs, or projects, as well as their management and implementation for decision making purposes" (Langbein, 2012, p. 3). Virtually every government department and every funded social program or intervention undergoes evaluation. For example, evaluation research was used to determine the effectiveness and management of the Canada Student Loans Program (Human Resources and Skills Development Canada, 2011), City-Street Video Surveillance Monitoring Programs (Lett, Hier, & Walby, 2012), the Nobody's Perfect Parenting Program (Skrypnek & Charchun, 2011), and the Language Instruction for Newcomers to Canada Program (Citizenship and Immigration Canada, 2010). The potential topics for evaluation research are endless.

Types of Evaluation Research

There are different kinds of evaluation research, depending on where a program is in terms of its existence and overall life course. For example, *before* a program is developed, evaluation research is informative for diagnosing what is required in the way of a program. "The main form of diagnostic research that centers on problems is the **needs assessment.** In needs assessment, the focus is on under-standing the difference between a current condition and an ideal condition" (Stoeker, 2013, p. 109). Goals of a needs assessment typically centre on identifying a problem, finding out who is affected by that problem, and coming up with a program to address the problem. Sample questions include:

Needs assessment
A systematic evaluation focused on improving an existing condition through the identification of a problem and a means for addressing it.

- What is the nature of the problem affecting this community (or group)?
- How prevalent is this problem?
- What are the characteristics of the population most affected by this problem?
- What are the needs of the affected population?
- What resources are currently available to address this problem?
- What resources are required to more adequately address this problem?

Needs assessments are largely focused on obtaining information that will help in the early planning and eventual development of a program. To learn as much as possible about members of a target community, researchers are likely to rely upon a range of methods, including existing documents, survey methods, observational analyses, and interviews (Sullivan, 2001).

Program evaluation
A systematic method for collecting and analyzing information used to answer questions about a program of interest.

Evaluation research that is conducted to examine and monitor *existing* programs is usually called **program evaluation** or program monitoring. The overarching question in a program evaluation is likely to take the form of: Did the program work? Evaluation directed at answering the question of whether a program, policy, or project worked usually entails a large-scale research project that combines multiple methods, such as site visits, the examination of existing program documents, and in-depth interviews with employees. The purpose is to gauge how well the major program components link up with the corresponding program goals.

Sample questions include:

- Is this program working? (Why or why not?)
- Is this program operating as it was intended?
- Are program objectives being met?
- Are the services reaching the intended target population?
- Were the program goals achieved?
- Did the program result in positive outcomes for the clients?

Program evaluations have historically relied on some form of system's model (see Figure 11.5). The model describes the program by depicting its organizational structure in terms of: interconnected inputs, including resources put into the program such as funding, other agency involvement, and certified staff; activities, including program offerings such as counselling sessions or skill development classes; outputs or results, including who attended the program; and outcomes, including the overall goals and benefits such as reduced recidivism or increased social development. While this might come across as a straightforward approach to evaluation, it is anything but. Many programs are not amenable to evaluation because they do not have clearly articulated goals and objectives, or the goals and objectives are not realistic or measureable. Wholey (1994) suggests first employing an evaluability assessment to see if minimum criteria can be met before embarking on a full-scale evaluation of a program. An evaluability assessment includes: 1) a description of the program's overall model; 2) an assessment of how amenable that model is to evaluation, such as whether the goals and objectives are clearly stated and whether performance measures can be obtained;

FIGURE 11.5   A System's Model of an Educational Program for Prostitution Offenders

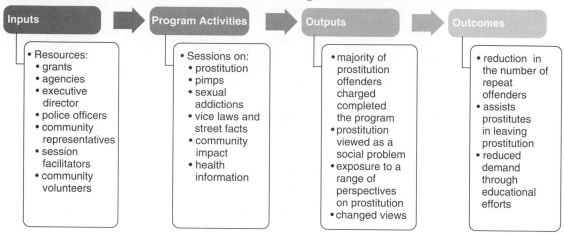

and 3) additional details on stakeholder views of the purpose and use of the evaluation findings, where possible (Rossi, Lipsey, & Freeman, 2001). The purpose of the evaluability assessment is to gauge whether a program can be meaningfully evaluated. For example, programs designed to reduce prostitution recidivism through educational efforts, also known as John School (see Symbaluk & Jones, 1998), are regularly criticized for having unclear or unmeasurable goals. For example, how would it be possible to show that there was a reduced demand for prostitution? Yet this is a claim frequently made by proponents of these programs as evidence of their success (Coté, 2009). It is possible, however, to show a reduction in the number of complaints about street prostitution to the police by business and community members in a particular location, or to measure whether or not known prostitution offenders reoffend. Except, in both cases, this still is not evidence that the program was effective because it could be that offenders are less likely to get caught a second time or that they learn to be more discrete, resulting in fewer complaints. You can download an exemplary evaluability assessment template from the United Nations Office on Drugs and Crime (go to unodc.org and search for "Evaluability Assessment Template").

Cost-benefit analysis A method for assessing the overall costs incurred by a program relative to outcome measures.

Because programs are typically very costly to operate, questions concerning whether or not a program is effective sometimes translate into a **cost-benefit analysis.** A cost-benefit analysis is a method for systematically assessing the overall costs incurred by the program, including the ongoing costs needed to run the program such as wages paid to employees, rent for the building, and materials, versus outputs or program results, such as who benefited and how did they benefit. Is the cost of the program justified given the overall benefit to the clients or to the wider society? For example, the cost-benefit analysis of a prostitution offender program might take into account the financial costs of running the program for one year, including educational resources such as skilled facilitators, police personnel, and rental space for the classroom, in relation to the risk of the same number of men reoffending in the absence of the educational program. Or a cost-benefit analysis might compare the financial costs and outcomes incurred by this particular program to other alternatives, such as criminal charges, fines, and vehicle seizures, to see whether the costs are warranted given the benefits achieved. Sample questions include:

- How costly is this program (i.e., operating costs)?
- Are there ways to quantify the benefits of the program (e.g., into dollars saved)?
- How do various operating costs compare to alternative resources (e.g., wages)?
- How do the overall costs of the program compare to alternatives to the program?
- Are the costs of the program justified given the overall benefits of the program?
- How do the costs and benefits of this program compare to alternate methods for dealing with this particular social problem?

Carrying Out Evaluation Research

The process for carrying out evaluation research will vary depending on the type of evaluation, the exact program, and the evaluation objectives. However, an evaluation generally proceeds through five stages, as simplified below and depicted in Figure 11.6:

1. Engage with stakeholders who provide valuable input.
2. Clarify the research problem—what question(s) are to be addressed in this evaluation?
3. Establish evaluation criteria (the criteria which the program is being evaluated against), including standards for indicating if the program meets or fails to meet these criteria.

FIGURE 11.6 **Steps for Carrying Out Evaluation Research**

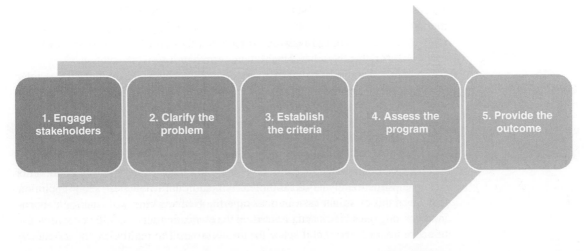

4. Assess the program, including selecting appropriate methods, data collection, and data analysis to measure performance against the established criteria.

5. Provide the outcome or the assessment or conclusion reached in the evaluation.

Engaging with Stakeholders

Because a program is generally set up to provide some kind of social service or resolve a particular social issue, a number of social relationships and roles exist within that program. For example, managers and other decisions makers supervise staff members who are responsible for delivering program services to intended target recipients. All of the various social relationships involve **stakeholders** who need to be considered as part of the evaluation. Stakeholders include any individuals, groups, and/or organizations that are directly or indirectly involved with or who are impacted by the program of interest. For example, the target recipient of an intended service or intervention would be considered a primary stakeholder, as would any staff member involved in the operation of the program, as well as any group that funds the program, such as program sponsors and donors. Stakeholders play a vital role in the creation, operation, and success of a program and they are usually identified early on so that their input can be sought at various stages throughout an evaluation (Rossi et al., 2003).

For example, in an evaluation of a Canadian workplace disability prevention intervention called Prevention and Early Active Return-to-work Safely (PEARS), Maiwald, de Rijk, Guzman, Schonstein, and Yassi (2011) sought feedback from three main groups of stakeholders: program designers, deliverers, and workers. The researchers used a variety of qualitative methods, including semi-structured interviews, participatory observations, and focus group sessions. Although the three groups of stakeholders similarly defined the causes of workplace disability, they placed emphasis on different aspects. For example, the deliverers explained disability largely in terms of risk factors and individual-level causes, while workers emphasized the importance of the workplace and organization contributors. In addition, while they agreed on the importance of workplace safety and the belief that workplace interventions can have a positive effect on work disability, stakeholders had very different ideas about how the intervention should work in practice. Deliverers, for example, largely targeted individual-directed measures, while workers felt these measures offered only short-term benefits rather than a sustainable long-term return-to-work solution.

From this example, it becomes apparent that while all stakeholders have a vested interest in how a program or initiative operates, they are unlikely to view the program similarly. While different perspectives clearly help an evaluator gain a richer understanding, they also add to the complexity of the evaluation as it becomes less clear which features should be changed and which ones should be retained. Guba and Lincoln (1994) suggest that one of the primary purposes of an evaluation is to facilitate negotiations among stakeholders so that they can come to a common or shared construction of the social program. In addition, Rossi et al. (2004) point out that "even those evaluators who do a superb job of working with stakeholders and incorporating their views and concerns in the evaluation plan should not expected to be acclaimed as heroes by all when the results are in. The multiplicity of stakeholder

Stakeholder An individual, group, or organization that is directly or indirectly involved with or impacted by the program of interest.

perspectives makes it likely that no matter how the results come out, someone will be unhappy" (p. 43). While a necessary and vital element in all program evaluations, stakeholders also constitute one of the main challenges in evaluation research.

Evaluator's Role in Relation to Stakeholders

Evaluation research designs can be fairly simple or highly complex depending on the nature of the program and the objectives of the evaluation. At a minimum, the design should specify the questions the evaluation seeks to answer, the methods that will be employed to answer the questions, and the nature of the relationship between the evaluator and the stakeholders. An evaluator is likely to assume one of two main roles in an evaluation. Either the evaluator works directly with the stakeholders who are part of the evaluation team with the evaluator acting as the team lead, or the program evaluator conducts research independent from the stakeholders but still consults with them at various points to establish the evaluation criteria and to obtain information used in the evaluation. In the case of the former, the research is often called partici-patory action research, collaborative research, or community-based research because the researcher is literally participating with the stakeholders to help them evaluate their own program. While there are some obvious disadvantages to this approach as the stakeholders who are typically the greatest proponents of the program are now in charge of evaluating it, there are also merits. People with a vested interest are also likely to be willing to commit their time and resources to a process that they feel is useful and is likely to lead to welcomed improvements. Compare this to an approach in which (often) underpaid and overworked stakeholders are asked to commit addi-tional time and resources on behalf of an outsider who is paid to assess their program and then tell them what their issues are (Stoecker, 2013).

Independent evaluation An evaluation that is headed up by a researcher who is not a primary stakeholder for the program under consideration.

A program evaluation most often takes the form of an **independent evaluation.** An independent evaluation is one led by a researcher who is not part of the organ-ization and who has no vested interested in that organization. The evaluator is not a stakeholder but a commissioned researcher and who designs the study, conducts the evaluation, and shares the findings with stakeholders (Rossi et al., 2003). Although the evaluator is not a stakeholder, he or she will still need to work closely with various stakeholders since they provide valuable data and they inadvertently set the agenda for the program evaluation through their vested interests. For example, funding agencies are interested in cost-benefit analyses and outcome measures since they want to know if a program is being run efficiently from a cost perspective and whether the program is meeting its intended objectives. In contrast, program man-agers are more concerned with questions pertaining to program monitoring since their vested interest has to do with how the program operates. Finally, in some cases, programs are examined and evaluated to determine where changes can and should be made, as discussed in a later section on action research.

Recognizing the Role of Politics in Evaluation Research

As a final comment on evaluation research, it is important be aware of how evaluation research takes place within a larger political framework that ultim-ately influenced how that particular program came to be, why it is currently being evaluated, and what will happen once the assessment is made available. As Carol H. Weiss explains in the opening of her 1973 paper "Where politics and evaluation research meet":

> Evaluation is a rational enterprise that takes place in a political context. Political considerations intrude in three major ways, and the evaluator who fails to recognize their presence is in for a series of shocks and frustrations:
>
> First, the policies and programs with which evaluation deals are the creatures of political decisions. They were proposed, defined, debated, enacted, and funded through political processes, and in implementation they remain subject to pressures—both supportive and hostile—that arise out of the play of politics.
>
> Second, because evaluation is undertaken in order to feed into decision making, its reports enter the political arena. There, evaluative evidence of program outcomes has to compete for attention with other factors that carry weight in the political process.
>
> Third, and perhaps least recognized, evaluation itself has a political stance. By its very nature, it makes implicit political statements about such issues as the problematic nature of some programs and the unchallengeability of others, the legitimacy of program goals and program strategies, the utility of strategies of incremental reform, and even the appropriate role of the social scientist in policy and program formation.
>
> Knowing that political constraints and resistance exist is not a reason for abandoning evaluation research; rather, it is a precondition for usable evaluation research. Only when the evaluator has insight into the interests and motivations of other actors in the system, into the roles that he himself is consciously or inadvertently playing, the obstacles and opportunities that impinge upon the evaluative effort, and the limitations and possibilities for putting the results of evaluation to work—only with sensitivity to the politics of evaluation research—can the evaluation be as creative and strategically useful as it should be. (P. 94)

Research on the Net

Canadian Evaluation Society

The Canadian Evaluation Society (CES) is a multidisciplinary association based on the advancement of evaluation theory and practice. The CES hosts an annual conference that serves as a forum for discussing current issues in evaluation. In addition, the CES and the Canadian Evaluation Society Educational Fund (CESEF) jointly host an annual Case Competition. In this student learning opportunity, teams compete for prizes and a trophy by first completing a preliminary round involving the analysis of a case file that is hidden on the Web. Each team has five hours to complete their evaluation and submit it for judging. The three highest-rated teams are invited to participate in the final round, held at the annual conference, where they receive a new case to evaluate and present their findings to a live audience. For more information, visit the CES website at evaluationcanada.ca.

LO5

Action research
Social research
carried out by a team
that encompasses
a professional
action researcher
and the members
of an organization,
community, or network
(stakeholders) who are
seeking to improve the
participants' situation.

Action Research

Action research, as its name implies, is a research strategy that attempts to better understand an area of interest in order to implement change within that area of interest. Greenwood and Levin (2007) define action research as "social research carried out by a team that encompasses a professional action researcher and the members of an organization, community, or network (stakeholders) who are seeking to improve the participants' situation" (p. 3). For example, action research is routinely employed in education where it serves as a transformational methodology used to determine how to optimize learning strategies and programs so that they work best for students with a range of learning needs and skills. Multiple methods used to explore an issue can include interviews, focus groups, surveys, archival analysis, and the secondary analysis of existing data.

As a simplified illustration, a teacher might begin by identifying a problem or concern, such as students are having difficulty understanding an important concept as evidenced by their grades on standard assessments as well as comments they have made in class. Once the problem is articulated via discussions with the class and in-depth interviews with a sample of students, the teacher needs to identify potential ways to resolve the issue. For example, other teachers might recommend strategies that have worked in their classrooms, there may be recommended strategies in the literature, and there may be potential solutions identified in the minutes from professional development meetings. After a period of reflection in which the teacher considers potential options, he or she will then determine the course of action most suitable for this particular class and then implement it for a trial period. Following this, the teacher will need to evaluate the success of the strategy by reassessing students' level of understanding on objective measures such as tests, as well as through informal discussions with the students. Once the evaluation has occurred, the teacher can begin to consider how to modify future instruction based on what worked and did not work. See Figure 11.7 for a summary of the logic underlying action research.

FIGURE 11.7
The Underlying Logic of Action Research

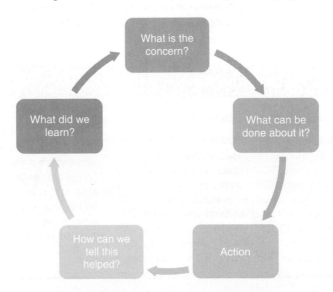

Action research is a continuous reflective, cyclical process that begins with observation, and is followed by reflection, action, evaluation, modification, and then subsequent observation (McNiff & Whitehead, 2006). In this sense, action research generally involves a series of cycles as opposed to one phase of research. Going back to the earlier example, a teacher might try a learning strategy and then discover that is was only effective for certain students. In this case, another action cycle will begin. The second cycle will retain successes of the first phase and add in a new course of action to try and further improve upon the learning environment. For instructors who strive to continuously improve upon their teaching, the action cycle can continue indefinitely (see Figure 11.8).

Research in Action

Collaborative Action Research

Assistant Professor Martine Pellerin came up with a collaborative action research model for the professional development of teachers. Teachers shared evidence of what worked and did not work in their own classrooms in a post-evaluation phase during a pilot project in four schools as part of the Alberta Initiative for School Improvement. As a result, they were able to learn from each other and gather strategies to strengthen subsequent plans of action. For more information on this initiative, refer to the Collaborative Action Research blog at blogs.rockyview.ab.ca/aisi/collaborative-action-research-model.

The purpose of action research is not only to improve conditions, but also to empower participants since it is the stakeholders who participate directly in identifying the issues and means for resolving them. For this reason action research is sometimes referred to as participatory action research or a participatory research process. For example, McKenzie, Seidl, and Bone (2010) relied on participatory action research to examine child welfare problems and practices in eight

FIGURE 11.8 **Action Research Cycles**

Source: Adapted from McNiff & Whitehead, 2006, pp. 9, 37.

Manitoba First Nations communities. During the first phase of the st__ groups and interviews were conducted with more than 200 individuals, ing Elders, Chiefs, and Council members; biological parents, foster parents, homemakers; local child and family service committee members and communi__ staff members; and youth between the ages of 13 and 18. After common themes were identified from the responses provided, the researchers engaged in a second round of consultation to evaluate and validate the findings.

Consistent with the literature on Aboriginal people, one of the common themes that emerged from this study was a traditional extended view of family that included aunts, uncles, cousins, and grandparents. In addition, along with concerns about the provision of good emotional and physical care and guidance, participants identified the common need to include the teaching of traditional values, language, and customs as part of the definition of what is in the "best interests of the child." Another main finding was that in cases where there are indicators of inadequate care, support should be provided to that family such that potential solutions are enacted within the family setting (McKenzie et al., 2010).

Research on the Net

Canadian Journal of Action Research

The *Canadian Journal of Action Research* is a free, full-text journal dedicated to action research for educators. Here, instructors and administrators share articles, book reviews, and notes from the field. You can find this journal on Nipissing University's site at cjar.nipissingu.ca.

Test Yourself

- What is case study research?
- For what reasons might a researcher choose a single-case study design over a multiple-case design?
- What is an independent evaluation?
- Why is it important to consult stakeholders in evaluation research?
- What is action research?
- What questions can be posed to depict the underlying logic of action research?
- What are the main steps in the process for carrying out an action research cycle?

Chapter Summary

LO1   **Compare and contrast quantitative and qualitative approaches.**

Quantitative approaches are grounded in the positivist paradigm and tend to be focused on objective methods that are based on deductive reasoning. Research questions are usually stated as hypotheses and data collection is carried out in experiments, surveys, or certain forms of unobtrusive methods such as the analysis of existing data. Quantitative methods are highly reliable but may be lacking in validity since findings from highly controlled experiments are difficult to generalize to the real world. Qualitative approaches, in contrast tend to be based in the interpretive paradigm that emphasizes subjectivity and inductive reasoning. Research questions tend to be broad and methods for data collection can include in-depth interviews, participant observations, focus groups, as well as various forms of unobtrusive methods such as content analysis. Qualitative methods tend to be higher in validity but lack reliability.

LO2   **Define mixed-methods approach, explain why a researcher might opt for a mixed-methods design, and differentiate between mixed-method designs.**

A mixed-methods approach always entails an explicit combination of qualitative and quantitative methods framed by the research objectives. Mixed methods can be useful for establishing the validity of measures and findings. For example, the results obtained in an experiment might be clarified by the results obtained through qualitative interviewing. In addition, mixed methods are useful for development purposes, such as when a researcher uses focus group findings to help inform categories that will later be used on a questionnaire. In a *convergent design,* both qualitative and quantitative methods are employed at the same time with equal priority. In an *explanatory design,* a quantitative method is used first and then the researcher follows up on the findings using a qualitative method. In an *exploratory design,* a qualitative method is prioritized and then, based on the findings from the qualitative study, the researcher develops and subsequently employs a quantitative method.

LO3   **Define case study research and explain why a researcher might choose a single-case design over a multiple-case study.**

Case study research is an intensive research strategy that uses multiple methods to describe or explain a phenomenon of interest in the context in which it occurs. A researcher might opt for a single-case study if the case selected represents a critical case for testing a theory, if the case is typical, if the case represents an extreme, if the case constitutes a rare opportunity, or if the researcher wishes to conduct a longitudinal analysis.

LO4   **Define evaluation research and explain what an evaluation design entails.**

Evaluation research is the application of social science research to the process of judging the effectiveness of policy, programs, or projects, as well as their management and implementation for decision-making purposes. At a minimum, an evaluation design outlines the questions of interest, the methods for obtaining answers, and the nature of the relationship between researchers and stakeholders.

LO5   **Define action research, describe the underlying logic of action research, and explain what an action research cycle entails.**

Action research is a research strategy that directly involves stakeholders in an attempt to better understand an area of interest to bring about improvement. The logic underlying action research centres on identifying a concern, determining what can be done about it, implementing an action, determining whether the action helped, and evaluating what was learned as a result. The process for carrying out action research entails observation, reflection, action, evaluation, and modification.

Research Reflection	1. Suppose you are interested in studying one program that is specifically geared toward students at the school you are currently attending. As a case study, provide rationale for examining this program using a single-case design.

1. Suppose you are interested in studying one program that is specifically geared toward students at the school you are currently attending. As a case study, provide rationale for examining this program using a single-case design.

2. If you were going to conduct an organizational case study of the school you are currently attending, describe two methods that you would use to collect suitable data.

3. If you were going to conduct a Bachelor of Arts degree program evaluation, what three questions would you pose to help focus the evaluation? In other words, what three questions do you think should be answered in the evaluation?

4. Thinking of the community in which you live, identify one main social issue that could be examined using participatory action research. List all of the relevant stakeholders you would include in a study designed to help address the social issue.

5. Of the four main paradigms discussed in Chapter 2 (positivist, interpretive, critical, and pragmatic), which best reflects the assumptions underlying action research? Explain your answer.

Learning Through Practice

Objective: Learning how to conduct case study research.
Directions:

1. Identify a local restaurant or coffee shop that you enjoy going to.

2. Describe some of the features that lead you to enjoy this particular restaurant.

3. Thinking of other restaurants or similar service providers, is this a typical case or more of an outlier? Explain your answer.

4. Visit the restaurant and conduct an observation to see if there is anything else you wish to add to your description.

5. Now suppose you have been asked by the owners to write a verifiable report on what makes this restaurant enjoyable.
   a. How could you go about proving your claims?
   b. How could you find out if others share similar views?

6. List and describe three methods you could use to help substantiate your description of what makes this restaurant special.

7. Based on the methods you selected and the potential order in which you could employ these methods, would your resulting design be best described as a mixed-methods design or simply a design that includes the use of multiple methods?

Research Resources

1. Although this book is meant to inspire product development as opposed to basic research, it is a worthwhile read for discovering a vast repertoire of innovative and more traditional methods that can be used to conduct social science research. For more information on artifact analysis, behavioural mapping, cognitive mapping, participatory action research, scenarios, shadowing, thematic networks, and much more, refer to Martin, B., & Hanington, B. (2012). *Universal methods of design: 100 ways to research complex problems, develop innovative ideas, and design effective solutions.* Beverly, MA: Rockport Publishers.

2. For a more in-depth look at mixed-methods research, including embedded, transformational, and multi-phase designs, see Creswell, J. W., & Clark, V. L. (2011). *Designing and conducting mixed methods research* (2nd ed.). Thousand Oaks, CA: Sage Publications.

3. To learn more about designing case study research, refer to George, A. L., & Bennett, A. (2005). *Case studies and theory development in the social sciences.* London, ENG: MIT Press.

4. For a comprehensive overview of evaluation research, I recommend Rossi, P. H., Lipsey, M. W., & Freeman, H. E. (2004). *Evaluation research: A systematic approach* (7th ed.). Thousand Oaks, CA: Sage Publications.

5. For more information on the purposes of action research and the methods used to carry it out, I recommend: McNiff, J., & Whitehead, J. (2006). *All you need to know about action research.* Thousand Oaks, CA: Sage Publications.

For more information on the resources available from McGraw-Hill Ryerson, go to www.mcgrawhill.ca/he/solutions.

References

Al-Mawali, H., & Al-Shbiel, S. O. (2013). Comprehensive evaluation of Jordanian companies' performance: A sequential explanatory study. *Journal of Accounting, Business & Management, 20*(1), 28–45.

Bryman, A. (2008). Why do researchers integrate/combine/blend/mix/merge/fuse quantitative and qualitative research? In M. M. Bergman (Ed.), *Advances in mixed methods research: theories and applications* (pp. 87–100). Thousand Oaks, CA: Sage Publications.

Citizenship and Immigration Canada (2010). *Evaluation of the Language Instruction for Newcomers to Canada Program (LINC).* Ottawa, ON: Evaluation Division. Retrieved from http://site.ebrary.com.ezproxy.macewan.ca/lib/macewan/docDetail.action?docID=10478640

Coté, J. (2009, Sept 20). Prostitution program badly flawed, audit finds. *San Francisco Chronicle (10/1/2007 to present)*. 9/20/2009, p. C1. Retrieved from http://ehis.ebscohost.com.ezproxy.macewan.ca/eds/detail?vid=2&sid=ad169edb-4b67-48bb-85ac-ddef1d40d81a%40sessionmgr12&hid=17&bdata=-JnNpdGU9ZWRzLWxpdmUmc2NvcGU9c2l0ZQ%3d%3d#db=bwh&AN=44239304

Creswell, J. W., & Clark, V. L. (2011). *Designing and conducting mixed methods research* (2nd ed.). Thousand Oaks, CA: Sage Publications.

George, A. L., & Bennett, A. (2005). *Case studies and theory development in the social sciences.* London, ENG: MIT Press.

Green, J. C., Caracelli, V. J., & Graham, W. F. (1989). Toward a conceptual framework for mixed-method evaluations designs. *Educational Evaluation and Policy Analysis, 11*(3), 255–274.

Greenwood, D. J., & Levin. M. (2007). *Introduction to action research: Social research for social change* (2nd ed.). Thousand Oaks, CA: Sage Publications.

Guba, E. G., & Lincoln, Y. S. (1994). Competing paradigms in qualitative research. In N. K. Denzin and Y.S. Lincoln (Eds.), *Handbook of Qualitative Research* (pp. 105–117). Thousand Oaks, CA: Sage Publications.

Hamm, S., MacLean, J., Kikulis, L., & Thibault, L. (2008). Value congruence in a Canadian nonprofit sport organization: A case study. *Sport Management Review, 11,* 123–147.

Harr, N., Dunn, & Price, P. (2011). Case study on effect of household task participation on home, community, and work opportunities for a youth with multiple disabilities. *Work, 39,* 445–453.

Human Resources and Skills Development Canada. (2011). *Summative evaluation of the Canadian Student Loans Program final report.* Ottawa, ON: Strategic Policy and Research Branch. Retrieved from http://site.ebrary.com.ezproxy.macewan.ca/lib/macewan/docDetail.action?docID=10527429

Langbein, L. (2012). *Public program evaluation: A statistical guide* (2nd ed.). Armonk, NY: M. E. Sharpe.

Lett, D., Hier, S., & Walby, K. (2012). Policy legitimacy, rhetorical politics, and the evaluation of City-Street Video Surveillance Monitoring Programs in Canada. *Canadian Review of Sociology, 49*(4), 328–349. DOI: 10.1111/j.1755-618X.2012.01298.x

Maiwald, K, de Rijk, A., Guzman, J., Schonstein, E., & Yassi, A. (2011). Evaluation of a workplace disability prevention intervention in Canada: Examining differing perceptions of stakeholders. *Journal of Occupational Rehabilitation, 21,* 179–189. DOI 10.1007/s10926-010-9267-z

Martin, B., & Hanington, B. (2012). *Universal methods of design: 100 ways to research complex problems, develop innovative ideas, and design effective solutions.* Beverly, MA: Rockport Publishers.

McKenzie, B., Seidl, E., & Bone, N. (2010). Child and family service standards in First Nations: An action research project. *Child Welfare League of America, LXXIV*(3), 633–653.

McNiff, J., & Whitehead, J. (2006). *All you need to know about action research.* Thousand Oaks, CA: Sage Publications.

Moubarac, J-C., Cargo, M., Receveur, O., & Daniel, M. (2012). Describing the situational contexts of sweetened product consumption in a Middle Eastern Canadian community: Application of a mixed-method design. *PLOS ONE, 7*(9), Special section, pp. 1–10. 10p. DOI: 10.1371/journal.pone.0044738

Padgett, D. K. (2012). *Qualitative and mixed methods in public health.* Thousand Oaks, CA: Sage Publications.

Rossi, P. H., Lipsey, M. W., & Freeman, H. E. (2004). *Evaluation research: A systematic approach* (7th ed.). Thousand Oaks, CA: Sage Publications.

Stoecker, R. (2013). *Research methods for community change: A project based approach.* Thousand Oaks, CA: Sage Publications.

Skrypnek, B. J., & Charchun, J. (2011). *An evaluation of the Nobody's Perfect Parenting Program* [electronic resource]. Ottawa, ON: Canadian Association of family resource programs, 2009 (Saint-Lazare, QC: Canadian Electronic Library, 2011). Retrieved from http://site.ebrary.com.ezproxy.macewan.ca/lib/macewan/docDetail.action?docID=10465255

Sullivan, T. J. (2001). *Methods of social research.* Orlando, FL: Harcourt, Inc.

Sussman, J., Barbera, L., Bainbridge, D., Howell, D., Yang, Y., Husain, A., Librach, S. L., Viola, R., & Walker, H. (2011). Health system characteristics of quality care delivery: A comparative case study of patients in four regions in Ontario, Canada. *Palliative Medicine, 26*(4), 322–335.

Symbaluk, D. G., & Jones, K. M. (1998). Prostitution offender programs: Canada finds new solutions to an old problem. *Corrections Compendium, 23*(8), 1–2.

Terrell, S. R. (2012). Mixed-methods research methodologies. *The Qualitative Report, 17*(1), 254–280.

Weiss, C. H. (1973). Where politics and evaluation meet. *Evaluation Practice, 14*(1), 93–106.

Wholey, J. S. (1994). Assessing the feasibility and likely usefulness of evaluation. In J. S. Wholey, H. P. Hatry, & K. E. Newcomer (Eds.), *Handbook of practical program evaluation* (pp. 15–39). San Francisco, CA: Jossey-Bass.

Wilson, D. W., Thomas, R., Burns, K. K., Hewitt, J. A., Osei-Waree, J., & Robertson, S. (2012). Canadian rural–urban differences in end-of-life care setting transitions. *Global Journal of Health Services, 4*(5), 1–13. http://dx.doi.org/10.5539/gjhs.v4n5p1

Yin, R. K. (2003). *Case study research: Design and methods* (3rd ed.). Thousand Oaks, CA: Sage Publications.

Endnote

[1] Cohen, L., Manion, L., & Morrison, K. (2011). *Research methods in education* (7th ed.). New York, NY: Routledge.

Writing Research Proposals and Reports

12

Learning Objectives

After reading this chapter, students should be able to do the following:

LO1 Outline the main components of a research proposal.

LO2 Explain the purpose of a method section in a research proposal.

LO3 Identify key ethical considerations that need to be addressed in a research proposal.

LO4 Outline the structure and format of a scholarly research report.

"Writing is not something you wait for (like an inspiration), nor is it a natural instinct (i.e., an inherent talent); it is a behaviour, and as such, it is something that can be shaped. And, if you persist, over time, it becomes something you learn to do well." (Symbaluk, 2006, p. vii)[1]

Introduction

Particular disciplines recommend their own writing style for academic papers and reports. Three common documentation styles used in the social sciences throughout North America are American Psychological Association (APA) format, Modern Language Association (MLA) style, and American Sociological Association (ASA) style. All three provide direction for quoting and paraphrasing the work of others, for setting up the format of documents (e.g., spacing, headers, and the presentation of material in tables and figures), and for referencing sources. APA format is based on the most current edition of the *Publication Manual of the American Psychological Association.* MLA style is based on the most current edition of the *MLA Handbook for Writers of Research Papers,* and ASA is based on the *American Sociological Association Style Guide.* Consult with your instructor, your course syllabus, your library's writing resources, or the instructions for contributors at a journal to determine the exact style you should use for preparing course work, research proposals, or research reports.

Research Proposals Versus Reports

Most everyone who takes a research methods course or who plans to carry out basic research for an honours project, an independent study, or for graduate studies (e.g., master's research or a research-based dissertation for a doctorate degree) is expected to develop a research proposal. Similarly, researchers and other academics who wish to carry out studies at universities and in the private or business sector typically submit a research proposal to an ethics board and/or to a funding agency prior to beginning the research project. A **research proposal** is a comprehensive plan created in advance of carrying out research that details what a research project is about and what the process entails for obtaining the data needed to address the research questions and objectives. Included in the proposal is a description of the relevant literature, the main research questions or hypotheses the study hopes to address, the methods for obtaining data, and anticipated ethical considerations. A **research report**, in contrast, is written after research is conducted. The report is a detailed account that describes the area of interest, outlines the specific research questions or hypotheses addressed in the study, spells out the methods used to obtain the data, and reports the results from the study. In addition, a research report discusses the findings in relation to the wider literature on the subject matter, indicates any limitations of the study, and offers suggestions for future research on that topic. The next section provides you with some guidance for what to include in a research proposal.

Research proposal
A comprehensive plan created in advance of carrying out research that details what the purpose of the project is and what the process will be for obtaining data.

Research report
A detailed account following research that describes the research interest, questions, or hypotheses addressed, methods used, and the findings from the study.

The Research Proposal

LO1

A research proposal is meant to address two primary questions: 1) What purpose does the research serve?; and 2) How will the research be carried out to meet the intended objective? The research purpose is articulated in the introduction section and the planned process for carrying out the research is detailed in the method section. A research proposal is usually divided into five main sections consisting of an introduction, a method section, a section on data analysis and dissemination, a section on ethical considerations, and a listing of prospective references. These sections are described in detail below.

Introduction Section

To explain the research purpose in a manner that is accessible to a wide audience of readers, a researcher should frame the general research interest within a theoretical context, briefly describe what other researchers have done and found on the topic, state the current research interest, and explain how the present study will contribute to the literature by posing specific research questions and/or by testing hypotheses. Begin with a broad, opening statement that identifies the area of interest. For example, a student of mine who planned to compare the portrayal of masculinity in the lyrics of country versus hip hop songs, began with: "Hiphop (or rap, the two terms are now used interchangeably) and country music are increasingly popular genres of music" and went on to point out the earnings and prevalence of the two genres to introduce the general topic (Holub, 2012). After introducing the general topic, a researcher can begin to narrow the topic by linking the topic to previous research on the proposed area of interest. This is where central concepts are discussed and the theoretical context is established. Continuing with the previous example, my student went on to point out prevalent masculinity themes identified in previous research on lyrics of music from the two genres. The same student ended the introduction section by noting that she planned to specifically compare depictions of masculinity across genres to see if there were common underlying features. A qualitative study with an exploratory focus includes a general question, such as: Are there similarities in the manner in which masculinity is depicted in country and hip hop music lyrics? In contrast, a quantitative study with a more descriptive focus would likely include a directional hypothesis, such as: H_1: The proposed study predicts that masculinity will be more evident in hip hop than in country music lyrics. Ask yourself the following questions as you prepare the introductory section:

- What is my broad area of interest?
- Did I identify a narrow focus within this area of interest?
- Did I summarize the relevant literature in this area?
- Did I include clear conceptual definitions for the main concepts?
- Is a theoretical context established for my study?
- What will my research contribute to this area?
- What is my research question or hypothesis?

Method Section

LO2

The method section outlines who the participants will be and how they will be selected. In addition, the method section includes details about the setting and materials needed to conduct the study, the procedures for carrying out the study, and the main variables examined in the study as discussed in more detail below.

Participants and How They Will Be Obtained or Sample Selection

First, if the study will include research participants, such as interview participants, survey respondents, or experimental subjects, a researcher needs to detail who the potential research participants will be and how they will be identified and recruited. In addition, the researcher should note any relevant criteria that may be used to include or exclude particular participants. For example, an honours student working under my supervision examined the prevalence of aggressive and dangerous forms of driving in a sample of 300 university students. In his ethics application, he proposed that participants would be recruited from the university's research subject pool in accordance with the department's procedures for online survey research participation. He also pointed that since this study was specifically about driving behaviours, the participants would need to include only volunteers who drive a motor vehicle at least on occasion.

Note that not all forms of research involve research participants. A researcher planning to use unobtrusive methods such as physical trace analysis or wanting to carry out a content analysis would instead describe proposed units of analysis. Recall Gackenbach, Sample, Mandel, and Tomashewsky's (2011) study on the video player's online dream diary. Although there was a person to whom the dreams belonged, it was the content of 447 of his 831 dream postings that constituted the units of analysis. In a qualitative study this section is usually called sample selection. Here, a researcher articulates how the sample (e.g., of dream postings) will be obtained, including any inclusion or exclusion criteria that will determine eligibility (Padgett, 2011). For example, of the 831 posted dreams, a dream was included in the analysis if it was more than 50 but less than 500 words, had a clear date as to when it occurred, included an activity blog entry from the night before the dream, and fit one of the defined dream categories, resulting in a sample of 447 dreams (Gackenbach et al., 2011).

Setting and Materials

In addition to describing the participants and how they will be recruited or the units of analysis, the method section also indicates the proposed setting or location for data collection and any materials that will be required to carry out the study. Research is often carried out at a university where the primary researcher holds a faculty position. However, if the study is an in-depth qualitative interview, the setting may be the respondent's place of residence or a public location that the respondent feels comfortable in and one that provides some degree of needed privacy, such as a booth in a local coffee shop. Similarly, if the study involves ethnographic fieldwork, the research setting is likely to be wherever that group or process is located and can best be examined from within a natural context.

Materials for a study include items that need to be purchased ahead of time to carry out the study. For example, to carry out my master's research on pain perception and endurance, I needed to purchase a heart rate monitor to monitor the participants for health and safety reasons throughout the exercise. I also needed to secure equipment that could be used to assist in the measurement of pain endurance. Specifically, participants performed an isometric sitting exercise above a box with a pressure plate. A participant who was too tired to continue sat down on the box, activating the pressure plate to stop a timer that recorded endurance.

As another example, an online ethnography might require a computer, Internet access, and possibly some kind of registration or software needed to gain access to a group of interest, such as through a membership or user account. Finally, a researcher conducting an interview-based study might wish to use incentives to compensate interviewees for their time and would therefore need to purchase gift cards or prepare some comparable remuneration in advance of the study.

Main Variables

Next, researchers describe the main variables or measures of interest. If the approach is quantitative, as in the case of an experimental method, this section describes the dependent variables. (The independent variables are discussed as part of the procedures for how the manipulation will be carried out.) For example, in the pain study, the main dependent variable was pain endurance defined as the length of a time a participant was able to maintain an isometric sitting exercise in minutes and seconds. Each dependent variable should be listed, along with the operational definition for how it will be measured. For a quantitative survey, each main variable is likely to be measured using a question or multiple questions on a self-report questionnaire. For example, in a study on aggressive driving, aggressive behaviour might be measured using Deffenbacher, Lynch, Oetting, and Swaim's (2002) shortened version of the Driver Anger Expression Inventory consisting of 21 items. The inventory assesses verbally aggressive behaviour (e.g., yelling at other drivers), physically aggressive behaviour (e.g., giving someone the finger), and/or constructive expressions of anger (e.g., thinking about other things). Survey items are usually summarized in this section and the full inventory is included in an appendix. If the measures are already established, you can report on the reliability and validity of the measures as described in the literature.

Alternatively, if a study is based on a qualitative content analysis, an in-depth interview, or an unstructured observation, this section elaborates on how the researcher plans to identify main themes and patterns from the data once it is collected and transcribed, as opposed to operationalizing variables ahead of time. The section is sometimes called coding procedures and it can take the place of the main variables and procedures sections. For example, a researcher who wishes to examine a particular television series for depictions of violence enacted by the main characters might indicate a plan to use an open coding scheme to detail every separate and distinct act of violence committed by a main character as a first cycle coding method. This can be followed by a second phase of coding directed at identifying main themes and categorizing the patterns to the violence identified in the first round of coding. Similarly, an ethnographer might plan to use descriptive coding for field notes and documents collected on a group of interest that will be later subjected to a more structured coding process. A qualitative researcher might also adopt existing coding schemes from the established literature to conduct a content analysis. When possible, the researcher should articulate the coding schemes and tie them back to the theoretical context in which they developed. Since the content of any method section is going to vary considerably depending on the approach and methodology (e.g., quantitative survey versus qualitative interview), you should examine published journal articles based on the same methodology you plan to use for a more definitive sense of what you need to include here.

Procedures

Finally, the procedures section outlines the detailed plan for carrying out the study as the last main component of the method section. This section needs to be written in so much detail that a reader could exactly replicate the study based on how it is described in writing. For example, if a researcher intends to conduct online survey research, the procedures will detail how the participants are to access the online survey, such as accessing the survey through a link they receive in an email invitation sent to their university email account. Once a participant clicks on the study link, what happens next? The procedures literally walk the reader through the study. For an online survey, the first page that is likely to appear on the screen following the link to the study is the informed consent statement. The procedures will then go into detail about how the online consent form describes the study, provides details about what is expected of participants, notes the benefits and risk of participation, indicates that participation is voluntary, explains how privacy will be maintained, and describes the plans for disseminating the findings. The procedures also indicate how consent is actually obtained. In the case of an online survey, potential participants are likely to be asked to click on a box that reads something like: "I agree to participant in this study" or "I do not agree to participate in this study." Procedures can also note that upon agreeing to participate in the study, the participants then receive the first screen page of the survey. What happens to those who choose not to participate? The procedures should also note that participants who do not consent to participate instead receive a debriefing statement that provides additional details about the study and contact information for the principal researcher.

In addition to describing the process leading up to survey access, the procedures also describe the survey instrument by noting how many questions are on the questionnaire, indicating whether questions are grouped into sections, noting the topic of each section, and listing the order in which the information will be received by the participant. For example, perhaps the questionnaire begins with ten items that assess background information, followed by a five-item personality scale or a 12-item behaviour inventory. The procedures also note what happens once participants complete the survey. In most cases, after completing an online survey, participants will receive the debriefing statement mentioned above. Finally, a copy of the questionnaire in its entirety, along with the consent form and debriefing statement, should be attached at the end of the proposal as an appendix.

Again, I would advise you to look at the procedures sections for a couple of published journal articles based on studies similar to the one you are planning for additional ideas on what you need to include as necessary steps. Ask yourself the following questions as you prepare the method section:

- Did I indicate who the target participants will be and how I plan to obtain them?
- If I don't have participants, did I explain what my units of analysis will be and how I plan to sample for them?
- Did I explain any relevant inclusion or exclusion criteria for selection?
- Have I noted where the proposed study will take place?
- Have I identified all materials that need to be obtained in advance of the study?
- For a quantitative study, have I listed and operationalized all of the main variables I plan to examine in my study?
- For a qualitative study, have I explained how I plan to code or categorize the information I will be collecting?
- Have I explained all of the steps I will undertake to carry out the study?

Data Analysis and Dissemination

In addition to describing the main variables and/or coding procedures, a research proposal also includes a brief section outlining the plan for data analysis and dissemination of findings. A quantitative study is likely to include statistical analysis using a software package especially designed for the social sciences, such as IBM SPSS or Stata statistical software. Data analysis in a qualitative study may be carried out by developing codes through transcription and textual analysis, or it can be assisted through specialized software programs such as NVivo, which helps to manage data by treating units of analysis as cases and organizing ideas, concepts, and themes into codes so that patterns and trends can be made apparent (Bazeley, 2007). Here researchers can also indicate any strategies they plan to use to establish reliability, including inter-rater reliability and methods for obtaining rigour. Finally, a proposal outlines the plan for what will be done with the data once it is collected. Perhaps the researcher intends to report on the findings at an upcoming conference or submit the main findings to a journal for peer review and possible publication.

LO3

Ethical Considerations

If a researcher plans to undertake a study that will include university students (or any humans) as research participants, as in the case of an experimental design, a survey project, an in-depth qualitative interview, or a focus group, the researcher needs to first obtain ethical approval through a university's research ethics board. Even in the case of non-reactive research, if a researcher wishes to carry out a project that will in some way involve a university's assets (directly or indirectly), as in the case of non-participatory observation in public spaces on campus, ethical approval will need to be sought from that university's research ethics board. A research proposal always includes relevant ethical concerns along with the ways in which the planned study will address the concerns.

Minimal Risk for Harm

Recognizing that all research involving humans has at least a minimum potential for harm, a researcher should identify whether the proposed study can be judged as a minimal risk. While it is up to the research ethics board to determine whether the study is deemed a minimal risk, a researcher can and should provide a rationale for why the proposed project should be assessed as such. For example, a researcher who plans to conduct a survey on driving may indicate that there are no anticipated risks associated with participating in the proposed study. However, since the participants are disclosing information about their own driving habits, there is a minimal risk that participants may experience psychological discomfort when answering questions about the extent to which they engage in dangerous or aggressive driving practices. Specifically, participants could feel remorse or embarrassment while responding to certain questions. In addition, participants could later reflect on responses given and regret having disclosed information about their driving.

Mitigating Minimal Risk of Harm

To help mitigate this potential likelihood of harm, a researcher can include fairly explicit information in the initial consent form to give the potential participant an idea of the type of questions he or she can anticipate being asked during the survey. For example, participants might be informed that they will be asked to report on safe and unsafe driving practices. In addition, the researcher can even include examples of specific items on the survey (e.g., Question #25 asks: How often do you send or receive text messages while stopped at a red light?).

Researchers can also include a statement within the questionnaire itself that reiterates that participation is voluntary, that participants may skip over questions they do not want to answer, and that they can choose to end their participation at any time without penalty. Finally, a researcher can include additional self-help resources with the debriefing statement, such as resources for driver education and training.

Addressing Beneficence

Recall from Chapter 3 the importance of designing a study in a manner that minimizes harm while maximizing the overall benefit of the research. Where possible, a research proposal should include a statement about the benefits of the proposed study for the researcher. For example, might the research help to fulfill the requirements for an honours project or a master's thesis? In addition, it is important to list potential benefits for the participants, such as the opportunity to learn more about themselves and research processes. Finally, the proposal should also indicate benefits to the wider research community and/or society as a whole. For example, may the proposed study contribute in particular ways to our understanding of some group, phenomenon, or process?

Upholding Privacy and Confidentiality

A researcher also needs to detail the planned procedures for upholding privacy through the anonymity of participants, how safe and secure storage of data will be achieved, and how confidentiality will be upheld in the disclosure of findings. For example, a researcher will need to note whether any personally identifying information is going to be collected and if so, how he or she plans to safeguard the identity of individual participants. Note that participants need to be made aware of this prior to providing consent.

Part of the process of ensuring privacy includes a consideration and disclosure of the following: who is going to participate in data collection (e.g., Will research assistants help to collect information?); who is expected to access the data once it is collected (e.g., Will anyone other than the principal researcher assist in the transcription or coding of coding?); and how is data going to be stored (e.g., Will the data be transferred onto a computer file that will be kept on a password-protected computer in a locked office of the principal researcher? Will field notes be kept in a locked cabinet in the secure office of the principal researcher?). A research ethics board will ask for information on all of these items, as well as additional information including how long the data will need to be stored (the recommended length is about two years) and how the data will eventually be disposed of (e.g., Will the notes be shredded?).

Prospective References

Finally, a research proposal ends with a list of relevant references. References included in a research proposal help to establish a scholarly context for the planned study. The references help identify, for example, the appropriate and relevant theories, theorists, and concepts that inform the proposed research. In addition, references can help to validate the proposed methodology. For example, perhaps the researcher plans to use a grounded theory approach such as the one described by Barney G. Glaser in 1992.

References are listed in a standard citation format such as the one provided by the sixth edition of the *American Psychological Association's Publication Manual* (APA format). In APA format, an author of a book is listed by last name, followed by first initials, year of publication, title, place, and then the publisher according to specific rules for style and punctuation. As illustrated below, the title of a book is capitalized and the title appears in italics. MLA and ASA format are similar, as shown below.

APA format:
Glaser, B. G. (1992). *Grounded theory analysis: Emergence vs. forcing.* Mill Valley, CA: Sociology Press.

MLA format:
Glaser, Barney. *Grounded Theory Analysis: Emergence vs. Forcing.* Mill Valley, CA: Sociology Press, 1992.

ASA format:
Glaser, Barney. 1992. *Grounded Theory Analysis: Emergence vs. Forcing.* Mill Valley, CA: Sociology Press.

Test Yourself

- What are the two primary questions addressed by a research proposal?
- Does the introduction section in a research proposal begin with a broad or narrow statement?
- In which section of a research proposal would you expect to find information on the setting and materials for a study?
- Which subsection of a research proposal literally walks the reader through the study?
- What suggestions might researchers propose to mitigate the risk of harm to participants?

The Research Report

A research report is a formalized summary of a completed research project. A research report is written in a standard format that you can use to describe the research you have carried out for an undergraduate research class, an honours project, an independent study, or a field placement. Whether you are writing up the research for class marks, to give to a supervisor or instructor as proof that you have completed your project, or you hope to submit the work to an academic journal for possible publication, these guidelines serve as a template for your finished product. A research report is structured so that it includes a number of standard components or features that are recognized by other researchers and academics in the field. This format, also required for publication in most professional journals, includes a title page, an abstract, an introduction, a method section, a results section, a discussion section, references, tables, figures, and an appendix, as described in detail in this section. Also refer to the appendix of this book for a sample research report that conforms to this format, written by a former student as part of the requirements for an undergraduate introduction to research methods course.

Title Page

The title page is much more than just a place holder for the title of the study—it not only identifies what was studied, it provides additional information that helps to locate and establish the study within the greater context of the discipline in which it is situated. First, a title page includes a *long title* that summarizes what the study is about. There is no required minimum or maximum word length; however, the title should contain enough information to give the reader a sense of the specific research objectives. For example, *Sleep Quality* as a title would help identify the area of interest, but not what the study was about. In contrast, Digdon and Koble's (2011) full title, *Effects of Constructive Worry, Imagery Distraction, and Gratitude Interventions on Sleep Quality: A Pilot Trial* informs readers that three specific techniques were used to try and (presumably) improve sleep quality.

In addition to the full title, a title page includes a *running head,* which is a shortened version of the title that appears in the header of the manuscript once it is published (e.g., in a journal). Digdon and Koble (2011) used *Effects of Interventions on Sleep Quality* as their running head. Finally, a title page includes a short list of relevant *key words,* which are concepts used to locate the article via database searches once it is in print. For example, readers interested in sleep quality, sleep improvement, constructive worry, and/or imagery distraction might benefit from reading Digdon and Koble's study.

A title page also includes additional details, including a recognition statement for the source of any relevant funding and how to correspond with the principal researcher for more information about the study. The recognition statement cites the source of support for the study, such as an external research grant (e.g., the Social Sciences and Research Council of Canada) or an internal source of funding (e.g., a research fund from within a department or school or a university's research office). The correspondence statement lists the name and email address of the main contact person or the principal researcher for the study so that interested readers and other researchers can reach the person for more information about the study.

Abstract

Abstract A brief overview of a research project that describes the participants or units of observation, the design, the procedures, and the main findings in 120 words or less.

Located at the beginning of a research report, an **abstract** is a brief overview of the research project. It summarizes what the research is about, how many participants there were and how they were obtained (or what the units of analysis were), what the procedures were for carrying out the study, what the design consisted of, and what the main findings were. This can be considered the most important section in the entire report as it is generally the first and sometimes the only section that is read by other academics and researchers conducting searches for relevant articles of interest. Although it appears at the beginning of a report, it should be the last thing the researcher writes to ensure that it is both succinct (usually less than 120 words) and comprehensive. This is one of the most difficult sections to write as it needs to include a lot of information in what amounts to only about six to eight sentences. A good strategy for writing an abstract that is under 120 words is to first write an abstract that includes all of the relevant information (this will likely be about 300 words on your first try). Then rework it a few times, paring it down word by word, until it is as concise as possible.

Introduction

An introduction section follows the abstract. Similar to the research proposal, an introduction in a research proposal should include a general opening and a broad discussion of the research interest and area, followed by a narrowing of the research topic. In addition, the research topic should be situated within the relevant literature, and the theoretical context and key concepts should all be well articulated. After summarizing the relevant literature, the introduction ends with a statement of the research problem, key question(s), issues explored, and/ or hypotheses tested.

For example, in a research project on pain that I conducted for my master's research, the broad opening statement in the journal article I published was "Pain is a fundamental fact of life" (Symbaluk, Heth, Cameron, & Pierce, 1997, p. 258). From there, the introduction narrowed to discuss forms of acute and chronic pain in everyday life. It further narrowed as we brought in the social psychology of pain and established how monetary incentives and social modelling have been used in experimental research to increase pain endurance. It continued to narrow as we identified gaps in the literature and explained how this experiment was the first to look at the role of self-efficacy and pain perception as potential mediators for the anticipated effects of money and modelling on pain endurance. The introduction ended with specific hypotheses, including one predicting that pain endurance would increase as a function of money for participants who were exposed to pain-tolerant social models.

Note that the introduction section for a qualitative research project also summarizes the relevant literature and ties that literature to the research interests of the present study. However, in lieu of hypotheses, this section is likely to conclude with a statement of the research objective or the main question (or questions) explored in the study that follow logically from the literature review (Pyrczak & Bruce, 2007). For example, a qualitative study conducted by one of my students in an introduction to research method course focused on the reproduction of common stereotypes in popular media. Finlay's (2012) research question was: Does the popular television series *Crime Scene Investigation* promote or resist common stereotypical media representations of gender?

Method

The method (sometimes called methodology) section of the research report is next. The method section is generally the longest in a report as it contains subsections on the participants or selection of a sample, setting and materials, procedures or coding scheme, dependent or main variables, and data analysis.

Participants and How They Were Obtained or Sample and Sample Selection

For research involving humans as participants, this section notes how many participants were included in the study, who the participants were, and how they were obtained. For example, Sabbane, Bellavance, and Chebat's (2009) experiment on the effects of antismoking warnings on attitudes and smoking intentions included 178 teenagers as participants. Specifically, participants were males and females between the ages of 12 and 17 years who were non-smokers (N = 158) or occasional smokers (n = 15) recruited from Secondary I classes in a Montreal secondary school with parental consent.

As a second example, Boyd, Jardine, and Driedger (2009) analyzed the content of media representations of bovine spongiform encephalopathy (BSE), more commonly known as mad cow disease, for the first ten days following an outbreak in Alberta on May 20, 2003. Their sampling frame consisted of *The Globe and Mail* and *The National Post* (as leading national papers), as well as *The Lethbridge Herald* (as a local Alberta newspaper) and *The Edmonton Journal* (as a regional newspaper). The sampling procedure involved online searches of these papers for articles on mad cow disease identified through key words. From this potential sample, articles were included if they met additional criteria. For example, articles that only peripherally mentioned BSE (i.e., it was not the main focus of the study) were excluded, resulting in 309 articles in the sample used (Boyd et al., 2009).

Finally, as a third example, Dr. Rosemary Ricciardelli interviewed 14 men as part of a study on the role of hair in self-identification. The interviewees were recruited through convenience sampling via four means of advertising the study, including business card advertisements for the study given out and left in coffee shops and shopping centres in the greater Toronto area, an email invitation sent out to students in a small suburban university, an advertisement in *FAB* magazine, and an ad in a free gay publication (Ricciardelli, 2011).

Setting and Materials

As addressed under research proposals, the setting refers to the location where the data collection takes place. For example, in a study looking at the meaning of recovery from the perspective of Canadian consumers receiving mental health services, Piat et al. (2009) conducted interviews at major mental health service sources, including the Wellington Centre of the Douglas Mental Health University Institute, the Canadian Mental Health Association Waterloo/Wellington-Dufferin branches, and the Programme d'encadrement clinique et d'hébergement. If the setting does not apply, as might be the case if the study was conducted over the Internet, then this section would refer to materials only.

The materials refer to the main instruments and supplies used to carry out the procedures of the study. In an experiment, whatever is manipulated as the independent variable likely constitutes a material that requires preparation in advance of the study. For example, in a study on social information processing as a function of psychopathic traits, Wilson, Demetrioff, and Porter (2008) showed participants artificially created characters and then examined recall and recognition. The characters were profiles developed ahead of time that consisted of eight stimulus characters created with images of faces from the Pictures of Facial Affect Series (POFA) put together with descriptions that contained a name, an occupation, and a set of likes and dislikes.

Note that indexes, scales, and other items used to make up a questionnaire given as part of survey research are generally described as main variables or measures after the procedures (not as materials needed to carry out the study).

Procedures

The procedures section of a research report details how the study was carried out. This subsection within the method section is written in past tense and includes a description of all phases of the study, beginning with any instructions given to participants and the consent process, followed by details on the type of techniques employed to gather data and to later examine it. For example, if interviews were conducted, the researcher needs to indicate how many times each participant was interviewed and the time frame over which data collection (interviewing) took place. Alternatively, if observations occurred, when, where, and under what conditions did these take place? As another example, if an experiment was employed, how did participants experience the independent variable? Instead, if the study was based on ethnography, how did the researcher access the setting? Who were the gatekeepers and how was the gatekeeping process navigated? How was rapport with group members established? What role did the researcher engage in for data collection purposes (e.g., participant observation)? What methods were used to collect data? How did the researcher disengage from the setting at the completion of the study?

Note that if the study was based on content analysis, instead of procedures, a research report can include a section on coding procedures or a coding scheme. Similarly, if the study was based on secondary analysis of existing data, this section would outline why and how that particular source was selected and obtained and how the archival material was organized and synthesized for subsequent data analysis (Neuman & Robson, 2012).

Main Variables or Measures

A research report always includes a section that outlines the main variables examined in the study. If the study is an experiment, the dependent variables are listed along with their operationalized definitions. For example, in the pain experiment I conducted for my master's research, *pain perception* was operationalized as the time elapsed prior to the first sensation of pain in seconds and *pain endurance* referred to how long a participant held an isometric sitting position in minutes and seconds (Symbaluk, Heth, Cameron, & Pierce, 1997).

As another example, in a study looking at alcohol content as a mediating factor for brand preference, Segal and Stockwell (2008) employed measures of intoxication and enjoyment completed by participants after they drank two low- or two regular-alcohol content beers. Their measures section included a description of an objective variable based on blood-alcohol content assessed using a standard instrument called the Alco-sensor IV, and it included a description of three subjective measures. Each subjective measure was listed along with appropriate citations for the originating source and an account of the measure. For example, one measure was *The Sensation Scale,* which they note was originally developed by Maisto, Conners, Tucker, McCollam, and Adesso (1980), and which consists of 31 items about effects of alcohol. It also notes that participants scored the items using Likert responses ranging from 0 (not at all) to 9 (extremely), with the higher ratings referring to higher intoxication.

If the study is based on qualitative research, as would be the case for in-depth interviews or most focus group sessions, the research report might not have a section for the main variables or measures. This is because concepts, themes, and main ideas may emerge during data collection and analysis in response to open-ended questions. However, if interviews or focus group sessions are fairly structured, a researcher may include the questions or describe items that make up an interview guide as part of a section titled "Interview Guide in lieu of Main Variables."

Data Analysis

The last part of the method section of a research report details how data analysis was carried out. For example, if content analysis was employed using the frequency of occurrence of certain categories of events, how were the categories developed? Specifically, did the researcher use categories already established in the literature, modify categories based on previous literature, or develop new ones? Were categories counted once or every time there was an instance of that category? And how was reliability assessed? Did the researchers employ inter-coder reliability and if so, what was the reliability rate achieved?

As another example, the process for data analysis in an ethnographic study of young homeless men in Calgary was described as follows:

> Interviews were transcribed verbatim and checked for accuracy against the digital recordings. A thematic framework was agreed upon by the authors (SP and LM), based on the reported significance of daily routines, coping strategies and access to services. This was used along with an open coding strategy to recursively analyze these findings using NVivo 7, a qualitative analysis software (QRS International 2007). Data analysis was concurrent with data collection and uncovered common themes among the interviewees. (Persaud, McIntyre, & Milaney, 2010, p. 345)

Research on the Net

Writing Guides

Colorado State University provides several beneficial guides to writing that are designed to help students and academics become proficient in writing scholarly papers and research reports and that are available on their website at writing.colostate. edu/guides. Under the section "Conducting Qualitative & Quantitative Research" you will find a link

called "Scholarly Publishing." Here you can learn more about each component of a research report and find research examples that illustrate each component. In addition, you can access commonly used guides for citing sources, such as APA format and MLA format, and even learn how to cite less commonly used sources, such as sound recordings or television shows.

Results

The results section of a research report outlines the main findings of the study in the appropriate technical terms. If there are several dependent variables or measures, each variable might be listed as a sub-heading in this section. Note that the results section states only facts as succinctly as possible. In the case of quantitative research, the results section for an experiment is likely to report on findings based on tests of differences between means using *t*-tests for two groups or analysis of variance for variation between and within more than two groups or categories. The results section for quantitative survey research is likely to describe main variables (e.g., using measures of central tendency and variability), as well as report on tests for associations between variables of interest, such as correlations, regression analysis, or non-parametric measures of association.

Coding and the Development of Categories

In a qualitative research report, results typically document the findings from the coding methods employed in the study. The coding methods involve a number of stages or phases beginning with initial codes. As described in various earlier chapters, a code "is most often a word or short phrase that symbolically assigns a summative, silent, essence-capturing, and/or evocative attribute for a portion of language-based or visual data" (Saldaña, 2009, p. 3). Recall that qualitative data includes a range of information, from narrative and text based on interviews and field notes to drawings and images presented in magazine ads, shown through character portrayals on television, and so on. A posting on RateMyProfessor.com, for example, might contain the passage "She really knows her stuff," coded as "instructor" and "knowledge" since the passage refers to the instructor and it contains a comment about an attribute of the instructor. To begin with, each unit of data is usually assigned its own specific code.

After the initial codes are determined, the next phase includes going back over the data to determine if there are patterns that can be coded into categories based on their common elements. For example, perhaps a large number of comments refer to the instructor. Some of the comments might pertain to instructor attributes, such as comments about the instructor's knowledge of the subject matter, and comments about the instructor's willingness to help students. Other items might have to do with an instructor's grading, such as "The instructor is a hard marker," "The instructor grades fairly," etc. Finally, other comments might pertain to assignments in the course, such as "This course has a lot of papers!" One large category that might emerge from this data might be "comments about the instructor." Another category might be "comments about the course content." Within the "comments about the instructor" category, other subcategories could also be identified. For example, there may be a subcategory for "instructor attributes." Within the subcategory for "instructor attributes," researchers could also list codes for "clarity," "helpfulness," "knowledge," and so on.

Qualitative data analysis is a lengthy process that eventually culminates in the development of themes. As Saldaña (2009) points out, "a theme is an outcome of coding, categorization, and analytic reflection, not something that is, in itself, coded" (p. 13). Results from qualitative studies, then, highlight main themes or claims that are descriptive outcomes identifying the main overall findings that emerged from the data collection and analysis processes. To substantiate the results, qualitative researchers need to carefully articulate each of the coding stages and the categories that developed within each stage. Each main theme is generally discussed within its own subsection in the results, similar to how each main dependent variable would be discussed for a quantitative study.

Figures

Figures Charts or graphs used to display results based on how a variable is measured.

Results from quantitative studies are often depicted in **figures**. Figures are charts or graphs used to display results based on how a variable is measured. A pie chart, for example, is used to depict the results in a picture format for a variable that is measured at the nominal level. For example, a researcher doing a content analysis on gender portrayals in the media might use a pie chart to convey that there are more males than females depicted as central characters shown on television. Or, a researcher conducting an online survey on attitudes toward health care might use a pie chart to describe the respondents who completed the survey. Perhaps the largest slice of the pie indicates that the majority of participants were married, followed by single, common-law, divorced, and separated (see Figure 12.1). If none of the respondents claimed they were in a particular category (e.g., widowed), that category would not be included in the pie chart.

FIGURE 12.1
Sample Pie Chart: Marital Status

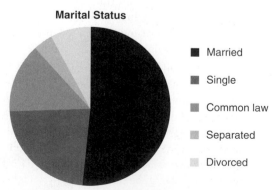

Marital Status

- Married
- Single
- Common law
- Separated
- Divorced

FIGURE 12.2   **Sample Bar Graph: Frequencies for Treatment Completion by Marital Status**

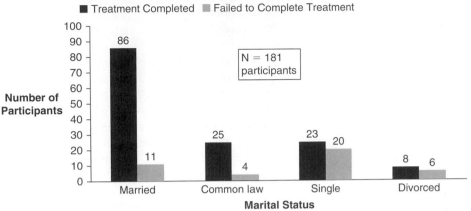

If it is important to indicate the frequency distribution for the categories of a variable, a bar graph would be used instead of a pie chart, since it emphasizes the number of respondents in each category of a variable and it can even be used to show the concurrent pattern of findings for two variables measured at the nominal level. In Figure 12.2 we can still determine that more than half of the participants in this fictitious study on the effectiveness of a drug treatment program were married (86 + 11 = 97 out of 181). However, we can also note that there may be a relationship between treatment completion and marital status, since a higher proportion of respondents who were in a relationship (married or common law) completed treatment relative to participants who were single or divorced (see Figure 12.2).

Bar graphs can also be used to display the distributions of responses across or within categories of a nominal variable shown in percentages. For example, Figure 12.3 shows the percent of respondents in each marital status category who completed or failed to complete treatment. This figure more clearly illustrates the link between relationship status and treatment completion, as it is now obvious to the reader that the vast majority of those in relationships completed treatment, whereas those who were not in relationships appear to have just slightly higher than a fifty-fifty chance of success (see Figure 12.3).

Tables

Tables are summaries of the main findings from quantitative research, such as the percentage of respondents who gave answers in each category of a variable on a questionnaire or the differences in means between groups on dependent measures. For example, Symbaluk and Howell's (2010) study showed that students gave higher ratings to instructors who won teaching awards than to research-award winners on the popular website RateMyProfessors.com. In the results section, they included a table that compared teaching-award winners and research-award winners by listing the mean rating given by students for easiness, helpfulness, and

Tables Summaries of main findings from quantitative research, such as the percentage of respondents who gave answers in each category of a variable on a questionnaire or the differences in means between groups on dependent measures.

FIGURE 12.3
Sample Bar
Graph: Percentage
of Treatment
Completion by
Marital Status

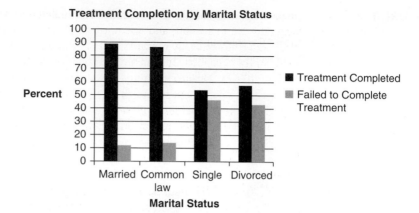

clarity for the two groups of instructors (see Table 12.1). Tables are also especially useful for indicating patterns in data over time (Nardi, 2006).

Discussion

In the discussion section of a research report, researchers summarize and elaborate on the main findings, highlight the importance of the findings, and tie them back into the wider literature. In addition, the discussion section notes limitations of the current study and identifies directions for future research. Since the results section focuses only on the findings, the discussion section is where the researcher can indicate what the results mean and whether the results are consistent with prior expectations, previous research, and/or the hypotheses tested

TABLE 12.1 **Comparison between Teaching-Award and Research-Award Recipients on Student Ratings of Easiness, Helpfulness, and Clarity**

Rating Variable	Teaching-Award Recipients	Research-Award Recipients
Easiness		
M	3.29	2.84
SD	.61	.81
Helpfulness		
M	4.10	3.42
SD	.76	1.07
Clarity		
M	4.10	3.51
SD	.72	1.10

Note: Means and standard deviations are based on sample sizes of 120 for teaching-award recipients and 119 for research-award recipients. Ratings were made on five-point scales, with higher scores reflecting greater ease, helpfulness, or clarity.

Source: Adapted from Symbaluk & Howell, 2010, p. 80.

in the study. In addition, researchers can elaborate on what the findings mean, why they are important, and how they can best be interpreted within the context of existing literature. A research report is often described as having the overall shape of an hourglass. Just as the introduction section begins broad and narrows to the focus of the current study where the method and the results sections are exclusive to the present study, the discussion broadens again until it finally generalizes back to the wider topic of interest.

After discussing the results in relation to the original research questions and wider literature, limitations are raised and suggestions for improvements are provided. All studies have strengths and weaknesses. Usually, a researcher will point out a few of the methodological limitations of the current study. Perhaps the sample size was smaller than desired, or perhaps the sampling method used was not ideal but was necessary under the present circumstances. Even if the most appropriate sampling method was used, as might be the case for a sample of convenience employed in an interview-based study on centenarians (people who live to be more than 100 years of age), inherent limitations such as the resulting inability to generalize the findings should be mentioned in the discussion. If secondary sources are used, there may be restrictions in terms of what can be explored given the different originating purposes of data collection. Usually a researcher will indicate ways to improve on the present study or offer suggestions for future studies given the limitations discussed. A discussion typically ends with a statement of direction for academics interested in conducting further research in this area. Note that some authors choose to include a conclusion section as a separate section to end the report. A conclusion section summarizes the contributions of the present study and provides suggestions for future research and/or includes directives for policy initiatives.

References

The last section of a research report is a list of all of the sources cited throughout the report. The list is generally double-spaced in accordance with the rest of the report and is written in a standard style, such as the one provided by the most current version of the American Psychological Association (APA format) discussed earlier on.

Research on the Net

APA Style

For questions you might have on how to cite special sources such as Facebook or interviews, visit the American Psychological Association's APA Style website at apastyle.org. You will find quick answers to frequently asked questions about referencing, such as how to cite Twitter and Facebook, as well as quick answers to questions about formatting tables, figures, or the table of contents. In addition, you can view a tutorial on the basics of APA style where you will learn more about how to apply the style in headings or for citing references in-text, for example.

Test Yourself

- What seven sections make up a standard academic research report?
- Why is an abstract so important?
- What is provided at the end of an introduction?
- What five subsections are described in the method section of a research report?
- Which section includes figures or tables?
- Where would a researcher indicate whether the findings obtained were the ones anticipated prior to the onset of the study?

Other Items

Other optional items that may be included in a research report are an appendix and a list of acknowledgments.

LO4

The Appendix

The appendix is a section or placeholder where a researcher can include additional information that may be relevant to other researchers, such as a scale or index used to construct questionnaire items, an interview guide used to assist a moderator in a focus group, a set of instructions provided to participants in an experiment, or a coding scheme adapted from the literature for use in a content analysis. Since the appendix is an extra section, it is generally not included in the page count for a research report.

List of Acknowledgments

A list of acknowledgments is included to pay tribute to individuals and organizations that helped to support the research. For example, research assistants, graduate students, or paid assistants who are not primary researchers or contributing authors are generally acknowledged at the end of the report. The researcher can also list agencies, groups, or organizations that provided funding in the form of grants, scholarships, and/or awards, along with any individual or organization that provided necessary materials, such as meeting space, for carrying out the study.

Test Yourself

- Why is a list of acknowledgments important to include in a research report?

Chapter Summary

LO1   **Outline the main components of a research proposal.**

A research proposal includes five main sections: an introduction, a method section, a section on data analysis and dissemination, a section on ethical considerations, and a listing of prospective references.

LO2   **Explain the purpose of a method section in a research proposal.**

The method section outlines who the participants will be and how they will be selected or how the sample will be obtained. In addition, a method section includes information on the setting and materials needed to conduct the study, the procedures for carrying out the study, and the main variables that are examined in the study.

LO3   **Identify key ethical considerations that need to be addressed in a research proposal.**

If a researcher plans to conduct research using humans as participants, the proposal should indicate why the study can be deemed minimal-risk for participants and how the minimal risk will be mitigated. The proposal should also include a statement that outlines the benefits of the study for participants, for the researchers, and for the wider academic community. Finally, the proposal should also include a discussion about how privacy and confidentiality will be upheld in the planned study.

LO4   **Outline the structure and format of a scholarly research report.**

A research report includes a title page, an abstract, an introduction, a method section, a results section, a discussion section, and references. The method section includes subsections on participants and how they were selected or the sample and how it was obtained, the setting and materials, the main variables or measures, and how data analysis was conducted.

Research Reflection

1. Suppose you are interested in studying the prevalence of texting while driving. What method do you think would be most suitable for examining this phenomenon? If you were going to use that method to study texting while driving, what ethical considerations would you need to address in a research proposal?

2. Suppose you are interested in learning about effective strategies used by post-secondary students to prepare for final exams. Indicate what you would include in a research proposal in the section on participants. Specifically, who would you hope to include in your sample and how you would go about obtaining participants?

3. Suppose you want to explore the ways in which people treat their pets similar to and different from how they treat members of their immediate family in an exploratory study for your master's thesis. What kind of method would you employ to study this topic? Based on your choice of method, what sorts of information would you need to include in the results section of a research report based on the findings?

Learning Through Practice

Objective: To develop a research outline.

Directions:

1. Suppose you plan to carry out your course-assigned research project on gender portrayals in the mass media. Use the following questions and steps to develop an outline that is 2–3 pages long that could serve as a starting point for a research proposal on this topic.

    a. First, decide on one area of the mass media where you wish to examine gender, such as music, television, magazines, the Internet, etc.

    b. Next, identify relevant secondary sources for data on gender within the selected area of the mass media. For example, if you want to study gender in music, a relevant source would be music lyrics in songs within a particular genre, such as rap.

    c. Develop one or two general research questions that you could (potentially) examine using the secondary source identified above.

    d. Explain whether your study will be based on qualitative or quantitative research. Justify your approach.

    e. Describe the main method you plan to use to examine your question of interest. For example, will you be conducting a content analysis?

2. Conduct a database search and locate one research article that examines gender and is relevant in some way to your proposed research topic.

    ○ Describe a main research question or hypothesis examined in the article.

    ○ Describe the method or methods used to answer the question of interest.

    ○ Explain whether this article has provided you with any ideas or guidance for how to develop your own study in the area.

3. Locate one secondary source of potential data for your study, such as finding and printing off the lyrics to one song.

    ○ Do you think this source of data is good one to include in your eventual sample? Why or why not?

    ○ Describe the sampling procedure you would use to conduct your planned study.

    ○ Examining the secondary source of data with your research questions in mind, what kind of data analysis do you think you would need to do? Explain the procedures for how you would carry out this analysis on a larger scale in your eventual study.

Research Resources

1. For step-by-step instructions on how to write research proposals and reports, refer to Chapters 7 and 8 in Symbaluk, D. G. (2006). *Thomson Nelson guide to success in social science: Writing papers and exams.* Toronto, ON: Nelson.

2. For guidance on writing qualitative and quantitative papers in sociology, see Edwards, M. (2012). *Writing in sociology.* Thousand Oaks, CA: Sage Publications.

3. For more detailed information on how to write quantitative reports and to learn how to prepare poster presentations based on research, refer to Rosnow, R. L., & Rosnow, M. (2012). *Writing papers in psychology* (9th ed.). Belmont, CA: Wadsworth.

4. For more information on a variety of methods used to code qualitative data, such as descriptive coding, process coding, emotion coding, axial coding, and theoretical coding, I highly recommend Saldaña, J. (2009). *The coding manual for qualitative researchers.* Thousand Oaks, CA: Sage Publications.

5. To learn how to code qualitative data using NVivo software, refer to Bazeley, P. (2007). *Qualitative data analysis with NVivo.* Thousand Oaks, CA: Sage Publications.

6. To learn more about descriptive and inferential statistics, refer to Colwell, S., & Carter, E. (2012). *Introduction to statistics for social sciences.* Toronto, ON: McGraw-Hill Ryerson.

 For more information on the resources available from McGraw-Hill Ryerson, go to www.mcgrawhill.ca/he/solutions.

References

Bazeley, P. (2007). *Qualitative data analysis with NVivo.* Thousand Oaks, CA: Sage Publications.

Boyd, A. D., Jardine, C. G., & Driedger, S.M. (2009). Canadian representations of mad cow disease. *Journal of Toxicology & Environmental Health, 72*(17/18), 1096–1105.

Colwell, S., & Carter, E. (2012). *Introduction to statistics for social sciences.* Toronto, ON: McGraw-Hill Ryerson.

Deffenbacher, J. L., Lynch, R. S., Oetting, E. R., & Swaim, R. C. (2002). The driving anger expression inventory: A measure of how people express their anger on the road. *Behaviour Research and Therapy, 40,* 717–737.

Digdon, N., & Koble, A. (2011). Effects of constructive worry, imagery distraction, and gratitude interventions on sleep quality: A pilot trial. *Applied Psychology: Health and Well-Being, 3*(2), 193–206.

Edwards, M. (2012). *Writing in sociology.* Thousand Oaks, CA: Sage Publications.

Finlay, J. (2012). *Portrayals of gender stereotypes in Crime Scene Investigation.* Unpublished report submitted as part of the course work for an Introduction to Social Research Methods, Fall, 2012.

Gackenbach, J., Sample, T., Mandel, G., & Tomashewsky, M. (2011). Dream and blog content analysis of a long term diary of a video game player with obsessive compulsive disorder. *Dreaming, 21*(2), 124–147.

Glaser, B. G. (1992). *Grounded theory analysis: Emergence vs. forcing.* Mill Valley, CA: Sociology Press.

Holub, J. (2012). *Themes surrounding masculinity within hip hop and country music: Portrayals of hegemonic masculinity common within each domain.* Unpublished report submitted as part of the course work for an Introduction to Social Research Methods, Fall, 2012.

Maisto, S. A., Conners, G. J., Tucker, J. A., McCollam, J. B., & Adesso, V. J. (1980). Validation of the sensation scale: A measure of subjective physiological responses to alcohol. *Behavior Research and Therapy, 18,* 37–43.

Nardi, P. M. (2006). *Interpreting data: A guide to understanding research.* Toronto, ON: Pearson Canada.

Neuman, W. L., & Robson, K. (2012). *Basics of social research: Qualitative and quantitative approaches* (2nd Can. ed.). Toronto, ON: Pearson Canada.

Padgett, D. K. (2011). *Qualitative and mixed methods in public health.* Thousand Oaks, CA: Sage Publications.

Persaud, S., McIntyre, L., & Milaney, K. (2010). Working homeless men in Calgary, Canada: Hegemony and identity. *Human Organization, 69*(4), 343–351.

Piat, M., Sabetti, J., Couture, A., Sylvestre, J., Provencher, H., Botschner, J., & Stayner, D. (2009). What does recovery mean for me? Perspectives of Canadian mental health consumers. *Psychiatric Rehabilitation Journal, 32*(3), 199–207.

Pyrczak, F., & Bruce, R. R. (2007). *Writing empirical research reports: A basic guide for students of the social and behavioral sciences.* Glendale, CA: Pyrczak Publishing.

Ricciardelli, R. (2011). Masculinity, consumerism, and appearance: A look at men's hair. *Canadian Review of Sociology, 48*(2), 181–201.

Rosnow, R. L., & Rosnow, M. (2012). *Writing papers in psychology* (9th ed.). Belmont, CA: Wadsworth.

Sabbane, L. I., Bellavance, F., & Chebat, J. C. (2009). Recency versus repetition priming effects of cigarette warnings on nonsmoking teenagers: The moderating effects of cigarette-brand familiarity. *Journal of Applied Social Psychology, 39*(3), 656–682.

Saldaña, J. (2009). *The coding manual for qualitative researchers.* Thousand Oaks, CA: Sage Publications.

Segal, D. S., & Stockwell, T. (2008). Low alcohol alternatives: A promising strategy for reducing alcohol related harm. *International Journal of Drug Policy, 20,* 183–187.

Symbaluk, D., Heth, C. D., Cameron, J., & Pierce, W. D. (1997). Social modeling, monetary incentives, and pain endurance: The role of self-efficacy and pain perception. *Personality and Social Psychology Bulletin, 23*(3), 258–269.

Symbaluk, D. G., & Howell, A. J. (2010). Web-based student feedback: Comparing teaching-award and research-award recipients. *Assessment and Evaluation in Higher Education, 35*(1), 75–86.

Symbaluk, D. G. (2006). *Thomson Nelson guide to success in social science: Writing papers and exams.* Toronto, ON: Nelson.

Wilson, K., Demetrioff, S., & Porter, S. (2008). A pawn by any other name? Social information processing as a function of psychopathic traits. *Journal of Research in Personality, 42,* 1651–1656.

Endnote

[1] Symbaluk, D. G. (2006). *Thomson Nelson guide to success in social science: Writing papers and exams.* Toronto, ON: Nelson.

Women's Roles in Advertisements in Car Magazines Targeting Young and Older Men

A title should be interesting enough to gain a reader's attention and be specific enough to describe the main topic.

Always include as an author anyone who has significantly contributed throughout the entire research process (e.g., the conception, design, data collection, data analysis, and report writing).

Articles that appear in scholarly journals include the date the article was first received, the date it was revised (if necessary), and the date of final acceptance.

An author note includes any relevant funding source as well as a corresponding mailing address or email address for the principal researcher.

An abstract provides a brief overview of the research project in under 120 words.

Try to select key words that are included as subject terms in databases for scholarly articles of similar content to the research report.

by
Bruno E. Haje
MacEwan University

Date submitted: April 05, 2012

Author Note

Funding of this research was provided by the Mad Hatters Gala scholarship from MacEwan University, Edmonton, Alberta, Canada. Correspondence should be addressed to Bruno E. Haje (howeb@mymail.macewan.ca).

Abstract

This study examined the prevalence of women as central figures in advertisements in car magazines targeting young and older men. A content analysis was performed on a sample of 18 car magazines published between November 2005 and September 2011. Results showed that in both types of magazines, women were featured as central figures in less than 12 percent of advertisements. In the car magazines targeting young men, 79 percent of advertisements featuring women were for the purpose of selling automobile accessories. In contrast, advertisements featuring women in older men's magazines were for dating service programs (33 percent) and health products (31 percent). These findings demonstrate how target audiences influence the content of advertisements and how advertisers use women to promote certain products.

Keywords: advertising, sexual objectification, content analysis

Women's Roles in Advertisements in Car Magazines Targeting Young and Older Men

For a research report written in APA style, the actual title appears in place of the word "Introduction."

The introduction section starts with a broad opening statement.

The topic is introduced and discussed within the context of relevant prior research.

Note: The student should have more thoroughly explained the critical feminist theoretical framework underlying these studies and guiding this project in the introduction section. For example, at minimum, there should be a discussion about the socially constructed nature of masculinity and femininity and more framing of women portrayed as sexual objects in advertising.

The introduction points out where there are gaps in the literature and establishes the purpose for the present study.

Always include a statement that summarizes the research question or intent of the current study.

For quantitative studies, the introduction section concludes with one or more hypotheses.

Read daily by millions of North Americans, magazines serve as an attractive place for advertisers to promote their products. From fashion and celebrity magazines, to those on home and gardening, readers encounter an abundance of advertisements. But, while most, if not all, magazines contain numerous ads, the types of advertisements shown can vary depending on the target audience. For example, in their study on nutritional messages in women's magazines, Hill and Radimer (1996) found that food advertisements varied drastically depending on whether the magazine targeted young or mature women. Results indicated that magazines targeting mature women often advertised foods belonging to the core food group (e.g., fruits, vegetables, dairy), while magazines targeting young women mostly advertised alcohol and food supplement products (Hill & Radimer, 1996).

Not only does the age of intended readers influence the types of advertisements presented in magazines, but also the gender of the target audience. This was illustrated by Monk-Turner et al. (2008) who looked at how women were depicted in advertisements in magazines for male, female, and gender-neutral audiences. Their results showed that in magazines targeting male audiences, 60 percent of advertisements had women depicted as a central figure. By contrast, 24 percent of advertisements in magazines targeting gender-neutral audiences featured women, while only 13 percent of advertisements in women's magazines did the same (Monk-Turner et al., 2008).

Although the use of women as central figures in magazine advertisements varies depending on the intended audience, studies have found that the way in which women are presented, when shown as a central figure, does not vary much according to the audience type. In fact, Massé and Rosenblum (1988) found that in both men's and women's magazines, women were often presented in subordinate poses (e.g., laying down wearing scant amounts of clothing). In a similar study, Reichert and Lambiase (2003) found that in both women's and men's general interest magazines, women were often shown engaging in sexually suggestive behaviour when advertising various products. Nevertheless, although research has shown that in both men's and women's magazines women are displayed in similar submissive fashions, other studies have shown that men's magazines, on average, include more advertisements with women as the central figure compared to women's magazines (Stankiewicz & Rosselli, 2008).

While many studies on advertisements have compared the prevalence and depiction of women in men's magazines to women's magazines, few have compared advertisements in magazines targeting young men to those targeting older men. Perhaps the magazine genre most associated with a male audience deals with the automobile sector. The purpose of the present study is to examine how often women are featured as central figures in advertisements in car magazines read by young and older men. Furthermore, this study looks at the overall purpose of advertisements that include women as the central focus. Based on past research showing that magazines for younger men often contain greater sexually provocative advertisements (Stankiewicz & Rosselli, 2008), the present study predicts that car magazines for young men will include more advertisements with women as the central figure and that these advertisements will primarily be for the purpose of selling automotive accessories since car customization is commonly associated with youth. Furthermore, this study predicts that car magazines for older men will have fewer ads featuring women as the main figure and that these ads will mostly focus on health-related products, as older men are more likely to experience health-related issues.

Method

Sample

The method section details how the study was carried out. It contains information on the participants or sample, setting and materials, procedures, and main variables examined in the study.

The purposive sample consisted of 18 automobile magazines on car customization that predominately target young men as a readership and monthly issued automobile magazines based on reviews and certified car sales programs that target older men. Magazines based on car customization included the following three publications: *Truckin', Rides,* and *Dub Magazine.* Although there are older men who take heavily to modifying their vehicles, car customization is an activity predominately performed by youth (Bengry-Howell & Griffin, 2007). In particular, *Truckin'* was selected because it appeals to readers interested in the "street struck" and "off-roading" scenes, which involves either lowering or lifting truck suspensions for a "custom look." *Rides,* on the other hand, is popular among those interested in custom stereos and features numerous articles on how to install stereo equipment. Lastly, *Dub Magazine* was selected as it also appeals to those interested in audio customizations. However, unlike *Truckin'* and *Rides, Dub Magazine* focuses on celebrities and their custom cars. Nevertheless, although *Dub Magazine* tends to include vehicles that are not affordable to the typical young male, its main emphasis is on customizations, making it appropriate for inclusion.

Magazines based on reviews and sales directed at older men included three publications: *Car and Driver, Motor Trend,* and *duPont Registry.* Unlike the magazines directed at young men, *Car and Driver* and *Motor Trend* rarely, if ever, include content pertaining to car customization. Instead, both magazines predominantly discuss topics on car reviews, the economic state of the automobile industry, and government regulatory policies (e.g., fuel economy regulations), which appeal to a more mature audience. Subtitled the "buyers' gallery of fine automobiles," *duPont Registry* was considered an older men's magazine as its main purpose is to provide a place for car enthusiasts to purchase classic and modern vehicles. Most of these vehicles, however, are not modified and are advertised for hundreds of thousands of dollars (e.g., Ferraris and Lamborghinis). Because this magazine focuses on the sale of non-customized vehicles for wealthy car enthusiasts, it was deemed appropriate as a sale-focused magazine targeting an older male market.

Sample Selection

Complete issues were available for *Truckin', Rides, Dub, Car and Driver, Motor Trend,* and *duPont Registry* for the years 2005 through 2011. Three issues were randomly selected from each of six categories of magazines (i.e., three from *Truckin'*'s 78 issues, three from *Rides*'s 42 issues, three from *Dub*'s 36 issues, three from *Car and Driver*'s 72 available magazines, three from *Motor Trend*'s 72 issues, and three from *duPont Registry*'s 78 issues) for a total of 18 magazines.

Inclusion and Exclusion Criteria   Because this study is specifically interested in how advertisers seek to draw the reader's attention, only ads larger than half a page were included in the analysis. Furthermore, since *duPont Registry* is essentially an advertisement magazine, advertisements from car dealerships and private individuals selling their vehicles were omitted from the analysis. Advertisements that exceeded one page were counted as one ad.

> Note how the magazines made up the sample but the units of analysis were the large advertisements contained within the magazines.

Units of Analysis

The units of analysis for this study were 1012 advertisements, including N = 198 from *Truckin'*, N = 156 from *Rides,* N = 215 from *Dub*, N = 134 from *Car and Driver,* N = 110 from *Motor Trend,* and N = 199 from *duPont Registry.*

Setting and Materials

Coding took place in the principal researcher's residence where the magazine collection was located. Necessary materials included the selected issues of *Truckin'* (March, 2008; May, 2008; and July, 2008), *Rides* (May, 2009; June, 2010; and January, 2011), *Dub* (November, 2005; October, 2007; and March, 2008), *Car and Driver* (July, 2009; September, 2009; and September, 2010), *Motor Trend* (March, 2008; August, 2009; and September, 2011), and *duPont Registry* (August, 2005; April, 2009; and July, 2009).

> Students and researchers alike tend to struggle with data analysis. Where possible, a researcher should explain how data analysis was carried out, including the type of coding process used in qualitative research or the type of statistical tests performed in quantitative research.

Coding Procedures

Each magazine was examined individually, page by page. For each magazine, the total number of advertisements meeting the size requirement for inclusion was recorded. Next, the number of advertisements featuring a female or multiple females as the central figure was also tabulated (see Appendix B). Next, any included advertisement featuring a female as a central figure was further coded for its overall purpose into one of the four pre-existing categories: dating services, health products, automobile products, and other. Data from each magazine publication was then aggregated and reported in percentages (see Table 1).

Main Variables

Two main variables were examined in this study: the predominance of ads featuring a woman (or female) and the purpose the advertisement categorized as dating service, health product, automobile product, or other. Ads with females as the central figure were operationalized as those in which upon initially looking at the advertisement, a woman was the first image one would most likely notice as a result of size

TABLE 1   **Percentage and Number of Advertisements Featuring Women by Publication**

Publication	Total ads	Ads featuring women	Purpose of ads featuring women			
			Dating services	Health products	Auto. products	"Other"
Truckin'	198	6% (12)	0%	16% (2)	42% (5)	42% (5)
Rides	156	9% (14)	0%	0%	93% (13)	7% (1)
Dub Magazine	215	17% (36)	0%	0%	86% (31)	14% (5)
Car and Driver	134	6% (8)	0%	50% (4)	0%	50% (4)
Motor Trend	110	8% (9)	0%	89% (8)	0%	11% (1)
duPont Registry	119	17% (34)	50% (17)	12% (4)	23% (8)	15% (5)

Note: The numbers in parentheses represent the total number of advertisements.

and central location). Advertisements categorized as *dating services* were designed to aid eligible men connect with single female. Advertisements placed in the *health products* category where those that dealt with health and fitness issues, such as hair restoration, food supplements, or male enhancement pills. Advertisements were defined as *automobile products* if the overall purpose of the advertisements was to sell automotive accessories, such as tires, stereo equipment, and engine-performance parts. Lastly, advertisements that did not fit any of the previously defined categories were placed in an *other* category (see Appendixes A and B).

Design

The results section is brief as it contains only the findings. Save comments and interpretation of the results for the discussion.

Content analysis was used to examine how the target audience of a magazine influenced the number of times a woman is shown as the central figure in an advertisements and the overall purpose of advertisements featuring these women.

Results

The nine magazines focused on car customization targeting younger males included a total of 569 advertisements. Of these, 11 percent (N = 62) featured a female as the central figure. The majority of advertisements (79 percent) that featured females were for the purpose of advertising automobile products. Furthermore, 18 percent of ads featuring women were placed into the "other" category. Most of the ads in this category were for magazine subscriptions or were designed to sell clothing. Lastly, 3 percent of advertisements including females in these magazines were for health products, while there were no advertisements for dating services.

Tables provide numerical summaries of main findings while figures provide visual displays.

Magazines focused on automobile reviews and car sales programs targeting older men had a total of 443 advertisements, with 11.5 percent (N = 51) portraying females as the central figure. Of these 51 advertisements featuring females, 33 percent were for dating services, followed closely by advertisements for men's health products such as Viagra (31 percent). Advertisements for automobile products made up 16 percent of total advertisements featuring females, while the "other" category encompassed 20 percent of advertisements including females (see Table 2 and Figures 1 and 2).

TABLE 2 Percentage and Number of Advertisements Featuring Women by Magazine Type

Magazine type	Total ads	Ads featuring women	Purpose of ads featuring women			
			Dating services	Health products	Auto. products	"Other"
Young men	569	11.0% (62)	0%	3% (2)	79% (49)	18% (11)
Older men	443	11.5% (51)	33% (17)	31% (16)	16% (8)	20% (10)

Note: The numbers in parentheses represent the total number of advertisements.

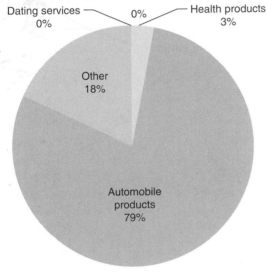

Ads Featuring Women in Car Magazines for Young Men

FIGURE 1

Purpose of Advertisements Featuring Women in Young Men's Car Magazines

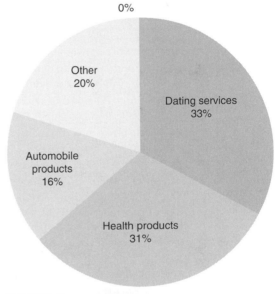

Ads Featuring Women in Car Magazines for Older Men

FIGURE 2

Purpose of Advertisements Featuring Women in Older Men's Car Magazines

Discussion

> The discussion usually begins by reiterating the hypotheses or research questions. The discussion section includes interpretations of the findings, linkages back to the literature and wider theoretical context, limitations of the present study, and suggestions for future research.

The results found did not support the initial hypothesis that car magazines targeting young men would have a greater number of advertisements featuring females as central figures compared to magazines for older men. In fact, the magazines targeting older men had almost the exact same percentage of advertisements featuring females (11.5 percent) compared to young men's magazines (11 percent). The fact that in both types of magazines less than 12 percent of the total advertisements featured females varied greatly from findings of past studies that have shown men's magazines to have significant numbers of advertisements with female characters (Monk-Turner et al., 2008). One possible explanation for why prior studies have found significant numbers of advertisements with women in men's magazines, while this study did not, is because most of the magazines sampled in the prior studies focused on health and fitness (e.g., *Sports Illustrated, Maxim*), which include topics that mesh with social constructions of both masculinity and femininity in terms of body image (i.e., the male who attains the perfect body can attract the female who is also portrayed with an idealized body). On the other hand, car magazine advertisements may be more reflective of the target audience that is historically and stereotypically male-dominated. Here, the emphasis might be more on having a certain type of car as part of the male persona, and hence the advertisements for car products.

Although the results did not support the first prediction, they did support the second hypothesis regarding the overall purpose of advertisements that featured women. As mentioned in the introduction, it was expected that advertisements featuring women as the central figure in young men's magazines would predominately be for automotive accessories. Indeed, this turned out to be true, as 79 percent of advertisements featuring women were for the purpose of selling automobile products. In fact, in one of the publications, *Rides,* 13 out of the 14 (93 percent) advertisements involving women were for automobile accessories, such as wheels and tires. This suggests that "having the right car" is necessary to attract a certain type of female. It is important to note that virtually all of the women featured in advertisements in young men's magazines were presented in sexually provocative postures and wore little to no clothing. Perhaps the best example of this sexual objectification came from an advertisement for a performance wheel specialist company in an issue of *Rides.* In this scene, a woman is reclining on a leather couch as a man stands over her with a cigar. However, unlike other derogative advertisements where women are wearing at least one or two pieces of clothing, she is wearing none. Instead, 18 one-hundred-dollar bills cover her body as she stares passively at the man holding the cigar. This ad clearly shows how, as Reichert and Lambiase (2003) have demonstrated, sexual imagery is often used by advertisers to draw attention to their products or services.

In addition to predicting that young men's magazines would have a greater number of advertisements with women for automotive accessories, this study expected advertisements with women in older men's magazines to be mostly for health products. In two magazine issues, *Car and Driver* and *Motor Trend,* this was indeed the case. In fact, close to 90 percent of the ads featuring women in *Motor Trend* were for health products, while 50 percent of ads in *Car and Driver* were for this reason. It was also expected, however, that these health products would consist of a variety of products, such as hair-growth products and diet programs, appropriate for aging men. Instead, results revealed that nearly 100 percent of the health product ads in *Car and Driver* and *Motor Trend* addressed one issue: erectile dysfunction. Mostly located toward the last few pages of each issue, drugs such as Viagra and Cialis were presented with young women often dressed in nightwear. The fact that in both magazines the ads featuring women were mostly for male enhancement pills, and that these magazines are primarily read by older men, suggests that advertisers are aware of and willing to capitalize on the "concerns" of their intended audience. In other words, because it is fair to say that erectile dysfunction is a condition more prevalent among older men, one will likely expect to see pharmaceutical companies featuring attractive women in advertisements in magazines read by older men. On the other hand, because erectile dysfunction is of less concern for young men, advertisers will be less inclined to include such ads with attractive women in young men's magazines. Results supported this assumption as only 3 percent of the advertisements featuring women in the young men's magazines dealt with erectile dysfunction issues. With the younger men, the point was to obtain the right automobile. Since older men may already have the "right" car, the focus shifts to sexual performance, indicating that females are still objectified in the magazines.

Another important finding in this study was the significant number of dating service advertisements in one of the older men's magazines, *duPont Registry.* Of all the advertisements in this magazine featuring women as the central figure, 50 percent were from dating agencies. As mentioned earlier, *duPont Registry* is a magazine primarily aimed at established and wealthy individuals. In fact, in one of the publications, there were a handful of vehicles with asking prices over one million dollars. The need to appeal to this well-to-do audience was quite evident in the dating service advertisements, as most stressed that their services were only for affluent persons. Nowhere can this appeal be better illustrated than in the following passage from a dating agency in one *duPont Registry* issue (Premier Mate, 2005):

> You are a high achiever; you worked all your life to cultivate wealth, power and independence.... For some reason, however, you still feel somewhat incomplete....Join us to discover ... beautiful, elegant, intelligent and committed-minded ladies. (P. 159)

Clearly, advertisers are aware that *duPont Registry* is primarily read by wealthy men. Furthermore, since, unless inherited, accumulating wealth often takes time, advertisers are aware that these readers are most likely of older age. To appeal to this audience, full-page ads with young models are included throughout the pages of this publication. Thus, just as with young men's magazines, advertisers seek to appeal to the specific "interests" of men, and attempt to draw attention to certain products by featuring women as central figures in their advertisements.

Limitations   Although this study provided interesting information into the nature of advertisements in car magazines, there are a few limitations to the methods of the data collection that are important to address. First, only advertisements featuring women were examined. Most of the magazines for both young and older men included a considerable number of advertisements featuring men as the central figure. Thus, to better understand the tactics used by advertisers to appeal to magazine readers, future research should examine how often men and women are featured as central figures in advertisements and compare for what purposes their signifying presence serves.

Another limitation of this study is that the sample was small and was restricted to automotive-based magazines. As result, the results found in terms of the prevalence and depiction of women in magazines may not represent the advertisements in these magazines as a whole. Future studies should therefore use a larger sample and extend the analysis to other types of magazines with a targeted male readership (e.g., hunting, fishing, computers, business, and finance) to examine whether the results found in this study are consistent across different magazine genres.

Certain journals require a conclusion for published articles. A conclusion wraps up the report with a succinct statement of the key findings.

Conclusion

This study demonstrates how advertisers feature women in car magazines to draw attention to certain products. Although no differences were found between young and older men's magazines in regards to the number of times women were featured, there were differences in the purposes of advertisements that included women. On the whole, advertisements featuring women in young men's magazines were for automotive products, while women featured in magazines for older men were often used to promote erectile dysfunction products or dating services. These findings illustrate how the nature of the content of advertisements in magazines is largely influenced by the targeted audience. Because car customization is most common among young men, advertisers of automotive accessories will often feature their products with attractive women in magazines read by young men. By contrast, since older men are more likely to experience certain health-related problems, advertisers of health products will often advertise their products with attractive women in magazines read by older men. Unfortunately, when women are featured in advertisements in both young and older men's magazines, they are often presented in submissive positions and have on little to no clothing. The prevalence of advertisements depicting women in these degenerate conditions is of great concern in our society as constant exposure to such sexually demeaning imagery may negatively influence men's attitudes toward women.

References are listed in a standard format such as APA.

References

Bengry-Howell, A., & Griffin, C. (2007). Self-made motormen: The material construction of working-class masculine identities through car modification. *Journal of Youth Studies, 10*(4), 439–458.

Hill, J. M., & Radimer, K. L. (1996). Health and nutrition messages in food advertisements: A comparative content analysis of young and mature Australian women's magazines. *Journal of Nutrition Education, 28*(6), 313–320.

Massé, M. A., & Rosenblum, K. (1988). Male and female created they them: The depiction of gender in the advertising of traditional women's and men's magazines. *Women Studies Int. Forum, 11*(2), 127–144.

Monk-Turner, E., Wren, K., McGill, L., Matthiae, C., Brown, S., & Brooks, D. (2008). Who is gazing at whom? A look at how sex is used in magazine advertisements. *Journal of Gender Studies, 17*(3), 201–209.

Premier Mate. (2005). Dating service advertisement for PremierMate.com. In *duPont Registry*. St. Petersburg, FL: duPont Publishing Inc.

Reichert, T., & Lambiase, J. (2003). How to get "kissably close": Examining how advertisers appeal to consumers' sexual needs and desires. *Sexuality and Culture, 7*(3), 120–136.

Stankiewicz, J. M., & Rosselli, F. (2008). Women as sex objects and victims in print advertisements. *Sex Roles, 58,* 579–589.

Appendix A: Sample Coding Sheet

Magazine #1

Magazine Information

Publication: _____

Issue date: _____

Intended audience: _____

Advertisement Totals

Number of total ads: _____

Number of ads with women as central figure: _____

Ads with women for dating services: _____

Ads with women for health products: _____

Ads with women for auto. products: _____

Ads with women that do not fit in above categories ("other"): _____

Appendix B: Advertisement Totals by Individual Magazine Issue

#	Publication	Issue date	Total ads	Total ads w/women	Dating service	Health products	Auto. products	Other
					Ads featuring women			
1	*Truckin'*	Mar. 2008	52	4	0	1	1	2
2	*Truckin'*	May 2008	72	3	0	1	1	1
3	*Truckin'*	July 2008	74	5	0	0	3	2
4	*Rides*	May 2009	44	4	0	0	3	1
5	*Rides*	June 2010	57	5	0	0	5	0
6	*Rides*	Jan. 2011	55	5	0	0	5	0
7	*Dub*	Nov. 2005	79	15	0	0	12	12
8	*Dub*	Oct. 2007	75	11	0	0	10	10
9	*Dub*	Mar. 2008	61	10	0	0	9	9
10	*Car and Driver*	July 2009	49	4	0	2	0	2
11	*Car and Driver*	Sep. 2009	43	3	0	2	0	1
12	*Car and Driver*	Sep. 2010	42	1	0	0	0	1
13	*Motor Trend*	Mar. 2008	41	3	0	3	0	0
14	*Motor Trend*	Aug. 2009	34	4	0	3	0	1
15	*Motor Trend*	Sep. 2011	35	2	0	2	0	0
16	*duPont Registry*	Aug. 2005	89	12	4	2	5	1
17	*duPont Registry*	Apr. 2009	63	10	6	1	1	2
18	*duPont Registry*	July 2009	47	12	7	1	2	2

Glossary

Abstract A brief overview of a research project that describes the participants or units of observation, the design, the procedures, and the main findings in 120 words or less.

Accretion measures Patterns of selective use and non-use based on accumulation.

Action research Social research carried out by a team that encompasses a professional action researcher and the members of an organization, community, or network (stakeholders) who are seeking to improve the participants' situation.

Active listening A technique in which the interviewer demonstrates an understanding of what is being said and expressed through appropriate feedback.

Alteration of documentation of informed consent An informed consent discussion that takes place with each participant in the setting in lieu of a signed informed consent statement.

Anonymity A state of being unknown. In the case of research, this means a researcher cannot link any individual response to its originator.

Applied research Scientific research that is conducted to address a problem or issue.

Archives Historical documents, records, or collections detailing the activities of businesses, agencies, institutions, governments, groups, or individuals.

Attitude questions Questions designed to measure points of view toward an attitude object such as a person or an event.

Audit trails Attempts made by a researcher to carefully document the research process in its entirety.

Authority A source of information that is perceived to possess specialized knowledge.

Basic experimental design An experimental design that includes random assignment, an experimental and control group, the manipulation of an independent variable, and a post-test measurement of the dependent variable.

Basic research Scientific research that is conducted to advance knowledge.

Behaviour questions Questions designed to find out more about the respondent's activities.

Beneficence A moral principle outlining that in the planning and conduct of research with human participants, the researcher maximizes the possible benefits and minimizes the potential harms from the research.

Between-subjects design A type of design in which the experimental group is exposed to only one level of the independent variable.

Case study Research on a small number of individuals or an organization carried out over an extended period of time.

Classic experimental design An experimental design that includes random assignment, an experimental and control group, a pre-test measure of a dependent variable, the manipulation of an independent variable, and a post-test measure of the same dependent variable.

Closed-ended question A question prompting an answer selected from a pre-determined set of responses provided.

Closing questions Questions used to bring closure to the interview by re-establishing distance between the interviewer and interviewee.

Cluster sampling A probability-based method for selecting groups for a sample, usually on the basis of their geographic location.

Codebook A detailed listing of how each variable is coded in the data set along with information on the methodology underlying the original study.

Coding The process of transforming raw data into a standardized form.

Cohort study Research on the same category of people carried out at multiple points in time.

Common sense Practical knowledge based on adaptive forms of prior learning.

Complete observer A participant observation role in which the researcher covertly observes a group but is not a group member and does not participate in any way.

Complete participation A covert participant observation role in which the researcher systematically observes a group as a full member whose true identity and research purpose is unknown to the group members.

Computer-assisted telephone interviews (CATI) A telephone-based interview method in which the interviewer inputs survey responses directly into a software program.

Concepts Abstract mental representations of important elements in our social world.

Conceptualization   The process where a researcher explains what a concept means in terms of a particular research project.

Concern for welfare   Steps taken to protect the welfare of research participants both in terms of harm and other foreseeable risks associated with participation in a given study.

Confidence interval   An estimated range that is likely to contain the true population value based on the sample value.

Confidentiality   The process of maintaining privacy. In research, this means even when a participant's identity is known to the researcher, steps are taken to make sure it is not made public.

Construct validity   The extent to which an instrument is associated with other logically related measures of the intended concept.

Constructs   Intangible ideas that do not exist independent of our thinking.

Content analysis   A repertoire of methods that allow researchers to make inferences from all kinds of verbal, pictorial, symbolic, and communication data.

Content validity   The extent to which an instrument contains the full range of content pertaining to the intended concept.

Context   The sets of conditions that give rise to problems or circumstances to which individuals respond by means of action/interaction/emotions.

Contingency question   A question prompting additional information about a previous item identified as relevant for the respondent.

Continuous real-time measurement   An observation-based data coding method in which every separate and distinct instance of a variable is recorded during an observation period.

Control group   The group that does not experience the independent variable in an experiment.

Convenience sampling   A non-probability method used to obtain a sample on the basis of availability alone.

Convergent design   A mixed-method design in which qualitative and quantitative methods are employed concurrently, with independent data collection and analysis compared in the final interpretation.

Cost-benefit analysis   A method for assessing the overall costs incurred by a program relative to outcome measures.

Coverage error   A type of error that results when not all members of the population have a known, non-zero chance of being included in the sample for the survey and when those who are excluded are different from those who are included on measures of interest.

Credibility   An assessment of the goodness of fit between the respondent's view of reality and a researcher's representation of it.

Criterion validity   The extent to which an instrument holds up to an external standard, such as the ability to predict future events.

Critical paradigm   A worldview that is critical of paradigms which fail to acknowledge the role of power in the creation of knowledge and is aimed at bringing about empowering change.

Cross-sectional research   Research conducted at a single point in time.

Cultural relativism   The non-judgmental view that a society's customs and ideas should be described objectively and understood in the context of that society's problems and opportunities.

Data   Information gathered through research techniques.

Data format   The statistical format in which data are saved or stored.

Data structure   The number and organizational nature of distinct files that compose a data collection and the relationship among those data.

Data triangulation   The reliance on multiple data sources in a single study.

Debriefing   The full disclosure and exchange of information that occurs upon completion of a study.

Deductive reasoning   A theory-driven approach that typically concludes with empirical generalizations based on research findings.

Demographic questions   Questions designed to collect facts about a respondent's age, race/ethnicity, education, job, gender, marital status, geographic place of residence, type of residence, size of family, and so on.

Dependability   An assessment of the researcher's process as well documented and verifiable.

Dependent variable   The variable that is measured in an experiment and is the outcome.

Descriptive research   Research undertaken to identify the main traits or characteristics of a particular population or phenomenon.

Disproportionate sampling   A sampling method used deliberately to obtain a different ratio of relevant characteristics than what exists in the population.

Double-barrelled question   A question prompting a single answer to a combination of questions.

Empirical methods   Data collection techniques carried out using logical and systematic procedures that are widely recognized by other researchers.

Encoding   A data-reduction method used to simplify observations through the use of categorizations.

Erosion measures   Patterns of selective use based on wear.

Essential questions   Questions that exclusively concern the central focus of the study.

Ethics   Conduct that is considered "morally right" or "morally wrong" as specified by codified and culturally ingrained principles, constraints, rules, and guidelines.

Ethnographers   Social scientists who undertake research and writing about groups of people by systematically observing and participating (to a greater or lesser degree) in the lives of the people they study.

Ethnography   A multi-method approach to field research that is used to study a social group or culture in its natural setting over time.

Evaluation research   Research undertaken to assess whether a program or policy is effective in reaching its desired goals and objectives.

Exhaustive   Comprehensive enough to include all likely responses.

Experience   First-hand observations or recollections of events that serve as sources of knowledge.

Experiment   A research method in which a researcher manipulates an independent variable to examine its effects on a dependent variable.

Experimental group   The group that experiences the independent variable in an experiment.

Experimental mortality   The course of participant drop-out over time.

Experimenter bias   The tendency for researchers to influence the behaviour of research participants in a manner that favours the outcomes they anticipate.

Explanatory design   A mixed-method design which a quantitative method is employed first and then the findings are followed up on using a qualitative method.

Explanatory research   Research undertaken to clarify the variation found between groups on some dimension of interest.

Exploratory design   A mixed-method design in which a qualitative method is employed first and then the findings are used to help develop a subsequent quantitative method-based phase.

Exploratory research   Research undertaken to find out more about a particular area of interest.

External validity   The generalizability of an experimental effect.

Extra questions   Questions roughly equivalent to essential ones that are used to assess reliability.

Face validity   The extent to which an instrument appears to be a good measure of the intended concept.

Factorial design   An experimental design that includes two or more independent variables.

Field experiment   A naturally-occurring experiment that takes place in a real-life setting.

Field notes   Detailed records about what a researcher hears, sees, experiences, and thinks about while immersed in the social setting.

Figures   Charts or graphs used to display results based on how a variable is measured.

Final question   The last interview question in the form of a general inquiry to determine if the participant has any questions about the study or further comments to make.

Focus group   A small discussion group led by a skilled interviewer that is designed to obtain views and feelings about a particular topic of interest through group interaction.

Follow-up questions   Questions specific to comments made that are used to clarify main ideas.

Garbology   The study of behaviour practices based on the analysis of waste.

Gatekeepers   People who have power to grant or deny permission to do a study in the field.

Graffiti   A form of visual communication, usually illegal, involving the unauthorized marking of public space by an individual or group.

Grounded theory   Theory discovered from the systematic observation and analysis of data.

History   Changes in the dependent measure attributed to external events outside of the experiment.

Hypothesis   A testable statement that contains at least two variables.

Ice breaker   An opening question that is used specifically to establish rapport.

Illogical reasoning   Faulty decision making based on a failure to take into account the most appropriate sources of information.

Imprecise observations   Everyday errors made as a function of our limited ability to perceive, store, and later accurately recall information.

Independent evaluation   An evaluation that is headed up by a researcher who is not a primary stakeholder for the program under consideration.

Independent variable The variable that is manipulated in an experiment and is presumed to be the cause of some outcome.

Index A composite measure of a construct comprising several different indicators that produce a shared outcome.

Indicator A measurable quantity that in some sense stands for or substitutes for something less readily measurable.

Inductive reasoning A bottom-up approach beginning with observations and ending with the discovery of patterns and themes informed by theory.

Informed consent A process where potential participants are provided with all of the relevant details of the study needed to make a knowledgeable judgment about whether or not to participate in it.

Instrumentation Differences produced by changes in the manner in which the dependent variable is measured.

Inter-item reliability Demonstrated associations among multiple items representing a single concept.

Internal validity The capacity to demonstrate an experimental effect and to rule out rival explanations for that effect.

Interpretive paradigm A worldview that rests on the assumption that reality is socially constructed and must be understood from the perspective of those experiencing it.

Inter-rater reliability Consistency between the same measures for a variable of interest provided by two independent raters.

Interval level A level of measurement in which the distance between categories of the variable of interest is meaningful.

Interview guide A series of key questions that provide the framework for an interview.

Justice A moral principle of rightness claiming that in the course of research, researchers behave and make decisions in a manner that demonstrates social responsibility in relation to the distribution of harm versus benefits.

Key insider A member of the setting who is willing to act as a guide or assistant within the setting.

Knowledge questions Questions designed to gauge whether respondents can retrieve and correctly report on factual information about some area of interest.

Latent content Implied meaning inferred by the message.

Longitudinal research Research conducted at multiple points in time.

Macro level The level of broader social forces.

Manifest content Stated content in the message itself.

Maturation Changes in the dependent measure that result from naturally occurring processes within the research participants themselves over the period of treatment.

Member checks Attempts made by a researcher to validate findings by testing them with the original sources of the data.

Micro level The level of individual experiences and choices.

Mixed-methods approach A research design that includes an explicit combination of qualitative and quantitative methods as framed by the research objectives.

Moderator A trained facilitator used in focus group research who guides the focus group discussion.

Multiple-case design A case study strategy that focuses on two or more persons, organizations, events, or programs selected for the explicit purpose of comparison.

Mutually exclusive Response categories are separate and distinct from each other.

Needs assessment A systematic evaluation focused on improving an existing condition through the identification of a problem and a means for addressing it.

Negative question A question made up of the negative form of a statement.

Nominal level A level of measurement used to classify cases.

Non-probability sampling A method in which the chance of selection of an individual or element in the population is unknown.

Non-response error A type of error that results when the people selected for the survey who do not respond are different from those who do respond in a way that is important to the study.

Nuremberg Code A set of ethical directives for human experimentation.

Observer as participant An overt participant observation role in which the researcher systematically observes a group but is not a group member and only interacts indirectly with the group.

One-shot case study A quasi-experimental design lacking a control group in which one group is examined following a treatment.

Open-ended question   A question prompting any response deemed appropriate in the participant's own words.

Operationalization   The process whereby a concept is defined so precisely that it can be measured.

Order effects   Differences in the dependent variable that result from the order in which the independent variable is presented.

Ordinal level   A level of measurement used to order cases along some dimension of interest.

Overgeneralization   The tendency to assume the existence of a general pattern based on a limited number of observed cases.

Panel study   Research on the same unit of analysis carried out at multiple points in time.

Paradigm   A model or framework for observation and understanding, which shapes both what we see and how we understand it.

Participant as observer   An overt participant observation role in which the researcher systematically observes a group by becoming a group member to establish relationships and interact directly with the group.

Participant observation   A research method in which the researcher is actively involved with the group being observed over an extended period of time.

Participant reactivity   The tendency for research participants to act differently during a study simply because they are aware that they are participating in a research study.

Peer debriefing   Attempts made by a researcher to authenticate the research process and findings through an external review provided by an independent researcher.

Periodicals   Publications that contain a number of articles written by different authors and are released at regular intervals.

Physical traces   The remnants, fragments, and products of past behaviour.

Population   The complete set of individuals, objects, or scores that the investigator is interested in studying.

Positivist paradigm   A worldview that upholds the importance of discovering truth through direct experience using empirical methods.

Pragmatic paradigm   A worldview that rests on the assumption that reality is best understood in terms of the practical consequences of actions undertaken to solve problems.

Premature closure   The tendency to stop searching for necessary observations due to an erroneous belief that the answer has already been determined.

Primary research   First-hand data collection and data analysis that is undertaken to answer an original research question.

Private archives   Personal records that are usually directed at a small known target or are produced only for use by the originating author.

Probability sampling   A method in which every individual or element in the population has a known chance of being selected.

Probes   Questions used to motivate an interviewee to continue speaking or to elaborate on a topic.

Program evaluation   A systematic method for collecting and analyzing information used to answer questions about a program of interest.

Public archives   Public records that are prepared specifically to be examined by others.

Purposive sampling   A non-probability method in which a researcher uses a combination of techniques to obtain all possible cases that possess the desired characteristics of the population of interest.

Qualitative interview   A technique used to understand the world from the subjects' point of view, to unfold the meaning of their experiences, and to uncover the world prior to scientific explanations.

Qualitative research method   A technique that seeks to explore, interpret, explain, or evaluate a phenomenon of interest and produces non-numerical data.

Quantitative research method   A technique that seeks to describe, explain, or evaluate a phenomenon of interest and produces numerical data.

Quasi-experimental design   An experimental design that lacks one or more of the basic features of a true experiment, including random assignment or a control group.

Questionnaire   A survey data collection instrument consisting of a series of questions or items to which a respondent provides responses containing the information of interest to the researcher.

Quota sampling   A non-probability method used to obtain a similar proportion of some characteristic of interest in a sample as exists in the population.

Random assignment   A method for assigning cases in which chance alone determines receipt of the experimental manipulation.

Random digit dialling   A technique used to create a sampling frame based on a computer-generated list of random phone numbers.

Random errors   Measurement miscalculation due to unpredictable mistakes.

Rate of response   The percentage of those sampled for whom data are actually collected.

Ratio level   An interval level of measurement with an absolute zero.

Reflexivity   A self-reflection process in which a researcher considers the ways in which his or her own subjectivities may have influenced the research outcomes.

Regression   Differences produced by the tendency for extreme scores to become less extreme.

Reliability   Consistency in measurement.

Representative sample   A sample with the same distribution of characteristics as the population from which it was selected.

Research design   The plan or blueprint for a study outlining the who, what, where, when, why, and how of an investigation.

Research ethics   An array of considerations that arise in relation to the morally responsible treatment of humans in research.

Research ethics board   A committee whose mandate is to review the ethical acceptability of research on behalf of the institution, including approving, rejecting, proposing modifications to, or terminating any proposed or ongoing research involving humans.

Research methods   Techniques for carrying out research to answer questions of interest.

Research proposal   A comprehensive plan created in advance of carrying out research that details what the purpose of the project is and what the process will be for obtaining data.

Research report   A detailed account following research that describes the research interest, questions, or hypotheses addressed, methods used, and the findings from the study.

Respect for human dignity   A value necessitating that research involving humans be conducted in a manner that is sensitive to the inherent worth of all human beings and the respect and consideration that they are due.

Respect for persons   A moral principle stressing that researchers respect the human participants in their investigations as persons of worth whose participation is a matter of their autonomous choice.

Rigour   A means for demonstrating integrity and competence in qualitative research.

Sample   A subset of the population of interest that represents the unit of analysis in a study.

Sampling   The technique or process used to acquire the unit of analysis from a population of interest.

Sampling error   The difference between the sample statistic and the population parameter.

Sampling frame   The complete list of individuals or elements making up the population.

Sampling interval   The fixed interval used to select every nth case listed after a random starting point is obtained.

Scale   A composite measure of a construct consisting of several different indicators that stem from a common cause.

Secondary analysis of existing data   Examination of data originally collected by someone other than the researcher for a different purpose.

Secondary research   The summation or analysis of research already collected by others.

Selection   Methods used to obtain groups that can result in differences prior to the experimental manipulation.

Selection by maturation interaction   A combined effect of initial differences in the groups at the onset of the study and maturation.

Selection by treatment interaction   A threat to external validity produced by the self-selection of participants susceptible to the independent variable.

Selective deposit   A bias resulting from the greater likelihood of establishing certain physical traces over others.

Selective observation   The tendency to assume a general pattern exists based on factors other than objective frequency.

Selective survival   A bias resulting from the greater likelihood of certain physical traces persisting over time.

Semi-structured interview   A somewhat flexible interview format in which main questions are prepared ahead of time but the questions are modified or clarified based on participant feedback.

Simple random sampling   A probability-based method used to obtain individuals or cases which make up a sample on the basis of chance alone.

Single-case design   A case study strategy that focuses on only one person, organization, event, or program as the unit of analysis as emphasized by the research objectives.

Snowball sampling   A non-probability method used to obtain a sample on the basis of one available case, followed by associated referrals.

Social domain personal archive   Personal information that is posted to public arenas using social media such as Facebook or Twitter.

Social research question   A question about the social world that is answered through the collection and analysis of first-hand, verifiable, empirical data.

Social science research   A process in which people combine a set of principles, outlooks, and ideas with a collection of specific practices, techniques, and strategies to produce knowledge.

Solomon four-group design   An experimental design that includes random assignments to one of four groups: an experimental group with a pre-test, the manipulation of an independent variable, and a post-test measure of the dependent variable; a control group with a pre-test, no manipulation, and a post-test measure; an experimental group with no pre-test, a manipulation, and a post-test measure; or a control group consisting of a post-test measure only.

Split-half reliability   Consistency between both halves of the measures for a variable of interest.

Stakeholder   An individual, group, or organization that is directly or indirectly involved with or impacted by the program of interest.

Static group comparison   A quasi-experimental design lacking random assignment in which two groups are compared following a treatment.

Step-wise consent process   A consent process that takes place in stages following the establishment of relationships within a group.

Stratified random sampling   A probability-based method used to obtain a sample on the basis of known population characteristics.

Structured observation   A quantitative approach in which behaviour is observed and coded using pre-determined categories.

Survey   An information-collection method used to describe, compare, or explain individual and societal knowledge, feelings, values, preferences, and behaviour.

Survey interview   A highly structured data collection method consisting of a series of prescribed questions or items asked by an interviewer who records the answers provided by the respondent.

Systematic errors   Miscalculation due to consistently inaccurate measures or intentional bias.

Systematic random sampling   A probability-based method used to obtain a sample on the basis of a fixed interval representing every *n*th case listed.

Tables   Summaries of main findings from quantitative research, such as the percentage of respondents who gave answers in each category of a variable on a questionnaire or the differences in means between groups on dependent measures.

Testing   Changes in the dependent measure that result from experience gained on the pre-test.

Test-retest reliability   Consistency between the same measures for a variable of interest taken at two different points in time.

Theoretical framework   A perspective based on core assumptions.

Theoretical sampling   A concept-driven method for obtaining data used in qualitative research.

Theory   A set of propositions intended to explain a fact or phenomenon.

Throw-away questions   Questions unrelated to the research topic that are used to take breaks in the conversation.

Time-interval sampling   An observation-based data coding method in which variables are recorded at the end of each set time interval throughout an observation period.

Time-series study   Research on different units of analysis carried out at multiple points in time.

Tradition   A familiar compilation of beliefs and practices passed down from one generation to the next.

Transcription   A data entry process in which the obtained verbal information is transferred verbatim into text.

Transition statements   Statements that move the conversation into the essential questions.

Triangulation   The use of multiple methods or sources to help establish rigour.

Unit of analysis   The object of investigation.

Unobtrusive research methods   Strategies in which the researcher examines evidence of people's behaviour or attitudes, rather than interacting directly with those being studied.

Unstructured interview format   A highly flexible interview format based on questions that develop during the interaction based on participant feedback.

Validity   The extent to which a study examines what it intends to.

Variable   A categorical concept for properties of people or events that can differ and change.

Virtual ethnography   An in-depth study of a group or culture that exists in an online environment.

Visual ethnography   Representations of culture as depicted in photographs and film documentaries.

Within-subjects design   A type of design in which the experimental group is exposed to all possible levels of the independent variable.

Photo Credits

Chapter 1

Page 2: CP/Andrea Gordon; p. 5: Eat Well and Be Active Poster. Health Canada, 2011. Reproduced with the permission of the Minister of Health, 2013.; p. 7: Brand X Pictures; 13: Maxexphoto/Dreamstime.com/GetStock.com; p. 16: © WoodyStock/Alamy.

Chapter 2

Page 26: Bradcalkins/Dreamstime.com/GetStock.com.

Chapter 3

Page 50: © Bettmann/CORBIS; p. 52: Courtesy of the National Archives at Atlanta; p. 55: Stanley Milgram papers, 1927–1993 (inclusive). Manuscripts & Archives, Yale University; p. 57: Philip G. Zimbardo, Inc.

Chapter 4

Page 81: Rayes/Getty Images.

Chapter 5

Page 103: Erica Simone Leeds; p. 104: © moodboard/Corbis; p. 117: Perfectlypure/Dreamstime.com/GetStock.com;

Chapter 6

Page 130: Photowitch/Dreamstime.com/GetStock.com; p. 141: Mario Beauregard/THE CANADIAN PRESS; p. 143: Reproduced with the permission of Law School Admission Council, Inc.

Chapter 7

Page 158: © Larry Lambert. www.Cartoonstock.com; p. 160: Arenacreative/Dreamstime.com/GetStock.com; p. 164: © Jose Luis Pelaez Inc/Blend Images LLC; p. 173: Photographer's Choice/SuperStock.

Chapter 8

Page 184: © George Redgrave; p. 185: © Huntstock/Getty Images; p. 186: © Trains and Planes/Alamy; p. 189: © Kathryn8/iStockphoto.com.

Chapter 9

Page 212: Design Pics/Steve Nagy; p. 214: Design Pics/Steve Nagy; p. 217: Brand X Pictures/Getty Images; p. 223: Monkey Business Images/Cutcaster.

Chapter 10

Page 235: Eric Audras/Getty Images; p. 236: BOAZ JOSEPH/THE LEADER; p. 240: © picturesbyrob/Alamy; p. 242: Hemant Mehta/Getty Images; p. 246: From People of a Feather, www.peopleofafeather.com.

Index